Critical Survey of Long Fiction

Fantasy Novelists

Editor

Carl Rollyson
Baruch College, City University of New York

Salem Press
Ipswich, Massachusetts • Hackensack, New Jersey

Cover photo:
Lewis Carroll (© Stapleton Collection/Corbis)

978-1-4298-3676-0

CONTENTS

Contributors iv

The Fantasy Novel 1

Richard Adams 11
Reinaldo Arenas 18
Marion Zimmer Bradley 24
Mikhail Bulgakov 32
James Branch Cabell 42
Lewis Carroll 54
Angela Carter 62
José Donoso 71
Anatole France 85
Julien Green 97
L. P. Hartley 108
Robert A. Heinlein 116
Alice Hoffman 123
E. T. A. Hoffmann 129
Stephen King 139
C. S. Lewis 160
Haruki Murakami 171
Juan Carlos Onetti 177
J. K. Rowling 189
José Saramago 195
Ramón José Sender 202
Andrei Sinyavsky 212
Jun'ichiro Tanizaki 222
J. R. R. Tolkien 232
Amos Tutuola 247
T. H. White 256
Jeanette Winterson 262

Bibliography 267
Glossary of Literary Terms 270
Guide to Online Resources 282
Geographical Index 287
Subject Index 288

CONTRIBUTORS

Linda C. Badley
Original Contributor

David Barratt
Farnsfield, England

Bernadette Lynn Bosky
Yonkers, New York

William Boyle
University of Mississippi

Joseph Bruchac
Original Contributor

Mitzi M. Brunsdale
Original Contributor

J. Madison Davis
Original Contributor

Thomas Du Bose
Louisiana State University in Shreveport

John R. Holmes
Franciscan University of Steubenville

Jane Anderson Jones
Original Contributor

Djelal Kadir
Original Contributor

Steven G. Kellman
University of Texas at San Antonio

Charles L. King
Original Contributor

Rebecca Kuzins
Pasadena, California

William Laskowski
Jamestown College

Charles E. May
California State University, Long Beach

Laurence W. Mazzeno
Alvernia College

P. Andrew Miller
Northern Kentucky University

David B. Parsell
Furman University

Janet Pérez
Original Contributor

Robert C. Petersen
Original Contributor

Murray Sachs
Original Contributor

Joachim Scholz
Original Contributor

Lynne P. Shackelford
Original Contributor

Paul Siegrist
Fort Hays State University

Brian Stableford
Reading, England

Christopher J. Thaiss
Original Contributor

Janet G. Tucker
Original Contributor

James Whitlark
Texas Tech University

Gay Pitman Zieger
Santa Fe College

The Fantasy Novel

The term "fantasy" refers to all works of fiction that attempt neither the realism of the realistic novel nor the "conditional realism" of science fiction. Among modern critics, the primacy of the realistic novel is taken for granted. Realistic novels not only describe normality but also constitute the normal kind of fiction; fantasy, in dealing with the supernatural, seems to be almost perverse. Prior to the rise of the novel in the eighteenth century, however, this was far from being the case. Prose forms such as the imaginary voyage, the dialogue, and satire blurred even the basic distinction between fiction and nonfiction, let alone that between "realistic" and "fantastic" subject matter. The separation of realistic and fantastic began not with the casting out of fantastic genres from the literary mainstream, but rather with the withdrawal of a realistic genre—the novel—from a mainstream that had easily accommodated fantastic motifs.

Eighteenth and nineteenth centuries

To speak of the "fantasy novel" in the context of the eighteenth century comes close to committing a contradiction in terms: Novels were about life as it was lived and had left behind the conventions of allegory and fable along with the decorations of the marvelous and the magical. It is arguable, though, that the withdrawal left behind a connecting spectrum of ambiguous works, and—more important—that it soon led to some important reconnections. Jonathan Swift's use of the techniques of narrative realism in his chronicling of the imaginary voyages of Lemuel Gulliver gave to his work a crucial modernity that is responsible for its still being widely read and enjoyed today.

The rise of the gothic novel in the last decades of the eighteenth century, in connection with the emergence of the Romantic movement that spread from Germany to France, England, and the United States, represents a definite reaction against the advancement of literary realism. The gothic novel, indeed, is almost an "antinovel" of its day, substituting a fascination with the ancient for a preoccupation with the modern, an interest in the bizarre for an obsession with the everyday, an exaltation of the mysterious for a concern with the intelligible, a celebration of the barbaric for a smug appreciation of the civilized. From the standpoint of today, the gothic can be seen to have been subversive in several different ways. It was subversive in a literary context because it opposed the dominant trend toward the development of the modern realistic novel. It was subversive in a sociological context because it reflected the fact that the values of the ancien régime were under stress and that the decadence of that regime was symptomatic of its imminent dissolution. It was subversive in a psychological context because it provided a parable of the impotence of the conscious mind to complete its oppressive victory over the forces of the unconscious, whose imprisonment could never be total.

Gothic novels dealt with strange events in strange environments, organized around the passions of the protagonists. The passions were frequently illicit in a perfectly straightforward sense, often involving incest and the breaking of sacred vows, but the more careful and controlled gothics—the archetypal example is *The Mysteries of Udolpho* (1794), by Ann Radcliffe—emphasized the extent to which the trend toward a less permissive morality would eventually rule, especially in England.

With the exception of the gothic novels, few of the products of the Romantic rebellion were cast in the form of long prose narratives. Short stories were produced in much greater quantity, and the evolution of the short story in Europe and America is closely intertwined with the Romantic reaction against realism and classicism. Poetry, too, was affected dramatically. Even the gothic novel underwent a rapid decline—not into nonexistence but into inconsequential crudeness. After the appearance, in 1824, of James Hogg's *The Private Memoirs and Confessions of a Justified Sinner*—a masterpiece of psychological terror involving paranoid delusions—there followed a long period in which gothic romance was primarily associated with the lowest stratum of the literary marketplace: with the partworks and "penny dreadfuls" marketed for the newly literate inhabitants of the industrial towns. Such interminable narratives as *Varney the Vampyre* (1847), by James Malcolm Rymer, and *Wagner the Wehr-Wolf* (1846-1847), by G. M. W. Reynolds, achieved considerable success in their own time but have little to offer modern readers.

Although the gothic novel was primarily a species of horror story, its supernatural trappings did overflow into moralistic fantasies that might be comic extravaganzas, such as James Dalton's *The Gentleman in Black* (1831) and *The Invisible Gentleman* (1833), or earnest parables, such as John Sterling's *The Onyx Ring* (1839). The themes of these novels—tricky deals with the devil, invisibility, wish-granting rings, and personality exchange—were to become the staples of what Nathan Drake had called "sportive gothic," while curses, ghosts, vampires, and madness remained the characteristic motifs of "gloomy gothic."

The writers who produced the most notable works of fantasy in the middle of the nineteenth century—including Edgar Allan Poe and Nathaniel Hawthorne in the United States, George MacDonald and William Gilbert in England, and Théophile Gautier and Charles Nodier in France—primarily worked in the short-story medium. The novels written by these authors often have fantastic embellishments, but for the most part they pay far more heed to the restraints of conventional realism than do these authors' short stories.

VICTORIAN ERA

The revival of the fantasy novel in the last two decades of the nineteenth century was associated with several trends that can be traced through the fiction of the twentieth century. The partial eclipse of substantial work in fantastic fiction in the mid-nineteenth century is clearly related to the repressive morality of that period—it is notable that in France, where the repression was less effective than in Great Britain, the United States, and Germany, the Romantic heritage was more effectively conserved. It is possible, in consequence, to see the various threads of the revival in terms of reactions against and attempts to escape from that repression.

During this repressive period, indulgence in fantasy came to be seen as a kind of laxity: It was in the Victorian era that the notion of escapism was born. An exception was made in the case of children's literature (though even here there was a period when fantasy was frowned upon), and there eventually arose in Britain a curious convention whereby fantasies were considered suitable reading for Christmas, when a little token indulgence might be overlooked, an idea that led to the emphasis on fantasy in the Christmas annuals to which Charles Dickens and William Makepeace Thackeray contributed. Such writers as Thackeray, MacDonald, and Lewis Carroll brought to the writing of books nominally aimed at children an artistry and seriousness that commended them to the attention of adults and helped to open a space for the production of fantastic novels within the British literary marketplace.

Another form of fantastic fiction that became to some extent associated with the British Christmas annuals was the ghost story, which became extremely popular in the 1880's and remained so for half a century, during which virtually all the classic British work in that genre was done. There is, however, something intrinsically anecdotal about ghost stories that keeps them more or less confined to short fiction. Though there have been some excellent novellas, there have never been more than half a dozen outstanding ghost novels. Joseph Sheridan Le Fanu, who stands at the head of the line of British ghost-story writers, produced several neogothic novels, but almost all of them are so ponderous as to be nearly unreadable. M. R. James wrote only short stories, and Algernon Blackwood's novels have not worn nearly as well as his shorter pieces.

The Victorian interest in ghosts, however, went far beyond the traffic in thrilling anecdotes. The influence of such contemporary fads as spiritualism and Theosophy sparked a new interest in the occult that began to be reflected quite prolifically in literary production. The great majority of the spiritualist fantasies of communication with the dead and accounts of the afterlife supposedly dictated by the dead through mediums are wholly inconsequential in literary terms, despite the eventual involvement in such movements of writers of ability, such as Arthur Conan Doyle. They did, however, lay important groundwork for those authors who followed. The fevered Rosicrucian romances of Edward Bulwer-Lytton, Marie Corelli's exercises in unorthodox theology, and commercially successful accounts of life "on the other side" by such writers as Coulson Kernahan and Elizabeth Stuart Phelps paved the way for much more substantial posthumous fantasies by Wyndham Lewis (*The Childermass*, 1928) and C. S. Lewis (*The Great Divorce*, 1945) and for the theological romances of Charles Williams and David Lindsay. Williams's *All Hallows' Eve* (1945) is possibly the best of the ghost novels, while Lindsay's *A Voyage to Arcturus* (1920) is a masterpiece of creative metaphysics.

The 1880's also saw a renaissance of comic fantasy, exemplified in Britain by the novels of F. Anstey and in the United States by Mark Twain's *A Connecticut Yankee in King Arthur's Court* (1889). The calculated irreverence of these stories reflects a self-confident rationalism that stands in opposition to the mystical movements inspiring most posthumous fantasy. The primary target held up for ridicule in these stories, however, is not the vocabulary of fantastic ideas itself but rather the moral pretensions of the contemporary middle classes. Anstey's stories use fantastic premises to expose the limitations of the attitudes that were rigidified within closed Victorian minds.

In the twentieth century, this tradition of humorous fantasy thrived more in the United States than in Britain—the leading American exponent of the species has been Thorne Smith—and this reflects, in part, the fact that as Britain has become somewhat less obsessed with the protocols of middle-class culture, the United States has become gradually more so. It was in the United States also that the absurd logical consequences of fantastic premises began to be exploited for pure amusement, largely in connection with the short-lived magazine *Unknown*, whose leading contributors were L. Sprague de Camp and Fletcher Pratt, who produced, in collaboration, a series of excellent comic fantasies.

A third species of fantastic fiction that first became clearly delineated in the last decades of the nineteenth century is the kind of story that translocates contemporary persons into fabulous imaginary worlds. Stories of this kind are among the oldest that are told. The mundane world has always had its fantastic parallels: its earthly paradises, the land of Cokaygne, and the land of Faerie. In the mid-nineteenth century these alternate worlds were retired into juvenile fiction, except for a few desert islands populated in a relatively mundane fashion. Victorian romances of exploration, however, celebrating the journeys of white men into the heart of the dark continent of Africa, reopened imaginative spaces for more exotic traveler's tales.

Numerous "lost race" stories and a few "hollow earth" romances were published before 1880, but the writer who first made a considerable popular impact with exotic romances of exploration was H. Rider Haggard, first in *King Solomon's Mines* (1885), and later in *She* (1887) and *The Ghost Kings* (1908). The example that he set was rapidly taken up by others, and the fantasization of the lands where adventurers went exploring proceeded rapidly. Because this was also the period when interplanetary stories were beginning to appear among early scientific romances, it was perhaps inevitable that writers began to displace their more exotic imaginary worlds to the surfaces of other planets. The example set by Edwin Lester Arnold in *Lieut. Gullivar Jones: His Vacation* (1905) was rapidly followed by Edgar Rice Burroughs and many others. In *The Lost World* (1912), Arthur Conan Doyle revitalized remote earthly locations with survivals from prehistory, and this too was an example enthusiastically followed. A new vocabulary borrowed from scientific romance allowed later writers to send heroes through "dimensional gateways" of one kind or another into magical fantasy worlds as exotic as could be imagined: The most determined of all writers of this kind of escapist fantasy was the American Abraham Merritt, author of *The Moon Pool* (1919) and *The Face in the Abyss* (1932).

Though the lost-land story set on the earth's surface was gradually destroyed by news of real explorations—the last classic example was James Hilton's *Lost Horizon* (1933)—the borrowing of conventions from science fiction has allowed the basic story framework to be retained to the present day. Contemporary humans can still be precipitated into magical imaginary worlds with the aid of a little fake technology or even a light sprinkling of jargon. The removal of imaginary worlds from darkest Africa to other planets and other dimensions, however, coincided with another and possibly more important innovation in the use of the theme, which was to dispense with the protagonist from the familiar world.

Fairy tales and heroic fantasy

Although traditional fairy tales had, at the time of their origin, been set in the believed-in world, their remote printed descendants could not help but seem to their consumers to be set in an entirely imaginary milieu. The magicalized medieval milieu of such stories became a stereotype useful to modern writers, who began to repopulate it with complex characters whose adventures were filled with allegorical significance. The pioneers of this kind of enterprise were the German Romantic Friedrich de la Motte Fouqué, in his novel *The Magic Ring* (1813), and George MacDonald, in *Phantastes* (1958), but their example was followed in far more prolific fashion by William Morris, whose several romances of this kind include *The Wood Beyond the World* (1894) and *The Water of the Wondrous Isles* (1897). The form gathered further momentum in the work of Lord Dunsany, most notably in *The King of Elfland's Daughter* (1924) and *The Charwoman's Shadow* (1926); other contemporary examples include Margaret Irwin in *These Mortals* (1925) and Hope Mirrlees in *Lud-in-the-Mist* (1926). These sophisticated but slightly effete fairy tales then began to give way to a more active brand of heroic fantasy, first featured to extravagant extent in E. R. Eddison's *The Worm Ourobouros* (1922).

Modified fairy-tale fantasy reached new heights of popularity in the fantastic volumes included in James Branch Cabell's "Biography of Manuel," set in the imaginary magical European kingdom of Poictesme. It was also developed in a much more extravagant way by several of the contributors to the magazine *Weird Tales*, who used imaginary lands set in remote eras of prehistory in order to develop the subgenre commonly known as "sword-and-sorcery" fiction. Because it was initially restricted to the pages of a pulp magazine, this subgenre was developed primarily in the short-story form, although it is actually better adapted to novel length. Its most famous progenitor, Robert E. Howard, wrote only one novel featuring his archetypal hero Conan: *Conan the Conqueror* (1950; originally "Hour of the Dragon," 1935-1936). The first important novel of this kind to be published initially in book form was *The Well of the Unicorn* (1948) by George U. Fletcher (Fletcher Pratt), but since the advent of the paperback book the species has become established as a successful brand of pulp fiction.

The most notable modern novels set entirely in imaginary worlds tend to give the appearance of being hybrids of sophisticated fairy romance and a variety of heroic fantasy not too far removed from American sword-and-sorcery fiction. The masterpieces of the genre are *The Once and Future King* by T. H. White—published in its entirety in 1958 but absorbing three earlier novels—and *The Lord of the Rings* by J. R. R. Tolkien, published in three volumes between 1954 and 1955.

One of the most striking side effects of the development of fantasy novels of this kind for adults was the revitalization of work done primarily for the juvenile market, which is often remarkably sophisticated in both technical and ideative terms. Tolkien's juvenile novel, *The Hobbit* (1937), is an old example; later ones include Ursula K. Le Guin's six novels set in the world of Earthsea and various works by Alan Garner, Susan Cooper, and Lloyd Alexander.

The paperback publication of Tolkien's *Lord of the Rings* in the 1960's and the feature films released to great acclaim in 2001-2003 sparked countless exercises in imitation that proved popular enough to make the trilogy the basic form of modern fantasy fiction. The reborn genre went from strength to strength in commercial terms, making best sellers out of dozens of writers, many of them direly mediocre in terms of the quality of their prose. Nor is it simply oral fairytales that were rehabilitated within modern commercial fiction; following the success of Richard Adams's *Watership Down* (1972), animal fables—which were also popular in medieval times—were similarly produced in some quantity. The leading examples of this form are the twenty-one novels in the Redwall series by Brian Jacques, in which generations of woodland creatures inhabit a vaguely medieval world.

This exploitation of imaginary worlds is the most striking aspect of the evolution of fantasy novels during the twentieth and twenty-first centuries, and it is not entirely surprising that the "fantasy" label is now retained for such novels by publishers. There has, however, been a parallel evolution of occult and horrific fantasy. The Decadent movements at the end of the nineteenth century saw the emergence of a kind of fiction that reveled in the unnatural, and though most of the fantastic fiction of this kind was cast in short-story form, there were a few notable novels, including Oscar Wilde's *The Picture of Dorian Gray* (serial 1890, expanded 1891) and Hanns Heinz Ewers's *The Sorcerer's Apprentice* (1907) and its sequels.

Twentieth century gothic fantasy

In parallel with these works appeared a new wave of stories that developed the gothic images of fear into new archetypes, treating them with a determined quasi-scientific seriousness. The great success in this line was Bram Stoker's *Dracula* (1897), which has remained in print and which surely stands as the most heavily plundered fantasy of all time, being the sourcebook for literally hundreds of vampire stories and films.

This resurgence of fiction that deals with the supernatural in a deadly earnest fashion may seem rather paradoxical. It was possible for nineteenth century rationalists to imagine that their victory over superstitious belief was almost won and to look forward to a day when the irrational might be banished from human affairs. If anything, the reverse is true: Superstition, mysticism, and irrationality now thrive to a greater extent than ever before, and modern fiction reflects that fact.

Fantasy novels intended to evoke horror and unease are more prolifically produced and consumed today than they were in the heyday of the gothic, and one of the world's best-selling novelists, Stephen King, is primarily a horror writer. In addition, the role played by occult forces within the neogothic novel is crucially different; in gothic novels, normality was usually restored, and when the forces of the supernatural did break free, they usually did so in order to punish the guilty and liberate the innocent. In later neogothic fantasies, however—whether one looks at the respectable middlebrow tradition that extends from Mervyn Peake's Gormenghast trilogy to the works of Angela Carter or the lowbrow tradition that extends from Dennis Wheatley to James Herbert and Clive Barker—the gothic elements were superimposed in a wholesale manner upon the mundane world, subjecting it to a surrealization from which there could be no possibility of redemption.

This situation has been complicated by a marked tendency among writers of dark fantasy to subject the traditional monsters of gothic fiction to moral reappraisal. In modern vampire fiction, particularly the lush historical romances of Anne Rice, Chelsea Quinn Yarbro, S. P. Somtow, and Elizabeth Kostovo, the male vampire is more hero than villain, and his unusual existential plight is subject to a sympathetically fascinated scrutiny. Modern awareness of the extent to which such figures as the vampire and the werewolf embodied and exaggerated the sexual anxieties of the nineteenth century has enabled writers to redeploy them in fictions that champion the cause of liberalism, although the question of whether understanding automatically paves the way to forgiveness remains interestingly and sometimes achingly open. The psychoanalytical sophistication of much modern horror fiction has moved so far beyond traditional considerations of good and evil that it seems to some critics to have turned from stigmatization to glamorization—an argument supported by the strangely reverent tone adopted toward their all-too-human monsters by such writers as Poppy Z. Brite and Thomas Harris.

The concerted attempt made by many modern writers of supernatural fiction to redeem the Byronic literary vampire from the negative image foisted on him by John Polidori and Stoker extends beyond the limits of literary fantasy into lifestyle fantasy. Similarly intricate relationships between literary and lifestyle fantasies, aided and abetted by extravagant scholarly fantasies—a process that began with the modern reformulation of the idea of witchcraft—have developed across the entire spectrum of New Age philosophies, pretenses, and practices. The relationship between fiction and action has been further complicated by virtue of the spectacular success of fantasy role-playing games, pioneered by Dungeons and Dragons, and fantasy-based computer games. Although play has always been a significant medium of fantasy, it has never been the case before that so much play (involving adults as well as adolescents) has drawn so extensively upon a vocabulary of ideas established and embodied by literary and cinematic fantasies.

POSTMODERNISM

While the contents of popular fantasy fiction have overspilled in this remarkable fashion, fantastic motifs and literary methods have been imported again into the literary mainstream on a considerable scale. The mid-1960's and early 1970's saw the beginnings of a significant break with the American realist tradition in novels by such fabulists as John Barth, Thomas Berger, Richard Brautigan, Thomas Pynchon, and Robert Coover, which eventually expanded in the 1980's into an entire field of postmodern fiction closely connected—at least in the eyes of critics—with a series of formal challenges to the very ideas of realism and reality. British writers of a broadly similar stripe whose work spanned the same period include Angela Carter, Peter Ackroyd, Alasdair Gray, Robert Irwin, and Russell Hoban, although the notion of postmodern British fiction never took hold to the extent that their work began to be aggregated into a symptom of some crucial cultural transition.

Although postmodern fiction borrowed a good deal of imagery from science fiction—and postmodern critics happily conscripted such science-fiction writers as Philip K. Dick, William Gibson, and Bruce Sterling into the field—its mainstream practitioners usually deploy such imagery as a set of metaphors commenting surreally and satirically on contemporary society, in the manner of Kurt Vonnegut and Don DeLillo. The typical materials of commercial fiction bearing the "fantasy" label are far less diverse, but their potential in this regard has been demonstrated by such works as Samuel R. Delany's Nevèrÿon series and Steven Millhauser's *Martin Dressler: The Tale of an American Dreamer* (1996).

The translation into English during this postmodern period of several highly esteemed Latin American novels that productively and provocatively mingle mundane and supernatural materials, including key examples by Gabriel García Márquez and Jorge Amado, introduced the concept of Magical Realism to contemporary literary criticism. The style is widely, and perhaps rather promiscuously, applied to works that owe some allegiance to alternative cultural traditions, whether or not it requires translation. Key examples can be found among the works of Ben Okri, Milorad Pavic, and Salman Rushdie. The increasing interest of African Americans and Native Americans in their traditional cultures—previously obscured by the dominant Euro-American culture—and increasing curiosity about the folkways of Asiatic and African cultures, have led to a steady flow of new works into the American book market, much of which is advertised as Magical Realism for want of any other convenient label.

The relaxation of the realist norm allowed several varieties of fantasy that had long been dormant to resurface in the 1970's and 1980's. Although the classical models of the *conte philosophique* established by Voltaire were mostly novellas, their modern equivalents frequently take the form of novels. Significant examples include Umberto Eco's *Il pendolo di Foucault* (1988; *Foucault's Pendulum*, 1989) and *L'isola del giorno prima* (1994; *The Island of the Day Before*, 1995) and the series of theological fantasies by James Morrow begun with *Towing Jehovah* (1994). The classical *Kunstmärchen* (art fairy tale) also was confined to shorter lengths, but its modern variants are similarly making increasing use of the novel form; key examples include John Crowley's *Little, Big* (1981) and Coover's *Briar Rose* (1996). Comic fantasy has been resuscitated with great success by such writers as Terry Pratchett—who was the best-selling novelist of the 1990's in Britain and whose work has been translated into dozens of languages—and by Pseudonymous Bosch, author of *The Name of This Book Is Secret* (2007) and *If You're Reading This, It's Too Late* (2008).

Although the bulk of the commercial fiction published under the fantasy label has become extraordinarily stereotyped and repetitive, with heavily promoted best sellers religiously following dumbed-down formulas derived from Tolkien, the fringes of the marketing category continue to play host to a number of highly imaginative and accomplished writers. These include Peter S. Beagle, Tim Powers, and James Blaylock. It is now commonplace for writers who produce excellent fantasy for children to extend their endeavors into adult fantasy; writers working with great facility on both sides of this increasingly ill-defined boundary include Jane Yolen, Patricia McKillip, and Nancy Willard. The Harry Potter series by J. K. Rowling, which has sold 400 million copies in dozens of languages, was marketed (if not written) for young adults but read by adults as well. In Britain, Rowling's publisher printed the books with alternate covers for adult readers who did not wish to be seen reading children's literature. Adults are also drawn to the witty absurdist *Artemis Fowl* series by Eoin Colfer and to Philip Pullman's *His Dark Materials* series. Pullman's books are marketed for young adults, yet their handling of complex religious—or antireligious—themes has made them a topic for serious scholarly debate.

The simultaneous extension of all these trends gives contemporary fantastic fiction such an extraordinary variety that it is becoming difficult to attach much meaning to the overarching notion of the fantasy novel—a difficulty clearly reflected in the comprehensive yearly summations of novel production offered by Terri Windling in her introductions to the annual *Year's Best Fantasy and Horror* anthologies that she coedits with Ellen Datlow. Windling routinely employs such fantasy categories as imaginary world, contemporary or urban, Arthurian, dark, religious, humorous, mysteries, historical, and literary fairytales but still requires such residual headings as "fantasy in the mainstream," "young adult fantasies," and "oddities" for the remainder. The priority traditionally awarded by critics to realistic fiction seems to be in the process of breaking down, and it may well be that a more elaborate literary taxonomy will have to be developed for the new millennium.

Brian Stableford

BIBLIOGRAPHY

Anatol, Giselle Liza, ed. *Reading Harry Potter: Critical Essays.* Westport, Conn.: Praeger, 2003. Fourteen scholarly essays examine the Harry Potter series, the biggest-selling fantasy series of all time. Topics include theories of adolescent development, book banning, literary influences, and morality and social values.

Attebery, Brian. *The Fantasy Tradition in American Literature: From Irving to Le Guin.* Bloomington: Indiana University Press, 1980. Comprehensive and intelligent study of the development of American fantasy, from Washington Irving to Ursula K. Le Guin.

Barron, Neil. *Fantasy Literature: A Readers's Guide.* New York: Garland, 1990. Guide with extensively annotated bibliographies of key texts. Includes a chapter on modern fantasy for young adults and sections on general reference works, history and criticism, author studies, and other sources for further study.

Bleiler, Everett F. *The Guide to Supernatural Fiction*. Kent, Ohio: Kent State University Press, 1983. Large collection of plot synopses and critical judgments of 1,775 books published between 1750 and 1960. A useful and near-comprehensive guide to the development and key themes of modern fantastic fiction.

Bleiler, Richard, ed. *Supernatural Fiction Writers: Contemporary Fantasy and Horror.* 2 vols. 2d ed. New York: Charles Scribner's Sons, 2003. Extensive collection of critical and biographical essays. The first volume deals with continental European and early British writers, the second with American and modern British writers.

Clute, John, and John Grant, eds. *The Encyclopedia of Fantasy.* New ed. New York: St. Martin's Griffin, 1998. Although less comprehensive and less well organized than its science-fiction companion, this remains one of the best general reference books on the fantasy genre that excludes horror and occult fiction.

Dickerson, Matthew T., and David O'Hara. *From Homer to Harry Potter: A Handbook on Myth and Fantasy.* Grand Rapids, Mich.: Brazos, 2006. Discusses Homeric and Biblical myth, Arthurian legend, nineteenth century fairytales, and contemporary writers including Ursula K. Le Guin, Philip Pullman, and J. K. Rowling.

Gray, William. *Fantasy, Myth, and the Measure of Truth: Tales of Pullman, Lewis, Tolkien, MacDonald, and Hoffmann.* New York: Palgrave Macmillan, 2009. Critical interpretations of the novelists' handling of reality, myth, and truth in their fantasy literature.

Hume, Kathryn. *Fantasy and Mimesis: Responses to Reality in Western Literature*. New York: Methuen, 1984. One of the best theoretical studies of the aesthetics of fantasy and its significance in postmodern fiction.

Lobdell, Jared. *The Rise of Tolkienian Fantasy.* Chicago: Open Court, 2005. One of dozens of scholarly books about Tolkien and the *Lord of the Rings* series, this book looks also to Tolkien's influences, and to his imitators.

Pringle, David, ed. *The St. James Guide to Fantasy Writers*. Detroit, Mich.: St. James Press, 1996.

_______. *The St. James Guide to Horror, Ghost, and Gothic Writers*. Detroit, Mich.: St. James Press, 1998. Matched pair of reference works on individual authors, with supportive bibliographies of their relevant books and biographical notes. These volumes cover more authors than Bleiler's *Supernatural Fiction Writers* and cover works untouched by Clute and Grant's *The Encyclopedia of Fantasy.*

Sandner, David. *Fantastic Literature: A Critical Reader.* Westport, Conn.: Praeger, 2004. Theoretical descriptions of fantasy literature, beginning with writings by Plato and Aristotle, through essays by Sigmund Freud and later twentieth century writers.

RICHARD ADAMS

Born: Newbury, Berkshire, England; May 9, 1920
Also known as: Richard George Adams

PRINCIPAL LONG FICTION

Watership Down, 1972
Shardik, 1974
The Plague Dogs, 1977
The Girl in a Swing, 1980
Maia, 1984
Traveller, 1988
The Outlandish Knight, 2000
Daniel, 2006

OTHER LITERARY FORMS

Richard Adams has written two collections of short fiction, one of which, *Tales from Watership Down* (1996), is in part a sequel to his most famous novel. His other works include several illustrated children's books in verse; an illustrated series of nature guides; an account of a journey to Antarctica, *Voyage Through the Antarctic* (1982), cowritten with Ronald M. Lockley, the author of the factual work that became the basis for *Watership Down*; and an autobiography covering the first part of his life through his demobilization after World War II, *The Day Gone By* (1990).

ACHIEVEMENTS

Called by English writer A. N. Wilson "the best adventure-story-writer alive," Richard Adams is most famous for taking the talking-animal story out of the genre of children's literature and informing it with mature concerns and interests, as in his first great success, *Watership Down*, which won the Carnegie Award and the Guardian Children's Fiction Prize. He continued this transformation in *The Plague Dogs* and *Traveller*. Adams also made his mark in fantasy literature; his imaginary kingdom of Bekla is the backdrop for *Shardik* and *Maia*, novels whose main concerns, slavery and warfare, definitely remove them from the realm of children's literature. He also wrote a less successful full-length ghost story, *The Girl in the Swing*, and later two historical novels, *The Outlandish Knight* and *Daniel*, the latter of which returns to his concern with the subject of slavery.

BIOGRAPHY

The youngest of three children, Richard George Adams spent an idyllic childhood ("the happiest [days] of my life") growing up on the outskirts of Newbury, England. His father, a local doctor, transmitted his knowledge of and love for the flora and fauna of the region to his son, whose later devotion to animal welfare was additionally inspired by Hugh Lofting's Dr. Dolittle books. Adams's father also instilled in his son a lifelong interest in storytelling, which Adams later honed in bedtime tales told to roommates at prep school. Other important influences included the Uncle Remus stories of Joel Chandler Harris, *Uncle Tom's Cabin* (1852) by Harriet Beecher Stowe, *The Three Mulla-Mulgars* (1910) by Walter de la Mare, and the silent Rin-Tin-Tin films. All would later echo in his fiction.

Although his time at prep school was often unpleasant, Adams thoroughly enjoyed his public school experience at Bradfield. The school put on a yearly play in its open-air theater, often a classical Greek drama, and Adams called the theater the place where he was "more consistently happy than anywhere else." Bradfield also encouraged his love of literature, the Greek and Roman classics, and history, the subject in which Adams won a scholarship to Worcester College, Oxford, in 1938. Adams was grateful to Oxford for its acceptance of what he calls one's "fantasy potential."

Adams's Oxford years were interrupted, as were those of so many others, by World War II. Adams chose to serve in the Royal Army Service Corps (RASC), which is mainly concerned with transport and communication duties, but later he volunteered for the airborne arm of the RASC and served in the Middle East and in Singapore. On his return to England, Adams was shocked to learn how many of his Oxford companions had died during the war.

After demobilization, Adams soon met Elizabeth Acland, whom he would later marry and with whom he would have two daughters. In 1948 he joined the British civil service, but he never abandoned his love for storytelling. *Watership Down* began, like many other "children's" classics, as a story initially told by the author to his children (in this case to entertain them on a long car trip); two years after its publication, Adams was able to retire from the civil service and write full time at his various homes in the south of England.

ANALYSIS

In each of his novels, Richard Adams adopts a different individual narrative voice: easygoing and colloquial in *Watership Down* and *Maia*, stately and epic in *Shardik*, ironic and densely allusive in *The Plague Dogs*, and the very different first-person voices in *The Girl in a Swing* and *Traveller.* On the surface, Adams's natural gift as a storyteller is his strongest talent, but his novels deserve to be read more for his habitual concerns: a love for "the surface of the earth," as George Orwell called it, as manifested in the English countryside and the creatures who inhabit it; a hatred for the cruelties that human beings inflict on the other inhabitants of this world as well as on themselves; and an acute awareness of the transitory nature of existence and the evanescence of friendship and love.

WATERSHIP DOWN

Watership Down burst on the literary scene in 1972, as unlikely a success as J. R. R. Tolkien's *The Lord of the Rings* (1955) had been almost two decades earlier. Its plot and characters seemed those of a children's book: A group of rabbits leave their threatened burrow and make a dangerous journey to find a new home as well as enough new rabbits to ensure its continuation. In its length and often violent action, however, it certainly went beyond the boundaries of a children's work, and it succeeded with many adults. It even led to some shameless imitations, such as William Horwood's mole epic, *Duncton Wood* (1980), but none had the imagination and freshness of the original.

As Tolkien did with the Hobbits, Adams made his exotic characters familiar by giving them an easily identifiable demotic speech. Hazel, Bigwig, and the others speak much as did the originals on which they are modeled: Adams's companions in the 205th Company of the RASC during World War II. (Hazel, according to Adams, is his commanding officer, John Gifford, and Bigwig is Paddy Kavanagh, who was killed in battle.) The rabbits, like their soldier counterparts, are believable everyday heroes. Their persistence in the face of daunting odds, their relatively unflappable demeanor as they are introduced into new and dangerous surroundings, their ingenuity in overcoming their difficulties—all recall the best qualities of those soldiers in the war.

The familiar speech is also reproduced in the novel's narrative voice, which is often that of a good oral storyteller; as Adams has noted, "A true folk-tale teller is usually rather colloquial." This informality helps to disguise the classical underpinnings of the work, the main one of which is Vergil's *Aeneid* (c. 29-19 B.C.E.; English translation, 1553). There are also echoes of Xenophon's *Kyrou anabasis* (c. fourth century B.C.E.; *Anabasis*, 1623) and Homer's *Iliad* (c. 750 B.C.E.; English translation, 1611) and *Odyssey* (c. 725 B.C.E.; English translation, 1614), with Hazel as a more trustworthy Odysseus and Bigwig a less belligerent Achilles. These archetypal characters and plot devices are also supported by the scientific accuracy of the details of the rabbits' lives, which Adams culled from *The Private Life of the Rabbit* by R. M. Lockley (1964). Familiar yet exotic characters, an epic story, and verisimilitude of milieu contribute to the lasting and deserved appeal of *Watership Down*. (*Tales from Watership Down*, in its latter half a sequel to the novel, also serves as an answer to those who accused the original of, among other charges, sexism.)

SHARDIK

Adams's next novel, *Shardik*, disappointed many of his readers, for although on the surface, like *Watership Down*, a fantasy, it was far removed from the first novel in setting, characters, and plot. Adams constructs the mythical land of Bekla, whose precarious peace is shattered by the emergence of a great bear, which is taken by many to be the avatar of the god Shardik. After a short rule by the bear's chief follower, Kelderek, the bear escapes, and Kelderek must learn the real meaning of the irruption of Shardik into the lives of so many people. For much of the book, the characters are unlikable, the setting is foreign without being exotic, and the plot seems to be nothing but one violent incident after another. The narration is also different from that in *Watership Down*, much more stately and epic in tone, with self-consciously Homeric similes interrupting the narrative flow.

In the end, however, *Shardik* is satisfying, once the reader grasps the greater themes of the novel. Shardik's reign has allowed slavery to flourish once again in Bekla, and only by suffering and death can Shardik and Kelderek redeem themselves and society. Adams's own horror at slavery, both literary and real, echoes in the plot: The evil slaver Genshed is consciously modeled on Stowe's great villain in *Uncle Tom's Cabin*, Simon Legree, and the mutilated beggar boys whom Adams had seen from a troop train in India are reproduced in some Beklan slaves. Adams's own hatred of war causes the first half of the book to be almost antiepic in its drive: The religious war it depicts is nasty, brutish, and long. Once the arc of the plot is evident, *Shardik* can be seen as an epic indictment of the horrors of epic war.

THE PLAGUE DOGS

The Plague Dogs is the most tendentious of Adams's novels. The title characters are trying to escape from a laboratory in England's Lake Country, where they have been subjected to cruel and unnecessary experiments. Although seemingly a return to the mode of his greatest success, the grown-up animal novel, it is much more a satire, filled with savage indignation at the lengths to which humans will use and abuse other species, a satire that gains effect from Adams's experience working in government bureaucracies. Like *Shardik*, it is an investigation of cruelty, this time toward what the novel calls "animal slaves": "It's a bad world for the helpless," as one of its characters says. Once again Adams adopts a new narrative voice, particularly in the sections concerning humans, this one arch and packed with literary allusions. The novel is not totally one-sided, the case being made near the end for useful animal medical experimentation. Yet again it is in his animal portrayals that Adams best succeeds, particularly those of the dog Snitter, whose nonsense language, caused by a brain operation, echoes that of dramatist William Shakespeare's fools, and of the wild fox, whose feral otherness seems to be an answer to criticisms of Adams's cozy rabbits.

THE GIRL IN A SWING

Adams's next two novels are major departures, explorations of the themes of sexuality and love, subjects he touched on only tangentially in previous work. *The Girl in a Swing* is nominally a ghost story, but in reality it is more a depiction of the obsessive love that the hero, Alan Desland, feels for Käthe, a German girl whom he meets in Copenhagen and swiftly marries, not knowing that she is trying to escape a ghost from her past. The work contains echoes of Emily Brontë's *Wuthering Heights* (1847), with Käthe as Cathy Earnshaw, but Alan is no Heathcliff, and while Adams's depictions of local scenery remain one of his strengths—much of the locale is again borrowed from Adams's childhood—the end of the novel is more deflationary than chilling. Adams has said that ghosts in English horror writer M. R. James's short stories are knowingly artificial, but the one in *The Girl in a Swing* is unfortunately no less an *umbra ex machina*, a ghost from the machine.

Maia

Maia returns to the fantasy world of Bekla, which Adams created in *Shardik*, to tell the story of the eponymous heroine, who undergoes a transformation from literal sex slave to country matron, all described at sometimes tedious length, in more than twelve hundred pages. Adams's narrative style here is more familiar than that in *Shardik*, his similes shorter, homelier, and less epic. However, the reproduction of the girl's countrified speech becomes irritating, and anachronisms such as discussions of infection and primitive vaccination are annoying. The plot is basic: Girl meets boy, girl loses boy, girl gets boy. The girl does not even meet the boy until almost halfway through the novel, however, making for difficult reading.

The underlying theme of *Maia* is much the same as that of *Shardik*, as the good side attempts to eradicate slavery in the Beklan empire, but this time the scenes of sadism that Adams describes become extremely uncomfortable. In *Shardik* such scenes had a moral point, but here their purpose seems cloudier: We know these characters are villains, so several scenes explicitly depicting their villainy are uncalled for. On the positive side, Adams once again depicts actions that undercut fantasy epic conventions: Maia's most heroic actions are undertaken to prevent, and not to further, violence and warfare. At the end, however, when Maia has become a contented country wife and mother, the reader wonders how this matron grew out of the girl who, some nine hundred pages earlier, had realized she possessed "an exceptional erotic attitude" and proceeded to use and enjoy it.

Traveller

Traveller is basically the story of the Civil War seen through the eyes and told by the voice of Confederate general Robert E. Lee's famous horse. In this novel, Adams plays to all his strengths, including a new narrative voice, this one a modification of Joel Chandler Harris's in the Uncle Remus stories; a singular, believable animal persona through which the action is described; and a depiction of his favorite themes—hatred of war, admiration for those who must suffer through it, and sorrow over the ephemerality of comrades and friendship. The bravery of Lee's Army of Northern Virginia is, as Adams elsewhere has noted, a reflection of Adams's own pride in the gallantry of the British First Airborne Division in the battle of Arnhem. Lee is Adams's quintessential hero because he treats both animals and people with dignity and respect. Traveller, like satirist Jonathan Swift's Houyhnhnms, a race of intelligent horses in *Gulliver's Travels* (1726), is aghast at humankind's capacity for cruelty, but he is not keen enough (or anachronistic enough) to see the cruelty that slavery commits. Traveller is, as another horse calls him, "thick": At Gettysburg, he thinks Pickett's charge succeeds, and at Appomattox, he thinks the Federals have surrendered to "Marse Robert." However, he gets the basic truth right: "Horses [are] for ever saying goodbye." It was the lesson Adams learned when he returned to Oxford after the war to learn of his friends' deaths, and it is the grave lesson that has informed his best fiction.

William Laskowski

OTHER MAJOR WORKS

SHORT FICTION: *The Unbroken Web: Stories and Fables*, 1980 (also known as *The Iron Wolf, and Other Stories*); *Tales from Watership Down*, 1996.

NONFICTION: *Nature Through the Seasons*, 1975 (with Max Hooper); *Nature Day and Night*, 1978 (with Hooper); *Voyage Through the Antarctic*, 1982 (with Ronald M. Lockley); *A Nature Diary*, 1985; *The Day Gone By*, 1990 (autobiography).

CHILDREN'S LITERATURE: *The Tyger Voyage*, 1976; *The Adventures of and Brave Deeds of the Ship's Cat on the Spanish Maine: Together with the Most Lamentable Losse of the Alcestis and Triumphant Firing of the Port of Chagres*, 1977; *The Legend of Te Tuna*, 1982; *The Bureaucats*, 1985.

EDITED TEXTS: *Sinister and Supernatural Stories*, 1978; *Occasional Poets: An Anthology*, 1980.

BIBLIOGRAPHY

Adams, Richard. *The Day Gone By*. London: Hutchinson, 1990. Provides information on Adams's childhood, his service in World War II, and how he developed both a love of nature and a skill for storytelling that would lead to his becoming a writer.

_______. "Richard Adams: Some Ingredients of *Watership Down*." In *The Thorny Paradise: Writers on Writing for Children*, edited by Edward Blishen. Harmondsworth, England: Penguin Books, 1975. Adams is one of more than twenty authors who contributed essays to this collection about why and how they write. His chapter focuses on *Watership Down*.

Bridgman, Joan. "Richard Adams at Eighty." *Contemporary Review* 277, no. 1615 (August, 2000): 108. Overview of Adams's personal and professional life, placed within the broader context of children's literature published in the United Kingdom and featuring an evaluation of *Watership Down*.

Harris-Fain, Darren. *British Fantasy and Science-Fiction Writers Since 1960*. Vol. 261 in *Dictionary of Literary Biography*. Detroit, Mich.: Gale Group, 2002. A brief biography of Adams and analysis of his books, along with a list of his works and a bibliography, are included in this standard reference book.

Kitchell, Kenneth F., Jr. "The Shrinking of the Epic Hero: From Homer to Richard Adams's *Watership Down*." *Classical and Modern Literature* 7 (Fall, 1986): 13-30. Detailed analysis of *Watership Down* makes a convincing argument that the novel is a twentieth century epic that treats its rabbit protagonist as a classical hero.

Meyer, Charles. "The Power of Myth and Rabbit Survival in Richard Adams' *Watership Down*." *Journal of the Fantastic in the Arts* 3, no. 4 (1994): 139-150. Examines the novel's treatment of reason and intuition and shows the connections between *Watership Down* and R. M. Lockley's *The Private Life of the Rabbit*.

Perrin, Noel. "An Animal Epic: Richard Adams, *Watership Down*." In *A Child's Delight*. Hanover, N.H.: University Press of New England, 1997. Collection of essays about thirty children's books that Perrin describes as "neglected," "ignored," or "under-appreciated" includes a brief discussion of *Watership Down*.

Watkins, Tony. "Reconstructing the Homeland: Loss and Hope in the English Landscape." In *Aspects and Issues in the History of Children's Literature*, edited by Maria Nikolajeva. Westport, Conn.: Greenwood Press, 1995. Assesses the treatment of the landscape in several works of English children's literature. Focuses on Kenneth Grahame's *The Wind in the Willows*, comparing it with *Watership Down* and J. R. R. Tolkien's *The Lord of the Rings* trilogy.

REINALDO ARENAS

Born: Holguín, Oriente, Cuba; July 16, 1943
Died: New York, New York; December 7, 1990

PRINCIPAL LONG FICTION

Celestino antes del alba, 1967 (revised as *Cantando en el pozo*, 1982; *Singing from the Well*, 1987; part 1 of *The Pentagonía*)
El mundo alucinante, 1969 (*Hallucinations: Being an Account of the Life and Adventures of Friar Servando Teresa de Mier*, 1971; also translated as *The Ill-Fated Peregrinations of Fray Servando*, 1987)
El palacio de las blanquísimas mofetas, 1975 (as *Le Palais des très blanches mouffettes*, 1980; *The Palace of the White Skunks*, 1990; part 2 of *The Pentagonía*)
La vieja Rosa, 1980 (novella; *Old Rosa*, 1989)
Otra vez el mar, 1982 (*Farewell to the Sea*, 1986; part 3 of *The Pentagonía*)
Arturo, la estrella más brillante, 1984 (novella; *The Brightest Star*, 1989)
La loma del ángel, 1987 (*Graveyard of the Angels*, 1987)
Old Rosa: A Novel in Two Stories, 1989 (includes the novella *Old Rosa* and the novella *The Brightest Star*)
El portero, 1989 (*The Doorman*, 1991)
Viaje a La Habana, 1990
El asalto, 1991 (*The Assault*, 1994; part 5 of *The Pentagonía*)
El color del verano, 1991 (*The Color of Summer: Or, The New Garden of Earthly Delights*, 2000; part 4 of *The Pentagonía*)

OTHER LITERARY FORMS

In addition to novels, Reinaldo Arenas (ah-RAY-nahs) wrote several collections of short stories, political essays, plays, poems, and an extensive autobiography, *Antes que anochezca* (1992; *Before Night Falls*, 1993). His short-story collections include *Con los ojos cerrados* (1972), *Adiós a mamá: De La Habana a Nueva York* (1995), and *Mona, and Other Tales* (2001). His poetry collections include *El central* (1981; *El Central: A Cuban Sugar Mill*, 1984) and *Voluntad de vivir manifestándose* (1989).

ACHIEVEMENTS

Reinaldo Arenas's first novel, *Singing from the Well*, was awarded first place by the Cuban Writers Union in 1965. *Singing from the Well* also was awarded a prestigious French literary award, the Prix Medici, in 1969. In the same year, *Hallucinations* received the award for Best Foreign Novel from *Le Monde* (France). In 1980, he was awarded the Cintas Foundation's Fellow honor. This was followed by other fellow honors, including from the Guggenheim Foundation in 1982 and the Wilson Center Foundation in 1987. His autobiography, *Before Night Falls*, was listed among the top ten books of the year by *The New York Times* in 1993. These literary awards were enhanced when the film based on his autobiography received both the Grand Jury Prize at the Venice International Film Festival (1999) and Movie of the Year award from the American Film Institute (2000).

BIOGRAPHY

Reinaldo Arenas was born on July 16, 1943, in Holguín, Oriente, Cuba. He was born into a rural setting, and his family suffered extreme poverty. According to his autobiography and interviews, his childhood was one of hunger and neglect. While a youth in rural Cuba under the harsh dictatorship of Fulgencio Batista, Arenas was marginally involved in the building insurrection that would eventually topple the oppressive regime in 1959. Several years after the Cuban Revolution, he moved to Havana (1961). He studied at the Universidad de Havana but did not graduate. Arenas also worked for a while in the José Martí National Library (1964).

In 1967, at the age of twenty-four, Arenas published his first novel, *Singing from the Well*. This work somewhat mirrored his childhood, presenting a young protagonist who suffers poverty—both physical and mental. It features a boy who must use independent thought to survive an oppressive reality. Arenas's literary works are not exemplary of the realism that the revolutionary authorities wanted to see published. His open advancement of independent thinking, coupled with his open homosexuality, soon led to his works being labeled antirevolutionary; they were then censored and banned in Cuba.

Nonetheless, Arenas secretly smuggled his writings out of Cuba. His works were published in Europe and the United States, where they received critical acclaim but led to further reprisals from the Cuban revolutionary regime. His works were removed from the lists of official Cuban literature and were confiscated throughout Cuba. Arenas was imprisoned several times for his defiant attitude. He was tortured in prison and forced to renounce his own works and his homosexuality. Although he was a nonperson in Cuba, he was not allowed to emigrate. His life was reduced to one of minimal existence in Havana, seeking marginal employment to survive. Because of a bureaucratic mistake, he emigrated to the United States in the 1980 exodus known as the Mariel Boat Lift.

In the United States, Arenas was free to publish and criticize the regime of revolutionary leader Fidel Castro. He insisted that his criticism was not only of the Cuban situation but of all types of dogmatic ideologies as well. His literary forms expanded to include poetry, essays, short stories, and journalism. On December 7, 1990, shortly after writing his definitive autobiography, Arenas committed suicide in New York City. In his parting words in a suicide letter, he made it clear that he was not leaving this world as a victim of the Cuban Revolution. To the contrary, he described his life as one of struggle and hope. He expressed his desire that one day all Cubans would be free, stating eloquently that in his death, he already was.

ANALYSIS

Reinaldo Arenas uses the written word to criticize all forms of authoritarianism, especially that which impedes independent thought and action. His most fervent and defiant works condemn the dictatorial regime of the post-Batista revolutionary junta in Cuba, headed by Castro (during Arenas's lifetime). However, he does not limit his criticism to Cuba. He once stated that both capitalism and communism severely limit freedom and expression, but in a capitalist society, one is free to complain openly; in a communist society, one must quietly accept repression. Many of Arenas's works also condemn adult authority over children. As in all authoritarian situations (political, societal, and familial), adult authority stifles the independence of children and adolescents. Arenas's works also contain much psychological and physical abuse.

Arenas presents the reader with a world where the protagonists must use their intellectual skills to survive in a world that is not logical, or just. The reader is confronted with unreliable narrations, descriptions, and dialogue. Indeed, Arenas writes as if truth is only to be found between fantasies, lies, distortions, exaggerations, and hyperbole. His works are often confusing counterpoints within perceived truths. For Arenas, truth is not universal, so the reader of his work is forced to decide for himself or herself what truth is being presented. Arenas reveals a society of humans who struggle for self-expression and self-esteem.

Arenas's textual style varies. In some novels, he uses neither paragraphs nor chapters. In others, he employs an inordinate amount of chapters and textual divisions. His language is generally quite graphic, to the point of being repugnant to some readers. Arenas is not concerned with convincing his readership of the innocence of his characters. To the contrary, he presents their actions as forms of fantasy, and it is up to readers to accept or deny the "reality" of the characters' actions. Extraordinary events are mingled with deceptions, half-truths, distortions, and confusion. The fictional is not obvious and neither is the truth. Furthermore, although Arenas's works are often fantastical and even magical, they are not examples of the Magical Realism employed by many Latin American writers.

SINGING FROM THE WELL

Singing from the Well is the first novel in a five-book series that Arenas called *pentagonía*, or five agonies. *Singing from the Well* is the first and only novel by Arenas to be published in Cuba. (His later works were banned there as well.) Like many of his works, there is no definite chronological order to the story, nor does it clearly delineate its characters. The only consistent linking of time and space is the dysfunctional relationship between the principal protagonist, a young boy growing up in rural poverty and confusion, and his mother. He is never named, unlike his imagined cousin, Celestino.

The world of the boy is a bizarre mixture of nightmare, punishment, and repression. His mother disciplines him with an ox prod, his cousins conspire to kill their grandfather, and his grandmother burns his beloved crosses. To survive this world of cruel fantasies, the boy splits himself into another imaginary being: Celestino, his deceased cousin. Celestino is a poet who carves his poems into trees and leaves.

The reader is never exposed to Celestino's poetry directly. Nonetheless, it is obvious that his poems are attempts to face the bleakness of his life. The wondrous world of nature that the boy and his imaginary cousin inhabit and narrate (through their poetry) is their imagined "real" world. The boy's grandfather, who cannot decipher the strangely coded texts that Celestino carves into trees and other plants, displays an ignorance and distrust that leads him to try to eliminate the texts by chopping them up with a hatchet. The word *hacha*, or hatchet, is used by Arenas more than hundred times over the course of one page of the novel.

Singing from the Well presents a poignant tale of imaginative self-expression. As with other novels by Arenas, the reader encounters a text full of dissonance and fantasy, and without normally accepted logic. The reader must determine the story's merits and truths.

The Palace of the White Skunks

In *The Palace of the White Skunks*, the childlike Celestino is replaced by an older adolescent narrator, Fortunato. Although not overtly stated, Fortunato is a chronological extension of the young boy from *Singing from the Well*. It is also an analogical extension of the anti-Batista revolutionary epic of rural Cuba.

In this work, there is a definite historical setting and time period: the revolutionary rebels fighting against the Batista regime in the Sierra Maestra of Cuba. The novel again describes a dysfunctional family and society. Fortunato faces many real challenges that often overlap with fantasy. The events could be described as forms of magical absurdism: Fortunato conversing with deceased characters, stabbing himself while continuing to amble along, and ghosts and demonic ghouls dancing in the home. Here, also, Fortunato's life is a series of frustrations, deceptions, and rejections. Extreme poverty, problems with the revolutionary insurrection, distrust and insults from family members, and even the sexual frustrations of others enter into impossible and improbable realities. The history presented is reliable, but the events and voices contained in the novel are inconsistent, conflicted, and confusing.

Arenas once again confronts the reader with surreal situations and characters that are not logically reliable. The reader must attempt to sort out the myriad textual transgressions and diversions. Fortunato realizes that he must find a form of self-expression to survive the oppressive situation in which he finds himself. He does so by starting to write his responses to the forces that are limiting his independent choices in life. Fortunato steals paper from his grandfather and begins to secretly express his inner revulsion with the outer life that he is experiencing. The reader is not privy to the actual words of the adolescent. However, it becomes clear that the writings represent a desperate defense mechanism. The text reveals a youth who is literally sweating-out a confrontation with an absurd reality that lurks in the background. He writes instead of sleeping or eating. As with other Arenas novels, the reader finds a protagonist who seeks to find an aesthetic and pure inner textual world that will address his need for self-expression.

FAREWELL TO THE SEA

In this novel, the reader finds an adult reincarnation of the central characters found in *Singing from the Well* and *The Palace of the White Skunks*. The main protagonist, Hector, lives in the institutionalized revolution of modern Cuba. He suffers for attempting to express independent thoughts and writings. In this work, Arenas confronts the Castro regime openly, presenting a postrevolution Cuba as intolerable of dissent. Hector confronts this world with a desperate desire to express his independence. He is an unpublished author, but in this novel, the reader is allowed to view his writings and hear his *cantos* (songs).

This novel is divided into two parts that feature events that follow Hector and his wife's return from the beach after six days of vacation from the totalitarian government in Havana. Part one consists of six chapters (one for each day at the beach) that straightforwardly reveal the unnamed wife's descriptions of a life devoid of tolerance, of unfulfilled intellectual and sexual expression. Part two is narrated by Hector and has six components labeled *cantos*. They are a blend of prose and poetry, fantasy and fact (as perceived by Hector).

As the couple approaches the outskirts of Havana, the reader discovers that the wife is actually a nonexistent creation of Hector. The car begins to accelerate, and the implied ending is that death by suicide is better than returning to a life of intolerance, oppression, and repression.

The reader is confronted by various analogies. The most obvious is the parallel of Hector's life with that of the author. Furthermore, this work was clearly important for Arenas, as he rewrote it twice, each time after it had been confiscated by the Castro government.

Paul Siegrist

OTHER MAJOR WORKS

SHORT FICTION: *Con los ojos cerrados*, 1972 (revised as *Termina el desfile*, 1981); *Adiós a mamá: De La Habana a Nueva York*, 1995; *Mona, and Other Tales*, 2001.

PLAY: *Persecución: Cuatro piezas de teatro experimental*, pb. 1986.

POETRY: *El central*, 1981 (*El Central: A Cuban Sugar Mill*, 1984); *Voluntad de vivir manifestándose*, 1989.

NONFICTION: *Necesidad de libertad*, 1986; *Antes que anochezca*, 1992 (*Before Night Falls*, 1993).

BIBLIOGRAPHY

Browning, Richard L. *Childhood and the Nation in Latin American Literature*. New York: P. Lang, 2001. A discussion of various Latin American authors and the specific correlations between their childhoods and the literature they produced as adults. Includes bibliographical references.

Ocasio, Rafael. *Cuba's Political and Sexual Outlaw: Reinaldo Arenas.* Gainesville: University Press of Florida, 2003. Good source for information on the life and self-exile of Arenas. Describes the relationship between his quest for self-determinism and living as an out gay man in Cuba and the United States. Includes bibliographical references.

Soto, Francisco. *Reinaldo Arenas.* Boston: Twayne, 1998. A comprehensive literary critique of most of the literature by Arenas. Includes bibliographical references and an index.

Vargo, Marc. *Scandal: Infamous Gay Controversies of the Twentieth Century.* New York: Harrington Park Press, 2003. A collection documenting the "gay" scandals of the twentieth century, including the political scandals involving an out Arenas in an intolerant Cuba. Includes bibliographical references.

Yozell, Erica Miller. "Writing Resistance Through Melancholy: Reinaldo Arenas's *El palacio de las blanquísimas mofetas* and *Otra vez el mar.*" *MLN* 123, no. 2, (March, 2008): 308-330. Argues that Arenas employs a "discursive melancholy" in these two novels "as a means of both resistance and escape."

MARION ZIMMER BRADLEY

Born: Albany, New York; June 3, 1930
Died: Berkeley, California; September 25, 1999
Also known as: Marion Zimmer

PRINCIPAL LONG FICTION

The Door Through Space, 1961
"The Planet Savers" and "The Sword of Aldones," 1962
The Bloody Sun, 1964
Star of Danger, 1965
The Winds of Darkover, 1970
The World Wreckers, 1971
Darkover Landfall, 1972
Hunters of the Red Moon, 1973 (with Paul Edwin Zimmer)
The Spell Sword, 1974
The Heritage of Hastur, 1975
The Shattered Chain, 1976
The Forbidden Tower, 1977
The House Between the Worlds, 1980
Two to Conquer, 1980
Sharra's Exile, 1981
The Mists of Avalon, 1983
Thendara House, 1983
Web of Light, 1983
The Firebrand, 1987
Witch Hill, 1990
Renunciates of Darkover, 1991
The Forest House, 1993
The Forest of Darkover, 1993
Rediscovery: A Novel of Darkover, 1993
Towers of Darkover, 1993
Glenraven, 1996 (with Holly Lisle)
Witchlight, 1996
Gravelight, 1997
Lady of Avalon, 1997
The Shadow Matrix: A Novel of Darkover, 1997
Heartlight, 1998
In the Rift, 1998 (with Lisle)
Traitor's Sun: A Novel of Darkover, 1998

Priestess of Avalon, 2000 (with Diana L. Paxson)
The Fall of Neskaya, 2001 (with Deborah J. Ross)
Zandru's Forge, 2003 (with Ross)
Flame in Hali, 2004 (with Ross)
The Alton Gift, 2007 (with Ross)

OTHER LITERARY FORMS

Although Marion Zimmer Bradley is known primarily as a novelist, she also wrote some short fiction as well as nonfiction, publishing several collections of short stories and a few essays. In addition to her writing, Bradley made a name for herself as an editor. She founded *Marion Zimmer Bradley's Fantasy Magazine* in 1988, and she also edited numerous anthologies, notably the Darkover anthologies and the Sword and Sorceress series. The Sword and Sorceress series has continued since her death as Marion Zimmer Bradley's Sword and Sorceress.

ACHIEVEMENTS

Marion Zimmer Bradley was one of the most prolific female science-fiction and fantasy authors, with more than sixty novels to her name and others written under pseudonyms. Although she was nominated for both the Hugo Award and the Nebula Award, science fiction's highest honors, she never won either, despite the fact that her novels contributed to the growth of science fiction and fantasy in numerous ways. After her death, she was honored with a World Fantasy Award for Life Achievement in 2000.

In her fiction, Bradley pushed the boundaries of sexual taboos, especially concerning homosexuality, with her sympathetic homosexual characters. It could also be argued that she, like fellow fantasy writer Andre Norton, served as a role model for many women who wanted to write science fiction and fantasy. As an editor, Bradley published many authors' debut stories and helped other women writers become established in what had traditionally been a male-oriented field. Her lasting contributions to the field of science fiction and fantasy are the Darkover and Avalon series, both of which continue after her death. Twenty-seven Darkover novels were published under her name, some of which were under way when she died and completed by others.

BIOGRAPHY

Marion Zimmer was born in Albany, New York, in 1930. As a teen, she was a science-fiction and fantasy fan. She made her first amateur sale to a fiction contest in *Fantastic/Amazing Stories* in 1949. That same year, she married Robert Alden Bradley. Her oldest son, David, was born in 1950. Bradley wrote during these early years, but only for fanzines and school magazines. Her first professional sale came in 1953, when she sold a short story to *Vortex Science Fiction*.

Bradley's first novel was published in 1961. In 1962, she published two novels together, including the first novel set on the planet Darkover. The Darkover novels eventually became her best-known works. She published several more novels in the 1960's, while going to college; some of her work at this time was done under various pseudonyms. She graduated from Hardin-Simmons University in Texas in 1964 with a B.A., and in 1966-1967 she did graduate work at the University of California, Berkeley. During this time she and Robert Bradley divorced. She then married Walter Breen, with whom she had two children, Patrick and Moira.

During the 1970's, Bradley published an average of two books per year, usually a Darkover novel and another novel. The Darkover series generated fan groups specifically dedicated to that series. Also in the 1970's, Bradley became a pastoral counselor in California and began to study religion and counseling. Her writing career continued to flourish in the 1980's. In 1983, she published *The Mists of Avalon*, a best seller. In 1980, she became an ordained priest of the Pre-Nicene Catholic Church and established the Centre for Nontraditional Religion. Religious themes also appear in her novels.

In the late 1980's, Bradley began editing her own magazine as well as anthologies. She helped nurture up-and-coming writers, particularly female authors. In her magazine and the Sword and Sorceress anthologies, she made an effort to publish first-time authors. In 1990, Bradley divorced Breen. Her writing and editing career continued, although she had some health problems. She died in 1999 after suffering a major heart attack, leaving behind many works in progress that were completed by other authors.

Analysis

Marion Zimmer Bradley's early years fit the conventional mold of the science-fiction and fantasy genres in which she was publishing. However, as she matured as a writer, she explored unconventional themes, particularly in the areas of religion and sexuality. She also moved away from hard science fiction into more traditional fantasy. Many of her characters possess psychic abilities or other kinds of powers that set them apart from others. Most of the criticism published on Bradley's work has focused on her as a woman writer and as a creator of female characters who is concerned with women's issues. Among her most memorable female characters are Morgaine from *The Mists of Avalon* and the members of her female sisterhoods, such as the Free Amazons of Darkover. Although Bradley did not call herself a feminist, she has been both criticized and applauded by others who have applied that label to her.

Darkover Landfall

Darkover Landfall is not the first book Bradley published about Darkover, but it is the first book in the chronological order of that series. *Darkover Landfall* details the origin of humans on the planet Darkover. A colonization ship, heading for another planet, crashes on the inhospitable planet. While trying to repair their ship, the crew and colonists are exposed to the Ghost Wind, a natural occurrence that spreads a psychoactive pollen over the crash party. The pollen activates latent psychic abilities, but, even more distressingly, it lowers sexual inhibitions. Various sexual unions occur among the survivors. Eventually, they realize that they will have to make their home on the world.

The plot is a fairly conventional one for a science-fiction novel. This book shows Bradley's interest in and use of psychic abilities in her novels. On a nonconventional level, the book, without giving details, explores alternate sexualities and alternate standards of marriage and partnerships. For the colonists to ensure a broad gene pool, everyone must have children with different partners. The biggest controversy raised by the novel when it appeared, however, stemmed from the fact that Camilla Del Rey, the first officer, is forbidden to have an abortion when she wishes one. If it had not been for the crash, her peers would have had no problem with her choice, but because the colonists know that fertility and infant survival rates will be low for the first several years on their new planet, they force her to have the child. This position, although defended in the world of the book, sparked controversy and ire among Bradley's fans, feminists, and other writers. It was not until her later books that Bradley changed their minds.

The Shattered Chain

The Shattered Chain is another Darkover novel, but it differs from earlier works because it focuses on the Free Amazons, or Renunciates, of Darkover. Centuries after the crash of the starship, Darkover has become a planet with a harsh caste system and a mostly feudal political and economic system. Women have few or no rights in most of this society. The exception is the Free Amazons. The Free Amazons have renounced their allegiance to and reliance on their former families and men. They renounce marriage, swearing an oath that they will give themselves to men and will have children only when they want to. They are often ridiculed by Darkoveran society. This novel in many ways answers the criticisms leveled at Bradley after the publication of *Darkover Landfall*. In this novel, the women are the protagonists and the capable characters.

The story is told in three sections, with twelve years separating part 1 from part 2. Parts 1 and 2 focus on rescues. In the first part, Rohanna Ardais, a telepathic noblewoman, hires the Free Amazons to rescue her abducted kinswoman because the men in her family have given up on her. Melora, Rohanna's cousin, is trapped in a Dry Town. In the Dry Towns, all women are chained, wearing the outward sign that they belong to the men. The Free Amazons rescue Melora and her daughter Jaelle so that Jaelle will not be chained. In part 2, Magda Lorne, a Terran sociologist, impersonates a Free Amazon to ransom her male friend, Peter Haldane, from a thief. She meets the grown Jaelle and her band and is forced to pledge the oath of the Amazons. She then realizes that she believes the oath. Part 3 focuses on the ramifications of Magda and Jaelle's oath.

While the first two parts of this novel carry most of the action for the story, it is the last section that reveals Bradley's themes. Throughout part 3, the three female protagonists confront the choices they have made and the prices they have paid or will pay. Rohanna renounced her freedom of choice for security in marriage. Jaelle gained her freedom but renounced the ability ever to marry. Magda has to renounce her Terran allegiance to live as a Free Amazon. Bradley's point is that what is important is the choice—a woman should always have a choice in what she does. Rohanna did not have that choice and learns to live with it. Jaelle did have that choice but realizes it requires a price. She eventually chooses to live as a freemate with Peter Haldane. That she wants to give herself to a man is her choice as well.

There is a brief mention of the theme of fate in this novel, a theme Bradley explores in greater depth in later works. It seems to be pure chance that Magda meets Jaelle on her way to free Haldane. However, Lady Rohanna does not think it mere coincidence that Haldane looks exactly like Rohanna's son or that Magda meets Jaelle, the one person who could uncover her masquerade as a Free Amazon. Bradley suggests that there is a higher power at work. While feminists hated *Darkover Landfall*, many hailed *The Shattered Chain* as a feminist novel. Reviewer Joanna Russ, critical of the earlier work, later included *The Shattered Chain* in a listing of books depicting feminist utopias. In her later works, Bradley continued her exploration of the theme of woman's choice.

THE MISTS OF AVALON

While she will be known forever among the science-fiction community for creating Darkover, Bradley is known to a wider literary audience for *The Mists of Avalon*. This novel, impressive in length, could be considered her magnum opus. It stayed on *The New York Times* best-seller list for months following its publication in 1983 and was Bradley's first and most successful crossover mainstream novel.

The themes that Bradley explores in *The Shattered Chain* reappear in *The Mists of Avalon*. This is the story of the women of the Arthurian legend and their struggles with fate, religion, and the social strictures of their time. The novel deals with the matter of choice, or lack thereof. Although it is principally the story of Morgaine and Gwenhwyfar, it also gives some attention to Igraine, the mother of Morgaine and Arthur; Viviane, the Lady of the Lake; Morguase, Morgaine's aunt and the mother of Gawaine; and Nimue, daughter of Lancelot and the nemesis of the Merlin, Kevin Harper. Through these women, Bradley reconfigures the Arthurian legends into a woman's history and story.

Bradley reimagines the thematic conflict of the legend. In the book, the old ways of the Goddess religion are dying out because of the encroachment of Christianity. The Lady of the Lake is the high priestess of the Goddess faith, with Avalon as her seat of power. The Merlin is the chosen messenger of the gods. Viviane, the Lady of the Lake, and Taliesin, the Merlin, plan to put Uther on the throne of Britain so that he can protect the people from both the Saxons and the Christians. They further arrange that Uther's son Arthur should be king of both Britain and Avalon. Their plans go awry when Gwenhwyfar turns out to be overly pious and converts Arthur to Christianity.

Morgaine is raised on Avalon as priestess of the Goddess and vows to do the Goddess's will. However, when Viviane arranges for Arthur and Morgaine to participate in the ancient rites and have sexual intercourse, Morgaine feels betrayed and leaves Avalon. She joins Arthur's court, though she never gives up her ways. She continually tries to make Arthur be true to his oath to Avalon. In Bradley's version of the legend, this is the source of the conflict between Arthur and Morgaine—the struggle of one religion over another. Mordred, the son of Arthur and Morgaine, is also incorporated into this struggle, as he has been raised in Avalon and sees himself as the one to return Britain to its old ways. To do so, he must remove his father. Morgaine never hates Arthur in this version; in fact, the siblings love each other. Morgaine has always been Arthur's first love.

The conflict between the religions spurs social conflict as well. Under the old ways, women had the choice of whom they would mate with or love. The priests bring patriarchy and the concept of adultery. Bradley makes it clear that few of these women have choices. Igraine, at the age of fifteen, is given in marriage to the old duke of Cornwall. Morgaine is given to Arthur in the rites. Gwenhwyfar is given to Arthur as part of a deal for horses. Arthur later arranges a marriage for Morgaine with the aged Uriens, king of North Wales. The women do what is expected of them, however much they internally question these rules. In addition to having no social choices, Bradley suggests, the women have no choices at all. Viviane and Morgaine both have the Sight, a gift from the Goddess that gives them knowledge of the future. The implication is that everyone has a destiny to be carried out, and there is little that can be done to change that destiny.

The success of *The Mists of Avalon* may be attributed to many things. First, the Arthurian legend holds a certain mystique of its own, and Bradley captures that sense of awe in her own way. Second, Bradley manages to portray the conflict that many women feel with traditional Judeo-Christian religions. Bradley, through Gwenhwyfar, often mentions how priests teach that sin came into the world through a woman, and therefore all women are evil. Morgaine's character dismisses that notion with contempt, and even Gwenhwyfar seems to finally reject it, entering the embrace of the Goddess in the aspect of the Virgin Mary.

LATER WORKS

Bradley reimagined another classic work in her 1987 novel *The Firebrand*, a retelling of the fall of Troy as told from Kassandra's point of view. The novel had some success, but it did not achieve the critical acclaim of *The Mists of Avalon*. Part of this could be that the source work did not resonate as strongly as the Arthurian literature with contemporary readers. Also, the thematic conflict of the older Goddess religion with Christianity is obviously absent from a book on the fall of Troy.

In 1993, Bradley returned to the Avalon series with a prequel, *The Forest House*, set in Briton during the Roman occupation. The title refers to the dwelling of the Druid priestesses who were resistant to the Roman occupation. The conflict revolves around a priestess in love with a young Roman during the collapse of the Roman Empire. Reviewers considered it a good companion novel to *The Mists of Avalon*, though it again did not receive as much critical attention as the earlier novel.

Bradley continued to write more stories in the Avalon series with *Lady of Avalon* and *Priestess of Avalon*. She died before she could complete the last novel, and it was finished by fantasy novelist Diana L. Paxson. Bradley's last two Avalon novels explore the same themes as the earlier books. Since Bradley's death, Paxson has continued writing in the series with such novels as *The Ancestors of Avalon* (2004), which links Avalon to Atlantis, and *Ravens of Avalon* (2007), which focuses on the historical figure of Queen Boudica.

P. Andrew Miller

OTHER MAJOR WORKS

SHORT FICTION: *The Dark Intruder, and Other Stories*, 1964; "A Sword of Chaos," 1981; "The Lesson of the Inn," 1981; *The Best of Marion Zimmer Bradley*, 1985; *Lythande*, 1986.

NONFICTION: "Responsibilities and Temptations of Women Science Fiction Writers," 1985.

CHILDREN'S LITERATURE: *The Brass Dragon*, 1970.

EDITED TEXTS: *Sword and Sorceress: An Anthology of Heroic Fantasy*, 1984-2003 (series); *Snows of Darkover*, 1994.

BIBLIOGRAPHY

Arbur, Rosemarie. *Marion Zimmer Bradley*. Mercer Island, Wash.: Starmont House, 1985. Provides a great overall look at Bradley's work, with biographical and chronological overviews as well as analyses of the fiction, divided into types such as Darkover, non-Darkover science fiction, and fantasy.

Hildebrand, Kristina. *The Female Reader at the Round Table: Religion and Women in Three Contemporary Arthurian Texts*. Uppsala, Sweden: Uppsala University Library, 2001. Places Bradley's work within the context of the history of the Arthurian legends and women's literature in general.

Kaler, Anne K. "Bradley and the Beguines: Marion Zimmer Bradley's Debt to the Beguinal Societies in Her Use of Sisterhood in Her Darkover Novels." In *Heroines of Popular Culture*, edited by Pat Browne. Bowling Green, Ohio: Bowling Green State University Popular Press, 1987. Discusses Bradley's use of elements from real medieval societies of women in creating her Darkover novels.

King, Betty. *Women of the Future: The Female Main Character in Science Fiction*. Metuchen, N.J.: Scarecrow Press, 1984. Provides background on how women characters have been portrayed in science fiction, placing Bradley's work in historical perspective.

Paxson, Diana L. "Marion Zimmer Bradley and *The Mists of Avalon*." *Arthuriana* 9, no. 1 (Spring, 1999): 110-126. The author who has continued the series of Avalon books examines the biographical roots of Bradley's female spirituality in *The Mists of Avalon*.

Riggs, Don. "The Survival of the Goddess in Marie de France and Marion Zimmer Bradley." *Journal of the Fantastic in the Arts* 9, no. 1 (1998): 15-23. Compares the depictions of the goddess in twelfth century writer Marie de France's *Lanval* and in Bradley's *The Mists of Avalon*.

Roberson, Jennifer, ed. *Return to Avalon: A Celebration of Marion Zimmer Bradley*. New York: DAW Books, 1996. Collection of appreciative essays—written primarily by other female luminaries writing in the science-fiction and fantasy genres—provides information about Bradley's fiction.

Russ, Joanna. "Recent Feminist Utopias." In *Future Females: A Critical Anthology*, edited by Marleen S. Barr. Bowling Green, Ohio: Bowling Green State University Popular Press, 1981. Draws comparisons among many different feminist utopias created in works of fiction, including Bradley's *The Shattered Chain*.

Schwartz, Susan M. "Marion Zimmer Bradley's Ethic of Freedom." In *The Feminine Eye*, edited by Tom Staicar. New York: Frederick Ungar, 1982. Discusses the portrayal of women in the Darkover novels, particularly *The Shattered Chain*. Examines Bradley's themes of choice and the price of choice and also emphasizes the importance of risk taking and choices involving tests of will and courage in the Darkover novels.

Tober, Lee Ann. "Why Change the Arthur Story? Marion Zimmer Bradley's *The Mists of Avalon*." *Extrapolation* 34, no. 2 (Summer, 1993): 147-157. Argues the feminist significance of Bradley's novel as an inversion of the male-centered Arthur legend.

MIKHAIL BULGAKOV

Born: Kiev, Ukraine, Russian Empire; May 15, 1891
Died: Moscow, Russia, Soviet Union (now in Russia); March 10, 1940
Also known as: Mikhail Afanasyevich Bulgakov

PRINCIPAL LONG FICTION

Belaya gvardiya, 1927, 1929 (2 volumes; *The White Guard*, 1971)
Teatralny roman, 1965 (*Black Snow: A Theatrical Novel*, 1967)
Master i Margarita, 1966-1967 (uncensored version, 1973; *The Master and Margarita*, 1967)
Sobache serdtse, 1968 (novella; wr. 1925; reliable text, 1969; *The Heart of a Dog*, 1968)

OTHER LITERARY FORMS

Mikhail Bulgakov (bewl-GAH-kuhf) wrote some thirty-six plays, of which eleven were published and eight performed during his lifetime. His writings for theater and film include adaptations from Miguel de Cervantes, Molière, Charles Dickens, Nikolai Gogol, and Leo Tolstoy. Only one of the opera libretti Bulgakov composed for the Bolshoi Theater, *Rachel* (wr. 1938, pr. 1947), based on a story by Guy de Maupassant, was ever produced. Among his more notable plays made available in English during the 1960's and 1970's are *Adam i Eva* (pb. 1971; *Adam and Eve*, 1971), *Dni Turbinykh* (pr. 1926; *Days of the Turbins*, 1934), *Beg* (pr. 1957; *Flight*, 1969), *Zoykina kvartira* (pr. 1926; *Zoya's Apartment*, 1970), *Ivan Vasilievich* (pb. 1965; English translation, 1974), and *Posledniye dni (Pushkin)* (pr. 1943; *The Last Days*, 1976). Bulgakov also wrote numerous short stories, many of them collected in the volumes titled *Diavoliada* (1925; *Diaboliad, and Other Stories*, 1972), *Zapiski iunogo vracha* (1963; *A Country Doctor's Notebook*, 1975), and *Traktat o zhilishche* (1926; *A Treatise on Housing*, 1972). He also published miscellaneous journalism. Bulgakov's close identification with the life of Molière produced one of his most interesting plays, *Kabala svyatosh* (pr. 1936; *A Cabal of Hypocrites*, 1972; also known as *Molière*), as well as a novelistic biography, *Zhizn gospodina de Molyera* (1962; *The Life of Monsieur de Molière*, 1970).

ACHIEVEMENTS

Some twenty-five years after his death, Mikhail Bulgakov began to receive increasing recognition—both in the Soviet Union and abroad—as a major figure in modern Russian literature. *The Master and Margarita* is a complex, ambitious masterpiece that has won an intensely loyal readership and much critical scrutiny since its first serialized publication in 1966-1967. This novel's posthumous success in turn began to direct attention to Bulgakov's other neglected works.

The hazards of cultural life under Soviet leader Joseph Stalin frustrated Bulgakov's aspirations in prose fiction, where he did his finest work, and channeled him into the theater, where, though productive, he was probably temperamentally out of place. Bulgakov's narratives combine acute, if perforce oblique, social analysis with a strain of playful fantasy. Beyond the deprivation, hypocrisy, and cruelty of contemporary Soviet life, his Horatian satires suggest a transcendent spiritual force. In *The Master and Margarita* and *The White Guard*, it is tender devotion to a beautiful, mysterious woman that represents the apocalyptic possibility of overcoming an oppressive present existence. *Black Snow* offers the advice that "you have to love your characters. If you don't, I don't advise anybody to try writing; the result is bound to be unfortunate." This sentimental belief in the liberating power of love—of characters for one another, of author for reader—is tempered by terminal melancholia. In the imperfect world portrayed by Bulgakov, those in power are never graced with imagination, though they must be humored, but it is the power of imagination and of humor that lifts the reader beyond the tyranny of the quotidian.

There is at least an allusion to Faust in almost all of Bulgakov's books, where the quest for an elusive truth becomes an explicit and central theme. Bulgakov's work frequently foregrounds itself, calling attention to its own formal inventions in the service of a sense of values against which the elaborate structures of society and art seem petty and transient indeed.

BIOGRAPHY

Mikhail Afanasyevich Bulgakov, the eldest of seven children, was born in Kiev on May 15, 1891, into a family that was both devout and intellectual. His father, who died when Mikhail was sixteen, was a professor of divinity at the Kiev Theological Academy. Bulgakov developed an early interest in music and the theater, but he pursued a medical degree at Kiev University. In 1913, he married Tatyana Nikolaevna Lappa, and in 1916 he graduated with distinction as a doctor. He subsequently served as a military doctor in remote village hospitals, settings that were to provide the material for the stories in *A Country Doctor's Notebook*. The isolation depressed him, and he attempted to obtain his release, only succeeding in 1918 after the Bolshevik Revolution.

Bulgakov returned to Kiev to establish a private practice in venereology and dermatology. During this time, the tense atmosphere of which is re-created in *The White Guard*, Kiev was a battleground for the Germans, the Ukrainian nationalists, the Bolsheviks, and the Whites. In November, 1919, Bulgakov fled south to the Caucasian town of Vladikavkaz. While he was confined to bed with typhus, Vladikavkaz was captured by the Bolsheviks. He abandoned the practice of medicine and began devoting himself entirely to writing.

In 1921, Bulgakov moved to Moscow, where, amid general hardship, he attempted to support himself and his wife through a variety of literary and journalistic jobs. In 1924, he divorced Tatyana and married Lyubov Yevgenievna Belozerskaya. Soon thereafter, with the publication of satiric stories later collected in *Diavoliada*, Bulgakov began achieving some recognition and was able to abandon the newspaper work he detested. The publication, in 1925, of parts of *The White Guard*, based on his experiences in Kiev during the civil war, dramatically changed his life in ways recounted in the autobiographical novel *Black Snow*. Bulgakov's work came to the attention of the producers of the Moscow Art Theater, and he was asked to adapt *The White Guard* for the stage. The result, after considerable revision, was *Days of the Turbins*, which opened in October, 1926, to intense, polarized reaction. Bulgakov was harshly attacked for portraying the opponents of Bolshevism too sympathetically, but the play proved enormously popular. During its lengthy run, Stalin himself saw it fifteen times.

A sudden celebrity, Bulgakov continued writing plays, but by the end of the decade, as Soviet cultural and political life became severely repressive, his works were banned, and his financial position deteriorated. Near despair, he sent letters in 1930 to Soviet officials complaining of the campaign of vilification against him and his inability to get his work accepted. Stalin's personal intercession resulted in Bulgakov's appointment as a producer at the Moscow Art Theater. His subsequent years in the theater were productive but frustrating, in part because of friction with the flamboyant director Konstantin Stanislavsky, whose production of *A Cabal of Hypocrites* in 1936 led Bulgakov to resign in disgust from the Moscow Art Theater. For the remainder of his life, he was employed by the Bolshoi Theater as librettist and consultant.

In 1929, Bulgakov had begun a clandestine love affair with Elena Sergeyevna Shilovskaya, wife of the chief of staff of the Moscow Military District. In 1932, after both succeeded in obtaining divorces, they were married, and Bulgakov adopted Elena's five-year-old son, Sergey. Bulgakov's happiness with and devotion to his third wife, to whom he, with failing eyesight, probably dictated *Black Snow* in 1939, are reflected in *The Master and Margarita*. The earliest version of the latter was begun as early as 1928, but Bulgakov destroyed that manuscript in 1929. He continued refining a revised version until his death, in Moscow, on March 10, 1940.

After Bulgakov's death, the official attitude toward his work in the Soviet Union ranged from indifference to hostility, and very few of his writings remained available. During the brief thaw in Soviet cultural repression following Stalin's death, a commission was established to rehabilitate Bulgakov's reputation, and by the late 1960's most of his major works were being published in the Soviet Union for the first time.

ANALYSIS

Mikhail Bulgakov never took advantage of the opportunity to flee Russia during the revolution and its turbulent aftermath, and his fiction is very much a product of Russian life during the first two decades of the Soviet regime. Bulgakov's social commentary is not oblique enough to have averted the ire and the proscription of powerful contemporaries, or to keep later readers from recognizing the quality of roman à clef in much of what he wrote. The key, however, is not simply in details of his own biography—friends, adversaries, and a pet cat persistently transposed into a fictional realm. More important, it is in his ability to render the plight of the creative individual in a system designed to subdue him. Within the carefully limned landscapes of modern Kiev and Moscow, Bulgakov's characters dramatize the limitations and hubris of temporal human power. His books, then, are not merely the frustrated effusions of an author encountering formidable obstacles to his ambitions, nor are they merely perceptive analyses of the kind of community Stalinist social engineering was begetting. Beyond Bulgakov's contempt for contemporary mischief is a veritably religious sense of a universal spiritual force and a conviction that *sic transit gloria mundi*. *The White Guard* thus concludes on a consoling note: "Everything passes away—suffering, pain, blood, hunger and pestilence." It is this spiritual perspective that endows Bulgakov's narratives with more than a parochial sociological or historical interest.

The tone of melancholy that suffuses Bulgakov's works is a consequence of the futility he sees in the artist's struggle against the mighty of this world, and most of his sympathetic characters are more than half in love with easeful death. Creativity, love, and good humor do, nevertheless, triumph. To reduce Bulgakov's fictions to the bare formula of a struggle between sensitivity and brutishness and between eternity and the moment is to miss the mournful exuberance of his *comédies larmoyantes*. Not only *Black Snow*, the subtitle of which proclaims it, but also Bulgakov's other books are theatrical novels. The spirited play of a harried author drawn to and disappointed by the theater, they employ self-conscious devices, such as apostrophes to the reader, impudent violations of verisimilitude, and encased narratives, to enact a liberation not only from the oppressive worlds they depict but also from the literary instrument of emancipation itself. *Black Snow* concludes with a deflationary fictional afterword, and it is night on the final pages of *The White Guard*, *The Master and Margarita*, and *The Heart of a Dog*. Like William Shakespeare's *The Tempest* (pr. 1611) abjuring its own magic, Bulgakov's novels provide bittersweet crepuscular valediction to the powers of temporal authority and to the verbal artifices that their inventive author assembles.

THE WHITE GUARD

Bulgakov's first novel, and the only one to be published (at least in part) in his lifetime, *The White Guard* is set in Kiev in the winter of 1918. It is the moment at which the hetman Pavel Petrovich Skoropadsky, who has ruled with the support of the Germans, flees the city, and the forces of the Ukrainian nationalist Semyon Petlyura prove temporarily triumphant over Whites and Bolsheviks. *The White Guard* is a polyphonic arrangement of a variety of characters and incidents within a brief, dramatic period in the history of modern Kiev. Its focus, however, is on the fate of one family, the Turbins, representative of a venerable way of life that is disintegrating as Ukrainian society undergoes radical change.

The Turbin children have recently buried their mother, and twenty-eight-year-old

Alexei, a physician, his twenty-four-year-old sister Elena, and their seventeen-year-old brother Nikolka, a student, attempt to maintain family traditions and values, which are those of a comfortable Russian intellectual home. Public events make this impossible, however, and the collapse of the kind of humane civilization that the Turbin family exemplifies—with which Bulgakov, whose background was similar, is, despite the censor, sympathetic—is inevitable with the victory of Petlyura's troops.

Captain Sergey Talberg, the opportunistic scoundrel to whom Elena is married, abandons her to seek safety and another woman in Paris. The hetman, in the cowardly disguise of a German officer, likewise deserts Kiev at its moment of greatest danger. Nevertheless, Alexei and Nikolka, along with many others, enlist in the loyalist army in a futile effort to repulse Petlyura's advance into the city. Bulgakov depicts a range of heroism and knavery on all sides during the months of crisis in Kiev. The narrative weaves multiple subplots of combat and domestic drama into a vivid account of an obsolescent society under siege.

Through it all, the Turbin house, number 13 St. Alexei's Hill, remains for the family and its friends a fragile sanctuary. Nikolka barely escapes the violence, and Alexei, who is wounded, miraculously survives battle and an attack of typhus with the gracious assistance of a mysterious beauty named Julia Reiss. Despite the grim situation, gentle comic relief is provided by characters such as the miserly neighbor Vasilisa and the benevolent bumpkin Lariosik, who comes to stay with his relatives, the Turbins.

The apocalyptic tone of *The White Guard* is supported by religious allusions, particularly to the biblical book of Revelation. The music for the opera *Faust* remains open on the Turbin piano from the beginning of the novel to its end, and the reader is reminded of enduring values that transcend the contingencies of politics:

> But long after the Turbins and Talbergs have departed this life the keys will ring out again and Valentine will step up to the footlights, the aroma of perfume will waft from the boxes and at home beautiful women under the lamplight will play the music, because *Faust*, like the Shipwright of Saardam, is quite immortal.

As the novel concludes, Petlyura's victory, too, is ephemeral, as the Bolsheviks advance. Night descends on the Dnieper, and each of several characters dreams of something far beyond the petty intrigues of daylight Kiev. As in all of Bulgakov's fictions, a foregrounded narrative voice, relying on rhetorical questions, playful and ingenious connections and summaries, and an overtly evocative landscape, impels the reader beyond the trifles of wars and words.

BLACK SNOW

Black Snow, an unfinished work, was discovered in 1965 by the commission established during the post-Stalin thaw to rehabilitate Bulgakov. An account of the emergence of an obscure hack named Sergey Leontievich Maxudov as a literary and theatrical celebrity in Moscow, it draws heavily on Bulgakov's own experiences in writing *The White*

Guard and adapting it for the Moscow Art Theater as *Days of the Turbins*. It provides a lively portrait of the artist as a melancholic and misunderstood figure and of a cultural establishment inimical to genuine creativity.

The novel begins with a letter from a producer named Xavier Borisovich Ilchin summoning Maxudov to his office at the Academy of Drama. Ilchin has read Maxudov's unacclaimed novel and is eager for him to adapt it for the stage. Next follows a flashback recounting how Maxudov conceived his book and how, as an obscure employee of the trade journal *Shipping Gazette*, he signed a contract for its publication in *The Motherland* shortly before that magazine folded. The flashback concludes with an account of how Maxudov's life is transformed after he signs a contract for the production of *Black Snow*, his stage version of the novel, by the Independent Theater.

Maxudov soon finds himself a victim of the rivalries and jealousies of figures in the theatrical world. In particular, he is caught between the two directors of the Independent Theater, Aristarkh Platonovich, who is currently off in India, and Ivan Vasilievich; neither has spoken to the other in forty years. Ivan Vasilievich is clearly modeled on Stanislavsky, and grotesque descriptions portray the tyrannical director at work, rehearsing his actors in *Black Snow* with his celebrated "method." The hapless dramatist makes a convincing case that "the famous theory was utterly wrong for my play."

Black Snow employs a sophisticated narrative perspective to distance the reader both from its inept protagonist and from the bizarre characters he encounters. Its two parts are both written by Maxudov himself in the form of a memoir. An afterword, however, introduces a new, anonymous voice who explains how Maxudov sent the manuscript to him shortly before killing himself by jumping off a bridge in Kiev. This second narrator describes the narrative that the reader has just finished as suffering from "slovenly style" and as the "fruit of a morbid imagination." Furthermore, he points out its egregious inaccuracies, among which is the fact that Maxudov never did have anything to do with the theater. The effect of this coda, as of those in Knut Hamsun's *Pan* (1894; English translation, 1920) and director Robert Wiene's film *The Cabinet of Dr. Caligari* (1920), is to cast retrospective doubt on the reliability of everything that precedes it. Is *Black Snow* a caustic mockery of philistine bureaucrats, or is it a case study in the psychopathology of a deluded author manqué? Or perhaps both? Maxudov, distraught over frustrations with the Independent Theater, does admit that he is a melancholic and describes an early suicide attempt, aborted when he heard a recording of *Faust* coming from the apartment downstairs. *Black Snow*, with its examination of the artist as victim—of powerful boors and of himself—and its lucid blend of whimsy and social observation, is a fitting commentary on and companion to Bulgakov's other works.

THE MASTER AND MARGARITA

Perhaps the supreme Russian novel of the twentieth century, and one of the most endearing modern texts in any language, *The Master and Margarita* was first published in abridged form in 1966-1967 and immediately created a sensation. It is a rich fusion of at least four realms and plots: the banal world of contemporary Moscow, containing the Griboyedov House, the Variety Theater, the apartments at 302-b Sadovaya, and a psychiatric hospital; ancient Jerusalem, where Pontius Pilate suffers torment over whether to crucify Yeshua Ha-Nozri; the antics of Woland and his satanic crew, including Koroviev, Azazello, Behemoth, and Hella; and the activities of the Master, utterly devoted to his art, and of Margarita, utterly devoted to him. Throughout, chapters of the novel crosscut from one of these subplots to another and ultimately suggest that perhaps they are not so distinct after all.

What sets the complex machinery of Bulgakov's novel in motion is a four-day visit to Soviet Moscow by the devil, referred to as Woland, and his assistants. They gleefully wreak havoc with the lives of the bureaucrats, hypocrites, opportunists, and dullards they encounter. They do, however, befriend and assist the Master, an alienated writer who has been hospitalized after the worldly failure of his literary efforts. The Master's beloved Margarita consents to serve as hostess at Satan's ball and is rewarded with supernatural powers. An inferior poet named Ivan Homeless finds himself in the same psychiatric clinic as the Master and gradually becomes his disciple. The lifework of the Master is a novel about Pontius Pilate, and chapters from it, with manifest parallels to the situation in contemporary Moscow, are interspersed throughout Bulgakov's novel.

Woland's performance at the Variety Theater is billed as a "black magic act accompanied by a full exposé," and *The Master and Margarita* itself, an absorbing blend of fantasy and verisimilitude presented with subversive self-consciousness, could be similarly described. The playful narrative voice that overtly addresses the reader mocks not only the characters but itself as well. Numerous authors among the *dramatis personae*, including Ivan, the Master, Matthu Levi, and Ryukhin, as well as characters given musical names such as Berlioz, Stravinsky, and Rimsky, foreground the process of fabrication and reinforce one of the novel's persistent themes—the elusive nature of truth.

Most of the characters in Moscow refuse to recognize anything problematic about truth. Arrogantly convinced that human reason is adequate to any cognitive task, they stubbornly deny the supernatural that erupts in the form of Woland or that is evoked in the story of Yeshua. Like the other hack writers who congregate at the Griboyedov House, Ivan Homeless would just as soon take life on the most comfortable terms possible, but his spirit will not permit him to do so. Torn between the material and the spiritual, the temporal and the eternal, the collective and the individual, Ivan is diagnosed as schizophrenic and is hospitalized. His progress as a patient and as a writer will be marked by his success in reconciling opposing realms. Bulgakov, the novelist as master weaver, seems to be suggesting that both artistic achievement and mental health are dependent on a harmony between ostensibly disparate materials.

The Master, like Bulgakov himself, attempted to destroy his book, but, as Woland points out, "manuscripts don't burn." Art survives and transcends the hardships and iniquities of particular places and times. It ridicules the obtuseness of temporal authorities with the example of immortal authority. In one of many echoes of the Faust legend, *The Master and Margarita* chooses as its epigraph Johann Wolfgang von Goethe's reference to "that Power which eternally wills evil and eternally works good." Bulgakov's ambitious novel certainly does not deny the oppressive reality of contemporary society, but its humor is restorative, and it moves toward an exhilarating, harmonious vision that would exclude nothing. It concludes with a benedictory kiss from a spectral Margarita.

THE HEART OF A DOG

The most overt of Bulgakov's statements on the Russian Revolution, *The Heart of a Dog*, though written in 1925, was published in English in 1968 and in Russian in 1969. It is a satiric novella about an experiment performed by the celebrated Moscow surgeon Philip Philipovich Preobrazhensky, who takes a stray mongrel dog, Sharik, and transforms him into a human being named Sharikov. Much of the tale is narrated by Sharikov himself, who is not necessarily better off for his transformation. To perform the operation, Preobrazhensky has inserted the pituitary of a vulgar criminal into the brain of the dog. The result is an uncouth, rowdy human being who, though adept at language and even at repeating the political slogans supplied by the officious house committee chairman, Shvonder, proves incapable of satisfying the standards of civilized behavior demanded by Preobrazhensky. Hence, convinced that the experiment is a fiasco, he reverses it and turns Sharikov back into Sharik.

The Heart of a Dog features Bulgakov's characteristic blend of fantasy and social analysis. It parabolically raises the question of the malleability of human nature and of the possibility of social melioration. Once again, it exposes to ridicule the arrogance of those who would presume to shape others' lives and raises doubts about the efficacy and desirability of social engineering, such as Russia was undergoing in the 1920's. The book suggests a fatal incompatibility between the proletariat and the intelligentsia, implying that the humane values of the latter are threatened by the former. It seems to counsel humble caution in tampering with the arrangements of the world.

Steven G. Kellman

OTHER MAJOR WORKS

SHORT FICTION: *Diavoliada*, 1925 (*Diaboliad, and Other Stories*, 1972); *Traktat o zhilishche*, 1926 (*A Treatise on Housing*, 1972); *Zapiski iunogo vracha*, 1963 (*A Country Doctor's Notebook*, 1975); *Notes on the Cuff, and Other Stories*, 1991.

PLAYS: *Dni Turbinykh*, pr. 1926 (adaptation of his novel *Belaya gvardiya*; *Days of the Turbins*, 1934); *Zoykina kvartira*, pr. 1926 (*Zoya's Apartment*, 1970); *Bagrovy ostrov*, pr. 1928 (adaptation of his short story; *The Crimson Island*, 1972); *Kabala svyatosh*, pr. 1936 (wr. 1929; *A Cabal of Hypocrites*, 1972; also known as *Molière*); *Don Kikhot*, pr. 1941; *Posledniye dni (Pushkin)*, pr. 1943 (wr. 1934-1935; *The Last Days*, 1976); *Beg*, pr. 1957 (wr. 1928; *Flight*, 1969); *Ivan Vasilievich*, pb. 1965 (wr. 1935; English translation, 1974); *Blazhenstvo*, pb. 1966 (wr. 1934; *Bliss*, 1976); *Adam i Eva*, pb. 1971 (wr. 1930-1931; *Adam and Eve*, 1971); *The Early Plays of Mikhail Bulgakov*, 1972; *Rashel*, pb. 1972 (wr. c. 1936; libretto; adaptation of Guy de Maupassant's short story "Mademoiselle Fifi"); *Minin i Pozharskii*, pb. 1976 (wr. 1936; libretto); *Batum*, pb. 1977 (wr. 1938); *Six Plays*, 1991.

NONFICTION: *Zhizn gospodina de Molyera*, 1962 (*The Life of Monsieur de Molière*, 1970).

TRANSLATION: *L'Avare*, 1936 (of Molière's play).

BIBLIOGRAPHY

Barratt, Andrew. *Between Two Worlds: A Critical Introduction to "The Master and Margarita."* New York: Oxford University Press, 1987. Puts forth an imaginative approach to understanding Bulgakov's most important work. Describes the genesis of the novel and its reception inside and outside the Soviet Union.

Curtis, J. A. E. *Manuscripts Don't Burn: Mikhail Bulgakov, a Life in Letters and Diaries.* Woodstock, N.Y.: Overlook Press, 1992. Contains previously unpublished letters and a diary that were believed to be lost. Groups of Bulgakov's letters, diaries, and speeches are arranged in chronological order and interspersed with biographical chapters, providing context for the primary source material.

Drawicz, Andrzej. *The Master and the Devil: A Study of Mikhail Bulgakov.* Translated by Kevin Windle. Lewiston, N.Y.: Edwin Mellen Press, 2001. Analyzes all of Bulgakov's prose and dramatic works, placing them within the context of the author's life and times. The initial chapters focus on Bulgakov's life, providing new biographical information, and subsequent chapters concentrate on his novels and other writings.

Haber, Edythe C. *Mikhail Bulgakov: The Early Years.* Cambridge, Mass.: Harvard University Press, 1998. Discusses Bulgakov's early life and career, describing how his novels and other works arose from his experiences during the Russian Revolution, civil war, and early years of Communism. Traces the themes and characters of his early works and demonstrates how he perfected these fictional elements in *The Master and Margarita.*

Milne, Lesley. *Mikhail Bulgakov: A Critical Biography.* New York: Cambridge University Press, 1990. Describes some of the features that are essential to understanding Bulgakov's outlook on life and the themes and techniques of his works. Includes detailed and original interpretations of some of Bulgakov's earliest works as well as a serious examination of *The Master and Margarita.*

_______, ed. *Bulgakov: The Novelist-Playwright.* New York: Routledge, 1996. Collection of twenty-one essays surveys Bulgakov's works from a wide variety of perspectives. Several essays examine *The Master and Margarita*, including one that compares the novel to Salman Rushdie's *The Satanic Verses* (1988). Includes an index of Bulgakov's works.

Proffer, Ellendea. *Bulgakov: Life and Work*. Ann Arbor, Mich.: Ardis, 1984. Comprehensive treatment of Bulgakov's career provides information and analysis of some early works that previously received little scholarly attention. Proffer's portrait of Bulgakov contrasts with that of other critics, who depict him as being a suppressed and haunted author under the Stalinist regime.

Weir, Justin. *The Author as Hero: Self and Tradition in Bulgakov, Pasternak, and Nabokov.* Evanston, Ill.: Northwestern University Press, 2002. Analyzes novels by three Russian authors—Bulgakov's *The Master and Margarita*, Boris Pasternak's *Doktor Zhivago* (1957; *Doctor Zhivago*, 1958), and Vladimir Nabokov's *Dar* (1952; *The Gift*, 1963)—to describe how these authors reveal themselves through their writing, transforming the traditional authors into the heroes of their novels.

Wright, A. Colin. *Mikhail Bulgakov: Life and Interpretations*. Toronto, Ont.: University of Toronto Press, 1978. Thorough critical biography examines *The Master and Margarita* and other works and places them within the context of Bulgakov's life. Includes indexes and bibliography.

JAMES BRANCH CABELL

Born: Richmond, Virginia; April 14, 1879
Died: Richmond, Virginia; May 5, 1958

PRINCIPAL LONG FICTION

The Eagle's Shadow, 1904
The Cords of Vanity, 1909
The Soul of Melicent, 1913 (republished as *Domnei*, 1920)
The Rivet in Grandfather's Neck, 1915
The Cream of the Jest, 1917
Jurgen, 1919
Figures of Earth: A Comedy of Appearances, 1921
The High Place, 1923
The Silver Stallion, 1926
Something About Eve, 1927
The Biography of the Life of Manuel: The Works of James Branch Cabell, 1927-1930 (18 volumes)
The White Robe, 1928
The Way of Ecben, 1929
Smirt, 1934
Smith, 1935
Smire, 1937
The King Was in His Counting House, 1938
Hamlet Had an Uncle, 1940
The First Gentleman of America, 1942
There Were Two Pirates, 1946
The Devil's Own Dear Son, 1949

OTHER LITERARY FORMS

James Branch Cabell (KAB-uhl) was both prolific and versatile. In addition to his many novels, he produced a volume of poetry titled *From the Hidden Way* (1916) and a play, *The Jewel Merchants* (pb. 1921). His short stories are collected in *The Line of Love* (1905), *Gallantry* (1907), *Chivalry* (1909), and *The Certain Hour* (1916). Included among his writings are critical volumes on his contemporaries Joseph Hergesheimer and Ellen Glasgow; *Taboo* (1921), a satire dedicated to Cabell's nemesis, John S. Sumner, who initiated obscenity charges against Cabell's novel *Jurgen*; *Some of Us* (1930), a defense of the individualism of such writers as Elinor Wylie, Sinclair Lewis, and H. L. Mencken; and *The St. Johns* (1943), a history of a Florida river written with A. J. Hanna, for Stephen Vincent Benét's book series titled The Rivers of America.

James Branch Cabell
(Library of Congress)

Perhaps Cabell's most interesting volumes are those that illuminate his life and literary development. He wrote two epistolary volumes: *Special Delivery* (1933), which presents both his conventional responses to letters he received and the unconventional replies he would have preferred to send, and *Ladies and Gentlemen* (1934), a collection of addresses to dead historical figures—from Solomon to George Washington, from Pocahontas to Madame de Pompadour—who have inspired myths and legends. He explores the past of his native region and its impact on his writings in his trilogy "Virginians Are Various," consisting of *Let Me Lie* (1947), *Quiet, Please* (1952), and *As I Remember It* (1955). Providing readers with insight into Cabell's art are *Beyond Life* (1919), which clarifies his values, literary precedents, and thematic concerns; *These Restless Heads* (1932), a discussion of creativity based on the four seasons of the year; and *Straws and Prayer-Books* (1924), an explanation of his reasons for writing *The Biography of the Life of Manuel*. Two volumes of Cabell's letters have been published: *Between Friends: Letters of James Branch Cabell and Others* (1962), edited by his second wife, Margaret Freeman Cabell, and Padraic Colum; and *The Letters of James Branch Cabell* (1975), edited by Edward Wagenknecht. His manuscripts and memorabilia are in the James Branch Cabell Collections at the University of Virginia in Charlottesville.

ACHIEVEMENTS

James Branch Cabell's aesthetic individualism—as expressed in his highly artificial style, his loose, episodic structure, and his peculiar synthesis of romance and comedy, idealism and cynicism, mythology and personal experience—has limited both his popular and critical appeal. As Arvin R. Wells observes in *Jesting Moses: A Study in Cabellian Comedy* (1962), "It seems fair to say that rarely has a serious literary artist had so little luck in finding a responsive, judicious, and articulate audience." The essays, short stories, and books that Cabell published from 1901 to 1919 received only a small readership along with generally negative reviews, although both Mark Twain and Theodore Roosevelt praised his collection of chivalric tales, *The Line of Love*. Most readers, advocates of realism, found his works too romantic, whereas those with a taste for romance complained that Cabell was too abstruse.

In 1920, when obscenity charges were brought against *Jurgen*, Cabell found himself in the public eye, perceived as a valiant iconoclast battling the forces of puritanical repression. Sales of *Jurgen* skyrocketed, and Cabell enjoyed praise from such respected literary figures as Vernon Louis Parrington, Carl Van Doren, H. L. Mencken, and Sinclair Lewis, who acknowledged Cabell's achievement in his Nobel Prize address of 1930. Suddenly, in critical studies, literary histories, and anthologies, Cabell was elevated to, as the critic Joe Lee Davis has put it, "the rank of a 'classic' and an 'exotic' in the movement of spiritual liberation led by H. L. Mencken, Theodore Dreiser, Eugene O'Neill, and Sinclair Lewis."

The public fanfare of the 1920's, however, inspired primarily by the eroticism in Cabell's works, proved to be short-lived—not to the surprise of Cabell, who, in *These Restless Heads*, predicted the decline of his literary generation. In the 1930's and 1940's, Cabell was viewed as a trifling talent, rooted to the 1920's and to his native Virginia. His aestheticism displeased the ethical neohumanists; his escapism annoyed the Marxists. The New Critics and mythic critics paid him scant attention. In the 1950's, three major literary historians—Edward Wagenknecht, Edd Winfield Parks, and Edmund Wilson—called for a reevaluation of Cabell's career, but they did little to change public opinion. Many of Cabell's books have been out of print at various times, although a late twentieth century surge of interest in fantasy literature brought some attention to his work, which has come to be appreciated primarily by a coterie of scholars and graduate students.

BIOGRAPHY

Born on April 14, 1879, in Richmond, Virginia, James Branch Cabell grew up there as a southern gentleman. His parents—Robert Gamble Cabell II, a physician, and Anne Branch—were both from distinguished southern families. Cabell's paternal great-grandfather was a governor of Virginia; his paternal grandfather held two claims to fame, having been a schoolmate of Edgar Allan Poe at the English and Classical School in Richmond and later a neighbor and the personal physician of General Robert E. Lee. On his mother's side of the family, Cabell was related through marriage to a number of prominent Virginia families and was cousin to a governor of Maryland. Fostering Cabell's aristocratic pride still further was his "mammy," Mrs. Louisa Nelson, who, in her several decades of service in the Cabell household, doted on James and encouraged him to consider himself a privileged member of society.

Cabell's outstanding intellect asserted itself early. He performed brilliantly at the College of William and Mary in Williamsburg, which he attended from 1894 to 1898. His professors suggested that he revise a sophomore paper titled "The Comedies of William Congreve" for publication and later asked him to teach courses in French and Greek at the college. The only blemish on Cabell's academic career was a scandal during his senior year. One of his professors was accused of having homosexual relations with his students; Cabell, because he had been friends with the man, was briefly implicated. The unpleasant episode had positive repercussions, however, for in wandering about Williamsburg alone and troubled, Cabell met Ellen Glasgow, who had come to town to research the background for a novel. She offered him sympathy, and thus began a lifelong friendship. Soon the charges against Cabell were dropped for lack of evidence, and he graduated with highest honors.

After his graduation, Cabell pursued writing both as a vocation and an avocation. He served as a copyholder on the *Richmond Times* in 1898, then spent two years working for the *New York Herald*, and in 1901 he worked for the *Richmond News*. For the next decade, he worked as a genealogist, traveling around the United States, England, Ireland, and France to examine archives. Not only did this occupation result in two volumes of the Branch family history—*Branchiana* (1907), a record of the Branch family in Virginia, and *Branch of Abingdon* (1911), a record of the Branch family in England—but it also prepared Cabell for his future literary endeavors in tracing the lineage of a character through twenty-two subsequent generations. During that same time, Cabell wrote several novels and steadily produced short stories, which he contributed to such periodicals as *The Smart Set*, *Collier's Weekly*, *Redbook*, *Lippincott's*, and *Harper's Monthly*. In 1911, Cabell, disappointed by his lack of acclaim as a writer, took a position in coal-mining operations in West Virginia; in 1913, he abandoned the experiment and returned to Richmond to resume work as a genealogist.

On November 8, 1913, at the age of thirty-four, Cabell gave up what had been a carefree bachelorhood, filled with romantic intrigues, to marry Rebecca Priscilla Bradley Shepard, a widow with five children. Marriage proved mutually satisfying to Cabell and Priscilla. He enjoyed the domesticity of his new lifestyle, including the rearing of their son Ballard Hartwell; she delighted in performing the literary and social duties that came with being his wife. Their thirty-five-year union was marked by undying affection and loyalty.

Literary prominence, or perhaps one should say notoriety, came to Cabell in 1920 when John S. Sumner, the executive secretary of the New York Society for the Suppression of Vice, seized the plates and copies of Cabell's novel *Jurgen* and accused the publishing company, McBride, of violating the antiobscenity statutes of the New York State penal code. Sumner's action proved ill-advised, for it only increased the public's interest in Cabell's writings during the two and a half years before the obscenity trial was finally held. On October 19, 1922, after a three-day trial, the jury acquitted McBride, and Cabell emerged as a celebrity.

During the 1920's, Cabell took a more active role as a literary leader and was instrumental, along with Ellen Glasgow, in making the nation aware of Richmond as a literary center. While writing books with great regularity (during the 1920's, he published seven novels, one play, and several works of short fiction and nonfiction), Cabell also entertained and corresponded with a number of important literary figures, including Sinclair Lewis, Hugh Walpole, and Carl Van Vechten. In addition, he served as a writer and guest editor for *The Reviewer*, Richmond's impressive contribution to the vogue of little magazines. As active as Cabell was on the literary scene, he was still able to continue his career as a genealogist, working for the Virginia Chapter of the Sons of the Revolution and other historical societies, as well as serving as editor of the Virginia War History Commission.

The last decades of Cabell's life were anticlimactic, fraught with physical ailments and an increasing disillusionment with the American reading public. With the advent of the Great Depression, his literary fame seemed to weaken and then die. From 1932 to 1935, Cabell—like Sherwood Anderson, George Jean Nathan, Eugene O'Neill, and Theodore Dreiser—attempted to rekindle the vital skepticism of the 1920's, serving as editor of the *American Spectator*; he soon realized, however, that his efforts to enlighten the public were useless. In the mid-1930's, Cabell suffered from repeated attacks of pneumonia, and Priscilla developed severe arthritis; thus, they frequently sought relief in the warm climate of St. Augustine, Florida. There, Priscilla died of heart failure on March 29, 1949. Her death left Cabell feeling bitter, lost, and angry, but he continued to write steadily. In 1950, he regained some of his former zest for life when he decided to wed Margaret Waller Freeman, a member of the Richmond literati whose acquaintance he had made years earlier while writing for *The Reviewer*. Cabell died of a cerebral hemorrhage on May 5, 1958, in Richmond.

Analysis

James Branch Cabell's art rests on a paradox. On one hand, the author contends that man is idealistic and must therefore create dreams to sustain himself. On the other, he mocks man's tendency "to play the ape to his dreams"—that is, to seek the unattainable foolishly. Manipulating the polarities of romance and comedy, Cabell responded to the predominant intellectual trend of the early twentieth century—naturalism. From a cosmic perspective, he had no difficulty accepting the premise that man is like a bit of flotsam in a deterministic universe, subject to environmental forces but unable to control or understand them. From a humanistic point of view, however, he could not tolerate the limitations that naturalism imposed on the human mind. For Cabell, man does not survive because he adapts to biological, social, or economic forces, but rather because he persists in believing in the products of his own imagination—what Cabell terms "dynamic illusions." These illusions, according to Cabell, emanate from the demiurge, or psyche, yet they are rooted in man's primitive, animal instincts. Their source of energy is the libido. Cabell's protagonists thus move between two realms of experience: They are romantic questers after ideal beauty, perfection, and salvation; they are also comic bumblers whose lusts, vanities, and misconceptions entangle them in a web of complexities. Cabell's narratives follow a Hegelian pattern. His thesis is that man desires to escape from the dull, routine world of actuality. His antithesis is that such a desire can never be attained; disillusionment is inevitable. In the synthesis, however, man achieves a degree of satisfaction. He learns that his ideals are illusions but also that they should be cherished, for in the realm of the imagination, dreams themselves have a reality.

Cabell's background explains his propensity for blending the romantic and the comic. Quite early, he developed a love for myth and legend. As a child, he delighted in such books as *Old Greek Stories Simply Told*, *Stories of Old Rome*, *Book of Bible Stories*, and *Stories of the Days of King Arthur*. Cabell gained a strong sense of aristocratic pride—an appreciation of the southern characteristics of chivalry and gallantry—yet he was no dreamy-eyed romantic. He saw the ironic underside of life. In growing up, he heard frank gossip, as well as heroic tales, from his elders. In college, Cabell became interested in the Restoration comedy of manners, which heightened his awareness of the hypocrisies and absurdities of human behavior. Such weaknesses became more immediately apparent when, as a bachelor in his twenties and early thirties, he vacationed at the Virginia resort of Rockbridge Alum. There, he witnessed and participated in affairs that assumed the facade of chaste, genteel encounters but were actually indulgences in lust. From his various experiences, Cabell developed a dichotomous concept of the artist, appropriate to his blending of romance and comedy. The artist assumes an exalted status, painting beautiful visions of life as it ought to be. Ironically, however, because of this detached, godlike perspective, skepticism intrudes. The world that the artist portrays becomes a caricature; it mocks and contradicts the idealistic presentation. For Cabell, the ideal and the real coexist.

THE BIOGRAPHY OF THE LIFE OF MANUEL

Cabell's major literary achievement is his eighteen-volume *The Biography of the Life of Manuel*, which he wished readers to regard as a single book. In 1915, Cabell conceived the idea of bringing together his writings into one vast architectural construct, and for the next fifteen years, he strove to achieve his plan: revising published works, deciding on a logical arrangement, and writing new tales and romances to clarify his design. The result was the Storisende Edition of *The Works of James Branch Cabell*, bound in green and gold. Cabell's magnum opus represents an ingenious application of his genealogical talents to the realm of fiction. Spanning seven centuries and moving from the imaginary medieval realm of Poictesme to modern Virginia, it celebrates the life force passed on by Manuel to his descendants.

The design of *The Biography of the Life of Manuel* is best viewed in musical terms. Whether one considers it to be a fugue or a sonata, it revolves on three themes and their variations. These themes are three philosophies of life: the chivalrous, the gallant, and the poetic. The chivalrous attitude views life as a testing; dominated by the will, it represents an ideal tradition in which men revere first God and then noble women. Quite the opposite, the gallant attitude views life as a toy; its social principle is hedonism. This attitude emphasizes the intelligence and is thus skeptical. Celebrating both chivalry and gallantry, the final attitude, the poetic, views life as raw material out of which it creates something that transcends life. It is controlled by the imagination.

These attitudes of the chivalrous, the gallant, and the poetic determine the structure of Cabell's work. In *Beyond Life*, the prologue to *The Biography of the Life of Manuel*, he defines them. Then, in *Figures of Earth*, Cabell presents the life of Manuel of Poictesme, who at various times is affected by all three codes, and follows it with *The Silver Stallion*, which traces the development of the legend of Manuel the Redeemer. The fourth volume—composed of *Domnei* and *The Music from Behind the Moon*—treats one aspect of the chivalric code: woman worship. Cabell then elaborates on the subject in his short-story collection titled *Chivalry*. He next examines the gallant attitude in *Jurgen*; inserts *The Line of Love*, which treats all three attitudes; then returns to gallantry in *The High Place* and the short-story collection *The Certain Hour*. The next four volumes move to the modern world: *The Cords of Vanity* presents Robert Townsend, a gallant; *From the Hidden Way* offers Townsend's verses; *The Rivet in Grandfather's Neck* portrays a chivalrous character; and *The Eagle's Shadow* examines the poet. Finally, *The Biography of the Life of Manuel* circles back on itself, as the soul of Felix Kennaston, the protagonist of *The Cream of the Jest*, journeys back to Poictesme through his dreams. Cabell's vast design concludes with an epilogue, *Straws and Prayer-Books*, and *Townsend of Lichfield*, containing notes and addenda.

FIGURES OF EARTH

Figures of Earth, one of Cabell's finest novels, follows its author's typical tripartite pattern of quest, ensuing disillusionment, and final transcendence, as it traces the career of the swineherd Manuel. Subtitled *A Comedy of Appearances*, it is a complex allegorical work peopled with supernatural and preternatural beings who reside in the imaginary medieval land of Poictesme. The tale begins when Miramon Lluagor, the master of dreams, appears to Manuel at the pool of Haranton. There, he convinces Manuel to abandon his job as a swineherd—that is, to rebel against the elemental forces of life—and to pursue knight-errantry in seeking the beautiful yet unattainable Lady Gisele. Eager to make a fine figure in the world, Manuel repudiates his lover Suskind, a mysterious creature who represents the unconscious desires of the libido, and sets forth, unaware that he is being victimized by Horvendile, the diabolical spirit of romance. On his journey, he has a series of encounters with allegorical women. He first meets Niafer, a rather plain kitchen servant, who symbolizes worldly wisdom and domesticity. Dressed as a boy, she accompanies Manuel on his quest until, when faced with his own death unless he gives up Niafer, Manuel decides to sacrifice her to Grandfather Death. His next encounter is with the Princess Alianora, who represents political power, worldly position, and the undercurrent of sexual excitement that accompanies them. Manuel surrenders to lust, but eventually rejects Alianora, discovering the limitations of self-seeking gallantry. His third important encounter is with the supernal Queen Freydis, who symbolizes creative inspiration. Using magic, Manuel persuades her to leave her realm of Audela and enter the ordinary world. She does so out of love for him and animates a set of clay figures that he sculpted as a swineherd. These eventually enter history as major writers.

Manuel soon discovers that Freydis cannot give him fulfillment; only Niafer can, so he submits to thirty years of slavery to The Head of Misery to bring Niafer back from the dead. Then he settles down to a comfortable existence as a husband, father, and the Count of Poictesme. One day, however, while watching his wife and daughter through the window of Ageus (Usage) in his palace study, he discovers to his horror that their figures are only scratched on the glass—that beyond the window is a chaos containing the images of preexistence, including the disturbing Suskind. Manuel must then choose whether to die himself or to allow his child Melicent to die in his place, while he resumes his relationship with Suskind. Acting decisively, he murders Suskind, bricks up the study window, and departs with Grandfather Death. In the last chapter, Grandfather Death accompanies him to the River Lethe, where he watches the images of his life as they sweep by him. Then the scene blurs, as Cabell moves his readers back to the pool of Haranton where Manuel began his quest. He repeats the dialogue of the first chapter, in which Miramon refers to Count Manuel, who has just died. Thus, Cabell ends with an appropriate reminder of his view of life as a cycle in which one life passes into other lives through heredity.

Manuel is Cabell's man of action, driven by dreams of a better life than that of a swineherd, yet the pursuit of dreams proves frustrating. Even in the mythical realm of Poictesme, Cabell constantly emphasizes through allegory the realities of death, misery, and madness. Life, Manuel learns, is full of obligations: to Alianora, Melicent, and especially to Niafer. Indeed, Cabell underscores this lesson by structuring his episodes into five books titled "Credit," "Spending," "Cash Accounts," "Surcharge," and "Settlement." It is in confronting his obligations, however, that Manuel finds fulfillment. The romantic quest results in a comic exposure of man's limitations, but the final picture is of human dignity in accepting those limitations. Manuel can never completely obliterate discontent, but he decides that the human possessions of a kingdom, a wife, and a family, even if they are illusions, are better than a return to the primitive unconsciousness. Thus, although he never achieves the object of his initial quest, he does transcend experience through belief in his destined role as the Redeemer of Poictesme and his ultimate rejection of lust for love.

Figures of Earth, because of its confusing cast of characters—some of whom are figures of earth and some unearthly—and the artificialities of Cabell's prose, makes difficult reading. The effort is rewarding, however, for Cabell offers some intriguing insights into man's values: that the demands of the family and the aspirations of the individual often conflict; that the world is duplicitous; and that the search for perfection involves paradoxically the self-realization of imperfection. The work is thought-provoking and timely.

JURGEN

Jurgen follows the same movement as *Figures of Earth:* the pursuit of perfection, the discovery that it does not exist, and then the satisfaction achieved through accepting actuality; it merely views these ideas from a different perspective. The controlling concept is justice, which to Cabell's title character, a poetry-producing pawnbroker, means that in the universe, every idealistic desire should have a means of being fulfilled. Jurgen's problem, however, is that existence is unjust; since man's intellect increases as his physical prowess diminishes, he can never completely realize his potential. Granting Jurgen a temporary respite from his dilemma, Cabell allows his middle-aged poet to retain his youthful body and then lets his reader see the subsequent effects on his protagonist's values.

Jurgen began as a tale titled "Some Ladies and Jurgen," which Cabell published in *The Smart Set* in 1918. His novel simply expands on the narrative of that story. The hero meets a monk, who curses the devil for causing him to trip over a stone. Jurgen, playing the devil's advocate, defends evil. Shortly thereafter, he meets a black gentleman who thanks him for the defense and expresses the hope that his life will be carefree. When Jurgen replies that such a life is impossible, since he is married, the stranger promises to reward him. The reward turns out to be the disappearance of Jurgen's wife, Dame Lisa. When he returns home, she is gone; he later learns that she has been seen near a cave outside town. Feeling an obligation, he goes there, only to encounter the black gentleman—who, he learns, is Koshchei the Deathless, the controller of the universe. Koshchei tempts Jurgen by evoking three women that he feels would be more suitable for a poet: Queen Guenevere, Queen Anaïtis, and Queen Helen—standing respectively for faith, desire, and vision. Jurgen rejects each, however, and asks for Dame Lisa back. She appears, lectures him, and then leaves for home. In response, Jurgen praises her as a source of poetic inspiration more valuable than faith, desire, and vision, and then follows her home.

Expanding his narrative for the novel, Cabell added two fantasy sequences that would explain Jurgen's ultimate attraction to Lisa. In the first, Jurgen visits the Garden between Dawn and Sunrise, where he relives falling in love with Dorothy la Désirée, one of the daughters of Manuel. She destroys his romantic bliss when she marries the wealthy Heitman Michael and then engages in adulterous affairs. Because of Dorothy's behavior,

Jurgen marries Lisa. In the second episode, Jurgen, having been granted by Mother Sereda the recovery of a bygone Wednesday, fantasizes about how his relationship with Dorothy might have developed. He imagines himself killing Heitman Michael and claiming her, but as the Wednesday ends, he finds himself embracing the Dorothy of reality, an aged femme fatale.

Cabell also expanded his original tale by depicting Jurgen's adventures in five realms: Glathion, Cocaigne, Leukê, Hell, and Heaven. Throughout these episodes, Jurgen assumes the roles of charlatan and womanizer, as he tests historical systems of values. In Glathion, he examines the medieval tradition of Christian chivalry, but rejects it as being irrational. In Cocaigne, he becomes equally dissatisfied with hedonistic paganism. Leukê, a stronghold of the Hellenic tradition, teaches him the danger of the realm of utilitarian Philistia. In Hell, Jurgen learns of the sin of pride, and in Heaven he encounters selfless love. Feeling the shadow of worldly wisdom trailing him, Jurgen finally decides to give up his youthful body and return to the domestic comforts that Dame Lisa can provide. He trades the ideal for the actual, yet in so doing bestows romantic value on his ordinary existence and his ordinary wife.

Although entertaining, *Jurgen* lacks clarity of design. The reader who is steeped in mythology may enjoy Cabell's manipulation of the legends of Faust, Don Juan, King Arthur, Troilus and Cressida, and Ulysses and Penelope, but somehow, the integration of the hero's adventures with the narrative line exploring the feelings between husband and wife is incomplete. The episodic looseness of the novel is distracting. Thus, modern readers, like those titillated readers of the 1920's, may be absorbed by Jurgen's amorous exploits without fully considering Cabell's analysis of the values that make life worth living.

Cabell's great achievement is that he celebrated the illusion-making capacity of the mind while simultaneously exposing man's follies in pursuing dreams. He merged the traditions of humanism and skepticism. Reacting against naturalism, Cabell had the courage to present a transcendent view of life—one that acknowledged not man's impotency, but his potential. A meticulous craftsman, a daring iconoclast, an imaginative thinker, Cabell deserves recognition as a major writer of the twentieth century.

Lynne P. Shackelford

Other major works

short fiction: *The Line of Love*, 1905; *Gallantry*, 1907; *Chivalry*, 1909; *The Certain Hour*, 1916; *The Music from Behind the Moon*, 1926.

play: *The Jewel Merchants*, pb. 1921.

poetry: *From the Hidden Way*, 1916.

nonfiction: *Branchiana*, 1907; *Branch of Abingdon*, 1911; *Beyond Life*, 1919; *The Judging of Jurgen*, 1920; *Joseph Hergesheimer*, 1921; *Taboo*, 1921; *Straws and Prayer-Books*, 1924; *Some of Us*, 1930; *These Restless Heads*, 1932 (includes two short stories and personal reminiscences); *Special Delivery*, 1933; *Ladies and Gentlemen*, 1934;

Of Ellen Glasgow, 1938; *The St. Johns*, 1943 (with A. J. Hanna); *Let Me Lie*, 1947; *Quiet, Please*, 1952; *As I Remember It*, 1955; *Between Friends: Letters of James Branch Cabell and Others*, 1962 (Margaret Freeman Cabell and Padraic Colum, editors); *The Letters of James Branch Cabell*, 1975 (Edward Wagenknecht, editor).

BIBLIOGRAPHY

D'Ammassa, Don. "James Branch Cabell: No Fit Employment for a Grown Man." In *Discovering Classic Fantasy Fiction: Essays on the Antecedents of Fantastic Literature*, edited by Darrell Schweitzer. San Bernardino, Calif.: Borgo Press, 1996. Essay on Cabell's fantasy fiction is part of a collection of essays focusing on the exploration of the origins of the modern fantasy genre. Contributors discuss how late nineteenth and early twentieth century writers' creation of places and people who could exist only in the imagination laid the groundwork for subsequent novels by J. R. R. Tolkien and others.

Davis, Joe Lee. *James Branch Cabell*. New York: Twayne, 1962. Reliable biography also presents analysis of Cabell's writings. Includes a list of bibliographical references.

Ginés, Montserrat. "James Branch Cabell: Quixotic Love, the Exercise of Self-Deception." In *The Southern Inheritors of Don Quixote*. Baton Rouge: Louisiana State University Press, 2000. Analyzes the work of five southern writers—Cabell, Mark Twain, William Faulkner, Eudora Welty, and Walker Percy—whose fiction expressed the ideals and spirit of Don Quixote. Describes how the writers were sympathetic to idealistic characters who tilted at windmills and points out the similarities between the Spain of Miguel de Cervantes and the social and economic conditions of the American South.

Himelick, Raymond. *James Branch Cabell and the Modern Temper: Three Essays*. New York: Revisionist Press, 1974. Explores realism and romance, the fact and the dream, in Cabell's novels. Himelick sees Cabell as an antiromantic whose novels convey his understanding of life as a "grotesque comedy."

Inge, Thomas M., and Edgar E. MacDonald, eds. *James Branch Cabell: Centennial Essays*. Baton Rouge: Louisiana State University Press, 1983. Compilation of essays, originally presented at a celebration of the centennial of Cabell's birth at Virginia Commonwealth University, provides both biographical information on the author and critical analysis of his works. Includes a bibliographical essay.

MacDonald, Edgar E. *James Branch Cabell and Richmond-in-Virginia*. Jackson: University Press of Mississippi, 1993. Very detailed, authoritative biography focuses on how Cabell was influenced by living in Richmond, Virginia, in the late nineteenth and early twentieth centuries. MacDonald is a senior Cabell scholar at the James Branch Cabell Library at Virginia Commonwealth University. Includes an excellent bibliography.

Riemer, James D. *From Satire to Subversion: The Fantasies of James Branch Cabell*. New York: Greenwood Press, 1989. Devotes separate chapters to *The Cream of the Jest*, *Jurgen*, *Figures of Earth*, *The High Place*, *The Silver Stallion*, and *Something About*

Eve—these books, Riemer argues, represent Cabell's greatest achievements. Includes an introduction that provides a good overview of the writer's career.

Tarrant, Desmond. *James Branch Cabell: The Dream and the Reality.* Norman: University of Oklahoma Press, 1967. Critical study of Cabell's work examines the author as mythmaker. Discusses both Cabell's early and later writings.

Van Doren, Carl, H. L. Mencken, and Hugh Walpole. *James Branch Cabell: Three Essays.* Port Washington, N.Y.: Kennikat Press, 1967. Valuable contribution to studies on Cabell presents criticism of a very high standard—both erudite and entertaining—by three eminent authors. Included in the appendix is a sampling of reviews of Cabell's works.

LEWIS CARROLL

Charles Lutwidge Dodgson

Born: Daresbury, Cheshire, England; January 27, 1832
Died: Guildford, Surrey, England; January 14, 1898
Also known as: Charles Lutwidge Dodgson

PRINCIPAL LONG FICTION

Alice's Adventures in Wonderland, 1865
Through the Looking-Glass and What Alice Found There, 1871
Sylvie and Bruno, 1889
Sylvie and Bruno Concluded, 1893
The Wasp in a Wig: The "Suppressed" Episode of "Through the Looking-Glass and What Alice Found There," 1977

OTHER LITERARY FORMS

Before and after writing his novels for children, Lewis Carroll published volumes in his primary vocation, mathematics: *A Syllabus of Plane Algebraical Geometry* (1860), *An Elementary Treatise on Determinants* (1867), *Curiosa Mathematica, Part I: A New Theory of Parallels* (1888), *Curiosa Mathematica, Part II: Pillow Problems Thought During Wakeful Hours* (1893), and *Symbolic Logic, Part I: Elementary* (1896). His gift for light verse, demonstrated in his novels, also led to four books of poems, with some duplication of content: *Phantasmagoria, and Other Poems* (1869), *The Hunting of the Snark: An Agony in Eight Fits* (1876), *Rhyme? and Reason?* (1883), and the posthumous *Three Sunsets and Other Poems* (1898). His literary and mathematical sides were fused in *A Tangled Tale* (1885), a series of mathematical word problems in the form of short stories, and *Euclid and His Modern Rivals* (1879), a closet drama in which Euclid is defended by various scholars and spirits.

ACHIEVEMENTS

In 1898, a few months after Lewis Carroll's death, the *Pall Mall Gazette* published a survey of the popularity of children's books, and the overwhelming front-runner was *Alice's Adventures in Wonderland.* Queen Victoria enjoyed *Alice's Adventures in Wonderland* so much that she asked Carroll to dedicate his next book to her (ironically, his next book, *An Elementary Treatise on Determinants*, proved to be nothing like the whimsical adventure the queen had admired).

Carroll encouraged the stage versions of the Alice books that appeared in his lifetime, though he was dismayed at his lack of legal control over adaptations. The Alice books have been translated into dozens of languages and are quoted more often than any English work, after that of William Shakespeare. *Alice's Adventures in Wonderland* is noteworthy for more than its popularity, however; it was the first work of literature for children that did

Lewis Carroll
(Library of Congress)

not have an overtly didactic or moralistic nature. In fact, Carroll parodied didactic children's works in verse, such as "You Are Old, Father William" in *Through the Looking-Glass and What Alice Found There*, and through characters such as the Duchess in *Alice's Adventures in Wonderland*. Writers as abstruse and complex as British philosopher Ludwig Wittgenstein and Irish novelist James Joyce were drawn to the deeper implications of Carroll's work, especially the lighthearted sense of play and the role of nonsense in human thought. The absurdist writers of the twentieth century saw Carroll as their prophet, and a few of his nonsense words, such as "Boojum," "Jabberwocky," and "chortle," have become seemingly permanent parts of the English language. His term for a particular method of coining compound words, "portmanteau," has since become a standard linguistic name for the process.

BIOGRAPHY

Charles Lutwidge Dodgson was the third of eleven children and the eldest son of the Reverend Charles Dodgson and Frances Jane Lutwidge. The younger Charles Dodgson was left-handed and spoke with a stutter, an affliction from which he would suffer his whole life. With eight younger siblings, he very early developed the knack of amusing children, an ability he would keep as an adult. For their amusement, he wrote and drew little magazines that demonstrated the whimsy later seen in his Alice books. Some of the verses in the Alice books received their first auditions in these family magazines.

At age twelve, Dodgson attended Richmond Grammar School, and the following year, the famous public school at Rugby. Nearly four years at Rugby, which he later recalled with displeasure, prepared him for Oxford University: He entered Christ Church College there on January 24, 1851. He distinguished himself in mathematics and classics, though difficulty with philosophy and history kept him in the lower third of his class. On December 18, 1854, he received his A.B. with first-class honors in mathematics. He stayed on at Christ Church as a tutor and lecturer. At this time his earliest stories and poems appeared in periodicals at Oxford and Whitby.

Early in 1856 Dodgson acquired his first camera, then a relatively rare and complicated device restricted to use by specialists. A large number of his photographs, mostly of young girls, survive, and one historian of photography has declared Dodgson the most outstanding child photographer of the nineteenth century. A month after he had purchased the camera, one young model, the four-year-old daughter of an Oxford dean, caught Dodgson's eye. Her name was Alice Liddell. Six years later he would extemporize, on a boating expedition, a story about Alice that was to become the famous Alice stories. However, until then, Dodgson's energies went into his vocations of mathematics and the clergy: He published his first book on mathematics in 1860, and he was ordained a deacon just before Christmas of 1861.

By February of 1863, Dodgson had committed to paper the story from the 1862 excursion with the Liddell sisters. He published it in 1865 (though it did not appear until 1866) as *Alice's Adventures in Wonderland*. Dodgson used the pseudonym Lewis Carroll for his publications, a name seemingly derived from the names Lutwidge and Charles. In 1867, Dodgson made the only voyage of his lifetime away from England, touring the Continent (mostly Russia). He had already begun his sequel to *Alice's Adventures in Wonderland*, which appeared near Christmas, 1871, as *Through the Looking-Glass and What Alice Found There*. When his father died in 1868, Dodgson moved his siblings to Guildford, and he moved into rooms at Tom Quad, Oxford, where he remained the rest of his life. In 1881 his income from writing was sufficient for him to resign his lectureship in mathematics, although he remained at Oxford. The following year he was elected curator of the Senior Common room, a post he held for ten years. He continued writing until his death in 1898, though he never equaled the success of the Alice books.

ANALYSIS

Lewis Carroll's first great contribution to children's literature is that he freed it from the heavy didacticism of previous children's books. The second is his legitimating of nonsense in children's literature, though in this claim he is preceded by fellow Victorian Edward Lear, whose *A Book of Nonsense* (1846) preceded the Alice books by two decades. It is perhaps in his nonsense that one can see the connection between Reverend Dodgson, the mathematician, and Lewis Carroll, the writer. Nonsense is self-referential; that is, it lacks "sense," if sense means a relationship to the world outside the work of nonsense. It is thus like certain mathematical systems or logic games. Carroll's works are in fact games, which is one of the reasons for their appeal to children.

ALICE'S ADVENTURES IN WONDERLAND

Lewis Carroll's first novel, *Alice's Adventures in Wonderland*, successfully creates and maintains a dream consciousness. Its dreamlike quality is revealed not merely in its conventional ending, with Alice waking up to discover her adventures in Wonderland were "all a dream"; its episodic movements are dreamlike in that one episode melts into the other and has no necessarily logical connection to the previous. Identities constantly shift: A baby turns into a pig; the Cheshire Cat fades away into a grin. Because the logic of dreams, like the logic of Wonderland, is closed, internal, and self-referential, *Alice's Adventures in Wonderland* resists interpretations that attempt to "explain" the novel by connecting its elements to structures outside it, such as biographical, historical, psychoanalytic, or political interpretations.

The story begins with Alice drowsing while her sister reads a boring book. Alice's attention is arrested by a white rabbit, which she follows, only to fall down a rabbit hole, where she finds a world where nothing is like the world she left. When she eats and drinks the Wonderland foods, she changes drastically in size, becoming small as a mouse, then large as a house. When small, she finds her way into a garden, where she meets a caterpillar, rescues a baby from a mean duchess, attends a mad tea party, plays croquet with the Queen of Hearts, listens to a mock turtle's life story, and attends the trial of the Knave of Hearts. When the angry subjects of the Queen rush at Alice, she awakens to find them to be only, in the real world, falling leaves.

The novel is narrated in the third person, but with limited omniscience, allowing the reader to view Wonderland from Alice's perspective. The creation of the Alice character (though it must be remembered that she is modeled on a real girl of the author's acquaintance) is one of Carroll's most stunning achievements. It is seen immediately in the opening paragraph, which presents her thoughts as she peers into a book her sister is reading; the book bores her because it has no pictures or conversations. This is clearly a child's perspective. Even Alice's precipitous changes in size reflect the point of view of children who are given contradictory messages: that they are too big for some things and too little for others. Alice is the most fully realized of the characters in the book, all others being functionally flat. The flatness of the characters is essential to the humor of the book, particularly the slapstick elements, for the whimsy of the Mad Hatter and the March Hare dunking the Dormouse in a teapot is lost if we sympathize with the Dormouse as a real character with feelings.

THROUGH THE LOOKING-GLASS AND WHAT ALICE FOUND THERE

Carroll's second novel is a sequel to the first, with the same main character. This time the "wonderland" is the looking-glass world, the world one sees when one looks in a mirror, a reverse image of the real world. As a photographer who needed to visualize finished photographs from their negative images, Carroll had an intuitive understanding of the implications of a "reverse" world. The consciousness of his "abnormality" of being a left-handed boy may also have played into the creation of *Through the Looking-Glass and What Alice Found There*.

In the novel's opening chapter, Alice passes through a mirror to find a house precisely the reverse of her own. She goes out into the garden, where she meets the Red Queen, then to the surrounding country, where she encounters strange insects, Tweedledee and Tweedledum, the White Queen, Humpty Dumpty, the lion and the unicorn, and the White Knight. In chapter 9, Alice becomes queen, and she upsets the board of chess pieces in a transition from dream to waking precisely like that of the first *Alice* book. The transition is handled in two truncated chapters, one of fifty-nine words, in which Alice shakes the Red Queen, and one of only six words, in which the Red Queen turns out to be Alice's kitten, and she is awake. The final chapter is an epilogue, in which Alice poses an unanswered question on the relation of dream to reality.

SYLVIE AND BRUNO

Carroll's last two novels were not as successful commercially as the Alice books, and, according to their earliest critics, they were unsuccessful artistically as well. Carroll continues to play with dreams and reality in the Sylvie and Bruno books, but this time waking and dream realities are interlaced in alternating chapters. In place of Wonderland or the looking-glass world, *Sylvie and Bruno* puts forth "the eerie state," in which one becomes aware of fairies. Thus, *Sylvie and Bruno* has two parallel plots: In the waking world, which Carroll's introduction calls "the ordinary state," there is a love triangle. The noble and selfless Dr. Arthur Forester loves Lady Muriel Orme but believes that she loves her cousin, Captain Eric Linden. The cousins, in fact, become engaged, but there is a grave religious impediment: Eric is not a Christian. The novel ends with Arthur accepting a medical post in India so as not to stand in Eric's way. Simultaneously in the fairy or "eerie" realm parallel to the human one of Arthur, Eric, and Muriel, Sylvie and Bruno are innocent fairy children of the Warden of Outland. This plot is a version of the ancient myth and fairy-tale motif of the disguised god or king. The Warden temporarily abandons his rule in order to travel the kingdom disguised as a beggar. In his absence, his wicked brother Sibimet conspires with his wife and selfish son Uggug to take over Outland.

SYLVIE AND BRUNO CONCLUDED

In the sequel to *Sylvie and Bruno*, the interactions between the fairy realm of Outland and the human realm of Arthur and Muriel are more causally connected, as Sylvie and

Bruno work "behind the scenes" to bring the true lovers together. Sylvie, in fact, appears to be the fairyland identity of Muriel. Through the invisible ministry of Sylvie and Bruno, Arthur and Muriel are married, but shortly after the wedding Arthur must go off to combat a plague in a nearby town. Muriel reads a false account of the death of Arthur from the plague, and Arthur, ironically, is rescued by Eric, who has come to accept the Christian faith and sees his assistance to a would-be rival as divinely directed. Meanwhile, the Warden (Arthur's counterpart) returns to Outland, thwarts Sibimet (Eric's counterpart), who repents, and regains his kingdom.

Perhaps it is no surprise that the human characters in both Sylvie and Bruno books are the least believable. They are the hackneyed stock characters of sentimental romance, though no worse than others of the same genre. As in the Alice books, the title characters, Sylvie and Bruno, are the more remarkable creations, though readers may have difficulty with the cloying baby talk of the fairies and the effusive affection they lavish on one another. Sylvie and Bruno are emblems of childlike innocence, which Carroll also tried to capture in the Alice books and in his photography.

John R. Holmes

OTHER MAJOR WORKS

SHORT FICTION: "Bruno's Revenge," 1867.

POETRY: *Phantasmagoria, and Other Poems*, 1869; *The Hunting of the Snark: An Agony in Eight Fits*, 1876; *Rhyme? and Reason?*, 1883; *Three Sunsets, and Other Poems*, 1898; *For "The Train": Five Poems and a Tale*, 1932; *The Collected Verse of Lewis Carroll*, 1932 (also known as *The Humorous Verse of Lewis Carroll*, 1960).

NONFICTION: *A Syllabus of Plane Algebraical Geometry*, 1860; *An Elementary Treatise on Determinants*, 1867; *Euclid and His Modern Rivals*, 1879; *Twelve Months in a Curatorship*, 1884; *Three Months in a Curatorship*, 1886; *The Game of Logic*, 1887; *Curiosa Mathematica, Part I: A New Theory of Parallels*, 1888; *Curiosa Mathematica, Part II: Pillow Problems Thought During Wakeful Hours*, 1893; *Symbolic Logic, Part I: Elementary*, 1896; *Feeding the Mind*, 1907; *The Diaries of Lewis Carroll*, 1954; *The Unknown Lewis Carroll*, 1961; *The Magic of Lewis Carroll*, 1973; *The Letters of Lewis Carroll*, 1979 (Morton N. Cohen, editor); *The Oxford Pamphlets, Leaflets, and Circulars of Charles Lutwidge Dodgson*, Vol. 1, 1993; *The Mathematical Pamphlets of Charles Lutwidge Dodgson and Related Pieces*, 1994.

CHILDREN'S LITERATURE: *A Tangled Tale*, 1885; *"The Rectory Umbrella" and "Mischmasch,"* 1932; *The Pig-Tale*, 1975.

BIBLIOGRAPHY

Blake, Kathleen. *Play, Games, and Sport: The Literary Works of Lewis Carroll*. Ithaca, N.Y.: Cornell University Press, 1974. Very insightful study of Carroll's work focuses primarily on the Alice books, *Sylvie and Bruno*, and *The Hunting of the Snark*. Emphasis is placed on systems of logic and language constructions. Supplemented by an index.

Bloom, Harold, ed. *Lewis Carroll's Alice's Adventures in Wonderland.* New York: Chelsea House, 2006. Collection of essays about the novel includes analysis of Alice's identity, elements of folklore and fairy tales in the work, and its treatment of love and death. Includes bibliography and index.

Carroll, Lewis. *The Annotated Alice.* Introduction and notes by Martin Gardner. 1960. Definitive ed. New York: W. W. Norton, 2000. Features abundant marginal notes that explain references in the Alice tales and *The Hunting of the Snark*, linking them to Carroll's life, events and controversies in Victorian England, and mathematics. Also includes reproductions of the works' original illustrations.

Cohen, Morton N. *Lewis Carroll: A Biography.* New York: Random House, 1995. Detailed work by an author who devoted more than three decades to Carroll scholarship. Using Carroll's letters and diaries, Cohen has provided what many regard as a definitive biography. Illustrated with more than one hundred of Carroll's photographs and drawings.

Collingwood, Stuart Dodgson. *The Life and Letters of Lewis Carroll.* New York: Century, 1899. As Carroll's nephew, Collingwood had firsthand knowledge of his uncle's life, and this biographical work is accordingly full of anecdotes. The letters quoted in the text often exemplify Carroll's dexterity with humor.

De la Mare, Walter. *Lewis Carroll.* London: Faber & Faber, 1932. Well-written volume places Carroll in historical context and analyzes the different genres he utilized. Contains a detailed discussion of the two Alice books and a brief treatment of other works. Supplemented by an index and a bibliography.

Gray, Donald J., ed. *Alice in Wonderland.* New York: W. W. Norton, 1992. Provides an ideal starting point for those interested in examining Carroll's novel. In addition to extensive background and critical essays, includes helpful annotations on the two Alice novels. Many of the best essays from other collections are reprinted here, making this a reference work of first resort.

Jones, Jo Elwyn, and J. Francis Gladstone. *The Alice Companion: A Guide to Lewis Carroll's Alice Books.* New York: New York University Press, 1998. Full of information and commentary on the people and places that make up Carroll's and Alice Liddell's world in mid-nineteenth century Oxford. Also an excellent source of information regarding the extensive literature on this period in Carroll's life.

_______. *The Red King's Dream: Or, Lewis Carroll in Wonderland.* London: Jonathan Cape, 1995. Places Carroll within his life and times through the discussion of his literary milieu, friends, and influences. Includes bibliographical references and index.

Leach, Karoline. *In the Shadow of the Dreamchild: A New Understanding of Lewis Carroll.* Chester Springs, Pa.: Peter Owen, 1999. Uses findings from new research to argue that many of the long-standing assumptions about Carroll—concerning his exclusively child-centered and unworldly life, his legendary obsession with Alice Liddell, and his supposedly unnatural sexuality—are nothing more than myths.

Pudney, John. *Lewis Carroll and His World*. London: Thames and Hudson, 1976. Historical study of Carroll and his culture is both insightful and broad in scope. Features more than one hundred illustrations as well as a chronology, a select bibliography, and an index.

Thomas, Donald. *Lewis Carroll: A Portrait with Background*. London: John Murray, 1996. Thomas surmises the formative influences on Carroll's personality and intellect as he describes Victorian England. An invaluable guide for readers who want to understand how manners and ideas changed during Carroll's lifetime.

ANGELA CARTER

Born: Eastbourne, Sussex, England; May 7, 1940
Died: London, England; February 16, 1992
Also known as: Angela Olive Stalker

PRINCIPAL LONG FICTION

Shadow Dance, 1966 (also known as *Honeybuzzard*, 1967)
The Magic Toyshop, 1967
Several Perceptions, 1968
Heroes and Villains, 1969
Love, 1971 (revised 1987)
The Infernal Desire Machines of Doctor Hoffman, 1972 (also known as *The War of Dreams*, 1974)
The Passion of New Eve, 1977
Nights at the Circus, 1984
Wise Children, 1991

OTHER LITERARY FORMS

Angela Carter is nearly as well known for her short fiction as she is for her novels. Her short-story collections include *Fireworks: Nine Profane Pieces* (1974), *Black Venus* (1985; also known as *Saints and Strangers*, 1986), the highly praised *The Bloody Chamber, and Other Stories* (1979), which contains her transformations of familiar fairy tales into adult tales with erotic overtones, and *American Ghosts and Old World Wonders* (1993). She also wrote a number of fantastic stories for children, including *Miss Z, the Dark Young Lady* (1970), *The Donkey Prince* (1970), and a translated adaptation of the works of Charles Perrault, *The Fairy Tales of Charles Perrault* (1977). In 1978, she published her first book of nonfiction, *The Sadeian Woman: And the Ideology of Pornography*, a feminist study of the Marquis de Sade that remains controversial among both literary and feminist critics. Other nonfiction essays by Carter have been published by British journals; *Nothing Sacred: Selected Writings* (1982) is a collection of her journalistic pieces, and *Shaking a Leg: Journalism and Writings* (1997) reprints other essays and reviews. She also wrote a screenplay adaptation of her novel *The Magic Toyshop* (1987) and cowrote, with Neil Jordan, the screenplay for the British film *The Company of Wolves* (1984), based on her short story of the same title.

ACHIEVEMENTS

With the publication of her first novels in the late 1960's, Angela Carter received wide recognition and acclaim in Great Britain for blending gothic and surreal elements with vivid portrayals of urban sufferers and survivors. She was awarded the John Llewellyn

Rhys Memorial Prize for *The Magic Toyshop* and the Somerset Maugham Award for *Several Perceptions*. Critics have praised her wit, inventiveness, eccentric characters, descriptive wealth, and strongly sustained narrative while sometimes questioning her depth of purpose and suggesting a degree of pretentiousness. Her imaginative transformation of folkloric elements and examination of their mythic impact on sexual relationships began to be fully appreciated on the appearance of *The Bloody Chamber, and Other Stories*, which received the Cheltenham Festival of Literature Award. *Nights at the Circus*, recipient of the James Tait Black Memorial Prize, helped to establish firmly for Carter a growing transatlantic reputation as an extravagant stylist of the Magical Realist school. Following her untimely death in 1992—which enabled her establishment in the syllabus of British universities traditionally reluctant to venerate living writers—Carter was immediately hailed as the most important English fantasist of her generation. Her critical writings, which add a robust and sometimes scathing rhetoric to the lucid prose of her fiction, also attracted new attention.

Biography

Angela Olive Stalker was born in Eastbourne, Sussex, England, on May 7, 1940. After working as a journalist from 1958 to 1961 in Croyden, Surrey, she attended Bristol University, from which she received a bachelor's degree in English literature in 1965. While married to Paul Carter between 1960 and 1972, she traveled widely and lived for several years in Japan. From 1976 to 1978, she served as Arts Council of Great Britain Fellow in Creative Writing at Sheffield University. She was a visiting professor at Brown University, the University of Texas, Austin, and the University of Iowa. She spent the last years of her life in London, living with Mark Pearce, the father of her son Alexander, who was born in 1983. She died of lung cancer in London on February 16, 1992.

Analysis

The search for self and for autonomy is the underlying theme of most of Angela Carter's fiction. Her protagonists, usually described as bored or in some other way detached from their lives, are thrust into unknown landscapes or embark on picaresque journeys in which they encounter representatives of a vast variety of human experience and suffering. These encountered characters are often grotesques or exaggerated parodies reminiscent of those found in the novels of Charles Dickens or such southern gothic writers as Flannery O'Connor. They also sometimes exhibit the animalistic or supernatural qualities of fairy-tale characters. The protagonists undergo voluntary or, more often, forced submission to their own suppressed desires. By internalizing the insights gained through such submission and vicariously from the experiences of their antagonists and comrades or lovers, the protagonists are then able to garner some control over their own destinies. This narrative structure is borrowed from the classic folktales and fairy tales with which Carter has been closely associated. Carter does not merely retell such tales in modern dress; rather, she probes and twists the ancient stories to illuminate the underlying hierarchical structures of power and dominance, weakness and submission.

In addition to the folkloric influence, Carter draws from a variety of other writers, most notably Lewis Carroll, Jonathan Swift, the Marquis de Sade, and William Blake. The rather literal-minded innocent abroad in a nightmarish wonderland recalls both Alice and Gulliver, and Carter acknowledges, both directly and obliquely, her borrowings from Carroll's *Alice's Adventures in Wonderland* (1865) and Swift's *Gulliver's Travels* (1726). She was also influenced by the Swiftian tool of grotesque parody used in the service of satire. It was through Swiftian glasses that she read Sade. While deploring the depredations on the human condition committed by both the victims and victimizers in Sade's writings, she interprets these as hyperbolic visions of the actual social situation, and she employs in her novels derivatively descriptive situations for their satiric shock value. Finally, the thematic concerns of Blake's visionary poetry—the tension between the contrarieties of innocence and experience, rationality and desire—are integral to Carter's outlook. The energy created by such tension creates the plane on which Carter's protagonists can live most fully. In Blake's words and in Carter's novels, "Energy is Eternal Delight."

Although Carter's landscapes range from London in the 1960's (*The Magic Toyshop*, *Several Perceptions*, *Love*) to a postapocalyptic rural England (*Heroes and Villains*), a sometime-in-the-future South America (*The Infernal Desire Machines of Doctor Hoffman*), a United States in which the social fabric is rapidly disintegrating (*The Passion of New Eve*), and London and Russia at the beginning of the twentieth century (*Nights at the Circus*), certain symbolic motifs appear regularly in her novels. Carter is particularly intrigued by the possibilities of roses, wedding dresses, swans, wolves, tigers, bears, vampires, mirrors, tears, and vanilla ice cream. Menacing father figures, prostitute mothers, and a kaleidoscope of circus, fair, and Gypsy folk inhabit most of her landscapes. It is unfair, however, to reduce Carter's novels to a formulaic mode. She juggles traditional and innovative elements with a sometimes dazzling dexterity and is inevitably a strong storyteller.

THE MAGIC TOYSHOP

At the opening of *The Magic Toyshop*, fifteen-year-old Melanie is entranced with her budding sexuality. She dresses up in her absent mother's wedding gown to dance on the lawn in the moonlight. Overwhelmed by her awakening knowledge and the immensities of possibility that the night offers, she is terrified and climbs back into her room by the childhood route of the apple tree—shredding her mother's gown in the process. Her return to childhood becomes catastrophic when a telegram arrives announcing the death of Melanie's parents in a plane crash. Melanie, with her younger brother and sister, is thrust from a safe and comfortable existence into the constricted and terrifying London household of her Uncle Philip Flower, a toy maker of exquisite skill and sadistically warped sensibility. He is a domestic tyrant whose Irish wife, Margaret, was inexplicably struck dumb on her wedding day. The household is also inhabited by Margaret's two younger brothers, Finn and Francie Jowle; the three siblings form a magic "circle of red people" that is alternately seductive and repulsive to Melanie.

Uncle Philip is a creator of the mechanical. He is obsessed by his private puppet theater, his created world to which he enslaves the entire household. In aligning herself with the Jowle siblings, Melanie asserts her affirmation of life but becomes aware of the thwarted and devious avenues of survival open to the oppressed. The growing, but ambivalent, attraction between her and Finn is premature and manipulated by Uncle Philip. Even the love that holds the siblings together is underlined by a current of incest. Finn is driven to inciting his uncle to murder him in order to effect Philip's damnation. The crisis arises when Uncle Philip casts Melanie as Leda in a puppet extravaganza. Her symbolic rape by the immense mechanical swan and Finn's subsequent destruction of the puppet release an orgiastic, yet purifying, energy within the "circle of red people." The ensuing wrath of Uncle Philip results in the conflagration and destruction of the house. Finn and Melanie are driven out, Adam-and-Eve-like, to face a new world "in a wild surmise."

In fairy-tale fashion, Melanie is threatened by an evil father figure, protected by the good mother, and rescued by the young hero. Even in this early novel, however, Carter skews and claws at the traditional fabric. The Jowle brothers, grimy, embittered, and twisted by their victimization at the hands of Philip Flower, are as dangerous as they are endangered. They are unable to effect their own freedom. Melanie's submission to Uncle Philip's swan catalyzes not only her own rescue but also, indeed, the release of the Jowle siblings. Melanie's sacrifice breaks the magic spell that held the Jowles imprisoned.

SEVERAL PERCEPTIONS

Several Perceptions, Carter's third novel, depends less on such folkloric structure. In this novel, her evocation of the late 1960's counterculture is so finely detailed that she manages to illuminate the thin line between the idealism and solipsism of that era, without denigrating the former or disguising the latter. The clarity of observation is achieved by viewing the culture through the eyes of Joseph Harker, a classic dropout. He has failed at the university, been dumped by his Jane Austen-reading lover, is disheartened by his job caring for dying old men, despises the contentment of his hippie peers, and, early in the novel, bungles a suicide attempt. Joseph, like his biblical namesake, is a dreamer of dreams: He dreams in the violent images of Vietnam War atrocities, the self-immolation of Buddhist monks, and assassinations. His schizophrenic perceptions are colored by shattered images from the books in his room, *Alice's Adventures in Wonderland* and Anne Gilchrist's *Life of William Blake* (1863), by memories of his grandfather, visions of his psychiatrist, the purring of his pregnant cat, Anne Blossom's custard, and the vanilla ice-cream breasts of Mrs. Boulder.

The novel narrates Joseph's slow crawl back into the world of the living. Despite a tough-minded acknowledgment of the grubby and quite desolate lives of the characters, the novel is written with a gentle touch and ends on an affirmative note. The Christmas party that takes place at the end of the novel, in which Joseph symbolically reenters society, stands as a classic description of a hippie-generation party, just as F. Scott Fitzgerald's description of Gatsby's party stands as the image for the flapper generation. The connected-disconnected flow, the costumes, the easy sexuality, the simple goodwill, the silliness, and the sometimes inspired personal insights are vividly re-created. Carter wrote the novel as this lifestyle was being played out, and it is much to her credit that she succumbed neither to sentimentality nor to parody.

SCIENCE-FICTION NOVELS

Parody and satire are, however, major elements in Carter's three novels that are often classified as science fiction or science fantasy. In *Heroes and Villains*, *The Infernal Desire Machines of Doctor Hoffman*, and *The Passion of New Eve*, Carter's protagonists dwell in societies that are described in metaphysical iconography. Carter seems to be questioning the nature and values of received reality. Marianne's world in *Heroes and Villains* is divided into high-technology enclaves containing Professors, the Soldiers who protect them, and the Workers who serve them. Outside the enclaves, in the semijungle/semicesspool wildernesses, dwell the tribes of nomadic Barbarians and the Out-people, freaks created by nature gone awry. Marianne, the daughter of a Professor, motivated mainly by boredom, escapes from her enclave with Jewel, a young Barbarian chieftain, during a raid.

In *The Infernal Desire Machines of Doctor Hoffman*, the aging Desiderio narrates his heroic exploits as a young man when he saved his City during the Reality War. Doctor Hoffman besieges the City with mirages generated from his Desire Machines. Sent by the Minister of Determination to kill Doctor Hoffman, Desiderio is initiated into the wonders of desires made manifest, Nebulous Time, and the juggled samples of cracked and broken reality. His guide is Hoffman's daughter, Albertina, who appears to Desiderio as an androgynous ambassador, a black swan, the young valet of a vampiric count, and finally as his one true love, the emanation of his whole desire.

The United States in *The Passion of New Eve* is torn apart by racial, class, and sexual conflicts. Evelyn, a young British teacher, travels through this landscape and is re-created. The unconsciously exploitative and disinterestedly sadistic narrator suffers a wild revenge when captured by an Amazon-like community of women. He is castrated, resexed, raped, forcibly wed and mated, and ultimately torn from his wife's love by a gang of murderous Puritanical boys.

Each of the protagonists of these novels experiences love but seems to be able to achieve wholeness only through the destruction of the loved one. Symbolically, the protagonists seem to consume the otherness of the loved ones, reincorporating these manifest desires back into their whole beings. Each, however, is left alone at the end of the novel.

Symbolic imagery of a harshly violent though rollicking nature threatens to overwhelm these three novels. The parody is at times wildly exaggerated and at times cuts very close to reality (for example, in *The Passion of New Eve*, the new Eve is incorporated into a polygamous group that closely resembles the so-called Manson family). Although some critics have decried Carter's heavy reliance on fantasies, visions, and zany exuberance, it is probably these qualities that have appealed to a widening audience. It must also be acknowledged that Carter continued, within her magical realms, to probe and mock the repressive nature of institutionalized relationships and sexual politics.

NIGHTS AT THE CIRCUS

With *Nights at the Circus*, Carter wove the diverse threads of her earlier novels into brilliantly realized tapestry. This novel has two protagonists—Fevvers, the Cockney Venus, a winged, six-foot, peroxide-blond aerialist who was found "hatched out of a bloody great egg" on the steps of a benevolent whorehouse (her real name is Sophia), and Jack Walser, an American journalist compiling a series of interviews titled "Great Humbugs of the World," who joins Colonel Kearney's circus, the Ludic Game, in order to follow Fevvers and who is "not hatched out, yet . . . his own shell don't break, yet." It is 1899, and a New World is about to break forth. The ambivalent, tenuous attraction between Fevvers and Walser is reminiscent of that between Melanie and Finn in *The Magic Toyshop* or Marianne and Jewel in *Heroes and Villains*, but it is now mature and more subtly complex. The picaresque journeyings from London to St. Petersburg and across the steppes of Russia recall the travels in *The Infernal Desire Machines of Doctor Hoffman* and *The Passion of New Eve* but are more firmly grounded in historical landscapes. The magic in this novel comes in the blurring between fact and fiction, the intense unbelievability of actual reality and the seductive possibilities of imaginative and dreamlike visions. Are Fevvers's wings real or contrived? Do the clowns hide behind their makeup and wigs or only become actualized when they don their disguises? As in most Magical Realist fiction, Carter is probing the lines between art and artifice, creation and generation, in a raucous and lush style.

Here, after a long hiatus from the rather bleak apocalyptic visions of her 1970's novels, in which autonomous selfhood is achieved only through a kind of self-cannibalization of destroyed love, Angela Carter envisions a route to self-affirmation that allows sexual love to exist. With shifting narrative focuses, Carter unfolds the rebirths of Walser and Fevvers through their own and each other's eyes. Walser's shells of consciousness are cracked as he becomes a "first-of-May" clown, the waltzing partner to a tigress, the Human Chicken, and, in losing consciousness, an apprentice shaman to a primitive Finno-Urgic tribe. As star of Kearney's circus, Fevvers is the toast of European capitals: an impregnable, seductive freak, secure in and exploitative of her own singularity. On the interminable train trek through Siberia, she seems to mislay her magnificence and invulnerability. She becomes less a freak and more a woman, but she remains determined to hatch Walser into her New Man. As he had to forgo his socially conditioned consciousness in order to recognize Sophia, however, so she has to allow him to hatch himself. It is as confident seers that Sophia/Fevvers and Jack Walser love at the close of the novel.

WISE CHILDREN

The fact that Carter produced only one novel during the last eight years of her life has more to do with the claims made on her time and attention by her son Alexander than the depredations of the cancer that killed her. This was a sore point—her much younger partner, Alexander's father, did not keep promises he made to take primary responsibility for child care—and some of that soreness is evident in the pages of the satiric comedy *Wise Children*, in which disowned and abandoned children are extravagantly featured. The story comprises a century-spanning memoir written by Dora Chance, one of the "lucky Chance" twins fathered—but swiftly disowned—by the Shakespearean actor Melchior Hazard in advance of the first of his three marriages.

Dora recalls that the identical Chance twins are indeed lucky, first by virtue of being informally adopted by Melchior's more colorful but less successful fraternal twin Peregrine, and second by virtue of developing a career as dancers in music halls. (Music halls were Britain's primary form of vulgar popular entertainment from the late nineteenth century to the end of World War II.) It subsequently transpires that Peregrine is the biological father of Melchior's supposedly legitimate identical twin daughters by his first marriage, Saskia and Imogen. The paternity of the fraternal twins of Melchior's third marriage, Gareth and Tristan, is never formally disputed, although Dora and her sister Nora cannot help but wonder why it is that one bears a far stronger physical resemblance to Peregrine.

The intricate comparisons and contrasts drawn between the fortunes and pretensions of the legitimate Hazards and the illegitimate Chances mirror and embody the fortunes and pretensions of "legitimate" theater and the music-hall tradition, as both are swallowed up by new media—first by Hollywood films and then by television. The contemporary events that surround Dora's recollections involve the effects of television game-show host Tristan's simultaneous sexual involvement with his much older half sister Saskia and the Chances' protégé Tiffany. The paradoxes of Melchior's theatrical career are summed up by the juxtaposition of his eventual knighthood with his attachment to the cardboard crown that was the chief legacy he received from his father, also a Shakespearean actor.

Although *Wise Children* is far more sentimental than the bleakly dark fantasies Carter penned while her own marriage was failing in the early 1970's, it is to some extent a revisitation of their themes. (The revised version of *Love*, which she prepared while struggling to find the time to write *Wise Children*, also softens the self-mutilatory aspects of the original, but only slightly.) What Carter's final novel adds to her jaundiced view of family life, however, is the legacy of her midperiod preoccupation with the processes by which the substance of childhood dreams and unfathomable experiences can be transmuted into high and low art. Beneath the surface of its comic exuberance, *Wise Children* achieves considerable intensity in its celebration of theatrical magic and its accounts of the redemption of wounded personalities by spirited performances.

Jane Anderson Jones
Updated by Brian Stableford

OTHER MAJOR WORKS

SHORT FICTION: *Fireworks: Nine Profane Pieces*, 1974; *The Bloody Chamber, and Other Stories*, 1979; *Black Venus*, 1985 (also known as *Saints and Strangers*, 1986); *American Ghosts and Old World Wonders*, 1993; *Burning Your Boats*, 1995.

SCREENPLAYS: *The Company of Wolves*, 1984 (with Neil Jordan; adaptation of her short story); *The Magic Toyshop*, 1987 (adaptation of her novel).

RADIO PLAYS: *Vampirella*, 1976; *Come unto These Yellow Sands*, 1979; *The Company of Wolves*, 1980; *Puss in Boots*, 1982; *Come unto These Yellow Sands: Four Radio Plays*, 1985 (includes previous 4 plays).

NONFICTION: *The Sadeian Woman: And the Ideology of Pornography*, 1978; *Nothing Sacred: Selected Writings*, 1982; *Expletives Deleted: Selected Writings*, 1992; *Shaking a Leg: Journalism and Writings*, 1997 (also known as *Shaking a Leg: Collected Writings*, 1998).

TRANSLATIONS: *The Fairy Tales of Charles Perrault*, 1977; *Sleeping Beauty, and Other Favourite Fairy Tales*, 1982.

CHILDREN'S LITERATURE: *The Donkey Prince*, 1970; *Miss Z, the Dark Young Lady*, 1970; *Moonshadow*, 1982; *Sea-Cat and Dragon King*, 2000.

EDITED TEXTS: *Wayward Girls and Wicked Women*, 1986; *The Virago Book of Fairy Tales*, 1990 (also known as *The Old Wives' Fairy Tale Book*).

MISCELLANEOUS: *The Curious Room: Plays, Film Scripts, and an Opera*, 1996.

BIBLIOGRAPHY

Day, Aidan. *Angela Carter: The Rational Glass*. New York: Manchester University Press, 1998. Presents an examination of Carter's fiction that is generally accessible to the nonspecialist. Notes the similarity of themes in Carter's work and describes how she was influenced by the books she read at various times in her life.

Gamble, Sarah. *Angela Carter: A Literary Life*. New York: Palgrave Macmillan, 2006. Critical biography analyzes the relationship between the events of Carter's life and her works. Examines how Carter was engaged in topical issues, such as politics, feminism, class, and national identity (particularly English identity).

_______. *Angela Carter: Writing from the Front Line*. Edinburgh: Edinburgh University Press, 1997. Comprehensive study of Carter's works. Argues that Carter intentionally undermined traditional ideas about history, social codes regarding propriety and "woman's place," and the distinction between "high" and "low" literature.

Landon, Brooks. "Eve at the End of the World: Sexuality and the Reversal of Expectations in Novels by Joanna Russ, Angela Carter, and Thomas Berger." In *Erotic Universe: Sexuality and Fantastic Literature*, edited by Donald Palumbo. Westport, Conn.: Greenwood Press, 1986. Examines the feminist mythology of Carter's work, in particular in the novel *Heroes and Villains*, and discusses Carter's confrontation of sexual stereotypes.

Lee, Alison. *Angela Carter.* New York: G. K. Hall, 1997. Presents critical discussion of all of Carter's novels in a clear and accessible style. Includes details of Carter's life and explains her ideas about nonfiction in order to provide insight into her fiction.

Munford, Rebecca, ed. *Re-visiting Angela Carter: Texts, Contexts, Intertexts.* New York: Palgrave Macmillan, 2006. Collection of essays focuses on Carter's extensive use of allusions and references drawn from a wide variety of sources. Among the topics discussed are the influences on Carter's writings of the works of Charles Dickens, Jonathan Swift, Edgar Allan Poe, and film director Jean-Luc Godard.

Peach, Linden. *Angela Carter.* New York: St. Martin's Press, 1998. Study of Carter's novels offers an overview of her work and close readings of the individual books. Argues that although Carter employed elements of fantasy literature, her novels still addressed "real-life" issues.

Rubinson, Gregory J. *The Fiction of Rushdie, Barnes, Winterson, and Carter: Breaking Cultural and Literary Boundaries in the Work of Four Postmodernists.* Jefferson, N.C.: McFarland, 2005. Compares and contrasts the work of the four authors, including an analysis of gender and sexuality in the writings of Carter and Jeanette Winterson and examination of *The Passion of the New Eve* and *Heroes and Villains.*

Sage, Lorna, ed. *Flesh and the Mirror: Essays on the Art of Angela Carter.* London: Chatto & Windus, 1994. Collection of thirteen essays on various aspects of Carter's work includes discussions of Carter's "political correctness," Carter and science fiction, and the novels *Love* and *Wise Children.*

Smith, Joan. Introduction to *Shaking a Leg: Journalism and Writings*, by Angela Carter. London: Chatto & Windus, 1997. Well-written essay on Carter's critical work links her social commentary to major themes in her long fiction.

JOSÉ DONOSO

Born: Santiago, Chile; October 5, 1924
Died: Santiago, Chile; December 7, 1996
Also known as: José Donoso Yañez

PRINCIPAL LONG FICTION

Coronación, 1957 (*Coronation*, 1965)
Este domingo, 1965 (*This Sunday*, 1967)
El lugar sin límites, 1966 (*Hell Has No Limits*, 1972)
El obsceno pájaro de la noche, 1970 (*The Obscene Bird of Night*, 1973)
Tres novelitas burguesas, 1973 (novellas; *Sacred Families*, 1977)
Casa de campo, 1978 (*A House in the Country*, 1984)
La misteriosa desaparición de la Marquesita de Loria, 1980
El jardín de al lado, 1981
La desesperanza, 1986 (*Curfew*, 1988)
Taratuta; Naturaleza muerta con cachimba, 1990 (novellas; *"Taratuta" and "Still Life with Pipe,"* 1993)
Donde van a morir los elefantes, 1995
El Mocho, 1997

OTHER LITERARY FORMS

José Donoso (doh-NOH-soh) was a superb storyteller, and his first literary efforts were in the area of the short story (curiously, his first stories were written in English and published in the Princeton University literary review *MSS*). His collections of stories include *Veraneo, y otros cuentos* (1955; summer vacation, and other stories); *Dos cuentos* (1956; two stories); *El Charlestón* (1960; abridged as *Cuentos*, 1971; *Charleston, and Other Stories*, 1977); and *Los mejores cuentos de José Donoso* (1965; the best stories of José Donoso). Little if any significant thematic or technical distinction can be drawn between Donoso's novels and shorter fiction, other than those imposed by the limits of the genres themselves. Regardless of length, all are superb blends of sociological observation and psychological analysis, in which realism never quite manages to eliminate fantasy, where madness, the supernatural, and the unknown hover just beyond the bounds of consciousness and reason.

Donoso also wrote essays of literary criticism and attracted attention with *Historia personal del "boom"* (1972; *The Boom in Spanish American Literature: A Personal History*, 1977). His *Poemas de un novelista* (1981) is a collection of thirty poems with a twelve-page authorial introduction explaining the personal circumstances that occasioned the verse.

ACHIEVEMENTS

Each of José Donoso's novels had its special success, and the writer's prestige grew with each stage of his career. Despite a slow beginning (he came to the novel at age thirty-three), Donoso published no novel that could be classed a failure by critics or the public, and several of his works have received awards, the most acclaimed being *The Obscene Bird of Night* (a favorite of reviewers and literary critics) and *A House in the Country*, which received the Spanish Critics' Prize, a coveted award despite its lack of endowment, since it reflects the esteem of the country's professional critics as a whole. Donoso was the recipient of two grants from the Guggenheim Foundation for the furthering of works in progress and served as writer-in-residence at various American universities, with stints at the University of Iowa Writers' Workshop (1965-1967) and teaching positions at Princeton University and Dartmouth College. In demand as a distinguished lecturer, he also held a number of editorial posts. His powers of sociopsychological penetration and his marvelous irony and skillful use of allegory, together with his masterful handling of existential themes and the abnormal or psychotic narrative perspective, place Donoso in the forefront of international fiction.

BIOGRAPHY

José Donoso is one of Chile's most widely known writers of prose fiction and one of the most outstanding and prestigious figures of his generation of narrators in Latin America. He was born José Donoso Yañez into an upper-middle-class family of Spanish and Italian descent in Santiago on October 5, 1924. His father (for whom Donoso was named) was a physician; his mother, Alicia Yáñez, came from a prominent Chilean family. It was she who, with the couple's servant, Teresa Vergara, reared Donoso and his two brothers. Until her death in 1976, Donoso's mother continued to live in the spacious home where the future novelist was born, and the atmosphere of decrepitude and decay in the labyrinthine mansion (property of Dr. Donoso's three elderly great-aunts) haunts his fiction.

When Donoso was seven years old, his father hired an English governess, the foundation of his excellent knowledge of the language, which he continued to study at the Grange, an English school in Santiago, from 1932 to 1942. During this period, Donoso's maternal grandmother returned from Europe to make her home with the family, an event that (together with her deteriorating mental and physical condition) left a mark on the future writer's development. A teenage rebel who disliked school and his father's imposition of the British sports ethic (personified in a boxing instructor), Donoso began feigning stomachaches, which led to a real appendectomy and subsequently an equally real ulcer.

Never serious about religion, Donoso proclaimed himself an atheist at the age of twelve. Equally cavalier about classes, he cared only for reading, and in 1943, he dropped out of school. After two years, during which he had not managed to hold a job for more than a few months, he set out for Magallanes at the southern tip of Chile, where he worked as a sheepherder on the pampas for about a year, subsequently hitchhiking through

Patagonia to Buenos Aires, where he lived as a dockhand until he contracted measles, which obliged him to return home. He finished high school in 1947, enrolling in the University of Chile with a major in English and completing his bachelor of arts degree at Princeton in 1951. His study with Allen Tate and his discovery of Henry James, as well as his introduction to the great paintings of the world, would all influence his future writings.

Returning to Chile, Donoso worked as a teacher, journalist, and literary critic but found himself estranged from his homeland and dissatisfied with his work. His ulcer returned, and he began psychoanalysis. He collaborated in launching the newsmagazine *Ercilla*, which he edited, and in 1954, his first short story written in Spanish ("China") was included in an anthology of Chilean short fiction. The following year, his first book, the collection *Veraneo, y otros cuentos*, was published and had a favorable critical reception, winning the Santiago Municipal Short Story Prize. This success and that of his first novel notwithstanding, Donoso found Chilean society oppressive and moved on to Buenos Aires, where he met his future wife and stayed for two years. He published his second collection of short stories upon his return to Santiago, and he became a leading literary critic, which led to teaching in the Writers' Workshop at the University of Iowa; he abandoned this position in order to move to Spain and finish a novel begun years before, which would become *The Obscene Bird of Night*.

Donoso and his wife, Mará del Pilar Serrano, whom he had married in 1961, adopted an infant daughter in Madrid and settled in Mallorca in 1967. Donoso's first Guggenheim award (1966) was followed by a lectureship at Colorado State University (1969). While in Colorado, his hemorrhaging ulcer required surgery; because of his inability to tolerate painkilling drugs, he subsequently went through a period marked by hallucinations, schizophrenia, and paranoia that resulted in suicide attempts. He returned to Mallorca, moved his family to Barcelona, and began to rewrite his novel, incorporating his nightmarish illness. Subsequently, still recuperating, he bought a seventeenth century home in Calaceite, remodeled it, and in 1971 moved to this village of some two thousand inhabitants in the center of Spain. Both his critical history, *The Boom in Spanish American Literature*, and his novellas in *Sacred Families* were published in Spain.

Donoso's second Guggenheim Fellowship, in 1973, enabled him to work on *A House in the Country*. His first trip to Chile in some nine years had to be canceled because of the military coup there (an event that colors both *A House in the Country* and *El jardín de al lado*). His next move, to the Mediterranean fishing and resort village of Sitges (1976), has obvious resonances in *El jardín de al lado*, which, like all of the author's fiction, has a strong autobiographical substratum. Donoso returned to Chile in 1980, winning the Chilean Premio National de Literatura in 1990. He died in Santiago in 1996.

ANALYSIS

José Donoso's first two novels are similar in a number of ways, which makes it convenient to consider them together, despite significant and perhaps fundamental differences in the level of style and technique. Both involve upper-class, traditional Chilean families, a decaying mansion, and the problem of the generation gap; both treat psychological abnormalities in a rigidly stratified society where a rich, decadent minority is contrasted with an impoverished lower class; and in both, members of the aristocracy become emotionally involved with members of the lower class. In *This Sunday*, however, there is a more adroit utilization of innovative techniques and more subtle thematic development, a contrapuntal effect and stream-of-consciousness narration rather than the omniscient narrator of *Coronation*, who summarizes events and describes places and people in photographic fashion, sharpening the narrative perspective and involving the reader's collaborative effort, using secondary characters as third-person reflectors.

Time in *Coronation* is treated in a linear, chronological manner, but in *This Sunday* it is subjected to a more fluid handling, reflecting the philosophical and literary theories of Henri Bergson and Marcel Proust while intensifying the latent Freudian and existential concepts of the first effort, with the result that the aesthetic and intellectual density of *This Sunday* is considerably greater.

CORONATION

Misiá Elisa Grey de Abalos in *Coronation* is a wealthy, demented nonagenarian who lives with her fiftyish bachelor grandson, Andrés, an asexual aesthete whose life is a prime example of abulia and existential inauthenticity, a man addicted to French history and collecting canes (possibly symbolic of his not standing on his own in life). Andrés's world, like that of his grandmother, is hermetic, monotonous, isolated from the "real" workaday world; virtually his only human contact is his lifelong friend, Dr. Carlos Gros. The two aging servants, Rosario and Lourdes, have devoted their lives to the service of the Abalos family but become unable to cope with and care for the bedridden Misiá Elisa; Estela, a sensual country wench, is brought in to care for her, introducing a new element into the previously closed system. Estela is something of a catalyst, awakening Andrés's dormant sexuality and introducing the neighboring shantytown's societal dregs into the mansion (and the novel) via her affair with Mario (whose older half brother, René, is a link with the criminal element).

Coronation is traditional in its technique and employs an almost naturalistic cause-and-effect sequence, portraying most of the characters as products of their environment, although Donoso's interest in psychological analysis transcends the usual naturalistic characterization. Social determinism underlies the formation both of Andrés, who studied law in his youth because it was the thing for young men of his class to do, and of Misiá Elisa, who is pathologically repressed, molded by the religious education and bourgeois puritanism of her family. A similar social determinism is responsible for Mario's fear of entrapment (partly cultural, partly based on his brother's unhappy marriage); Estela's pregnancy thus inspires in Mario panic and instinctive flight.

Following Freudian psychology, Donoso stresses the importance of early-childhood experiences, the power of the unconscious, and the central role of sexuality in other areas of human life, with much of the characters' conduct being irrational, neurotic, or motivated by repressed erotic urges. In her senile dementia, Misiá Elisa becomes overpoweringly obsessed with sexuality, which she suppressed during most of her life, and gives way to obscene outbursts. Obsessions are a recurring motif in *Coronation* and in Donoso's fiction as a whole, and often are associated with recurring symbols, false rituals, repetitive or symbolic dreams, existential themes, and rigid daily routines that acquire an unconscious, magical, or supernatural character for the participants. Any break in the routine, therefore, is a transcendent disruption of order—hence the ultimately catastrophic ramifications of bringing Estela, the new servant, into the rigid and ritualistic existence of the mansion.

Misiá Elisa's conversations with Estela include warnings of the dangers of seduction and reveal that she considers all men "pigs" while considering herself a saint (having never let her husband see her naked). Life for the old lady is a gutter, a sewer, a cesspool from which religion is the only escape; thus she is also obsessed with sin, although for her, sexuality and sin are essentially identical. His grandmother's stern warnings and prohibitions and the inculcation of childhood fears and exaggerated taboos fill the boy Andrés with dread and apprehension, leading ultimately to his falsifying his first confession and, disappointed that instant fire and brimstone is not the result, to a loss of faith and rejection of religion, without any accompanying loss of inhibitions.

Plagued by a recurring nightmare in which a long bridge over an abyss suddenly ends, precipitating him into the void, Andrés experiences extreme existential anguish as he comes to realize the inability of philosophy or science to replace the security promised by faith and to assuage the fear of death, of the infinite, and of nothingness. Existentially, he is also radically alone, his solitude and loneliness so extreme that his abulia and inability to act are the visible result of the isolation and meaninglessness of his life. More than two decades spent in idle alienation, avoiding any engagement with life, end abruptly for Andrés when the terror inspired by his grandmother's approaching death is combined with the disturbing attraction of Estela's presence, bringing the realization that he has never really lived (in contrast with his friend, Carlos Gros, who represents an acceptance of life and love, believes both in science and religion, and exemplifies an existential exercise of free will). Where Misiá Elisa sees life as a sewer, Andrés sees it as chaos, terror, absurdity, a mad trick played upon humankind by an unjust or insane god. Both grandmother and grandson thus exemplify alienation so extreme that it borders upon the psychotic, their fragile equilibrium maintained by a series of obsessive routines and rituals—as in the case of Andrés limiting his cane collection to ten.

Donoso employs an indirect, third-person narration or monologue (comparable to the procedure of James) to plumb the psychological depths of his characters and thereby provide a multiplicity of perspectives, augment dramatic intensity, and allow the reader to identify more directly with a given character's viewpoint. The novel raises serious psychological, social, and philosophical issues, often through Andrés's very avoidance of them (an ironic technique that requires the reader to face the conclusions that Andrés has refused to contemplate), but Donoso also employs humor and numerous aesthetic ingredients. Incongruity is essential to many moments of humor, with the best examples involving Misiá Elisa, who, in her madness, swings like a pendulum from prudishness to obscenities to exaggerated religiosity. Similarly, the ironic contrast between Andrés's adolescent ignorance (in flashbacks to his childhood and youth) and the mature knowledge of narrator and reader provides much black comedy; for example, the young Andrés imagined that there was some connection between hell and the school restroom because the latter was a filthy place, and it was there that he first overheard a conversation about sex.

One of the recurring symbols or images of Donoso's fiction is the decaying mansion, often a Victorian monstrosity replete with gables and turrets, balconies whose only function is decorative, passages leading nowhere, closed or walled-up rooms, and other elements representative of a decadent or outmoded lifestyle. The mansion in *Coronation*, similarly constructed, also exemplifies Donoso's fascination with Art Nouveau—with its opulence of detail, decorative floral borders, and curving lines—while the depictions of the grandmother, her "coronation" and death (amid rococo bows, streamers, and billowing folds of cloth), function to complement and emphasize the theme of conspicuous consumption. The decadent mansion is a transparent allegory of a decadent upper class, while on an individual, psychological level, it also frequently symbolizes existential or emotional emptiness, isolation or alienation, and lack of contact with reality.

Another important symbol in *Coronation* is Andrés's collection of canes, rigidly limited to ten to exteriorize or make visible the rigid, self-imposed limits on his sterile, monotonous, routine existence. When the existential crisis provoked by confrontation with two of life's most powerful forces—love and death, both of which he has previously avoided—obliges Andrés to take radical measures, the one step he is able to visualize is raising the limit on his cane collection. He visits the home of an antique dealer whose wife—with her pink shawl and naked palms, evoking a powerful subconscious association with Estela—profoundly disturbs him; thus brought to an awareness of his desire for Estela, he resolves to win her, a decision that, if carried out, would constitute his first step toward existential engagement and authenticity. As he returns home, however, an accidental glimpse of the girl with her lover beneath a streetlight mortifies him and brings realization of his own absurdity and that of his situation; unable to return to his once-comfortable abulia and solitude, he gradually retreats into madness (a denouement that, in naturalistic terms, might be implicit in his heredity), succumbing to the pernicious influence of his grandmother, whose pervasive madness has gradually undermined his own rationality.

Similarly, Mario's fear of becoming a criminal, arising from his brother's criminal nature, the family's increasingly desperate financial straits, and the injustices of society, presages his fall into crime: He is induced to participate in the theft of the Abalos family silver, thereby setting the stage for the grotesque denouement that combines the frustrated robbery attempt, Andrés's madness, and Misiá Elisa's death.

THIS SUNDAY

The themes of alienation and existential anguish reappear in *This Sunday*, but Donoso's interest in abnormal psychology and the exploration of the unconscious of each of his protagonists are much more visible than in the earlier novel. Don Alvaro Vives and his wife, Chepa, a wealthy, middle-aged couple, live in another of Donoso's mansions, where they are visited by their five grandchildren (one of whom narrates portions of the novel). Other characters include Violeta, a retired former servant of the Vives household and onetime mistress of Alvaro; Maya, a lower-class psychopath who has been convicted of murder; Marujita, a peddler; Mirella, Violeta's illegitimate daughter; and her husband, Fausto.

In brief, the plot revolves around the activities of Chepa, a volunteer welfare worker, and her infatuation with Maya and use of the family's influence to obtain his parole. Settled by Chepa in Violeta's house, Maya is both attracted to his benefactor and fearful of her, and his pathology determines a path of escape through violence once again—this time through the murder of Violeta, which allows him to return to the comfortable alienation of prison, where no existential decisions are required. Rather than a straightforward narrative, *This Sunday* employs an ironic alternation between the naïve or limited vision of characters—first-person narrators who are participants in the action—and the occasional interventions of an omniscient narrator, thereby stressing the characters' ingenuousness, self-deception, or unawareness.

Much of the narrative is retrospective, via the use of Proustian flashbacks (for example, Alvaro's recollections of the beginning of his affair with Violeta are stimulated by the smell of meat pastries, experienced years previously when he had gone to her house). Free association and indirect third-person, stream-of-consciousness narrative are combined in reconstructing Alvaro's life as a weak young man whose social position enabled him to exploit Violeta without assuming responsibilities, avoiding the threats represented by both university girls and prostitutes while preventing the servant girl from living an authentic existence of her own. A victim of the social conventions by which "decent" girls of his own class were sacred, meant only for marriage, Alvaro is unable to truly love Chepa and other upper-class girls, although on the basis of established mores, he assumes that he will love her; actually, he manages to consummate the marriage only by closing his eyes and imagining that he is making love to Violeta.

In their fifties, Alvaro and Chepa have ceased sleeping together, and both live behind masks, maintaining a facade that serves as a substitute for authentic relationships as well as an escape from unpleasant reality. Alvaro's inability to love having become more pronounced with time, he appears narcissistic, withdrawn, and slightly ridiculous—aspects emphasized by his grandchildren's nicknaming him the Doll, his interminable games of chess and solitaire, his deafness, his lack of concern for things other than his health, and his rituals. Chepa, a victim of a loveless marriage that has increased her basic insecurity, provides a self-portrait in a number of interior monologues, most of them precipitated by contact with Maya. As a lonely, aging woman whose children have left home, she seeks to give some meaning to her existence by works of charity—by helping the poor and through her work at the prison—in an attempt to compensate for the knowledge that for Alvaro she is an object devoid of significance.

A good deal of sadomasochism inheres in Chepa's relationships with "her" poor; she imagines herself as "a littered bitch" with a compulsive need to feed the hungry mouths fastened to her. Her philanthropy is a substitute for the normal human relationships that are lacking in her life as well as a mask for less admirable motivations of her own, the desire to dominate or control, and to indulge her more (or less) than maternal interest in Maya. She helps him to set up a leather-goods shop, but her vigilance arouses his resentment and desire to escape; despite his derangement, Maya intuits in Chepa the devouring female, the Jungian evil mother.

Seeking Maya at Violeta's house, Chepa learns both that he has become Violeta's lover and that Violeta had an affair with Alvaro before his marriage to Chepa, provoking the latter's decision to throw off convention and look for Maya in the shantytown. Unfamiliar with the sprawling slums, she becomes lost in the twilight maze of alleys, but she fortuitously encounters Maya's mistress, Marujita, whose revelations of Maya's mixed emotions concerning Chepa inflame her and bring on a surrealistic, nightmarish experience as she is set upon by slum children who rob her of her furs and purse and leave her exhausted, on a trash heap. The inferno of the slums into which Chepa descends is a symbolic, expressionistic representation of her own subconscious with its hidden, conflicting sexual desires. Maya's murder of Violeta has been seen by critics as an instance of transferring his repressed aggression for Chepa to one socially weaker; the murder frees him from his obligations to her as benefactor, and to society.

The differences between Alvaro and Chepa are not so marked as the grandchildren imagine; their inability to communicate with Alvaro leads them to see him as cold, absurd, and slightly grotesque, while the grandmother is perceived in an unrealistically positive fashion as generous and loving (perhaps a result of her own altruistic self-image), a participant in the children's games of fantasy. Actually, both Alvaro and Chepa suffer from inauthenticity, solitude, and unfulfilled emotions, but Chepa is close to achieving authenticity when she recognizes and accepts her desire for Maya and determines to seek him, while Alvaro has lived so long in egotistic aloofness, exploiting without giving, that no self-redemption appears possible.

The novel's title refers to the family's habitual Sunday gatherings for dinner at the grandparents' residence, highlighting an incident of one specific Sunday, when Chepa searches for Maya, returning from the slums so traumatized that her subsequent life is almost that of a catatonic. Maya's murder of Violeta, who is vicariously Chepa, symbolically signals Chepa's death, and although she lives for many years, she spends them in isolation, essentially as dead to her grandchildren as if she were deceased. The rituals in the lives of adults are paralleled by the children's games, and additional parallels and contrasts throughout the novel lend symmetry: Alvaro's relationship with Violeta is socially similar to that of Chepa with Maya (a superior-inferior involvement); Alvaro and Violeta are passive, inert, making no effort to change their lives, while Chepa and Maya are active, attempting to improve their situations or to change them. *This Sunday* explores more complicated relationships, with more tragic repercussions, than those plumbed in *Coronation*, and it does so in a more objective fashion, given the lessening of authorial intervention. Both novels, however, re-create the surrealistic and nightmarish effects of subconscious, irrational, or instinctive forces, achieving especially memorable portraits in the matriarchs (Misiá Elisa and Chepa), who undoubtedly hark back to the mental deterioration of Donoso's own maternal grandmother.

HELL HAS NO LIMITS

Hell Has No Limits, which was published one year after *This Sunday*, provides a departure from the novelist's previous urban settings, being set in a somber, sordid brothel in a backwater rural winegrowing area. Although the existential issues of authenticity and alienation, solitude, and a lack of communication found in the earlier novels are again present to some degree, there is an increased emphasis on absurdity and the grotesque, and Donoso begins to employ mythic elements and ambiguity, symbolically alluding to biblical myths of the Creation and the Fall in depicting the results of a failed economic experiment by a local politician, Don Alejo, who is a sort of local god, even said to resemble the Lord.

The village, Estación El Olivo, created by Don Alejo, a wealthy landowner and area boss, was touted as an earthly paradise at its inception, but some twenty years later, during the novel's present, it has become a caricature of itself, where physical and moral stagnation make it something of a hell on earth. Don Alejo had originally owned the brothel, but as the result of a bet between himself and the madam, Big Japonesa, he signed the property over to her (the wager involved Japonesa's managing to seduce Manuela, a gay cross-dresser who imagines that he is a flamenco dancer). Japonesa won, thanks to her astuteness in manipulating Manuela's erotic fantasy and a promise to make him her partner in the brothel, but during the incident she became pregnant and subsequently gave birth to an unattractive girl, Japonesita, who operated the brothel business following her mother's death. Japonesita, at the age of twenty still a virgin despite her managing a house of prostitution, is a rival of her gay father in a subliminal competition for the affections of Pancho Vega, a truck driver, bully, and closeted gay man whose return precipitates the novel's climax.

Although Don Alejo, as "creator" of Estación El Olivo, is a benign god figure, he is ambiguous by reason of being politically and morally corrupt (he also plots the destruction of the town, since he has decided to convert the whole area to vineyards). His wager, the precipitating factor that brings Manuela's family into being, is a parodic perversion of the concept of Christian marriage, and his association with the powers of evil is symbolized by four vicious black dogs that accompany him (similar dogs appear in *The Obscene Bird of Night*). The ambiguity of Manuela is primarily sexual, for he desires ardently to be a woman; some similar ambiguity appears in Pancho, who is muscular and seemingly virile but in reality is cowardly and in the closet. The ambiguity of Japonesita, virgin madam of the bordello, is underlined by her lack of sexual maturity, her exaggerated thrift, and illusions that hinge on her buying a phonograph—a pathetically unrealistic hope, given the reality of her economic situation.

The catalyst in *Hell Has No Limits* is Pancho, who decides after a meeting with Don Alejo that he will enjoy one last spree at the brothel. He makes sexual advances toward Japonesita, but having aroused her (all the while thinking of his truck—both a Freudian sexual symbol and an instrument of suicidal escape), he sadistically rejects her for Manuela, whose dance provokes him, not so much to sexual desire as to murderous fantasies of disemboweling and leaving her lifeless.

The novel's brutal climax resolves Manuela's existential identity crisis (brought on by age and the depressing material situation). Leaving the brothel with Pancho and his brother-in-law, Octavio, after the flamenco performance, Manuela makes the mistake of kissing Pancho, who fears exposure of his homosexuality; this unleashes a nightmarish flight-and-pursuit sequence in which Manuela is beaten and attempts to seek refuge in the home of Don Alejo. Caught and beaten again, Manuela is sodomized by Pancho and Octavio and left nearly dead by the river. Whether this episode is fatal is also ambiguous; the novel ends on a note of pessimism as Japonesita extinguishes the brothel light and retires to the howling of Don Alejo's dogs and the sobs of a prostitute's child, traditional motifs of doom that combine with the blackness of night to underscore the impression of impending death and oblivion. Because of his psychological complexity, existential revolt, and commitment to ideals of art and beauty, Manuela is one of Donoso's most memorable characters.

The Obscene Bird of Night

The Obscene Bird of Night, considered by critics an antinovel because of Donoso's abandonment of traditional plot, character, and thematic development in favor of a more spontaneous depiction of reality and a virtuosic display of stylistic artistry, is the author's most complex work. Filled with grotesque fantasies, characters with multiple and fluctuating identities or protean, disintegrating personalities, the novel does away with conventions of logic and of mimetic literature, discarding any portrayal of objective reality to present the dilemma of humanity before the existential void.

Humberto Peñaloza, narrator and protagonist, begins as an incipient or would-be writer whose poverty obliges him to accept the job of secretary to Don Jerónimo Azcoitía, a wealthy aristocrat and influential politician. Jerónimo's wife, Inés, inspires Humberto's erotic fantasies, although her witchlike old servant, Peta Ponce, intrudes upon many of them, preventing the consummation—even in his mind—of Humberto's desire. When

Jerónimo and Inés fail to have a son to carry on the family's distinguished name, Peta Ponce supposedly arranges for Humberto to have intercourse with Inés, who conceives and gives birth to Boy, a repugnant little monster, deformed to such an extreme that Jerónimo has him reared on an isolated, distant estate that is placed under the direction of Humberto. Whether Humberto fathers Boy is highly questionable; it may be only another fantasy, as are many other incidents in the novel (the ultimate reality of Boy is also questionable).

The distant estate, La Rinconada, peopled by monsters—gathered by Jerónimo so that Boy will not believe himself abnormal—is a grotesque, absurd mirror image of the Azcoitía estate and a possible expressionist allegory of Chilean society. Years later, after surgery for an ulcer, Humberto becomes obsessed with the notion that his physician, Dr. Azula, has removed eighty percent of his organs; Humberto abandons La Rinconada to take refuge in La Casa—a former convent that has become a domicile for retired female servants—where he retreats into silence and is called Mudito (mute).

Inés, now aging and frustrated in her aspirations to maternity, fails in a mission to the Vatican in which she seeks symbolic perpetuity, via the quest for beatification of a homonymic forebear, and also takes refuge in La Casa, where she spends her time despoiling the grotesque old inmates of their few miserable belongings in a dog-racing game that she always wins. Or does she? The visionary and phantasmagoric world of the protagonist-narrator is so fluctuating, so surrealistic and ambiguous, that the reader assumes the narrative consciousness to be schizophrenic or psychotic and mistrusts his representation of events. Humberto's schizophrenic symptoms include withdrawal from reality, hallucinations, living in a world of fantasy, systems of false selves, masks or personas, fear or terror of engulfment by others or the world, a feeling of imprisonment, and the imagining of himself as an infant. Donoso's uncanny capturing of the schizophrenic's perceptions undoubtedly owes something to his own experience of mental illness, with transient schizophrenia and paranoia induced by his inability to tolerate the painkillers given him after his operation. It is possible—and even plausible—that most of the novel's characters are phantoms generated by Humberto's deteriorating mind, and that the two worlds of the Azcoitía estate and the isolation of La Rinconada respectively represent the rational world of visible reality and the dangers of the invisible world of the unconscious.

A House in the Country

Although the labyrinthine, dilapidated casa has been seen as an archetypal Jungian symbol of terror, it may also be related to Donoso's use of the decaying mansion throughout his fiction as a symbol of Chilean society with its archaic social structures and decadence. Yet another such house, a seemingly limitless labyrinth with miles of underground passages, secret rooms, false or hollow walls, and hidden doors, appears in *A House in the Country*, seen by some as an allegory of Chilean politics and referring concretely to the military coup of 1973, following in the wake of other novels about Latin American dictators, such as Alejo Carpentier's *El recurso del método* (1974; *Reasons of State*, 1976), Augusto Roa Bastos's *Yo el Supremo* (1974), and Gabriel García Márquez's *El otoño del patriarca* (1975; *The Autumn of the Patriarch*, 1975). If this is true, Donoso's novel does not present the biography of a dictator so much as the ideological configurations of a historical event, alluding to the opponents, victims and villains, the personal concentration of power and attendant aspiration to perpetuity, physical and intellectual repression, official rhetoric, and external intervention, with the house or mansion and its surrounding outbuildings constituting a metaphor for the totalitarian state, especially for the political prison, concentration camp, or detention center.

Beyond allusions to specific concepts or historically recognizable persons, *A House in the Country* is significant for its portrayal of a general problem in Latin America, a vast complex transcending geographical and political boundaries and involving the unholy alliance between oligarchies and foreign interests, militarism and dictatorships, the exploitation of the lower class and the lack of freedom of speech and of the press. It is an abstract political allegory of the abuse of power based on bureaucratic structures, the novel of a family dynasty whose fortune is based on mining in a remote rural area of lush vegetation and unreal, stylized geography, with significant subthemes such as adolescent rebellion, the conflict between idealism and materialism, the generation gap, psychosexual repression, conformism and hypocrisy, inauthentic values and lifestyles, and radical solitude and the inability to communicate.

Set in an imaginary country whose flora and fauna appear to be drawn from all of South America, *A House in the Country* employs a vague chronology, as befits its mythic and ahistorical nature. As something of a dystopia with strong existentialist undercurrents, it portrays a Kafkaesque world where utopia has gone awry via the symbolic narration of a "revolution": Children who take advantage of their elders' absence on an extended and unexplained trip take over the estate and set up their own regime, instituting some reforms among the natives but eventually quarreling among themselves and finally being discovered and chastised after a parental display of force involving the use of troops. *A House in the Country* is thus no more a realistic portrayal of recognizable reality than is *The Obscene Bird of Night*, although powerful realities of another order are captured and conveyed with forceful impact.

Donoso's later novels also display vanguardist tendencies, employing variants of the metanovel and self-conscious fiction, the purpose of which is to erase the boundaries between the real and fictitious worlds, with the author being simultaneously creator and novelistic character, the novel both that which the reader peruses and another work whose genesis is subject or problem of the text at hand. The problem of the relationships among author, text, and reader is a leitmotif in *The Obscene Bird of Night*, *A House in the Country*, and *El jardín de al lado*, where it assumes preponderant proportions. In an encounter between the novelist and one of the Ventura dynasty in *A House in the Country*, the character criticizes many details of the narrative, a situation elaborated in *El jardín de al lado*; in both works, Donoso presents his literary theories or comments upon them, burlesques the expectations of the reader of conventional novels, parodies literary convention, and repeatedly destroys the mimetic illusion in favor of an investigation into the problems of the novel as genre, thereby further separating his last five novels from those of the 1950's and 1960's. Without ceasing to write of Chile, he became more cosmopolitan in his choice of settings and characters; without abandoning social concerns, he incorporated broader themes and more universal literary preoccupations.

Janet Pérez

Other major works

SHORT FICTION: *Veraneo, y otros cuentos*, 1955; *Dos cuentos*, 1956; *El Charlestón*, 1960 (abridged as *Cuentos*, 1971; *Charleston, and Other Stories*, 1977); *Los mejores cuentos de José Donoso*, 1965; *Cuentos*, 1971; *Seis cuentos para ganar*, 1985.

PLAYS: *Sueños de mala muerte*, pb. 1985; *Este domingo: Versión teatral de la novela homónima*, pb. 1990.

POETRY: *Poemas de un novelista*, 1981.

NONFICTION: *Historia personal del "boom,"* 1972 (*The Boom in Spanish American Literature: A Personal History*, 1977).

Bibliography

Callan, Richard J. *Jung, Alchemy, and José Donoso's Novel "El obsceno pájaro de la noche."* Lewiston, N.Y.: Edwin Mellen Press, 2000. Examines *The Obscene Bird of Night* from the perspective of Carl Jung's analytical psychology. Callan explains how Donoso created his own literary version of Jungian psychology to focus on themes of imprisonment and disguise.

Carbajal, Brent J. *The Veracity of Disguise in Selected Works of José Donoso: Illusory Deception*. Lewiston, N.Y.: Edwin Mellen Press, 2000. Carbajal discusses the use of masks, both literal and metaphorical, in four of Donoso's novels. One chapter focuses on the role of the double in his lesser-known novel *Donde van a morir los elefantes*.

Finnegan, Pamela May. *The Tension of Paradox: José Donoso's "The Obscene Bird of Night" as Spiritual Exercises*. Athens: Ohio University Press, 1992. Finnegan examines the novel as an expression of humanity's estrangement from the world. A difficult but rewarding study for advanced students. Includes a bibliography.

Friedman, Mary Lusky. *The Self in the Narratives of José Donoso: Chile, 1924-1996*. Lewiston, N.Y.: Edwin Mellen Press, 2004. A detailed examination of a major theme in Donoso's writing: the perils of establishing a self. Friedman focuses on his later works, including the novels *The Garden Next Door*, *Curfew*, and *Donde van a morir los elefantes*, to describe how Donoso's works expressed his conception of selfhood.

González Mandri, Flora. *José Donoso's House of Fiction: A Dramatic Construction of Time and Place*. Detroit, Mich.: Wayne State University Press, 1995. A study of

Donoso's incorporation of masks and houses in his fiction, the latter implicating allusions to Henry James. González Mandri focuses on his novels and the novella *Taratuta* (1990). Includes detailed notes, an extensive bibliography, and an index.

King, Sarah E. *The Magical and the Monstrous: Two Faces of the Child-Figure in the Fiction of Julio Cortázar and José Donoso*. New York: Garland, 1992. Informative, although the short citations in Spanish are not translated into English. Nevertheless, this comparative study of two figures of the Spanish American boom in literature is valuable.

McMurray, George R. *Authorizing Fictions: José Donoso's "Casa de Campo."* London: Tamesis Books, 1992. Chapters on Donoso's handling of voice and time, his narrative strategies (re-presenting characters), and his use of interior duplication and distortion. Includes a bibliography.

_______. *José Donoso*. Boston: Twayne, 1979. An excellent introductory study, with chapters on Donoso's biography, his short stories, *The Obscene Bird of Night*, and *Sacred Families*. Includes a chronology, detailed notes, and an annotated bibliography.

Magnarelli, Sharon. *Understanding José Donoso*. Columbia: University of South Carolina Press, 1993. Thoroughgoing study of Donoso's works. The first chapter, "How to Read José Donoso," offers an introduction to his work. Separate chapters analyze his novels *Coronation*, *This Sunday*, *Hell Has No Limits*, *The Obscene Bird of Night*, *A House in the Country*, and *Curfew*.

ANATOLE FRANCE

Born: Paris, France; April 16, 1844
Died: La Béchellerie, near Tours, Saint-Cyr-sur-Loire, France; October 12, 1924
Also known as: Jacques-Anatole-François Thibault

PRINCIPAL LONG FICTION

Le Crime de Sylvestre Bonnard, 1881 (*The Crime of Sylvestre Bonnard*, 1890)
Les Désirs de Jean Servien, 1882 (*The Aspirations of Jean Servien*, 1912)
Thaïs, 1890 (English translation, 1891)
La Rôtisserie de la Reine Pédauque, 1893 (*At the Sign of the Reine Pédauque*, 1912)
Le Lys rouge, 1894 (*The Red Lily*, 1898)
L'Histoire contemporaine, 1897-1901 (collective title for the first 4 novels that follow; *Contemporary History*)
L'Orme du mail, 1897 (*The Elm Tree on the Mall*, 1910)
Le Mannequin d'osier, 1897 (*The Wicker Work Woman*, 1910)
L'Anneau d'améthyste, 1899 (*The Amethyst Ring*, 1919)
Monsieur Bergeret à Paris, 1901 (*Monsieur Bergeret in Paris*, 1922)
Histoire comique, 1903 (*A Mummer's Tale*, 1921)
L'Île des pingouins, 1908 (*Penguin Island*, 1914)
Les Dieux ont soif, 1912 (*The Gods Are Athirst*, 1913)
La Révolte des anges, 1914 (*The Revolt of the Angels*, 1914)

OTHER LITERARY FORMS

Of the twenty-five volumes that make up the standard French edition of the complete works of Anatole France (frahns), more than fifteen are given over to one form or another of prose fiction: ten novels (thirteen if one counts the tetralogy *Contemporary History* as four separate novels), ten collections of short stories, and four volumes of fictionalized autobiography. The remainder of the twenty-five-volume set exhibits a startling variety of literary forms: poetry, theater, biography, history, literary criticism, philosophy, journalism, and polemical writings.

France's first publication was a book-length critical study of the French Romantic poet Alfred de Vigny (1868), after which he published two volumes of his own poetry, one containing lyric poems, the other a play in verse, and several long narrative poems. In the 1880's and 1890's, he wrote a regular weekly column, mostly about books and the literary world, for a prominent Paris newspaper, *Le Temps*. The best of those columns were republished in five volumes under the title *La Vie littéraire* (1888-1892; *On Life and Letters*, 1911-1914). His major venture into the writing of history was *La Vie de Jeanne d'Arc*

Anatole France
(Library of Congress)

(1908; *The Life of Joan of Arc*, 1908), published after a quarter of a century of research. That same year, he published his one original prose work for the theater, *La Comédie de celui qui épousa une femme muette* (1903; *The Man Who Married a Dumb Wife*, 1915), a farce based on a well-known medieval fabliau.

France's major speeches and occasional writings, on such issues of the times as the Dreyfus affair, socialism, and pacifism, were collected and published in several volumes under the title *Vers les temps meilleurs* (1906, 1949). Philosophical meditations on human nature and civilization can be found in a volume titled *Le Jardin d'Épicure* (1894; *The Garden of Epicurus*, 1908), consisting of pieces on general subjects originally written for his weekly newspaper column and not included in the volumes of *On Life and Letters*. One may say, in sum, that France was the complete man of letters, who tried his hand at just about every form of writing practiced in the literary world of his time. It is nevertheless accurate to say that the writing of fiction so dominated his output, throughout his career, that it constituted his true vocation.

Achievements

The election of Anatole France to the French Academy in 1896 and his winning of the Nobel Prize in Literature in 1921 were the major public landmarks of the great success and recognition he achieved during his career as a writer, first in his own country and then in the international arena. At the height of his fame, in the early years of the twentieth century, he was widely regarded as France's greatest living author, celebrated for his wit, his wisdom, and his humanitarian vision. The paradoxes of that fame, however, were multiple and heavy with irony: The fame had been an unusually long time in coming (he was nearly fifty years old before he had his first significant success with the public), it was based largely on his association with public events rather than on his genuine but esoteric literary talent, and it lasted only briefly. Indeed, the greatest paradox of his fame was its bewilderingly rapid eclipse after his death. His reputation would not regain the luster of his glory years, around the turn of the twentieth century.

France himself lived long enough to be the saddened witness of a major erosion of his fame in a storm of bitter controversy, which made him an object of both worship and hatred but for purely nonliterary reasons. The truth is that the great fame he enjoyed, during a brief period of his life, was of the public sort, only indirectly occasioned by his writings, which, even at their most popular, appealed to a rather narrowly circumscribed audience. One must separate his fame from his achievements as a writer—which is not to say that his achievements were minor, but only that they were literary and aesthetic, hence accessible to relatively few at any time.

As a novelist and short-story writer, France made his mark in the fiction of ideas, and as a literary critic, he established, by personal example, the validity of subjective impressionism as a method. Those are the two major achievements of his career in letters, the accomplishments that have affected literary history. To those literary achievements, one should add a more personal achievement: the creation of a highly distinctive, instantly identifiable style of classic purity and elegance, with subtle rhythms and limpid clarity, which perfectly translated the skeptical and gently ironic view he held of the human condition.

Biography

Anatole France, born Jacques-Anatole-François Thibault in 1844, was the only child of a well-established Parisian bookdealer and was seemingly predestined to the world of books. His father, Noël-François Thibault, ran the sort of bookshop that was also a gathering place of the literati, who would come as not only customers but also friends. They would sit and talk with the owner, whom they called by the familiar diminutive France, an abbreviation of François. Once the son was old enough to help in the shop and participate in the daily conversations, he was naturally called le jeune France, a custom that suggested to young Anatole the pen name he would choose when he began to write.

Shy and unassertive by nature and unprepossessing physically, France matured into an unworldly and bookish young man, easily intimidated by the "real" world and much given to periods of solitude and quiet reverie. In his twenties, he did occasional research and editing chores for the publishers of dictionaries and encyclopedias, having definitely decided against following in his father's footsteps as a bookseller. Eventually, he became a reader of manuscripts for a publisher, wrote articles for ephemeral journals, and took a civil servant's position, working in the senate library, all the while using his leisure moments to learn the craft of writing. He was thirty-three years old, and a published but thoroughly obscure and unknown author, when he overcame his timidity long enough to marry, in 1877. The marriage produced one child, a daughter born in 1881, but was otherwise an unhappy relationship for both sides that ended in a bitter divorce in 1893, after a prolonged separation.

France's unhappy domestic life was the backdrop for his long personal struggle to find his own "voice" and establish himself as a writer. By the 1880's, he had abandoned poetry and was experimenting with different modes of prose fiction, trying both the novel and the short-story forms but attracting very little attention from the reading public. Only after he became the regular literary critic for *Le Temps* and had published a genuinely popular work, the novel *Thaïs*, did he feel securely established enough as a writer to give up his post at the senate library.

Thereafter, all through the 1890's, France's books sold well, and he rose rapidly in public esteem, aided in part by a newfound interest in and involvement with politics and public affairs. In particular, the Dreyfus affair outraged his sense of justice and galvanized him into public action for the first time in his life. He was then in his fifties, and he discovered, a bit to his own surprise, a radical social thinker beneath the placid and conservative exterior he had always presented to the world. During the first years of the new century, he became outspokenly anticlerical and socialistic in his views but was soon plunged into disillusionment when he saw that even victory, as in the Dreyfus affair, produced little real change in society, and that his own activism served only to make him controversial and the object of vicious attacks, which he found especially painful to endure. This mood of disillusionment drove him to withdraw into himself once more and to give up active involvement in public affairs. His work increasingly concerned the past and took on an unaccustomed satiric edge.

The outbreak of World War I tempted France briefly into the public arena once more, to proclaim his pacifist views, but when he was assailed as unpatriotic, he retreated, this time definitively, into the private world of letters. It is perhaps suggestive of the depth of his wounds from the public fray that his literary preoccupations during the final decade of his life were almost exclusively autobiographical. His career as a novelist had effectively ended with the publication of *The Revolt of the Angels* in 1914.

ANALYSIS

The world of books into which Anatole France was born was surely the strongest influence in determining his vocation as a writer, but that influence went far deeper still, for it also determined the kind of writer he would be. Almost all the subjects he chose to write about, in his long career, were derived from or related to books in some way. He was a voracious reader all of his life, and the many books he wrote not only reflect that wide reading but also reveal that what he read was more immediate and more vital to him—more nourishing to his creative imagination, indeed more *real* to him—than the quotidian reality in which he lived. Even when most actively involved in public events, as he was in the years immediately before the end of the nineteenth century and the beginning of the twentieth, he tended to approach events as abstractions, dealing with them as intellectual issues, somehow detached from specific occurrences involving specific human beings. This conscious need to convert real events into matter for books can be seen most clearly in the tetralogy that he so pointedly titled *Contemporary History* and in which he contrived to write about current events as though they were already in the distant past or even the stuff of legend.

Concomitant with his irreducibly bookish view of the world was his almost instinctive taste for storytelling. Whether as reader or as writer, nothing charmed him more than the unfolding of a narrative. Even factual writing—history and biography, for example—he treated as an exercise in storytelling, going so far as to characterize good literary criticism as a kind of novel in which the critic "recounts the adventures of his soul among masterpieces," as he put it in the famous preface to *On Life and Letters*. The art of storytelling was the art he set out to master in his long and difficult apprenticeship, and the storytelling impulse can be identified as the very heart of his vocation as a writer.

To the mind of the man of letters and the instinct of the teller of tales must be added a third characteristic: the outlook of the determined skeptic. France trained himself, from an early age, to question everything and to discern the contradictions and ironies in all forms of human behavior, including his own. He cultivated a perspective of distance and detachment from both people and events, but he learned to temper the bleakness and isolation of such a perspective with feelings of sympathetic recognition of the folly common to all humankind. A subtle blend of pity and irony came to be the hallmark of his view of the affairs of this world, expressed in the tone of gentle mockery with which his celebrated style was impregnated in the works of his maturity. Indeed, all three central characteristics of France—the literary turn of mind, the narrative impulse, and the ironic perspective—can be found in everything he wrote, including the youthful works of poetry, fiction, and literary criticism through which he gradually learned the writer's trade. Those three traits can be seen fully developed for the first time in the novel that won for him his first public recognition, *The Crime of Sylvestre Bonnard*, in 1881.

THE CRIME OF SYLVESTRE BONNARD

Published to the accolades of the French Academy, *The Crime of Sylvestre Bonnard* provided France with his first taste of success. The improbable hero of the book is an elderly, unworldly scholar and bibliophile who explains, in his own words, in the form of diary entries, how he came to acquire a coveted medieval manuscript and how he rescued a young girl from poverty and oppression. What holds the reader's interest is not the trivial plot but the character of Sylvestre Bonnard, whose naïve narrative style, in his diary, constantly and unwittingly reveals his own bumbling incompetence in dealing with the practical side of life.

The reader quickly recognizes as comical the dramatic earnestness with which the simpleminded scholar narrates the only two "adventures" that have ever intruded into his serene existence. The ironic discrepancy between the excited tone of the narrator and the mundane character of the events he narrates is echoed suggestively in the title, which promises a thriller but delivers nothing more violent than a book lover's crime: Having promised to sell his personal library in order to create a dowry for the damsel in distress he has rescued, Bonnard confesses, at the end of the diary, that he had "criminally" withheld from the sale several items with which he could not bear to part.

Perhaps the greatest skill the author displays in this book is that of artfully concealing the inherent sentimentality of the material. The key device of concealment is mockery: Bonnard's interest in old books and manuscripts is magnified, in both incidents, into a grand and criminal passion by a transparently mock-heroic tone. This device distracts and amuses the reader, preventing inopportune reflections about the "fairy-tale" unreality of the happy ending of each incident. It is also true that the eccentric character of Bonnard is charming and that the novelty of a gentle fantasy, published at the height of the popularity of the naturalistic novel in France, must have struck many readers of the day as a welcome relief. It was for such reasons, no doubt, that the novel enjoyed mild critical acclaim and modest sales in 1881, even as its author, sternly self-critical, recognized its limitations of both form and content and set about immediately trying to do better.

What France retained from *The Crime of Sylvestre Bonnard* for future use was the tone of gentle and sympathetic irony about human foibles. In the decade that followed, he experimented with fictionalized autobiography, tales of childhood, and themes borrowed from history or legend, seeking above all a composition that he—and his readers—could recognize as a fully realized work of art. He reached that goal with the publication of *Thaïs* in 1890—his first critical and popular success.

Thaïs

The story of Thaïs, the courtesan of Alexandria, has a bookish source, as does most of France's fiction; he changed the legend of Thaïs, however, by giving the central role in the tale to the monk, Paphnuce, whose ambition for saintliness inspires in him the project of converting the notorious actor and prostitute to Christianity. The well-known plot, in which the saintly monk succumbs to sin even as the notorious sinner seeks salvation in piety, is thus, in France's version, seen almost exclusively from the point of view of the monk. The character of Thaïs is developed hardly at all, while the complex motivations of Paphnuce are analyzed and explored in detail. This imbalance in the point of view, however, does not affect the fundamental irony of the story. Thaïs, though superficially presented, is shown clearly to be a seeker of pagan pleasure and prosperity, who yet was influenced in early youth by piety, having been secretly baptized, and whose growing fear of death and damnation happens to make her receptive to the preaching of Paphnuce at that particular time of her life.

Paphnuce, on the other hand, has had a long struggle against his own sensuality in trying to live as a monk, and is unaware that his sudden project of converting Thaïs is really prompted by his unconscious but still unruly sensual yearnings. When the two meet, therefore, each is ignorant of the other's true disposition, and Paphnuce, moreover, is ignorant of his own desires. Their encounter is thus fated to be sterile, for by that time, Thaïs is already on her way to salvation, and Paphnuce is proceeding precipitously in the opposite direction. France exploits the irony of their opposing trajectories by making the occasion of their meeting the longest and most concentrated episode in the book. The effect is structural: The book is designed as a triptych, with the shorter first and last segments employed to introduce the protagonists and then to record the ultimate fate of each, while the middle segment, equal in length to the other two combined, examines and analyzes their encounter from every angle and demonstrates the impossibility of any fruitful contact between them, because by that time each is in an unanticipatedly different frame of mind.

The structure of the book is perhaps what critics and public admired most about *Thaïs*. It has a satisfying aesthetic quality that announced that France had mastered the sense of form necessary for the achievement of a work of art. The book's success must also, however, be attributed to the subtle complexity of the ideas the author was able to distill from what is, after all, little more than a mildly indecorous comic anecdote. *Thaïs* is a profound and suggestive exploration of the hidden links between religious feeling and sexual desire and, beyond that, of the intricate and unexpected interplay between pagan and Christian ideals and thought and between worldliness and asceticism as patterns of human behavior. In this novel, characterization and realistic description count for comparatively little, and in spite of the daring subject matter, there is not a hint of prurience. The best effects are achieved by a tasteful and harmonious blend of elegant style, well-proportioned structure, and subtle ideas, all presented with gentle irony through the eyes of an amused and skeptical observer. *Thaïs* remains a delight for the thoughtful and attentive reader, one of France's finest achievements.

At about the same time as *Thaïs* was being composed, France was also diligently exploring the short-story form. Employing similar material from history or legend, he was striving to find the ideal fusion of form and content that would yield a work of art in that genre also, and in some of the stories of the volume titled *L'Étui de nacre* (1892; *Tales from a Mother of Pearl Casket*, 1896), notably the famous "Procurator of Judea" and "The Juggler of Our Lady," he succeeded as fully as he had for the novel in *Thaïs*. Thereafter, having earned his artistic spurs in both the novel and the short story, France developed his career in both domains, alternating a novel and a volume of short stories with something approaching regularity over the next twenty years. What is notable in the work of those years is the visible effort he made to avoid the facile repetition of past successes, to explore and experiment with new techniques, and to strive to develop and grow as an artist. During the 1890's, for example, he followed the gemlike stories of *Tales from a Mother of Pearl Casket* with a comic fantasy of a novel called *At the Sign of the Reine Pédauque*, then used a trip to Florence, Italy, as inspiration for a volume of short stories, *Le Puits de Sainte-Claire* (1895; *The Well of Saint Clare*, 1909), and a surprisingly conventional love story, *The Red Lily*, appearing in 1894. Those publications confirmed his newly won stature as a major writer and earned for him election to the French Academy in 1896.

CONTEMPORARY HISTORY

France's next project, *Contemporary History*, began as a series of weekly newspaper articles commenting on current events by means of anecdotes and illustrative tales. Soon he began interconnecting the articles by using the same set of characters in each. The articles could have formed the basis for a volume of short stories, but instead, France conceived the notion of weaving selected articles from one year's output into a novel that would record the main events of that year in a kind of fictionalized history. It was a bold experiment, which eventually ran to four volumes and occasioned some brilliant writing and the creation of one truly memorable character, Monsieur Bergeret, a scholar and teacher of a wittily ironic turn of mind, who usually articulated the author's own skeptical view of public events.

Some consider *Contemporary History* to be France's finest work, but while it does make unflaggingly entertaining reading, as well as offer a valuable historical record, it may be too randomly structured and too variable in tone to be artistically satisfying for the sophisticated modern reader. It deserves respect, however, both as an interesting experiment in a new kind of fiction and as the inauguration of a new thematic vein in France's work: the overt exploitation of public events, especially politics, in the writing of fiction.

The novels and short stories published between 1900 and 1914 are almost all in this new political vein, sometimes seriously polemical, more often comic and satiric. The most widely read work of that period is the amusing and clever *Penguin Island*, which gives a brief and jaundiced view of French history as though it were a history of a society of penguins. The masterpiece of this period, however, and probably the finest of all France's novels, is his reconstruction of the atmosphere of the French Revolution, called *The Gods Are Athirst*, published in 1912.

THE GODS ARE ATHIRST

France's strong interest in the period of the French Revolution was undoubtedly inspired by his youthful browsing in his father's bookshop, which specialized in that subject. During the 1880's, France began work on a novel about the revolutionary period, but he abandoned it, rearranging some of the completed fragments into short stories that turned up, a few years later, in the collection *Tales from a Mother of Pearl Casket.* By 1910, when he began to work on a new novel of the Revolution, he had been through his own personal revolution—involvement in the Dreyfus affair and public espousal of socialism—only to suffer rapid disillusionment with the way human nature seems inevitably to distort and betray ideals. Something of that disillusionment must have shaped *The Gods Are Athirst*, for it concentrates on the process by which the Reign of Terror developed out of revolutionary zeal for liberty, equality, and fraternity and, by means of the inclusion of a large and varied cast of characters, seeks to depict how daily life was affected by this process. The novel is set in Paris and covers a time span of about two years, from 1792 to 1794.

At the very heart of the novel, France places a struggling young painter, a pupil of Jacques Louis David, whose name is Évariste Gamelin and who, in 1792, is active in the revolutionary committees of his quarter. Gamelin is depicted as a mediocre artist but one who is serious in his devotion both to art and to the humanitarian ideals of the new Republic. His seriousness is a function of his youthful innocence, which is unrelieved by any element of gaiety or humor but which endows him with a capacity for tender feelings of affection or sympathy. Those tender feelings are the noble source of his support for the Revolution, but he gets caught up in complex and emotionally charged events that he is incapable of understanding, and, as a member of a revolutionary tribunal, he unwittingly betrays his own humanitarian principles by voting for the execution of innocent people to satisfy the bloodthirsty mob of spectators. Gamelin thus embodies the book's fundamental and deeply pessimistic theme, which is that even decent individuals and noble ideals will fall victim to the winds of fanaticism. At the ironic end of the novel, Gamelin the terrorist is himself condemned and executed by the Reign of Terror.

Gamelin is surrounded by an array of different types who give magnificent density to the novel's re-creation of the past. Most memorable, perhaps, is Maurice Brotteaux, a neighbor of Gamelin and a former member of the nobility, now earning his living by making puppets to sell in toy shops. Brotteaux is a skeptic and a witty ironist—unmistakably the author's alter ego—who, though not unsympathetic to the Revolution, deplores its decline into fanaticism, consoling himself by reading his ever-present copy of Lucretius's *De rerum natura*. The author's intentional irony in this detail is that the Latin poet's work had the original purpose of explaining nature to his contemporaries without reference to the supernatural, in order thus to liberate his compatriots from their superstitious fear of the gods. As the novel's title suggests, Lucretius's noble project is a futile exercise when the gods thirst for blood. Gamelin's fiancé, the voluptuous Élodie, adds a fascinating psychological element to the novel, for as her lover Gamelin grows more and more savage in his condemnation of his fellow citizens, she is surprised to discover that, her horror of him notwithstanding, her sensual attraction to him intensifies: The more blood there is on his hands, the more uncontrollable her passion becomes.

The novel is masterful in its smooth handling of the welter of significant characters and details, the unobtrusive integration of known historical figures and events into an invented narrative, and the creation of both a sense of inevitable tragedy in the action and the feel of epic grandeur in the composition as a whole. It is an impressively vast canvas the author attempts to encompass here—the greatest and most complex of his career. Although there is, of necessity, much weaving back and forth from setting to setting and from one group of characters to another, the clarity and focus of the narrative line are never blurred, and the careful structure accentuates for the reader the inexorability of the mounting dramatic tension enveloping more and more of the novel's characters. In the manner of a classical tragedy, the novel closes with the return of uneasy calm after the catastrophe and the indication that the dead will be quickly forgotten and that life will go on as before. The final paragraph shows Élodie taking a new lover and employing the same endearments to him as she had used at the start of her affair with Gamelin.

The Gods Are Athirst does not quite attain the majestic historical sweep that a subject such as the French Revolution might be expected to command, perhaps because the figure at its center, Évariste Gamelin, is deliberately not cast in the heroic mold. Yet it is a fine and powerful novel, and its unforgettable images carry their intended message to issues beyond the events described, revealing something fundamentally important about human conduct in any revolution and, indeed, in any group situation subject to the volatile incitements of mob psychology. This brilliant novel, written when the author was nearly seventy years old, proved to be the artistic culmination of France's long career. The novel that followed it, *The Revolt of the Angels*, is a merry fantasy of anticlerical bent, amusing to read but making no artistic or intellectual claims to importance. It proved, simply, that this veteran teller of tales still had the skill and magic, at seventy, to hold the attention of the reading public.

THE RED LILY

As a writer of fiction, France has always eluded classification. He showed little interest in the precise observation of daily reality that was the hallmark of his naturalist contemporaries, nor did he strive to win fame with sensational plotting, flamboyant characters, or studies in spicily abnormal psychology. Though allied, at certain times, with the Parnassians and the Symbolists, he never submitted himself fully to their aesthetic discipline in his own art. He followed his own bent, and because he was so steeped in books and erudition, so unsociable and so fond of solitude, and so little driven by ambition, he tended to cut a strange and solitary figure in the literary world.

In both manner and matter, he was really quite unlike anyone else then writing. Probably nothing contributed more to his uniqueness as a writer than his absolute addiction to ideas. The originating inspiration for everything he wrote was neither an event nor a character nor a situation nor even a new literary trick to try out, but ever and always an idea, a concept, an abstraction that he wanted to bring to life by means of a story, a play, or a poem. Even his most conventional novel, *The Red Lily*, seems to be only a routine story of frustrated love and jealousy. What truly animates this novel is the daring concept of female independence, which entrenched social attitudes and the habits of male possessiveness in love relationships put out of the reach of even the most lucid and intelligent women, even in that haven of enlightened individualism, Florence.

Though not a great novel, *The Red Lily* penetratingly probes an idea that was very advanced for the time: the idea that a woman who conceives the ambition to be a person in her own right, rather than an accessory to someone else's life, faces tragically insuperable obstacles. One can identify a seminal idea of that kind at the very center of the concerns of every novel and every short story France wrote. Ideas are his trademark—not surprisingly, because his literary imagination was so completely grounded in books, rather than in life, and because his carefully maintained view of the world was a skepticism so systematic, and so bathed in irony, that it kept reality at a distance and made the life of the mind virtually the only life he knew. Such a writer is not for everyone, but in spite of the low ebb of his reputation since his death, his audience will never entirely vanish as long as there are those who relish the pleasures of the intellect.

Murray Sachs

OTHER MAJOR WORKS

SHORT FICTION: *Nos enfants*, 1886; *Balthasar*, 1889 (English translation, 1909); *L'Étui de nacre*, 1892 (*Tales from a Mother of Pearl Casket*, 1896); *Le Puits de Sainte-Claire*, 1895 (*The Well of Saint Clare*, 1909); *Clio*, 1900 (English translation, 1922); *Crainquebille, Putois, Riquet, et plusieurs autres récits profitables*, 1904 (*Crainquebille, Putois, Riquet, and Other Profitable Tales*, 1915); *Les Contes de Jacques Tournebroche*, 1908 (*The Merry Tales of Jacques Tournebroche*, 1910); *Les Sept Femmes de la Barbe-Bleue, et autres contes merveilleux*, 1909 (*The Seven Wives of Bluebeard*, 1920); *The Latin Genius*, 1924; *The Wisdom of the Ages, and Other Stories*, 1925; *Golden Tales*, 1926.

PLAYS: *La Comédie de celui qui épousa une femme muette*, pb. 1903 (*The Man Who Married a Dumb Wife*, 1915); *Crainquebille*, pb. 1903 (English translation, 1915).

NONFICTION: *Alfred de Vigny*, 1868; *La Vie littéraire*, 1888-1892 (5 volumes; *On Life and Letters*, 1911-1914); *Le Jardin d'Épicure*, 1894 (*The Garden of Epicurus*, 1908); *Vers les temps meilleurs*, 1906, 1949; *La Vie de Jeanne d'Arc*, 1908 (*The Life of Joan of Arc*, 1908); *Le Génie latin*, 1913 (*The Latin Genius*, 1924); *Sur la voie glorieuse*, 1915.

MISCELLANEOUS: *The Complete Works*, 1908-1928 (21 volumes); *Œuvres complètes*, 1925-1935 (25 volumes).

BIBLIOGRAPHY

Auchincloss, Louis. "Anatole France." In *Writers and Personality*. Columbia: University of South Carolina Press, 2005. Auchincloss, himself a novelist, has compiled his observations about writers in this collection. The chapter on France discusses how France's personality was reflected in his own fiction.

Axelrad, Jacob. *Anatole France: A Life Without Illusions*. New York: Harper & Brothers, 1944. In this dated but eminently readable biography, Axelrad focuses on France's impact as a social critic and partisan of justice. While the research is carefully undertaken and generally accurate, the point of view is overly sentimental, unabashedly admiring, and insufficiently critical and analytical.

Chevalier, Haakon M. *The Ironic Temper: Anatole France and His Time*. New York: Oxford University Press, 1932. Although dated, this book is insightful and engagingly written. Its purpose is to study a character, not to evaluate the artistic achievement of its subject. It sets an excellent analysis of France's ironic view of the world against a detailed portrait of the political climate in which he lived and wrote. Includes photographs and a bibliography.

Emery, Elizabeth. "Art as Passion in Anatole France's *Le Lys rouge*." *Nineteenth Century French Studies* 35, no. 3/4 (2007): 641-652. An analysis of the novel *The Red Lily*, describing it as a "mordant satire of [France's] contemporaries' aesthetic pronouncements" and focusing on its detailed descriptions of fin-de-siècle aesthetic tastes and attitudes about art.

Hamilton, James F. "Terrorizing the 'Feminine' in Hugo, Dickens, and France." *Symposium* 48, no. 3 (Fall, 1994): 204-215. An analysis of France's novel *The Gods Are Athirst* and novels about the French Revolution by Victor Hugo and Charles Dickens. Hamilton argues that these authors repress the feminine side in their depiction of the Reign of Terror, relying on cold mechanical reasoning that creates a self-defeating force of violence.

Jefferson, Carter. *Anatole France: The Politics of Skepticism*. New Brunswick, N.J.: Rutgers University Press, 1965. This work emphasizes the historical and political, as opposed to the literary, ideas of France and is especially informative with respect to the complex and shifting political positions he assumed in the last two decades of his life. The book's five chapters cover the conservative, anarchist, crusader, socialist, and "bolshevik" stages of France's thought. Contains a bibliography.

Stableford, Brian M. "Anatole France." In *Supernatural Fiction Writers: Fantasy and Horror, 1: Apuleius to May Sinclair*, edited by Everett Franklin Bleiler. New York: Scribner's, 1985. Stableford provides a brief introduction to France's treatment of the Christian myth and to his fantastic fiction, discussing some of the individual works.

Virtanen, Reino. *Anatole France*. New York: Twayne, 1968. Intended as a general introduction to the author's work, this insightful volume is accurate and sound in its evaluation of France's life and career. It is also of use to general readers in its detailed analysis of France's most significant literary works.

JULIEN GREEN

Born: Paris, France; September 6, 1900
Died: Paris, France; August 13, 1998
Also known as: Julien Hartridge Green

PRINCIPAL LONG FICTION

Mont-Cinère, 1926 (*Avarice House*, 1927)
Adrienne Mesurat, 1927 (*The Closed Garden*, 1928)
Léviathan, 1929 (*The Dark Journey*, 1929)
L'Autre Sommeil, 1931 (*The Other Sleep*, 2001)
Épaves, 1932 (*The Strange River*, 1932)
Le Visionnaire, 1934 (*The Dreamer*, 1934)
Minuit, 1936 (*Midnight*, 1936)
Varouna, 1940 (*Then Shall the Dust Return*, 1941)
Si j'étais vous, 1947 (*If I Were You*, 1949)
Moïra, 1950 (*Moira*, 1951)
Le Malfaiteur, 1955 (*The Transgressor*, 1957)
Chaque homme dans sa nuit, 1960 (*Each in His Darkness*, 1961)
L'Autre, 1971 (*The Other One*, 1973)
Le Mauvais Lieu, 1977
Les Pays lointains, 1987 (*The Distant Lands*, 1990)
Les Étoiles du sud, 1989 (*The Stars of the South*, 1996)
Dixie, 1995

OTHER LITERARY FORMS

Julien Green first drew critical attention in the late 1920's as a writer of short fiction (*Le Voyageur sur la terre*, 1930; and *Les Clefs de la mort*, 1927) before attempting the longer narratives that became his forte. Green, however, is almost as well known for his autobiographical works as for his novels. His *Journal*, begun in 1928, has appeared in eighteen volumes published between 1938 and 2006 (partial translations in *Personal Record, 1928-1939*, 1939, and *Diary, 1928-1957*, 1964); a second series, begun in 1963, is more personal and frankly confessional in tone: *Partir avant le jour* (1963; *To Leave Before Dawn*, 1967), *Mille chemins ouverts* (1964; *The War at Sixteen*, 1993), *Terre lointaine* (1966; *Love in America*, 1994), and *Jeunesse* (1974; *Restless Youth, 1922-1929*, 1996). An additional volume, *Memories of Happy Days* (1942), was written and published in English during Green's self-imposed wartime exile in the United States.

Encouraged by Louis Jouvet to try his hand at writing plays, Green achieved moderate success as a playwright with *Sud* (pr., pb. 1953; *South*, 1955), *L'Ennemi* (pr., pb. 1954), and *L'Ombre* (pr., pb. 1956), but he soon concluded that his true skills were those of a novelist. In any case, Green's plays are seldom performed and are of interest mainly to readers already familiar with his novels.

ACHIEVEMENTS

In 1971, shortly after publication of his novel *The Other One*, Julien Green became, at the age of seventy, the first foreigner ever elected to membership in the French Academy; his election brought sudden and considerable attention to a long, distinguished, but insufficiently appreciated literary career. Green, born in France to American parents, had been writing and publishing novels in French since the age of twenty-five, attracting more critical attention in France than in the United States, despite the availability of his work in English translation. Even in France, however, his novels have not received extensive critical notice, owing in part to his work being difficult to classify.

Encouraged by the success of his earliest writings, Green lost little time in developing a characteristic mode of expression, alternately mystical and sensual, often both at once. Many critics, as if willfully blind to the erotic dimension of Green's work, sought to classify him as a "Catholic" writer in the tradition of Georges Bernanos and François Mauriac. Others, focusing on the oppressive atmosphere pervading many of his novels, sought to place Green closer to the gothic tradition. Neither classification is quite accurate, yet it was not until after Green's autobiography began to appear in 1963 that reassessment of his novels began in earnest.

Using a clear, ornament-free style that has been described as classical, Green quickly involves his readers in the solitary lives of tortured characters obsessed with the need to escape. Often, the compulsion toward escape leads to violence, madness, or death; when it does not, it produces an implied "leap of faith," which is not, however, totally satisfying to those who would see Green as a religious writer in the Catholic tradition. Even in those rare cases in which solutions are offered, it is still the problems that dominate the consciousness of author and reader alike. Endowed with keen powers of observation, Green excels in the portrayal of psychological anguish that any thoughtful reader can understand, even if he or she does not share it.

The publication of Green's autobiography beginning in the 1960's permitted at last a demystification of the novels—in Green's case, more help than hindrance. In the light of Green's frankness, many of the tortures undergone by his characters stood revealed as artistic transpositions of the author's own private anguish as he sought to reconcile his spiritual aspirations with a growing awareness of his homosexuality. Far from detracting from the power of Green's novels, such disclosures shed valuable light on his life in art, allowing critics and casual readers alike to appreciate the true nature of Green's novelistic achievement. Whatever their source, Green's novels remain powerful portraits of alienation and estrangement unmatched in contemporary French or American literature.

Biography

Julien Hartridge Green was born in Paris on September 6, 1900, the youngest of eight children. His father, Edward Moon Green of Virginia, had since 1895 served as European agent of the Southern Cotton Seed Oil Company. Green's mother, Mary Hartridge of Savannah, Georgia, dominated her son's early life with a curious blend of love and Puritan guilt; her death in 1914, instead of liberating the young Green from the tyranny of her moods and ideas, seems rather to have increased her hold upon his developing conscience. Green grew to adulthood torn between a strong, if repressed, sensuality and a mystical desire for sainthood, often equally strong. Converted to Catholicism within a year after his mother's death, he seriously considered entering a monastic order but deferred his plans for the duration of World War I. In 1917, he served as an ambulance driver, first for the American Field Service and later for the Red Cross; the following year, still (as he remained) a U.S. citizen, he obtained a commission in the French army by first enlisting in the Foreign Legion. Demobilized in 1919, he returned to Paris and soon renounced his monastic vocation, a loss that caused him considerable anguish.

Unable to decide on a career, he accepted with some reluctance the offer of a Hartridge uncle to finance his education at the University of Virginia. Enrolled as a "special student," Green read widely in literature, religion, and sociology; in 1921, after two years in residence, he was appointed an assistant professor of French. Still homesick for his native France, more at ease in French than in English, Green returned to Paris in 1922 to study art, gradually discovering instead his vocation as a writer and attracting the attention of such influential literary figures as Jacques de Lacretelle and Gaston Gallimard. By the age of twenty-five, already an established author with a growing reputation, Green had found his lifework.

During his thirties, Green read widely in mysticism and Eastern religions. Returning to the Catholic Church as early as 1939, Green was soon thereafter obliged to leave Paris by the onset of World War II. After the fall of France in 1940, he moved to the United States for the duration, teaching at various colleges and universities before and after brief service as a language instructor in the U.S. Army. Returning to Paris in September, 1945, he remained there, pursuing the life and career of a French man of letters until his death on August 13, 1998.

Analysis

Educated primarily in the French tradition, Julien Green brought to his novels a distinctly French concern for the presentation and development of character. Whether his novels are set in France, the United States, or elsewhere, his characters are observed and portrayed with the psychological precision that has characterized French fiction from Madame de La Fayette down through Honoré de Balzac and Gustave Flaubert to Marcel Proust. With critical and seemingly pitiless exactitude, Green takes the reader inside his characters to show their thought and motivations, achieving considerable identification even when the characters tend toward violence or madness. On the surface, few of Green's characters would appear to invite identification on the part of the reader; they tend to be misfits of one sort or another, haunted by strange fears and insecurities. It is Green's singular talent, however, to present them and their thoughts in such a way that they seem almost instantly plausible and authentic, and to hold the reader's interest in what will happen to them. Life, as particularized in Green's characters, emerges as both threat and promise, most often as a trap set for the unwary.

Typically, Green's protagonists, often female with one surviving and insensitive parent, find themselves trapped in an existence that they can neither tolerate nor understand; not infrequently, they contribute to their own misfortune through a stubborn refusal to express themselves. Even so, the reader senses that to speak their minds would render them vulnerable to even greater assaults from a hostile environment. Locked within themselves, they suffer all the tortures of an earthly hell from which they yearn to escape. In his autobiography, Green observes that a feeling of imprisonment was a recurring childhood nightmare; in his novels, the theme is enlarged to archetypal proportions, assuming the authority of fable. Green's characters, for all their particularities, emerge as highly convincing exemplars of the human condition.

Escape, for all of its apparent promise, offers no relief to the suffering of Green's characters. Adrienne Mesurat, among the most convincing of Green's early heroines, gradually retreats into madness once she has achieved through an act of violence the freedom for which she has longed; Paul Guéret, the ill-favored viewpoint character of *The Dark Journey*, strikes and disfigures the young woman whose attentions he has sought, thereafter becoming a fugitive. Manuel, the title character of *The Dreamer*, retreats from the undesirable world into a fictional universe of his own making, only to die soon thereafter. Elisabeth, the protagonist of *Midnight*, seeks to escape with her lover, only to be killed with him in a fall. Clearly, the oppressive atmosphere that stifles Green's characters is internal as well as external; like Adrienne Mesurat, they remain imprisoned even when they are free to come and go as they please. Even in the later novels, such as *The Other One*, death is frequently the only means of escape available.

The power of Green's novels derives in no small measure from the author's skill in providing motivation for the behavior of his characters. In the case of Adrienne Mesurat, for example, Green quickly and convincingly shows normal desire stifled by silence until it becomes first an obsession, then true madness. Philippe Cléry, the main viewpoint character of *The Strange River*, passes the age of thirty before being obliged to examine his life; thereafter, he becomes most convincingly self-conscious, questioning his every move in an authentically ineffectual way. Sympathetic or not (and most are not), Green's characters are inescapably human and believable, commanding the reader's identification; although they seem to exist in a world of their own, they are unmistakably drawn from life, the products of Green's keen powers of observation.

It is possible, that, had Green not been reared in a time less tolerant than the twentieth century, his novels might never have come into being. Arguably, Green's expression has responded somewhat to the temper of the times, dealing more and more openly with homosexual attraction in such novels as *The Transgressor*; indeed, by the time Green wrote and published his autobiography in the 1960's, his revelations seemed less scandalous than timely and enlightening. The restraint that helped to shape his earlier works was in a sense no longer necessary. It seems likely, moreover, that the writing of the autobiographical volumes lessened the sense of creative urgency that marks the best of Green's earlier writing. In fact, Green's later novels (*Le Mauvais Lieu* in particular), while still holding the reader's attention, cover little new ground and move perilously close to self-parody.

THE CLOSED GARDEN

Green's second novel, *The Closed Garden*, written and published within a year after the success of *Avarice House*, ranks among his best and is perhaps the most memorable. Refreshingly normal at the start of the novel, eighteen-year-old Adrienne quickly erodes into madness and amnesia as a result of the stifling circumstances of her life. Recently out of school (the time is 1908), she lives in a provincial French town with her retired father and her thirty-five-year-old spinster sister, Germaine. A chronic invalid whose illness their autocratic father refuses even to recognize, Germaine rules over Adrienne with the authority of a mother but with none of the attendant love. As in Green's *Avarice House*, kinship is no guarantee of understanding or even friendship; indeed, the family emerges as perhaps the most inimical and threatening of human institutions. Using heavy irony, Green shows Adrienne's daily interaction with her hostile relatives; the reader, privy to Adrienne's innermost thoughts, looks on with horror as she is repeatedly unable to express them.

At the start of the novel, Adrienne is looking with healthy scorn at a group of family portraits to which she inwardly refers as "the cemetery," concluding with some satisfaction that her own features place her on the "strong" side of the family. Dressed as a servant, she is doing the family housework, exhibiting physical strength by moving heavy furniture with ease. It is precisely such apparent strength that will soon prove to be her undoing, as it turns inward upon herself, accomplishing in several weeks a deterioration that otherwise might take years. Deprived of normal human companionship, Adrienne becomes infatuated with a neighboring physician, Dr. Maurecourt, whom she has seen but once; such adolescent passion, harmless enough at face value, functions rather in Green's universe as an instrument of destruction. Adrienne, unable to confide to her father or sister the relatively innocent causes of her slightly irregular behavior, retreats further and further into her fantasy with each new demand for an explanation.

Steadfastly refusing to name the object of her secret passion, she soon finds herself literally locked up in the house, forbidden to leave but still dreaming of escape. Ironically, it is the nearly bedridden Germaine, rather than the healthy Adrienne, who in fact does manage to escape the father's tyranny, sneaking out of the house with Adrienne's help in order to seek refuge in a convent near Paris. Germaine's departure triggers a rare and violent dispute between Adrienne and her father, who reveals that he, like Germaine, has guessed the identity of Adrienne's lover. Overcome with shame and grief, Adrienne runs toward her father and pushes him downstairs; she is never quite sure whether she intended to kill him. In any case, he dies, and although Adrienne is never formally charged with his murder, she is eventually convicted of the crime by the tribunal of malicious gossip. Indeed, the entire village soon takes on the sinister aspect of Adrienne's now-absent family, hemming her within a circle of watchful and accusing eyes.

A brief attempt at leaving the village finds Adrienne drifting aimlessly from one provincial town to another, beset by nightmares as she sleeps fitfully in seedy hotels, imagining that she is being watched. Returning home to live among her tormentors, she falls physically ill; Dr. Maurecourt is summoned, and at the end of a lengthy and difficult conversation, she blurts out her unrequited love for him. Maurecourt, a frail widower of forty-five, is understandably nonplussed; with genuine compassion, he explains to Adrienne that he is mortally ill, having hardly more than a year left to live, while she, Adrienne, has her whole life ahead of her. For all practical purposes, however, Adrienne's life is as good as over; she again leaves the house, intending to escape but succeeding only in wandering aimlessly about the town until she is found suffering from amnesia.

Like other novels and plays of the period—John O'Hara's *Appointment in Samarra* (1934) and Jean Cocteau's *La Machine infernale* (1934; *The Infernal Machine*, 1936) come readily to mind—*The Closed Garden* is the carefully recorded history of what can happen to a human life and mind when everything possible goes wrong. Subjected to torture such as might be inflicted upon a steel rod in laboratory tests, Adrienne's mind eventually snaps. Until very near the end, however, Adrienne remains painfully lucid, aware of all that is happening to her yet powerless to stop it. Unlike such characters as O'Hara's Julian English and Cocteau's Oedipus, Adrienne seems singularly undeserving of her cruel fate; neither arrogant nor thoughtless, she seems to have been chosen almost at random by unseen forces bent upon destroying her for no good reason.

The Dark Journey

The Dark Journey, Green's third novel, breaks new ground in presenting several viewpoint characters and a number of interlocking subplots. Each of the main characters, reminiscent of Balzac's provincial "monomaniacs," is governed and identified by a ruling passion, much as Adrienne Mesurat is governed by her passion for the helpless Dr. Maurecourt. The main viewpoint character, whose life provides a link among the others, is Paul Guéret, an ill-favored and unhappily married man in his thirties who is obsessed by his passion for the young and attractive Angèle. A typical Green heroine, Angèle has been thrust by circumstances into a thankless and sordid existence from which she longs to escape, presumably in the loving company of a young man her own age. A launderer by day, she moonlights by sleeping with various gentlemen who frequent the restaurant owned and operated by the insatiably curious Madame Londe. In a sense, Angèle is less prostitute than spy, engaged by Madame Londe to supply her with useful information concerning the gentlemen's private lives. Guéret, to his consternation, is excluded from Angèle's regular clientele because he is simply not interesting enough, either as a person or because of his station in life, to warrant Madame Londe's interest. Angèle, meanwhile, is flattered and at least amused by Guéret's awkward attentions, even if she cannot bring herself to return his love in kind.

Guéret, driven nearly to distraction by Angèle's flirtatiousness and inaccessibility, becomes increasingly obsessed with his need to possess the girl, and before long his obsession leads to violence. First, after a long and painful struggle to scale the wall of Angèle's building, he breaks into her room, only to find that she is not there. The next day, unable to tolerate her taunting behavior, he beats her and goes into hiding, leaving her for dead on a riverbank. Angèle survives, although disfigured for life. Guéret, meanwhile, is in fact guilty of murder, having bludgeoned to death an old man who stumbled upon his hiding place. After several months as a fugitive, he is given asylum by the bored and sadistic Eva Grosgeorge, mother of a boy he once tutored. Eventually, Madame Grosgeorge tires of Guéret and denounces him to the police against the protestations of Angèle, still convalescent, who does her best to rescue him. Unsuccessful, Angèle lapses into a dreamlike state and, like Adrienne Mesurat before her, wanders about town in what she thinks is an attempt to escape; delirious, she dies of exposure soon after being brought back to her room. Madame Grosgeorge, meanwhile, having shot herself melodramatically at the moment of Guéret's arrest, is expected to survive.

The Dark Journey differs from Green's earlier novels in both the depth and the scope of its character development. Although both Guéret and Angèle show clear lines of descent from Green's earlier protagonists, such characters as Madame Londe and the Grosgeorge couple bear witness to a broadening of Green's psychological and social observation; Eva Grosgeorge, in particular, is a most convincing grotesque, the bored and self-indulgent younger wife of a rather bovine industrialist. Guéret, the misfit, serves unwittingly as the link between these various social types, whose paths would otherwise be unlikely to cross. As elsewhere in Green's work, interpersonal love is shown to be an unattainable illusion. Guéret's passion for Angèle, among the more normal obsessions portrayed in the book, is doomed by its own intensity. Angèle, meanwhile, is too lost in her own romantic fantasies to see beyond Guéret's ugliness to her own genuine feelings toward him until it is too late for them both.

The Strange River

Less sensational in subject matter and in treatment than *The Closed Garden* or *The Dark Journey*, Green's fifth novel, *The Strange River*, remains one of his least known; nevertheless, it ranks among his best. Nearly devoid of external action or incident, *The Strange River* presents social and psychological analysis of rare accuracy and power, approaching Flaubert's ambition to write a book about "nothing." To a far greater degree than in *The Dark Journey*, Green reveals his seldom-used gifts as a social satirist, here portraying in painful detail the empty existence of the idle rich. *The Strange River* is, moreover, the only one of Green's novels to be set in Paris, where he himself resided.

As in *The Dark Journey*, Green derives considerable effect in *The Strange River* from the presentation of multiple viewpoints, primarily those of Philippe Cléry and his sister-in-law, Eliane, but not excluding that of Philippe's wife, Henriette. Philippe, rich through inheritance, suffers in his own ineffectual way the double torture of being superfluous and knowing it. As titular head of a mining company about which he knows nothing and cares even less, he need only appear (and remain silent) at monthly meetings in order to do all that society expects of him. The rest of the time, he is free to remain in his elegant apartment (he owns the building) or go for long walks dressed as the gentleman he is. At thirty-one, he is aware that his marriage has long since become as meaningless and hollow as his professional title; Henriette goes out on the town without him nearly every evening and has taken a lower-class lover to occupy the rest of her time. Their only child, ten-year-old Robert, spends most of the year out of sight and mind in boarding school; his rare presence during school vacations, when he has nowhere else to go, proves irritating to his parents and aunt, as they have no idea what to say to him. Philippe, meanwhile, unless he is out walking, usually finds himself in the company of Henriette's elder sister, Eliane, who secretly loves Philippe even as she comes to despise him for what he is.

Against such a background of silence and mistrust, Green sketches in the private thoughts and feelings of his characters, expressing the pain of existence in all of its contingency. The plot of *The Strange River*, such as it is, turns upon an incident that Philippe thinks he may have witnessed in the course of one of his long walks: A middle-aged, shabbily dressed couple appeared to be struggling on the banks of the Seine, and the woman may or may not have called out to Philippe for help. In any case, Philippe went on his way, not consulting the police until hours later. As the novel proceeds, the incident often returns to haunt Philippe with its implications.

Anticipating by some twenty-five years the central incident of Albert Camus's *La Chute* (1956; *The Fall*, 1957), Philippe's experience disrupts the balance of a previously unexamined life; Philippe, however, is already too weak to do much of anything with what he has learned about himself. For months after the incident, he scans the papers for reports of bodies fished from the Seine; at length he finds one, and it is quite likely that he was in fact witness to a murder. In the meantime, another of his nocturnal walks has provided him with further evidence of his own cowardice; accosted by a stranger, he hands over his billfold at the merest threat of violence. Attending a monthly board meeting, he impulsively takes the floor and resigns his post, to the astonishment of his sister-in-law and wife, who fear that he has lost his mind; his life, however, goes on pretty much as before, closely observed by the lovesick spinster Eliane. Like Adrienne Mesurat, Eliane is both powerless and lucid in her unrequited love, increasingly attached to Philippe even as she begins to deduce his guilty secret concerning the couple on the riverbank.

Unlike all but one of Green's other novels (*The Other Sleep*), *The Strange River* is open-ended, leaving the main characters with much of their lives yet before them. The action is not resolved in violence, as in *The Dark Journey*, or in madness, as in the case of Adrienne Mesurat. Philippe, of course, is too weak to do much of anything except worry about himself.

Not until *The Transgressor*, written a quarter of a century later, did Green again try his hand at the sort of social satire so successfully managed in *The Strange River*; despite his skill in such portrayal, it is clear that Greene's true interest lay elsewhere, deep within the conscience of the individual. *The Strange River* is thus in a sense a happy accident; Green, in order to probe the inmost thoughts of a Philippe Cléry, had first to invent Philippe and place him against a social background. The result is a most satisfying work, rather different from Green's other novels but thoroughly successful in accomplishing what it sets out to do.

For a period after *The Strange River*, Green's novels tended increasingly toward fantasy, taking place in a real or fancied dreamworld fashioned by individual characters. It is perhaps no accident that these novels, atypical of Green's work taken as a whole, were written during the time of Green's estrangement from Catholicism, when he was reading extensively in mysticism and Eastern religions. Reconciled with the Church in 1939, Green was soon thereafter to leave France and his career as a novelist for the duration of World War II. *Moira*, the first of Green's true postwar novels, returns to the familiar psychological ground of his earliest work, going even further in its portrayal of the conflict between the mystical and the sensual.

MOIRA

Returning to the time and setting of his American university experience, Green presents in *Moira* the thoughts and behavior of Joseph Day, a Fundamentalist rustic who is even more of an outsider to the university life than Green himself must have been. Joseph is at odds with the school from the first day of his enrollment, horrified by the license and corruption that he sees all around him. His landlady, Mrs. Dare, smokes cigarettes and wears makeup, and his classmates discuss freely their relations with the opposite sex. His missionary zeal fueled by a truly violent temperament to match his red hair, Joseph seeks to save the souls of those around him; thus inclined, he is quite unable to see either himself or his fellows as human beings. Derisively nicknamed "the avenging angel," he burns with a white heat, quite unaware of the eroticism at its source. Early on, he unwittingly rebuffs the sexual advances of a young, male art student, who later commits suicide as a result; meanwhile, Joseph feels mysteriously drawn to the elegant, aristocratic Praileau, who has made fun of Joseph's red hair. Challenging Praileau to a fight, Joseph is so overcome by an excess of clearly sexual frenzy that he nearly kills the young man, who tells him that he is a potential murderer.

Unable to reconcile his Protestant faith with his increasingly violent feelings and behavior, Joseph confides in a fellow ministerial candidate, David Laird, whose vocation is both stronger and less temperamental than Joseph's own. David, however sympathetic, is quite unprepared to deal with the problems of his tortured friend, who proceeds toward the date with destiny suggested in the book's title. Moira, it seems, is also the name of Mrs. Dare's adopted daughter, a licentious young woman who emerges as almost a caricature of the flapper. Even before he meets the girl, Joseph is scandalized by all that he has heard about her; even so, he is quite unprepared for her taunting, loose-mouthed treatment of him.

Another apparent gay man, Killigrew, tries and fails to get close to Joseph. Joseph does, however, vividly recall Killigrew's description of Moira as a she-monster whenever thoughts of the girl invade his daydreams. At length, Joseph, having changed lodgings, returns to his room to find Moira planted there as part of a prank perpetrated upon the "avenging angel" by his classmates. Moira, of course, is a most willing accessory, her vanity piqued by the one man, Joseph, who has proved resistant to her rather blatant charms. By the time the planned seduction occurs, it is Moira, not Joseph, who believes herself to have fallen in love. In the morning, however, Joseph strangles Moira in a fit of remorse over what they have done. After burying her body without incident, he twice considers the possibility of escape but finally turns himself in to the police, who have sought him for questioning.

Despite a plot almost too tightly rigged to seem quite plausible, *Moira* ranks with the best of Green's earlier novels, showing considerable development in the depth and scope of his literary art. As in *The Dark Journey* and *The Strange River*, Green shows himself to be a shrewd and discerning observer of society and its distinctions. Characteristically, however, he remains concerned primarily with the inner workings of the human mind and emotions, and the variety of characters portrayed in *Moira* affords him ample opportunity to display his talents. Freed from taboos (both internal and external) against the depiction of homosexuality in literature, Green in *Moira* seemed to be moving toward a new, mature frankness of expression. However, the novels that he wrote after *Moira*, though explicit, fail to match that work either in suggestive power or in tightness of construction. The first novel of Green's "mature" period thus remains quite probably that period's best.

David B. Parsell

Other major works

SHORT FICTION: *Le Voyageur sur la terre*, 1930 (*Christine, and Other Stories*, 1930).

PLAYS: *Sud*, pr., pb. 1953 (*South*, 1955); *L'Ennemi*, pr., pb. 1954; *L'Ombre*, pr., pb. 1956.

NONFICTION: *Journal*, 1938-2006 (18 volumes; partial translations in *Personal Record, 1928-1939*, 1939, and *Diary, 1928-1957*, 1964); *Memories of Happy Days*, 1942; *Partir avant le jour*, 1963 (*To Leave Before Dawn*, 1967; also known as *The Green Paradise*); *Mille chemins ouverts*, 1964 (*The War at Sixteen*, 1993); *Terre lointaine*, 1966 (*Love in America*, 1994); *Jeunesse*, 1974 (*Restless Youth, 1922-1929*, 1996); *Memories of Evil Days*, 1976; *Dans la gueule du temps*, 1979; *Une Grande Amitié: Correspondance, 1926-1972*, 1980 (with Jacques Maritain; *The Story of Two Souls: The Correspondence of Jacques Maritain and Julien Green*, 1988); *Frère François*, 1983 (*God's Fool: The Life and Times of Francis of Assisi*, 1985); *Paris*, 1983 (English translation, 1991); *The Apprentice Writer*, 1993; *Jeunesse immortelle*, 1998.

BIBLIOGRAPHY

Armbrecht, Thomas J. D. *At the Periphery of the Center: Sexuality and Literary Genre in the Works of Marguerite Yourcenar and Julien Green*. Amsterdam: Rodopi, 2007. Ambrecht compares the representation of homosexuality in the work of Green and Yourcenar, comparing their depiction of gay characters in their novels and plays. Includes a bibliography.

Burne, Glenn S. *Julian Green*. New York: Twayne, 1972. Provides a comprehensive overview of the first forty-five years of Green's career, culminating in his induction into the French Academy in 1971. Includes a bibliography.

Dunaway, John M. *The Metamorphoses of the Self: The Mystic, the Sensualist, and the Artist in the Works of Julien Green*. Lexington: University Press of Kentucky, 1978. Dunaway's study traces the sources and evolution of Green's narrative art, exploring the biographical genesis of his major fiction. Includes a bibliography and an index.

O'Dwyer, Michael. *Julien Green: A Critical Study*. Portland, Oreg.: Four Courts Press, 1997. O'Dwyer provides a biographical introduction and a critical assessment of Green's novels, short stories, plays, autobiography, journals, and other miscellaneous writings. Highlights the importance of Green's American background for a full appreciation of his work. Includes a foreword by Green.

_______. "Toward a Positive Eschatology: A Study of the Beginning and Ending of Julien Green's *Chaque homme dans sa nuit*." *Renascence* 49, no. 2 (Winter, 1997): 111-119. An analysis of *Each in His Darkness* within the context of Green's ideas about the end of the world. Examines the negative elements of Green's spiritual vision, the identical structure of the first and final chapters, and the echoes, resonances, and parallels between these two chapters.

Peyre, Henri. *French Novelists of Today*. New York: Oxford University Press, 1967. Provides a good overview of Green's career, presenting him as standing outside both the French and the American traditions from which his work derives. Includes useful readings of Green's early and midcareer fiction.

Stokes, Samuel. *Julian Green and the Thorn of Puritanism*. 1955. Reprint. Westport, Conn.: Greenwood Press, 1972. A study of Green's novels, concentrating on the various intellectual influences that help explain the spiritual background of his work. Discusses Green's use of fiction to relate the lives of individuals to the society in which they live.

L. P. HARTLEY

Born: Whittlesea, England; December 30, 1895
Died: London, England; December 13, 1972
Also known as: Leslie Poles Hartley

PRINCIPAL LONG FICTION

Simonetta Perkins, 1925
The Shrimp and the Anemone, 1944
The Sixth Heaven, 1946
Eustace and Hilda, 1947
The Boat, 1949
My Fellow Devils, 1951
The Go-Between, 1953
A Perfect Woman, 1955
The Hireling, 1957
Facial Justice, 1960
The Brickfield, 1964
The Betrayal, 1966
Poor Clare, 1968
The Love-Adept, 1969
My Sisters' Keeper, 1970
The Harness Room, 1971
The Collections, 1972
The Will and the Way, 1973

OTHER LITERARY FORMS

L. P. Hartley published, in addition to eighteen novels, six collections of short stories: *Night Fears* (1924), *The Killing Bottle* (1932), *The Traveling Grave* (1948), *The White Wand* (1954), *Two for the River* (1961), and *Mrs. Carteret Receives* (1971). Reprinted in *The Complete Short Stories of L. P. Hartley* (1973), with the exception of ten apprentice pieces from *Night Fears*, the stories reveal Hartley's reliance on the gothic mode. At their least effective, they are workmanlike tales utilizing conventional supernatural machinery. At their best, however, they exhibit a spare symbolic technique used to explore individual human personalities and to analyze the nature of moral evil. The best of Hartley's ghost and horror stories include "A Visitor from Down Under," "Feet Foremost," and "W. S.," the last dealing with an author murdered by a character of his own creation. "Up the Garden Path," "The Pampas Clump," and "The Pylon" reveal a more realistic interest in human psychology, and they deal more directly with the theme central to Hartley's major fiction: the acquisition, on the part of an innocent protagonist, of an awareness of the existence of evil.

A frequent lecturer, and a reviewer for such periodicals as *The Observer, Saturday Review*, and *Time and Tide* from the early 1920's to the middle 1940's, Hartley published a volume of essays titled *The Novelist's Responsibility: Lectures and Essays* (1967), in which he deplored the twentieth century devaluation of a sense of individual moral responsibility. These essays explain Hartley's fictional preoccupation with identity, moral values, and spiritual insight. His choice of subjects, particularly the works of Jane Austen, Emily Brontë, Nathaniel Hawthorne, and Henry James, suggests the origins of the realistic-symbolic technique he employs in both his short stories and his novels.

ACHIEVEMENTS

While L. P. Hartley's novels from *Simonetta Perkins* to *Facial Justice* were published in the United States, they did not enjoy the popularity there that they earned in England. *The Go-Between*, for example, continued to be in print in England since its publication in 1953, and the *Eustace and Hilda* trilogy—comprising *The Shrimp and the Anemone*, *The Sixth Heaven*, and *Eustace and Hilda*—was given a radio dramatization by the British Broadcasting Corporation (BBC). In the course of a literary career of roughly fifty years, Hartley came to be a noted public figure, and his work received favorable attention from Lord David Cecil, Walter Allen, and John Atkins. Only in the United States, however, did his novels receive detailed critical attention. The three full-length studies of his fiction—Peter Bien's *L. P. Hartley* (1963), Anne Mulkeen's *Wild Thyme, Winter Lightning: The Symbolic Novels of L. P. Hartley* (1974), and Edward T. Jones's *L. P. Hartley* (1978)—are all American, as are the notable treatments of Hartley's work by James Hall and Harvey Curtis Webster.

BIOGRAPHY

Born on December 30, 1895, near Whittlesea in Cambridgeshire, Leslie Poles Hartley was named for Sir Leslie Stephen, the father of Virginia Woolf and himself a noted late Victorian literary man. According to Edward T. Jones, whose book *L. P. Hartley* contains the most complete biographical account, Hartley's mother, Mary Elizabeth Thompson, was the daughter of a farmer named William James Thompson of Crawford House, Crowland, Lincolnshire. His father, H. B. Hartley, was a solicitor, justice of the peace, and later director of the successful brickworks founded by the novelist's paternal grandfather. This information figures as part of the background to Hartley's *The Brickfield* and *The Betrayal*.

Hartley was the second of his parents' three children; he had an older sister, Enid, and a younger, Annie Norah. None of the three ever married. Reared at Fletton Tower, near Peterborough, Hartley was educated at Harrow and Balliol College, Oxford, his stay at the latter interrupted by military service as a second lieutenant in the Norfolk Regiment during World War I. He was discharged for medical reasons and did not see action in France. In Oxford after the war, Hartley came into contact with a slightly younger generation of men, among them Anthony Powell, Graham Greene, and Evelyn Waugh. His closest literary friend at this period, however, may have been Lord David Cecil. After leaving Balliol with a second honours degree in 1921, Hartley worked as a reviewer for various periodicals, wrote the stories later collected in *Night Fears* and *The Killing Bottle*, and cultivated friendships with members of both bohemian Bloomsbury and British society. His novella *Simonetta Perkins*, a Jamesian story of a young American woman's inconclusive passion for a Venetian gondolier, was published in 1925.

Hartley made many trips to Venice. From 1933 to 1939, he spent part of each summer and fall there, and he drew on this experience for parts of *Eustace and Hilda*, *The Boat*, and *My Fellow Devils*. Returning to England just before the start of World War II, Hartley started work on the series of novels that earned for him a place in the British literary establishment. Given the James Tait Black Memorial Prize for *Eustace and Hilda* in 1947 and the Heinemann Foundation Prize for *The Go-Between* in 1953, he served as head of the British Association of Poets, Playwrights, Editors, Essayists and Novelists (PEN) and on the management committee of the Society of Authors. In 1956, he was created a Commander of the British Empire by Queen Elizabeth II. In his later years, Hartley gave frequent talks, most notably the Clark lectures delivered at Trinity College, Cambridge, in 1964. Joseph Losey won the Grand Prize at Cannes, France, in 1971 for a film version of *The Go-Between*, for which Harold Pinter wrote the script, and in 1973, Alan Bridges's film of *The Hireling*, from a script by Wolf Mankowitz, won the same prize. Hartley died in London on December 13, 1972.

ANALYSIS

Indebted to Bloomsbury, as shown by a concern with personal conduct and a highly impressionistic style, L. P. Hartley betrays affinities with D. H. Lawrence, Aldous Huxley, and George Orwell in a more fundamental concern with larger social and moral issues. His best books argue for the existence of a spiritual dimension to life and demonstrate that recognition of its motive force, even union of oneself with its will, is a moral imperative. In this emphasis on connection, his novels recall those of E. M. Forster, but unlike his predecessor, Hartley insists that the nature of the motive force is supernatural, even traditionally Christian. In his most successful books, Hartley draws upon elements of both novel and romance, as Richard Chase defines them in *The American Novel and Its Tradition* (1957), and the uniqueness of the resulting hybridization precludes comparisons with the work of most of his contemporaries.

Hartley's moral vision, revealed by the gradual integration of realism and symbolism in his novels, is the most striking characteristic of his long fiction. In a book such as *The Go-Between*, he shows that all people are subject to the power of love, even when they deny it, and that achievement of insight into love's capabilities is a prerequisite of achieving moral responsibility. This pattern of growth at the center of Hartley's novels is conventionally Christian in its outlines. The protagonist of each book, beginning with Eustace

Cherrington in the *Eustace and Hilda* trilogy, accepts his status as a "sinner" and experiences, if only briefly and incompletely, a semimystical transcendence of his fallen state.

The epiphanic technique Hartley develops in the trilogy to objectify these moments of insight recurs in various forms in all of his novels, coming in time to be embodied not in symbolism but in the pattern of action in which he casts his plots. Without suggesting that Hartley's fiction is about theology, it is clear that his concern with the subject of morality cannot avoid having religious overtones. Like Nathaniel Hawthorne, he traces the process of spiritual growth in innocent, morally self-assured, and thereby flawed personalities who experience temptation, even commit sins, and eventually attain spiritual kinship with their fellow people. These encounters, in a book such as *Facial Justice*, occur in settings symbolic of traditional religious values, and so while Hartley's novels may be read from psychoanalytic or mythic points of view, they are more fully comprehended from a metaphysical vantage point.

There is a thematic unity to all of Hartley's longer fiction, but after 1960, there is a marked decline in its technical complexity. In one sense, having worked out his thematic viewpoint in the process of fusing realism and symbolism in his earlier books, Hartley no longer feels the need to dramatize the encounter of good and evil and to set it convincingly in a realistic world. His last novels are fables, and in *The Harness Room*, the most successful of them, the lack of realism intensifies his treatment of the psychological and sexual involvement of an adolescent boy and his father's slightly older chauffeur. This book brings Hartley's oeuvre full circle, back to the story of the American spinster and the Venetian gondolier he produced in *Simonetta Perkins* at the start of his career.

Eustace and Hilda trilogy

The three novels constituting the *Eustace and Hilda* trilogy—*The Shrimp and the Anemone*, *The Sixth Heaven*, and *Eustace and Hilda*—objectify a process of moral growth and spiritual regeneration to be found in or behind all of Hartley's subsequent fiction. The process is not unlike that which he describes, in the Clark lectures reprinted in *The Novelist's Responsibility*, as characteristic of Hawthorne's treatment of the redeeming experience of sin in *The Marble Faun* (1860). The epiphanic moments Hartley uses to dramatize his protagonist's encounters with Christ the Redeemer reveal truths that can be read on psychological, sociological, and theological levels.

In *The Shrimp and the Anemone*, Hartley depicts the abortive rebellion of Eustace Cherrington, aged nine, against the moral and psychological authority of his thirteen-year-old sister, Hilda. Set in the summers of 1905 and 1906, the novel reveals young Eustace's intimations of a spiritual reality behind the surface of life. Unable to act in terms of these insights, for they are confused with his aesthetic sense, Eustace feeds his romantic inclination to construct an internal fantasy world and refuses to see the moral necessity of action.

In *The Sixth Heaven*, Hartley details Eustace's second effort to achieve his freedom from Hilda, this time by engineering a socially advantageous marriage for her with Dick Staveley, a war hero and rising young member of Parliament. This novel focuses on a visit the Cherringtons make in June, 1920, to the Staveleys, acquaintances who live near their childhood home at Anchorstone. Eustace's adult epiphanic experiences are more insistent. Less tied to his childish aestheticism, they emerge in the context of the novel as hauntingly ambiguous intimations of a moral and spiritual realm that he unconsciously seeks to avoid acknowledging.

In *Eustace and Hilda*, the final novel in the trilogy, Hartley brings his protagonist face-to-face with Christ during the Venetian Feast of the Redeemer, the third Sunday in July, 1920. This encounter leads to Eustace's return to Anchorstone and acceptance of moral responsibility for the emotionally induced paralysis Hilda experienced at the end of her love affair with Dick Staveley. Back in his childhood home, Eustace learns the lesson of self-sacrificial love in Christ's example, and he effects a cure for Hilda by staging a mock accident for her at the edge of Anchorstone Cliff. Because of the strain this involves, he suffers a fatal heart attack, and the novel ends. His death signals the genuineness of the moral growth and spiritual regeneration that had begun in Venice. The interpenetration of realistic narrative and symbolic subtext that occurs by the end of the *Eustace and Hilda* trilogy objectifies Hartley's vision of the world.

THE BOAT

Hartley's equivalent of Ford Madox Ford's and Evelyn Waugh's treatments of men at war, *The Boat* presents the mock-epic struggle of Timothy Casson, a forty-nine-year-old bachelor writer, to gain permission to use his rowing shell on the fishing stream that runs through Upton-on-Swirrell. Timothy, settling back in England in 1940 after an eighteen-year stay in Italy, consciously attempts to isolate himself from the effects of the war in progress in the larger world. He devotes himself to collecting china, to cultivating friends, to raising a dog, and to forcing the village magnates to allow him to row on the Swirrell. In the process, Timothy violates his own self-interest, as well as that of his nation and his class, but he is not the tragicomic figure that Eustace Cherrington becomes in the trilogy. In Hartley's hands, Timothy achieves only a degree of the self-awareness that Eustace does, and this enables the novelist to label him the "common sinner" that all people are, a figure both sinned against and sinning.

Timothy's desire to take his boat out on the river is an assertion of individuality that polarizes the community. His attachment to his boat becomes a measure of his moral and political confusion, for Timothy is torn between the influences of Vera Cross, a Communist secret agent sent to Upton-on-Swirrell to organize unrest among the masses, and Volumnia Purbright, the wife of the Anglican vicar and an unconventional, perhaps mystical, Christian. The emblematic names suggest the comic possibilities Hartley exploits in his treatment of the two, but *The Boat* is a serious novel. Vera represents a social disharmony resultant upon the advocacy of ideology, while Volumnia reflects both social harmony and personal tranquillity resulting from sacrifice of self. Indeed, when Timothy persists in his protest against the prohibition against rowing and sets forth on the flooded Swirrell with two children and his dog as passengers, Volumnia confronts Vera on the riverbank. Vera attacks the vicar's wife, and the two women tumble into the water. When Vera drowns in the Devil's Staircase, Volumnia blames herself for the younger woman's death and subsequently dies from exposure and pneumonia. When at the end of *The Boat* Timothy, who had to be rescued from the river when his boat capsized in the flooded stream, dreams he receives a telephone call from Volumnia inviting him to tea, he hears Vera's voice as well as Volumnia's, and the two women tell him that they are inseparable, as are the moral and ethical positions they represent.

Near the end of the novel, Timothy prepares to leave Upton-on-Swirrell in the company of two old friends, Esther Morwen and Tyrone MacAdam. The two discuss the prospects for Timothy's acceptance of himself as an ordinary human being. At the time of the boating accident, he had managed to rescue one of the children with him, but he needed the fortuitous help of others to rescue the second child and to reach safety himself. Timothy is clearly partially responsible for the deaths of Vera Cross and Volumnia Purbright, and the "true cross" he must bear is an acceptance of moral complexity. Whether he will achieve this insight is an open question at the end of *The Boat*, and Hartley's refusal to make the book a neat statement reinforces its thematic point.

The Go-Between

Hartley's *The Go-Between*, arguably his finest novel, is the only one with a first-person narrator as protagonist. Leo Colston, like the focal characters of the *Eustace and Hilda* trilogy and *The Boat*, frees himself from psychological constraints and achieves a measure of moral insight. Indeed, Leo's story amounts to a rite of passage conforming to the pattern of initiation characteristic of the bildungsroman. More significantly, *The Go-Between* is a study of England on the verge of its second Elizabethan Age, and the patterns of imagery that Hartley uses to reveal the personality of Leo suggest indirectly that the Age of Aquarius will be a golden one.

These linguistic patterns, introduced into the novel by Leo himself, derive from the signs of the zodiac. On one hand, they are a pattern manufactured by Leo as a schoolboy and utilized to explain his conviction that the start of the twentieth century, which he dates incorrectly as January 1, 1900, is the dawn of a second Golden Age. On the other hand, the zodiac motifs, as associated with Leo and other characters in the novel, underscore Hartley's thematic insistence on the power of self-sacrificial love to redeem both individuals and society from error.

At the start of the novel in 1951 or 1952, Leo is an elderly man engaged in sorting through the accumulated memorabilia of a lifetime. Coming upon his diary for the year 1900, inside the cover of which are printed the zodiac signs, he recalls his experiences at Southdown Hill School and his vacation visit to a schoolmate, Marcus Maudsley. In the body of the novel, the account of that nineteen-day visit to Brandham Hall, the narrative voice is split between that of the thirteen-year-old Leo of 1900 and that of the aged man with which the book begins. Used by Marcus's sister Marian to carry messages to her lover, the tenant farmer Ted Burgess, Leo finds himself faced with the dubious morality of his actions when Marcus tells him that Marian is to marry Viscount Trimingham, the owner of Brandham Hall and a scarred veteran of the Boer War.

In Leo's mind, Marian is the Virgin of the zodiac, Trimingham the Sagittarian archer, and Burgess the Aquarian water-carrier. Determined to break the bond between Marian and Ted and to restore her to Viscount Trimingham, Leo resorts to the schoolboy magic with which he had handled bullies at school. He plans a spell involving the sacrifice of an *atropa belladonna* or deadly nightshade growing in a deserted outbuilding, but the ritual goes awry and he finds himself flat on his back with the plant on top of him. The next day, his thirteenth birthday, Leo is forced to lead Marian's mother to the spot where the girl meets her lover, and they discover the pair engaged in sexual intercourse. For Leo, whose adult sexuality has just begun to develop, this is a significant shock, and he feels that he has been defeated by the beautiful but deadly lady, both the deadly nightshade and Marian herself.

In the epilogue to *The Go-Between*, the elderly Leo Colston returns to Norfolk to find out the consequences of the mutual betrayal. Encountering Marian, now the dowager Lady Trimingham, once more, he undertakes again to be a messenger. This time he goes to her grandson Edward in an effort to reconcile him to the events of the fateful year 1900, to the fact that his father was really the son of Ted Burgess. This action on Leo's part embodies the theme of all of Hartley's fiction: The only evil in life is an unloving heart. At the end of his return journey to Brandham Hall, Leo Colston is a more vital man and a more compassionate one. Having faced the evil both inside and outside himself, he is open to love, and the Age of Aquarius can begin. That it will also be the age of Elizabeth II, given the political and sociological implications of the central action, gives Hartley's *The Go-Between* its particular thematic rightness.

Robert C. Petersen

OTHER MAJOR WORKS

SHORT FICTION: *Night Fears*, 1924; *The Killing Bottle*, 1932; *The Traveling Grave*, 1948; *The White Wand*, 1954; *Two for the River*, 1961; *Mrs. Carteret Receives*, 1971; *The Complete Short Stories of L. P. Hartley*, 1973.

NONFICTION: *The Novelist's Responsibility: Lectures and Essays*, 1967.

BIBLIOGRAPHY

Bien, Peter. *L. P. Hartley*. University Park: Pennsylvania State University Press, 1963. The first book on Hartley's fiction, important for its Freudian analysis of his novels; its identification of his indebtedness to Nathaniel Hawthorne, Henry James, and Emily

Brontë; and its examination of Hartley's literary criticism. At its best when discussing the novels about the transition from adolescence to adulthood.

Bloomfield, Paul. *L. P. Hartley*. 1962. Rev. ed. Harlow, England: Longman, 1970. Bloomfield, a personal friend of Hartley, focuses on character analysis and thematic concerns, providing a brief discussion of Hartley's novels. Laudatory, perceptive, and very well written.

Fane, Julian. *Best Friends: Memories of Rachel and David Cecil, Cynthia Asquith, L. P. Hartley, and Some Others*. London: Sinclair-Stevenson and St. George's Press, 1990. Fane writes about his friendship with Hartley and others, which helps to situate Hartley's fiction in terms of his sensibility and his time.

Hall, James. *The Tragic Comedians: Seven Modern British Novelists*. Bloomington: Indiana University Press, 1963. Claims that the Hartley protagonist possesses an inadequate emotional pattern that leads inevitably to failure. This neurotic behavior is discussed in his major fiction: *The Boat*, *Eustace and Hilda*, *My Fellow Devils*, and *The Hireling*. In these novels, Hartley demonstrates that confidence is accompanied by a contradictory desire to fail.

Jones, Edward T. *L. P. Hartley*. Boston: Twayne, 1978. An excellent analysis of Hartley's literary work, particularly of his novels, which are conveniently grouped. Also contains a chronology, a biographical introductory chapter, a discussion of Hartley's literary criticism, and an excellent annotated bibliography. Of special interest is Jones's definition of the "Hartleian novel."

Mulkeen, Anne. *Wild Thyme, Winter Lightning: The Symbolic Novels of L. P. Hartley*. Detroit, Mich.: Wayne State University Press, 1974. Focuses on Hartley's fiction until 1968, stressing the Hawthornian romance elements in his early novels. Particularly concerned with his adaptations of the romance and how his characters are at once themselves and archetypes or symbols.

Webster, Harvey Curtis. *After the Trauma: Representative British Novelists Since 1920*. Lexington: University Press of Kentucky, 1970. The chapter on Hartley, entitled "Diffident Christian," concerns his protagonists' struggles to distinguish between God's orders and society's demands. Discusses *Facial Justice*, *Eustace and Hilda*, *The Boat*, and *The Go-Between*, concluding that Hartley merits more attention than he has been given.

Wright, Adrian. *Foreign Country: The Life of L. P. Hartley*. London: A. Deutsch, 1996. A good biography of Hartley for the beginning student, providing a balanced account of Hartley's life and information about his novels and other works. Includes a bibliography and an index.

York, R. A. " L. P. Hartley: *The Go-Between*." In *The Rules of Time: Time and Rhythm in the Twentieth-Century Novel*. Madison, N.J.: Fairleigh Dickinson University Press, 1999. York's examination of Hartley's book and novels by other authors focuses on the rhythm and pace of reading, maintaining that these elements affect readers' perception of time—a conspicuous presence in all twentieth century fiction.

ROBERT A. HEINLEIN

Born: Butler, Missouri; July 7, 1907
Died: Carmel, California; May 8, 1988

Principal long fiction

Rocket Ship Galileo, 1947
Beyond This Horizon, 1948
Space Cadet, 1948
Red Planet, 1949
Sixth Column, 1949 (also published as *The Day After Tomorrow*, 1951)
Farmer in the Sky, 1950
Between Planets, 1951
The Puppet Masters, 1951
The Rolling Stones, 1952
Starman Jones, 1953
The Star Beast, 1954
Tunnel in the Sky, 1955
Double Star, 1956
Time for the Stars, 1956
Citizen of the Galaxy, 1957
The Door into Summer, 1957
Have Space Suit—Will Travel, 1958
Methuselah's Children, 1958
Starship Troopers, 1959
Stranger in a Strange Land, 1961
Glory Road, 1963
Podkayne of Mars: Her Life and Times, 1963
Farnham's Freehold, 1964
The Moon Is a Harsh Mistress, 1966
I Will Fear No Evil, 1970
Time Enough for Love, 1973
The Notebooks of Lazarus Long, 1978
The Number of the Beast, 1980
Friday, 1982
Job: A Comedy of Justice, 1984
The Cat Who Walks Through Walls, 1985
To Sail Beyond the Sunset, 1987
For Us, the Living, 2004
Variable Star, 2006 (with Spider Robinson)

OTHER LITERARY FORMS

Robert A. Heinlein (HIN-lin) was a best-selling writer of science-fiction short stories for ten years before his first novel appeared. Those stories were published in more than one dozen collections, with a great deal of overlap. He cowrote the screenplays for two films, *Destination Moon* (1950) and *Project Moonbase* (1953). He did not publish nonfiction during his lifetime, but his wife, Virginia Heinlein, published his 1946 typescript "How to Be a Politician" as *Take Back Your Government: A Practical Handbook for the Private Citizen Who Wants Democracy to Work* in 1992. His 1953 travelogue *Tramp Royale* was published in 1992.

Heinlein edited *Tomorrow, the Stars* (1952), a collection of short stories by other science-fiction writers. In his introduction to the book, he discusses the terms "science fiction" and "speculative fiction," telling readers that he prefers the term "speculative fiction." His letters, which were published as *Grumbles from the Grave* (1989), were selected and edited by his wife.

ACHIEVEMENTS

Known since the 1950's as the dean of science fiction, Robert A. Heinlein was the top-selling author of the golden age of pulp-magazine science fiction (1930's-1940's), the first to sell science fiction to the "slick" magazines (prestigious glossy-paper periodicals such as *The Saturday Evening Post*), and the first major science-fiction author to write for film.

Heinlein's science fiction is of the nuts-and-bolts variety, in which space travel and other future technologies are presented realistically; their engineering is worked out in detail, yet that detail does not intrude on the narrative. Examples of Heinlein's technologies include the space suit, descriptions of which borrow from his own wartime research at the Philadelphia Navy Yard. In fact, his research led to the development of space suits long after he had described them. (Also, he had envisioned and then detailed the water bed.)

Heinlein received the Hugo Award for best science-fiction novel four times, and Science Fiction Writers of America honored him with its first Grand Master award for lifetime achievement. His fiction introduced several words and phrases to the English language, including "free fall" for zero gravity, "waldo" for a mechanical arm (named after a Heinlein character), and his acronym TANSTAAFL (There Ain't No Such Thing As A Free Lunch) for a popular phrase, perhaps borrowed from Rudyard Kipling. The acronym became a byword for libertarians and economists such as Milton Friedman.

BIOGRAPHY

Robert Anson Heinlein was born in Butler, Missouri, and grew up in Kansas City, immersed in what he thought was a Bible Belt culture. His relationship with that culture, as displayed in his fiction, would be partly adversarial.

Heinlein entered the U.S. Naval Academy at Annapolis, from which he emerged as a naval officer in 1929. He served on one of the first aircraft carriers, the USS *Lexington*

(1931), and the Wickes-class destroyer, the USS *Roper* (1933-1934). He married Eleanor Curry from his Kansas City hometown, but the marriage lasted only one year. In 1932, he married Leslyn Macdonald. Heinlein's military career was cut short with a diagnosis of tuberculosis, leading to a medical discharge. He dabbled in mining and politics, assisting novelist Upton Sinclair's unsuccessful bid for governor of California in 1934 and running for a seat in the California State assembly in 1938.

In 1939, Heinlein's short story "Life Line" was published in *Astounding Science Fiction*, marking his first publication. A flurry of similar stories in the following years determined his career. In fact, he was so prolific that he began competing with himself: Fan polls in *Astounding Science Fiction* rated him number one, followed by Anson MacDonald—one of his many pseudonyms.

The year 1947 was portentous for Heinlein. First, he broke into the upper echelon of the magazine fiction market with "The Green Hills of Earth" in the February issue of *The Saturday Evening Post*. Second, he began his lucrative and influential series of juvenile novels for Scribner's with *Rocket Ship Galileo*. Third, he divorced his second wife and, the following year, married fellow engineer and naval officer Virginia Gerstenfeld, whom he had met at the Naval Air Experimentation Station in Philadelphia during World War II. Gerstenfeld was the model for many of the celebrated "strong red-headed women" in his fiction.

Heinlein's contract with Scribner's guaranteed him one novel a year, timed for a Christmas release. Scribner's, however, broke the contract in 1959 by rejecting "Starship Troopers." Heinlein sold the manuscript to G. P. Putnam's Sons, which published the book the same year. His next novel, *Stranger in a Strange Land*, created controversy with its frank sexual and religious themes, but it proved that science fiction could be a medium of social criticism. His later novels continued exploring similar controversial themes, while mixing the hard, nuts-and-bolts science fiction with pure fantasy, in a type of magical realism in which the most fantastic events are given scientific plausibility.

Heinlein was a guest commentator for CBS television's coverage of the first U.S. spaceflight to the Moon, and his works were discussed on the Moon by Apollo 15 astronauts in 1971. He almost died from peritonitis in the early 1970's and was ill through most of the decade and unable to write much. In his last decade, however, he wrote five well-regarded novels. He died in his sleep on May 8, 1988, from emphysema and congestive heart failure.

ANALYSIS

The science fiction of Robert A. Heinlein became, by the second half of the twentieth century, the gold standard by which the genre was measured. Along with his friend Isaac Asimov and British author Arthur C. Clarke, Heinlein became one of the "big three" writers of English-language science fiction in the twentieth century.

Heinlein's specialty was twofold: the well-engineered, scientifically plausible exposition of future technologies, and his success at weaving those technologies into his fiction unobtrusively. He also was recognized as one of the pioneers in the integration of the social sciences into science fiction, and many of the major themes of his fiction concern social issues: individual liberty, the nature of authority and civil disobedience, nonconformity, sexual and religious morality, and the role of the military in society. Critics sometimes overstate the importance of sexual, religious, and military themes in Heinlein's fiction, but his conviction was that all three would be impacted by space travel and that speculative fiction—the term Heinlein preferred for the genre in which he wrote—would not give a complete picture of possible futures if it did not take these themes into account.

THE PUPPET MASTERS

One of the marks of this novel's success is that its plot (human bodies being invaded by aliens who control their minds) has become a cliché, particularly in film. *Invasion of the Body Snatchers* (1956, 1978; based on the 1955 novel *The Body Snatchers* by Jack Finney), *I Married a Monster from Outer Space* (1958), and *The Brain Eaters* (1958) are all similar in plot, but Heinlein's *The Puppet Masters* preceded them all. In fact, *The Brain Eaters* so clearly "borrowed" from his 1951 novel that Heinlein sued for plagiarism and won an out-of-court settlement. Readers who can get beyond the echoes of later imitators will find a novel of surprising psychological depth that forces its characters to reevaluate the nature of human relationships.

Like most of its imitators, *The Puppet Masters* gains much of its energy from the instinctive horror at the thought of another creature controlling a person completely. That horror is not mitigated by knowing that the alien creatures controlling the humans remove any trace of negative feeling about the experience. The first-person narrator of the novel, Elihu Nivens, is a government agent known by his codename Sam, and he is humanity's last best hope for saving the world from the creatures that attach themselves to the human spinal cord. In the process, Sam's disgust at the prospect (and at one point the reality) of being controlled by another creature forces him to confront the ways in which the human spirit can be dominated without alien interference—through such cultural bulwarks as filial piety (the head of the secret service agency Sam works for turns out to be Sam's father), marriage (Sam's emotional connection with his wife, Mary, also an agent, is used to manipulate him into taking an alien parasite on his back), and religion (Sam wonders if Mary had been a member of a cult known as the Whitmanites).

The book ends with the eradication of the alien puppet masters that are immanent, but more important, the story ends with Sam coming to terms with the imitations of the puppet masters in his social, vocational, and emotional relationships.

DOUBLE STAR

Heinlein's first Hugo Award winner, *Double Star,* is a science fiction version of Anthony Hope's *Prisoner of Zenda* (1894), in which a look-alike is groomed to stand in for a kidnapped monarch. In *Double Star*, the captured leader, John Joseph Bonforte, is not a monarch (though the solar system is presented in the book as a constitutional monarchy, with an emperor), but the leader of an expansionist coalition. Bonforte's party wants the human government of the solar system to form an alliance with the nonhuman Martians, but there is a great deal of race prejudice against the Martians among Earth's humans (Bonforte's opponents are known as the Humanity Party).

One of the novel's racist humans is the first-person narrator, the egotistical actor Lorenzo Smythe, billed as the Great Lorenzo. Because of his resemblance to Bonforte and because of his acting ability, Smythe is tapped to stand in for Bonforte at a Martian ceremony. Smythe, however, cares little for politics. By projecting the psychology of racism in 1950's America as future prejudice against an alien other, Heinlein took science fiction beyond its literary ghetto and showed that it could engage contemporary social issues—though in this novel the connection was not overt, and certainly not allegorical. The triumph of this novel, however, lies not in any implicit critique of racism but in the development of the character of Smythe.

An egotistical, vain, bigoted aesthete at the beginning of the story, Smythe "modulates" to something nobler. He had expected to play Bonforte only for a single event, but when Bonforte dies in the hands of his captors, Smythe is faced with the prospect of either continuing the charade for the rest of his life or allowing an entire government to collapse. This most selfish of men is poised to sacrifice his entire career for a cause that was not his. This unlikely outcome is possible because of the metamorphosis of Smythe's character from a cad to a hero so likeable that Bonforte's secretary, who hated Smythe from the start, falls in love with him. Fellow science-fiction writer James Blish called Lorenzo Smythe Heinlein's most successful first-person narrator.

STARSHIP TROOPERS

Reminiscent of the boot-camp films of World War II, this study of the nature of the military mind in an interplanetary future scandalized many readers who considered the novel militaristic and even fascist. Heinlein's editor at Scribner's refused to publish the work, but Putnam's jumped at the chance to publish anything from the popular novelist. The novel led to Heinlein's second Hugo Award.

Starship Troopers posits of a future society in which government service (including, but not limited to, military service) is a prerequisite for citizenship. Some readers chafed at the book's supposed didacticism. It is certainly more discursive than most Heinlein novels: Each difficulty in narrator Juan "Johnny" Rico's training results in a flashback to a lecture in Johnny's high school civics class (a required course designed to prepare students for their government service). The novel's real protagonist might well be the power suit that is the all-purpose soldier's weapon. Heinlein describes the armored suit with the same detail he uses to describe the regular space suit in *Have Space Suit—Will Travel*.

STRANGER IN A STRANGE LAND

Heinlein's third Hugo-winning novel, *Stranger in a Strange Land*, is probably his best-known and most influential work. The basic premise of the "Martian-eye view" of Earth society had long been a natural narrative device for writers of science fiction. Because the novel's protagonist, Valentine Michael Smith, is biologically human but had been raised by Martians, he arrives as a cultural outsider on Earth. This plot line allows Heinlein to critique his own culture indirectly. While doing so, Heinlein also delves into the science of linguistics by applying the hypotheses of Edward Sapir and Benjamin Whorf.

Indeed, Heinlein's use of linguistic theory in his novels had a major effect on science fiction. The hypothesis is simple: Grammatical categories of a language determine how a speaker of that language views the world. In the novel, Smith has a number of unique abilities, which no other human has. He tries to teach his Earth friends these abilities (telekinesis, voluntary control of autonomic bodily functions, and others) but cannot do so until they learn the Martian language. In the process, Smith creates precedents in international (and interplanetary) law, starts a new religion, and invents unconventional family arrangements, which became actual models for many communes of the 1960's.

John R. Holmes

OTHER MAJOR WORKS

SHORT FICTION: *The Man Who Sold the Moon*, 1950; *Waldo and Magic, Inc.*, 1950; *The Green Hills of Earth*, 1951; *Universe*, 1951 (as *Orphans of the Sky*, 1963); *Assignment in Eternity*, 1953; *Revolt in 2100*, 1953; *The Menace from Earth*, 1959; *The Unpleasant Profession of Jonathan Hoag*, 1959 (as *6 × H*, 1962); *The Worlds of Robert A. Heinlein*, 1966; *The Past Through Tomorrow*, 1967; *Destination Moon*, 1979; *Expanded Universe: The New Worlds of Robert A. Heinlein*, 1980; *Requiem: New Collected Works by Robert A. Heinlein and Tributes to the Grand Master*, 1992; *The Fantasies of Robert A. Heinlein*, 1999; *Off the Main Sequence*, 2005.

SCREENPLAYS: *Destination Moon*, 1950 (with James O'Hanlon and Rip Van Ronkel); *Project Moonbase*, 1953 (with Jack Seaman).

NONFICTION: *Of Worlds Beyond: The Science of Science-Fiction Writing*, 1947 (with others); *The Science Fiction Novel*, 1959 (with others); *Grumbles from the Grave*, 1989 (Virginia Heinlein, editor); *Take Back Your Government: A Practical Handbook for the Private Citizen Who Wants Democracy to Work*, 1992; *Tramp Royale*, 1992 (wr. 1953).

EDITED TEXT: *Tomorrow, the Stars*, 1952.

MISCELLANEOUS: *The Best of Robert A. Heinlein, 1939-1959*, 1973.

BIBLIOGRAPHY

Franklin, H. Bruce. *Robert A. Heinlein: America as Science Fiction*. New York: Oxford University Press, 1980. A study of Heinlein's entire corpus, biased in its Marxist readings. Franklin, unaware of Heinlein's socialist activities in the early 1930's, paints him as a knee-jerk conservative capitalist.

Gifford, James. *Robert A. Heinlein: A Reader's Companion*. Sacramento, Calif.: Nitrosyncretic Press, 2000. Commentary on all known Heinlein works, including each of his short stories. Gifford attempts to balance what he sees as anti-Heinlein rant (Alexei Panshin) and Heinlein chauvinism (Spider Robinson).

Heinlein, Robert A. *Grumbles from the Grave*. Edited by Virginia Heinlein. New York: Del Rey, 1989. Heinlein's letters are helpful not only for biographical background but also critical comment on Heinlein's own fiction.

Olander, Joseph D., and Martin Harry Greenberg. *Robert A. Heinlein*. New York: Taplinger, 1978. This collection includes critical articles that vary in quality. Jack Williamson's article on Heinlein's juvenile articles and Ivor A. Rogers's study of Heinlein's work through the spectrum of folklore are of particular interest.

Panshin, Alexei. *Heinlein in Dimension*. Chicago: Advent, 1968. Now dated, and marred by Panshin's love-hate relationship with Heinlein's fiction, this book-length study of Heinlein's works nevertheless has some value for the perspective of a fellow science-fiction writer (Panshin won a Hugo Award in 1967).

Patterson, William H., Jr., and Andrew Thornton. *The Martian Named Smith: Critical Perspectives on Robert A. Heinlein's "Stranger in a Strange Land."* Sacramento, Calif.: Nitrosyncretic Press, 2001. Criticism of Heinlein's well-known novel, as well as a thorough study of his works overall.

Stover, Leon E. *Robert Heinlein*. Boston: Twayne, 1987. A volume in a standard series of U.S. authors, this is an ideal starting point for most research. Fans have criticized its supposed inaccuracies, but these are all addressed by James Gifford (2000). Includes a helpful annotated bibliography.

ALICE HOFFMAN

Born: New York, New York; March 16, 1952

PRINCIPAL LONG FICTION

Property Of, 1977
The Drowning Season, 1979
Angel Landing, 1980
White Horses, 1982
Fortune's Daughter, 1985
Illumination Night, 1987
At Risk, 1988
Seventh Heaven, 1990
Turtle Moon, 1992
Second Nature, 1994
Practical Magic, 1995
Here on Earth, 1997
Local Girls, 1999
The River King, 2000
Blue Diary, 2001
The Probable Future, 2003
The Ice Queen, 2005
Skylight Confessions, 2007
The Third Angel, 2008

OTHER LITERARY FORMS

Alice Hoffman's short stories and nonfiction have appeared in such notable publications as *The New York Times*, *Boston Globe* magazine, *Kenyon Review*, *Boulevard*, *Architectural Digest*, *Gourmet*, *Premier*, *Self*, *Southwestern Review*, and *Redbook*. Her work also has been published in the anthologies *Family*, *Thirty-Three Things Every Girl Should Know*, and *Cape Cod Stories*. In addition, she has written novels for young adults as well as children's books.

ACHIEVEMENTS

Alice Hoffman's novels have been recognized as notable books of the year by *The New York Times*, the *Los Angeles Times*, *Library Journal*, and *People* magazine. In 2007, her teen novel *Incantation* won the Massachusetts Book Award. A number of her works have been adapted for film, and she was the original screenwriter for the film *Independence Day* (1983). Her 1997 novel *Here on Earth* was selected for Oprah Winfrey's Book Club, which helped her gain more readers as well as international acclaim. Her books have been translated into more than twenty languages. Her 1988 novel *At Risk* is included as required reading on many academic reading lists. After successful treatment for breast cancer in 1998, she established the Hoffman Breast Center at Mount Auburn Hospital in Cambridge, Massachusetts.

BIOGRAPHY

Alice Hoffman was born in New York City on March 16, 1952, and grew up on Long Island. Her mother was a teacher and social worker, and her father was a real estate agent. Though her parents divorced when she was eight years old, her father remained a constant in her life because he had left her his vast collection of fantasy and science-fiction magazines and novels, including the works of Robert A. Heinlein and Ray Bradbury. She became an insatiable reader. She loved fairy tales and myths, which she later deemed the inspiration for all literature to follow. The dark, scary tales by the Grimm brothers appealed to her more than the lighter offerings of Mother Goose and Hans Christian Andersen.

After graduating from high school, Hoffman entered the workforce, but a single morning in the factory of Doubleday convinced her that she was not suited for supervised eight-hour days and restroom passes; she quit that job at noon. Though she had not considered herself college material, she enrolled at Adelphi University, graduating with a degree in English and anthropology in 1973. She was awarded a Mirrellees Fellowship and studied at Stanford University, earning her master of arts degree in 1975.

Hoffman attributes her motivation to become a writer to her mentor and professor, Albert J. Guerard, and to Maclin Bocock Guerard, both accomplished authors who encouraged her to publish her first short story. Her first novel, *Property Of*, was published in 1977. From then on, aside from establishing a home and raising two children with husband Ted Martin, writing has been her life.

Neither her breast-cancer diagnosis in 1998 nor the yearlong radiation treatments could interfere with Hoffman's will to keep writing. She has said that when she was too sick to sit at her desk, she would move to her office futon, switching from one to the other throughout the day while she explored plot ideas and characters. Hoffman has said that she is not always comfortable in the world, often feeling horrified and adrift, like an outsider looking in, a state that helps her powers of observation when studying people as potential characters. Having struggled with phobias, panic attacks, a lingering fear of bridge crossings, as well as a natural cynicism and fatalism, she has always considered writing a means of healing. She believes that in giving life to inner terrors, she can help readers recognize the truth of emotional illness.

ANALYSIS

Alice Hoffman writes for a wide audience of adults, teenagers, and children. Her works grow from her belief that the greatest reality is in fiction, that all lives contain elements of fantasy. She finds the stuff of fairy tales in everyday life. Monsters and compassionate people live side by side. The woods hold mysteries, if only of the mind. Some dwellings might as well be palaces, in their distancing of ordinary folks. Animals have distinct personalities and can communicate with humans. Children are abused by wicked adults and sometimes rescued by forces of good. Partners and loved ones are abandoned, and people die. Dreams and other images can be haunting, and sounds and smells can evoke memories that seem otherworldly.

Hoffman bases some of her works on fairy tales because she appreciates their emotional truths; the lessons they teach about human nature, love, and hatred. Though a witch may not wait before an open fire for Hansel and Gretel, there are purveyors of evil in the world and sometimes a long-toothed slathering wolf will drape himself in the coat of a kindly sheep.

Hoffman often lulls readers by beginning her stories simply, with characters seeming to live perfect lives; but the asp is in the garden, ready to change things. Children, the most vulnerable of creatures, die or are kidnapped; old people wither into death; people divorce, drink, philander, take drugs, commit suicide, abuse the less powerful, murder, engage in incest, and succumb to mental illness. Women give in to their attractions to bad men. They suffer. Some evolve, some never recover. Many need to sink to the depths of darkness before they can emerge into the light.

Hoffman's method of introducing otherworldly themes in her narrative is so subtle, so natural, that even readers who prefer straight-on fiction often overlook what they would otherwise consider lapses. Her stories are true psychologically. Who, on occasion, has not sensed the identity of the caller on a ringing phone or had a dream become a life event?

Hoffman uses recurring themes that follow familiar patterns, mainly because, she notes, there are just so many variations on what can happen to people. The key, she says, is in the voice, how the writer makes basic plots seem new and exciting. One of her favorite devices is having a mysterious stranger enter the scene, upsetting the lives of otherwise unremarkable people in their undistinguished towns. Readers recognize and appreciate these elements of her fiction because of the familiarity, and then they wait to find the twists or new ways of expressing old truths.

In many of Hoffman's novels, nature has magic properties, casting a spell that makes it almost another character. Growing things seem to respond to human actions. In one novel, a garden begins producing poisonous blooms with evil names, such as black nightshade, hemlock, and thorn apple.

Hoffman notes that all of her characters contain a bit of herself, that she writes emotional autobiography rather than using actual events in her life. Her depiction of a woman whose simmering sense of dread leads to full-fledged panic attacks, brain-chemistry disorders that strike randomly, will ring true to readers who suffer the same condition. The "Force," as Hoffman labels it, may lead a character to narrow her realm of experience until she is no longer able to leave the house (the disorder is called agoraphobia).

Hoffman's novels always include outsiders, people who do not fit easily into the greater world: the lonely, the frightened, and the socially inept; sometimes the scar-faced, leather-jacketed hoods; girls of easy virtue; junkies; and scholastic achievers who must downplay their intelligence to fit in. Hoffman's love of folk tales has led her to create such characters as an eight-foot-tall man, a child of possible stunted growth, and assorted women trapped like princesses in towers, who also have to rescue themselves.

AT RISK

At Risk details the impact of AIDS on a family of four, and on the people of the town in which they live. Eleven-year-old Amanda, an accomplished gymnast and possible Olympics contender, is infected with the virus that causes the disease after getting a blood transfusion. The blamelessness of the child and the waste of a life would make this novel unbearably sad were it not for the greater story of people of indomitable spirit who adjust to a situation that can only be endured. Hoffman also brings to light an alternate reality: the anger people have at the disease, and also at the victim, the all-too-real feeling of blaming the one who is afflicted.

Amanda is not simply a sweet, curly-haired cherub. Eleven-year-olds, including Amanda, can be willful, manipulative, nasty, unthinking, demanding, and bratty. Her mother understands this, but is constrained by her adored daughter's impending death and becomes tired of always putting the situation in its proper perspective. What difference does it make if Amanda snaps at her, given that one day she will not be there to snap? Her mother is wracked with guilt and sapped by her impatience.

Eight-year-old Charlie can be a typical bratty younger brother, but he loves his sister. Now he is hateful, resentful, and jealous of the attention she is getting. There is much self-recrimination in the novel, with characters appalled at their thoughts, attempting to deny their uncharitable feelings. Added to this situation are the fears of the community that lead to the family's isolation.

HERE ON EARTH

Here on Earth has many of the elements of one of Hoffman's favorite authors, Emily Brontë, and of her novel *Wuthering Heights* (1847). *Here on Earth* is similar with its dramatic landscape and clearly defined characters. The location is a small town outside Boston, where nature looms as a constant backdrop with stygian nights and exploding August heat.

The heroine, March Murray, returns to her childhood home after twenty years to attend the funeral of Judith Dale, her beloved housekeeper. She brings her snarly daughter Gwen and leaves behind the man she had married when Hollis, the boy she loved as a youth, had abandoned her. A foundling, Hollis is now wealthy and in the process of buying up the whole town. He, too, had married, but his wife died under mysterious circumstances. He is determined to claim March. His allure is so great that she allows her world to be subverted, her friends hurt. Hoffman uses this plot angle frequently to show the ramifications of following the heart instead of the head and to portray women who find the strength to rise from the depths of destructive obsessions.

As the plot unfolds, March learns a great deal about her past. Her brother became an incapacitated alcoholic who now lives in a shack deep in the woods. Hollis was a hired horse killer who helped owners collect insurance money on their prize winners by making the deaths seem natural or necessary. Judith Dale has her own secrets.

March soon moves in with Hollis, and Gwen develops a fondness for both Hollis's farm help, Jody, and his nearly wild horse. The horse responds to her soft words. Gwen's powers seem magical. Jody is torn between his allegiance to the man who gave him a job and a place to live and the woman he has come to love. Hoffman's common plot elements are here: deception, mental and physical abuse, dysfunctional relationships, alcoholism, obsession, mental illness, people unwise in love, alienation, and despair.

ILLUMINATION NIGHT

Illumination Night takes place in Martha's Vineyard, where once a year the townspeople gather in the town square, which has been illuminated with candles. The central characters, Andre and Vonny, are worried about their four-year-old son Simon because he is short in stature. He is often mistaken for a much younger child and refuses to celebrate another birthday until he grows more. The elderly woman next door, in a literal flight of fancy, flaps her arms out of an upper-story window, leading her sixteen-year-old granddaughter Jody to monitor her behavior. Jody finds her neighbors fascinating and begins babysitting for Simon and flirting with Andre. Emotional conflicts and hostility arise, as do resolution, love, and acceptance.

Jody and her grandmother have always found themselves outside the realm of ordinary interactions, Andre has always been too close-lipped to attract serious friends, and Vonny has fallen into a pattern of agoraphobia that threatens her own existence, her ability to even walk out her front door in comfort.

Add to this mix Ed, the giant of a man who lives just outside the town, mostly isolated from those who fear him. The reader sees seemingly ordinary people experiencing self-doubt, isolation, deception, guilt, and terror, a whole range of common human emotions.

Gay Pitman Zieger

OTHER MAJOR WORKS

SHORT FICTION: *Blackbird House*, 2004.

SCREENPLAY: *Independence Day*, 1983.

CHILDREN'S/YOUNG ADULT LITERATURE: *Fireflies*, 1997; *Horsefly*, 2000; *Aquamarine*, 2001; *Indigo*, 2002; *Green Angel*, 2003; *The Foretelling*, 2005; *Incantation*, 2006.

BIBLIOGRAPHY

Aguiar, Sarah Appleton. *The Bitch Is Back: Wicked Women in Literature*. Carbondale:

Southern Illinois University Press, 2001. Examination of the presence of the archetypal "bitch" character in modern fiction includes brief discussion of Hoffman's novel *Here on Earth*.

Brown-Davidson, Terri. "'To Build Is to Dwell': The Beautiful, Strange Architectures of Alice Hoffman's Novels." *Hollins Critic* 33, no. 5 (December, 1996). Provides an extensive literary critique of Hoffman's work. Brown-Davidson tends to incorporate her own rather vast awareness of literature, sometimes filling her prose with references that may be obscure to general readers.

Hoffman, Alice. "At Home with Alice Hoffman: A Writer Set Free by Magic." Interview by Ruth Reichl. *The New York Times*, February 10, 1994. Hoffman answers penetrating questions, dealing frankly with her life and work.

E. T. A. HOFFMANN

Born: Königsberg, East Prussia (now Kaliningrad, Russia); January 24, 1776
Died: Berlin, Prussia (now in Germany); June 25, 1822
Also known as: Ernst Theodor Wilhelm Hoffmann

Principal long fiction

Die Elixiere des Teufels: Nachgelassene Papiere des Bruders Medardus, eines Kapuziners, 1815-1816 (*The Devil's Elixirs: From the Posthumous Papers of Brother Medardus, a Capuchin Friar*, 1824)

Lebensansichten des Katers Murr, nebst fragmentarischer Biographie des Kapellmeisters Johannes Kreisler in zufälligen Makulaturblättern, 1819-1821 (*The Life and Opinions of Kater Murr, with the Fragmentary Biography of Kapellmeister Johannes Kreisler on Random Sheets of Scrap Paper*, 1969; also known as *The Educated Cat*)

Other literary forms

For most of his life, E. T. A. Hoffmann (HAWF-mahn) cherished the hope that he would one day be remembered as a composer, and it was only late in his career as an artist that literary preoccupations began to outweigh his interest in music. By the time of his death, Hoffmann had nevertheless produced a considerable literary oeuvre that included two novels and more than seventy tales. Hoffmann gathered most of the tales into three collections. He published the first under the title *Fantasiestücke in Callots Manier* (1814-1815; *Fantasy Pieces in Callot's Manner*, 1996). Included in this collection are Hoffmann's important first story, "Ritter Gluck: Eine Erinnerung aus dem Jahr 1809" ("Ritter Gluck"), as well as his most famous fairy tale, "Der goldene Topf: Ein Märchen aus der neuen Zeit" ("The Golden Flower Pot"). Hoffmann's second collection, *Nachtstücke* (1817; night pieces), contains his most ghostly, even ghoulish, creations. Its opening story, "Der Sandmann" ("The Sandman"), still served Sigmund Freud in 1919 as a case study of the human sense of the uncanny. Into the four volumes of *Die Serapionsbrüder* (1819-1821; *The Serapion Brethren*, 1886-1892) Hoffmann incorporated "Rat Krespel" ("Councillor Krespel"), "Die Bergwerke zu Falun" ("The Mines of Falun"), and—immortalized by Peter Ilich Tchaikovsky in 1892 as *The Nutcracker Suite*—the fairy tale "Nussknacker und Mausekönig" ("Nutcracker and the King of Mice"). The first detective story in European literature and Hoffmann's most popular tale during his lifetime, "Das Fräulein von Scudéri" ("Mademoiselle de Scudéri"), also appeared in *The Serapion Brethren*.

During the last three years of his life, Hoffmann wrote three lengthy, complex tales in which he tried to achieve a unique blend of fairy tale, social satire, and aesthetic speculation: *Klein Zaches, genannt Zinnober* (1819; *Little Zaches, Surnamed Zinnober*, 1971),

E. T. A. Hoffmann
(Library of Congress)

Prinzessin Brambilla: Ein Capriccio nach Jakob Callot (1821; *Princess Brambilla: A "Capriccio" in the Style of Jacques Callot*, 1971), and *Meister Floh: Ein Märchen in sieben Abenteuern zweier Freunde* (1822; *Master Flea: A Fairy Tale in Seven Adventures of Two Friends*, 1826). Hoffmann's letters and diaries were published in the four-volume *Tagebücher* in 1971, and a volume of his letters was published in English in 1977.

ACHIEVEMENTS

In his own day, E. T. A. Hoffmann became a successful writer in a remarkably short time. His ghost and horror stories were received with favor by critics and with enthusiasm by the general reading public. Still, few would have considered Hoffmann to be more than an admittedly original and masterful entertainer. With his mixture of the miraculous, the fantastic, and the horrible, he clearly catered to his generation's fascination with the occult and his readers' thirst for the thrill of a spine-chilling story.

After Hoffmann's death, his reputation as a writer diminished rapidly and was finally destroyed by a formidable opponent from abroad. In 1827, Sir Walter Scott published in *Foreign Quarterly Review* a scathing attack against the excessive employment of supernatural elements in fiction titled "On the Supernatural in Fictitious Composition; and Particularly on the Works of Ernest Theodore William Hoffmann." Using the works of Hoffmann to make his point, Scott concluded that only an opium-inflamed mind could have conceived such frightful chimeras. Scott's assault on Hoffmann's reputation proved fatal, because Johann Wolfgang von Goethe then made it his personal mission to recommend Scott's indictment of the unsavory Hoffmann to the sane sensibilities of his German compatriots.

That Hoffmann's writings survived this Olympian disapproval is largely the result of their success in France. Though none of Hoffmann's works had been translated into a foreign language during his life, French translations of several of his tales appeared shortly after his death and were quickly followed by a veritable Hoffmann vogue among France's most distinguished writers. Honoré de Balzac and Charles Baudelaire showed themselves to be greatly impressed, and in 1836, Gérard de Nerval summarized the French conception of Germany's literary pantheon by speaking of Germany as the land of Friedrich Schiller, Goethe, and Hoffmann. Stimulated by the French reception, enthusiasm for Hoffmann caught fire in Russia as well. Indeed, no major Russian writer of the nineteenth century—from Alexander Pushkin and Nikolai Gogol to Fyodor Dostoevski and Leo Tolstoy—failed to acknowledge Hoffmann's impact on his work.

In the Anglo-Saxon world, by contrast, Scott's article squelched whatever interest there might have been in the achievements of Hoffmann. Still, as if by an ironic twist, it is in that world that Hoffmann doubtless found his most congenial successor, Edgar Allan Poe. The precise nature and extent of Hoffmann's influence on Poe, however, remains a much-debated and apparently elusive issue among literary historians.

Hoffmann would certainly have derived special gratification from the fact that, while his own musical compositions did not bring him fame, composers throughout the nineteenth century set his literary inspirations to music. Thus, for a wide and international audience, Hoffmann's name is often linked, if not identified, with the names of his greatest musical admirers. Robert Schumann's *Kreisleriana* (1838; eight fantasies for keyboard devoted to Kreisler, the hero of Hoffmann's second novel), Jacques Offenbach's opera *Les Contes d'Hoffmann* (1881; *The Tales of Hoffmann*), and Tchaikovsky's ballet *The Nutcracker Suite* are only the best known of many musical offerings to the genius of Hoffmann.

In the twentieth century, Hoffmann finally emerged, even in Germany, as one of that country's most brilliant writers of fiction. He became especially valued as a fearless explorer of the labyrinthine qualities of the human psyche in its desperate search for inner order in the face of instinctual lust and aggression. Hoffmann's works definitely began to cast their spell again, although more than ever before readers often found themselves feeling ambivalent about what is charm and what is curse within that spell's obsessive power.

BIOGRAPHY

Ernst Theodor Wilhelm Hoffmann—who in later life replaced his third baptismal name with Amadeus, in honor of Wolfgang Amadeus Mozart—was born in Königsberg, then the capital of East Prussia, now a Russian city known as Kaliningrad. The disastrous marriage between his father, an alcoholic lawyer, and his mother, a mentally unstable recluse, was dissolved when Hoffmann was only three years old. He subsequently grew up under the pedantic tutelage of a bachelor uncle. The precocious boy spent a loveless and lonely childhood from which only his instructions in music and painting provided some much-needed relief.

At the age of sixteen, Hoffmann enrolled as a student of law at the University of Königsberg. Three years later, he passed his examinations with great distinction. He then joined the legal branch of Prussia's civil service and was employed in various capacities in Glogau (1796-1798), Berlin (1798-1800), Posen (1800-1802), Plock (1802-1804), and Warsaw (1804-1806). All through these years, Hoffmann combined a punctilious execution of his official duties with an increasing interest in music as well as a wild bachelor existence in which the consumption of alcohol played an increasingly significant part. Hoffmann's marriage in 1802 to Michalina Rohrer, the daughter of a minor Polish civil servant, was entered into almost casually and seems to have been of little consequence to Hoffmann for the rest of his life.

It was in Warsaw that Hoffmann seriously started to cultivate a second career as composer and conductor. When, in 1806, the collapse of Prussia's Polish empire under the Napoleonic onslaught deprived him of his position and livelihood in Warsaw, he decided to embark on a musical career. For more than a year, he tried to establish himself in Berlin—an impossible task, as it turned out, in the defeated and impoverished capital of Prussia. He finally accepted a position as music director at the theater and opera house of Bamberg, a small town in northeastern Bavaria.

Hoffmann began his career in music with great expectations and, in spite of an almost immediate disenchantment with the new occupation, remained in Bamberg for four and a half years, supplementing his frequently uncertain income by giving music lessons to members of patrician families in town. His hopeless passion for the gifted vocal student Julia Marc was to become the most embittering experience of his stay. In 1813, Hoffmann joined an opera company that traveled between Leipzig and Dresden, yet this change only caused his professional frustrations to reach new heights. When an influential friend, Theodor Gottlieb von Hippel, managed to have him reinstated in Prussia's legal service in 1814, Hoffmann eagerly jumped at the chance. He returned to his beloved Berlin, where he was to reside until his death in 1822.

In 1814, Hoffmann was thirty-eight years old. Until that time, little in his life suggested that during the eight years left to him he was to become one of the most prominent writers of his age. In the preceding ten years, he had made a concerted effort to establish himself as a composer. By 1814, the list of his compositions included several operas, two masses, and one symphony as well as a considerable quantity of vocal and instrumental music, yet it was only with the publication of his first collection of tales, during the same year, that Hoffmann finally gained the recognition that had eluded him in all of his musical productivity. Obviously exhilarated by the experience of success, Hoffmann set out to write with single-minded fervor. Publishers sought him out, and so did the literary salons of Berlin. The publishers Hoffmann tried to satisfy; the literary salons, however, he more and more regularly exchanged for the wine cellar of Lutter and Wegener, where he and his alter ego, the famous actor Ludwig Devrient, drank themselves into states of fantastic exaltation.

In spite of his private excesses, Hoffmann's professional career—he was to become vice president of the Supreme Court of Prussia—and literary career proceeded with unimpeded speed until his body gave way under the triple strain. In 1821, Hoffmann began to suffer from a rapidly advancing paralysis, perhaps the result of a syphilitic infection. Writing—finally dictating—at a feverish pace, Hoffmann died several months later, at the age of forty-six.

ANALYSIS

E. T. A. Hoffmann's literary work constitutes a compelling and insightful expression of the prevailing anxieties of a deeply unsettled age. The rational improvement of the private self and the enforced stability of the social self were severely shaken by the upheavals of the French Revolution and the rise of Napoleon I's will to power. The heroes of this restless time revealed to the perceptive observer unexpectedly atavistic passions compared to which all existing social and ethical norms proved exceedingly insubstantial. People came to the realization that they had hardly known themselves to that point and that it was critical for them to learn more about what was asserting itself so menacingly in their lives. Interest in marginal, even pathological, states of the mind—in hypnosis, telepathy, magnetism, somnambulism, dreams, and trances—became a widespread obsession. In the wake of this trend, there arose the specter of a human existence threatened from within by chaotic instincts and threatened from without by capricious turns of events.

Probably more than any other writer of his time, Hoffmann delved into the vicissitudes that the defenseless psyche undergoes as it finds itself in the grip of conflicting demands that it can neither adjudicate nor deny. To introduce the reader to the torture chambers of the mind, Hoffmann employed an arsenal of literary devices that his audience knew well from gothic horror stories. Madness, witchery, cloak-and-dagger intrigues, secret passageways, mysterious doubles, incest, rape, and human sacrifice follow one another with baffling speed in mystifying plots that disorient readers until they can no longer tell what is real and what is imagined, what is mere wish and what is accomplished fact.

THE DEVIL'S ELIXIRS

In *The Devil's Elixirs*, the plot of which was clearly inspired by Matthew Gregory Lewis's gothic novel *The Monk: A Romance* (1796; also known as *Ambrosio: Or, The Monk*), the Capuchin friar Medardus recounts the story of his rebellious flight from the monastery and his repentant return to it. Medardus is born within the precincts of a monastery, grows up in the vicinity of a nunnery, and promptly resolves to live a religious life himself. After having become an extraordinarily successful preacher at his monastery, he suddenly experiences a breakdown of his rhetorical abilities and is desperate for a cure from the mysterious ailment. He knows that among the monastery's sacred relics is preserved a flask filled with a potent elixir that the Devil had once offered to the hermit Saint Anthony during his temptations in the desert. Medardus takes a drink from the flask and finds his powers restored, but he also senses new and ominous passions rushing through his veins. Medardus's superior, concerned about the peace of the monastic community, soon finds himself forced to send the agitated and arrogant monk on a mission to Rome.

From the moment Medardus leaves the monastery, the reader is hard put to assess the actual nature of the monk's frenzied adventures. Torn between contradictory desires, Medardus's personality repeatedly breaks apart, integral elements battling one another as life-size enemies. Presented with a chance to assume another identity—which in fact appeals to everything he has suppressed during his years as a monk—Medardus wantonly enters an adulterous affair with a baroness while, at the same time, falling in love with her angelic stepdaughter, Aurelie. The resulting emotional turmoil culminates in a scene of horror in which Medardus poisons the baroness and tries to rape Aurelie. Momentarily exorcised from his evil self by the enormity of the crime, he hurries away in frantic fear of his own passions.

After further wanderings, Medardus meets Aurelie again. This time, he is determined to court her with genuine love and devotion, yet the demoniac compulsion to subjugate and destroy the love he awakens never completely leaves him. On their wedding day, the indomitable strain in Medardus's soul flares up with renewed ferocity. As he sees his alter ego carted off to execution, he refuses to let it die, rejects Aurelie and everything noble in himself, and runs off, his satanic double on his back, until rage and frustration deprive him of his senses. Several months later, Medardus revives, finding himself in an Italian insane asylum. He proceeds to submit his body to a rigorous course of penance, and, after many additional adventures, he returns to the monastery from which he had set out. He arrives the day before Aurelie is to take her religious vows in a nearby convent. Overwhelmed by the coincidence, Medardus feels rent apart again. He claims Aurelie for himself and slays her on the steps of the altar. Having thus destroyed the object of his passion, Medardus is at last free to reject the call of instinct and to reenter the tranquillity of monastic life.

The Devil's Elixirs can be read on at least two levels. Late in the novel, the reader is told that the main characters are, unbeknown to themselves, members of one family that for several generations has lived under a curse resulting from a sacrilege committed by an ancestor. That curse can be laid to rest only if the remaining members of the family renounce earthly love and thus mark the family for extinction. Medardus and Aurelie, the last of the unholy clan, embrace the necessary self-denial and break the chain of sin and guilt. The notion of an inherited curse was the stock-in-trade of the gothic novel. The introduction of supernatural agencies allowed authors to explain the many otherwise inexplicable coincidences needed to sustain the suspense of their stories. The real impact of *The Devil's Elixirs*, therefore, does not arise from Hoffmann's belated revelations about Medardus's guilt-ridden family but rather from his relentless depiction of a man's fearful struggle with instincts that lie, in stubborn and hostile cynicism, beyond the reach of his moral self.

Medardus, of course, does put an end to the curse, not only for his family but also for his own troubled self. *The Devil's Elixirs*, after all, is his autobiography; it contains his retrospective creation of a continuous self and signals a significant victory over his chaotic past. The success with which Medardus has managed to construct—from the fragmented impulses of his psyche—the notion of a responsible personality shows that he has established for himself a basis for moral behavior. Still, he has stabilized his personality at a high price: the exclusion of all instinct, the truncating of his very life. Secure as Medardus's self now might be, a unified self it is not, and no amount of Catholic pageantry can disguise the pessimism of that conclusion.

The Life and Opinions of Kater Murr

Hoffmann's second novel, *The Life and Opinions of Kater Murr*, remained a fragment, a fact that—considering the less-than-convincing end of *The Devil's Elixirs*—rather enhances its effectiveness. In contrast to *The Devil's Elixirs*, which in spite of its confusing plot follows the traditional technique of a chronological narration, *The Life and Opinions of Kater Murr* surprises the reader with one of the most amusingly original structures in German literature. The novel is composed of two distinct narratives bewilderingly conflated: the autobiography of a tomcat (Murr) and the biography of a musician (Kreisler). Murr, so the editor apologizes, had, while writing his memoirs, torn up the biography of Kreisler in order to use its pages as writing pad and blotting paper. When Murr had his work published, the printer mistakenly thought the sheets from Kreisler's life to be part of the tomcat's autobiography, so that in the finished product two very dissimilar stories interrupt each other with maddening regularity.

In Murr's account, Hoffmann parodies the educational novel, the bildungsroman, of his day. Murr, a smugly egotistical tomcat, pompously details the stages by which he planned to advance himself in the world. With all the naïveté of his inflated ego, he tells how he first embarked on an academic career, then felt free to pursue romantic love, became involved in the political arena, and finally aspired to be recognized as a true gentleman. At the end, the reader is informed that the splendid cat has unfortunately died, a fate common to those who achieve too much at too early an age.

That Murr's penmanship at least left much to be desired might be gathered from the fact that about two-thirds of all pages in the book were apparently needed as blotting paper. These pages tell of the life of Johannes Kreisler. The story opens at the small court of Sieghartsweiler, where for some time now the former mistress of Prince Irenäus has spun an intrigue that is to lead to a marriage between Irenäus's half-witted son Ignaz and her own daughter, the beautiful and sensitive Julia.

The plot gets under way as the eccentric musician Kreisler joins the tedious life at the miniature court. He soon is asked to give Julia and Hedwiga, Prince Irenäus's only daughter, music lessons, and the two girls are quickly attracted to Kreisler by the strange powers that his curiously extravagant behavior reveals. Their idyllic association is destroyed by the news that Hedwiga is to marry the handsome but unscrupulous Prince Hektor. Hektor, assured that in time he will possess Hedwiga, promptly sets out to seduce Julia. For a while, Kreisler manages to foil Hektor's plans, until an attempt on Kreisler's life forces the musician to flee from court. He takes up residence in a nearby Benedictine abbey and there resumes work as composer and music director. Unfortunately, Kreisler has barely achieved peace in his new surroundings when an urgent letter from Sieghartsweiler implores him to return to court, where a double wedding joining Hektor and Hedwiga as well as Ignaz and Julia is about to take place. Whether Kreisler was able to prevent this impending misfortune remains unclear, as the novel breaks off in the middle of a sentence.

Throughout the story, evidence accumulates suggesting that Kreisler, whose identity is the central mystery of the plot, may well be the victim of a long-standing court intrigue. The attraction that Kreisler's character exerts, however, seems to depend even less on the unraveling of a web of fateful family relations than does the account of the friar Medardus. What the torn-out pages of Kreisler's biography tell about the torn-up life of its hero, no clandestine schemes could possibly bind together. Kreisler's existential rootlessness is ultimately the result not of clever machinations from without but of his own self-lacerating quest for human perfection in a petty environment. Sheltering a highly idealistic and highly vulnerable personality behind masks of cynicism and eccentricity, Kreisler is plagued by the sudden shifts of an artistic vision that shows the trivial to be sublime as often as it shows the sublime to be trivial. Thus barred from any consistent perspective on world or self, he is forced to vacillate between ecstatic joy and despondent frustration: ecstatic joy at the world's grandeur, despondent frustration at its inevitable depreciation at the hands of unresponsive men. In contrast to Medardus, who could still reconstruct his divided will from the secure vision of an undisputed faith, Kreisler's divided perception finds no such security; even his monastic retreat offers him hardly more than a brief respite from his self-tormented life.

It would be inaccurate, however, to think of *The Life and Opinions of Kater Murr* as a thoroughly pessimistic novel. It must not be forgotten that Hoffmann chained Kreisler's volatile idealism to the pedestrian common sense of the tomcat Murr. If the musician unmasks the cat's vain shallowness, Murr, too, provides a mocking mirror for Kreisler's pursuit of perfection at the Lilliputian court of Sieghartsweiler. How serious Hoffmann was about seeing the perspectives of the conformist animal and of the nonconformist artist as complementary becomes clear when Murr ends his memoirs with the remark that henceforth he will live with a new master, the concertmaster Kreisler.

Murr's death, of course, leaves it to the reader to imagine what the unlikely companions could have meant to each other. For Hoffmann, the outcome of their partnership cannot be in doubt. Whenever people admit to being part self-serving cat and part self-effacing idealist, self-irony—the tolerant smile at one's own incongruous personality—will turn the menace of a divided ego into the promise of a healthily deflated, less commanding but also less aggressive self. Although Hoffmann's creatures have not yet attained their creator's humorous wisdom, the reader understands and is invited to rise to its challenge.

Joachim Scholz

Other major works

SHORT FICTION: *Fantasiestücke in Callots Manier*, 1814-1815 (*Fantasy Pieces in Callot's Manner*, 1996); *Nachtstücke*, 1817; *Klein Zaches, genannt Zinnober*, 1819 (*Little Zaches, Surnamed Zinnober*, 1971); *Die Serapionsbrüder*, 1819-1821 (4 volumes; *The Serapion Brethren*, 1886-1892); *Prinzessin Brambilla: Ein Capriccio nach Jakob Callot*, 1821 (*Princess Brambilla: A "Capriccio" in the Style of Jacques Callot*, 1971); *Meister Floh: Ein Märchen in sieben Abenteuern zweier Freunde*, 1822 (*Master Flea: A Fairy Tale in Seven Adventures of Two Friends*, 1826); *Four Tales*, 1962; *The Best Tales of Hoffmann*, 1967; *Selected Writings of E. T. A. Hoffmann*, 1969 (2 volumes); *The Golden Pot, and Other Tales*, 1992.

NONFICTION: *Briefwechsel*, 1967-1969 (3 volumes; correspondence); *Tagebücher*, 1971 (4 volumes; diaries); *Selected Letters*, 1977.

MUSICAL COMPOSITIONS: *Liebe und Eifersucht: Oper*, 1807; *Trois Canzonettes*, 1808; *Arlequinn: Ballett*, 1811; *Undine*, 1816; *Musikalische Werke*, 1922-1927.

Bibliography

Chantler, Abigail. *E. T. A. Hoffmann's Musical Aesthetics*. Burlington, Vt.: Ashgate, 2006. Hoffmann was a music critic and composer as well as a writer, and this book describes his aesthetic ideas about music, placing them within the context of late eighteenth and early nineteenth century philosophy. Also discusses the significance of Hoffmann's literary works.

Daemmrich, Horst S. *The Shattered Self: E. T. A. Hoffmann's Tragic Vision*. Detroit, Mich.: Wayne State University Press, 1973. Important study of Hoffmann's literary work begins with an introduction that places Hoffmann in historical context and outlines critical appraisals of his work. Analysis of Hoffmann's major themes and motifs finds in the author's work a portrayal of "the disintegration of the individual in a world of uncontrolled forces." Includes extensive notes, bibliography, and index.

Hewett-Thayer, Harvey W. *Hoffmann: Author of the Tales*. Princeton, N.J.: Princeton

University Press, 1938. Classic work, intended as an introduction for both students and general readers, that provides a comprehensive biography of Hoffmann and discussion of his works, with very readable story analyses. Informative footnotes include suggestions for further reading as well as the original German for many passages when these appear in English translation in the main text. Supplemented by a listing of Hoffmann's literary works with dates of publication, a bibliography, and an index of names and works.

Kohlenbach, Margarete. "Women and Artists: E. T. A. Hoffmann's Implicit Critique of Early Romanticism." *Modern Language Review* 89, no. 3 (July, 1994): 659-673. Examines the Romantic philosophy of love in the novel *The Life and Opinions of Kater Murr* and in Hoffmann's other works. Argues that the character Johannes Kreisler expresses ideas about love that are at variance with Hoffmann's writings as a whole and explains the significance of this divergence.

McGlathery, James M. *E. T. A. Hoffmann*. New York: Twayne, 1997. Interesting introduction to Hoffmann's life and work analyzes his major works of fiction and also discusses the critical reception of Hoffmann's writings and Hoffmann's own works of criticism.

Negus, Kenneth. *E. T. A. Hoffmann's Other World: The Romantic Author and His "New Mythology."* Philadelphia: University of Pennsylvania Press, 1965. Very readable monograph focuses on Hoffmann's development of a coherent body of myth in his fantasy world—a "new mythology" founded on an inner spiritual (or psychological) world but extending to form a "cosmic myth." Examines all of Hoffmann's major literary works as well as many of his minor works with a view to laying a critical foundation for his narrative art. Includes select bibliography and index.

Riou, Jeanne. *Imagination in German Romanticism: Re-thinking the Self and Its Environment*. New York: Peter Lang, 2004. Examines the works of Hoffmann and other German writers and philosophers to explore the Romantic concept of the imagination and the imagination's critique of reason.

STEPHEN KING

Born: Portland, Maine; September 21, 1947
Also known as: Stephen Edwin King; Richard Bachman; John Swithen; Eleanor Druse

Principal long fiction

Carrie, 1974
'Salem's Lot, 1975
Rage, 1977 (as Richard Bachman)
The Shining, 1977
The Stand, 1978 (unabridged edition 1990)
The Dead Zone, 1979
The Long Walk, 1979 (as Bachman)
Firestarter, 1980
Cujo, 1981
The Gunslinger, 1982 (revised 2003; illustrated by Michael Whelan)
The Running Man, 1982 (as Bachman)
Christine, 1983
Cycle of the Werewolf, 1983 (novella; illustrated by Berni Wrightson)
Pet Sematary, 1983
The Eyes of the Dragon, 1984, 1987
The Talisman, 1984 (with Peter Straub)
Thinner, 1984 (as Bachman)
The Bachman Books: Four Early Novels by Stephen King, 1985 (includes *Rage*, *The Long Walk*, *Roadwork*, and *The Running Man*)
It, 1986
The Drawing of the Three, 1987 (illustrated by Phil Hale)
Misery, 1987
The Tommyknockers, 1987
The Dark Half, 1989
Needful Things, 1991
The Waste Lands, 1991 (illustrated by Ned Dameron)
Gerald's Game, 1992
Dolores Claiborne, 1993
Insomnia, 1994
Rose Madder, 1995
Desperation, 1996
The Green Mile, 1996 (six-part serialized novel)
The Regulators, 1996 (as Bachman)

Wizard and Glass, 1997 (illustrated by Dave McKean)
Bag of Bones, 1998
The Girl Who Loved Tom Gordon, 1999
Storm of the Century, 1999 (adaptation of his teleplay)
Black House, 2001 (with Peter Straub)
Dreamcatcher, 2001
From a Buick Eight, 2002
Wolves of the Calla, 2003 (illustrated by Bernie Wrightson)
The Journals of Eleanor Druse: My Investigation of the Kingdom Hospital Incident, 2004 (as Eleanor Druse)
The Dark Tower, 2004 (illustrated by Michael Whelan)
Song of Susannah, 2004 (illustrated by Darrel Anderson)
The Colorado Kid, 2005
Cell, 2006
Lisey's Story, 2006
Blaze, 2007 (as Bachman)
Duma Key, 2008

Other literary forms

In addition to his novels, Stephen King has published many short stories, including the collections *Night Shift* (1978), *Nightmares and Dreamscapes* (1993), and *Everything's Eventual: Fourteen Dark Tales* (2002). The collections *Different Seasons* (1982) and *Four Past Midnight* (1990) contain novellas, two of which are of central importance to King's body of work. In *The Body*, a boy's confrontation with mortality shapes his developing identity as a writer. In *The Mist*, King in his satirical and apocalyptic mode brings Armageddon to the Federal Foods Supermarket as an assortment of grade-B film monsters that inhabit a dense fog.

The relations of King's fiction with the electronic media are many and complex. Much of his fiction has been adapted to both the large and small screens, although it usually plays best in the mind's eye. Several of King's screenplays have been produced, including *Maximum Overdrive* (1986), a film he also directed. A relatively successful mixed-media venture was his collaboration with George Romero on *Creepshow* (1982), a film anthology inspired by the D.C. Comics' blend of camp and gore and based on King's own book version. *Creepshow II*, written by Romero and based on King's stories, appeared in 1987. King's teleplays include *The Stand* (1994), which is based on his novel, and *Storm of the Century* (1999), which was written expressly for television broadcast. In 2002, he wrote the script for the television miniseries *Rose Red*. In addition to his works of fiction, King has published numerous articles as well as a critical book, *Danse Macabre* (1981). In 2000, he published *On Writing: A Memoir of the Craft*, and in 2003, he began to publish occasional columns on popular culture in *Entertainment Weekly* magazine.

Achievements

Stephen King is perhaps the most widely known American writer of his generation, yet his distinctions include publishing as two authors at once: Beginning in 1966, he wrote novels that were published under the pseudonym Richard Bachman. He won many British Fantasy and World Fantasy Awards, including the latter for overall contributions to the genre in 1980. King was at first ignored and then scorned by mainstream critics, but by the late 1980's his novels were reviewed regularly in *The New York Times Book Review* with increasing favor. Beginning in 1987, most of his novels were main selections of the Book-of-the-Month Club, which in 1989 created the Stephen King Library, committed to keeping King's novels "in print in hardcover."

King was *People* magazine's Writer of the Year in 1980. One of his most appropriate distinctions was the October 9, 1986, cover of *Time* magazine, which depicted a reader, hair on end, transfixed by "A Novel by Stephen King." The cover story on the "King of Horror" correctly suggested that his achievement and the "horror boom" of the 1970's and 1980's are inseparable. Like Edgar Allan Poe, King turned a degenerated genre—a matter of comic-book monsters and drive-in films—into a medium embodying the primary anxieties of his age. His revitalization of the horror genre and his increasingly good reviews from mainstream newspapers and journals culminated in his receiving his most illustrious award in 2003: the National Book Award for Distinguished Contribution to American Letters.

King's detractors attribute his success to the sensational appeal of his genre, the main purpose of which, as King readily confesses, is to scare people. His fiction is graphic, sentimental, and predictable. His humor is usually crude and campy. His novels are often long and loosely structured: *It*, for example, comprises more than eleven hundred pages. In an environment of "exhaustion" and minimalism, King's page-turners are the summit of the garbage heap of a mass, throwaway culture. Worst of all, he is "Master of Postliterate Prose," as Paul Gray stated in 1982—his writing takes readers mentally to the movies rather than making them imagine or think.

On the other hand, King's work provides the most genuine example of the storyteller's art since Charles Dickens. He has returned to the novel some of the popular appeal it had in the nineteenth century and turned out a generation of readers who vastly prefer some books to their film adaptations. As Dickens drew on the popular culture of his time, King reflects the mass-mediated culture of his own. His dark fantasies, like all good popular fiction, allow readers to express within conventional frames of reference feelings and concepts they might not otherwise consider. In imagination, King is not merely prolific; his vision articulates universal fears and desires in terms peculiar to contemporary culture.

Biography

The second son of Donald and Nellie Ruth Pillsbury King, Stephen Edwin King has lived most of his life in Maine, the setting for most of his fiction. Two childhood traumas, neither of which he remembers, may have been formative. In 1949, when he was two years old, his parents separated and his father disappeared. In 1951, he apparently saw a train dismember a neighborhood friend.

King's conservative Methodist upbringing was supplemented early with a diet of comic books and *Weird Tales*. When twelve, he began submitting stories for sale. In 1970, he graduated from the University of Maine, Orono, with a B.S. in English and a minor in dramatics. He encountered two lasting influences: the naturalist writers and contemporary American mythology. He also met Tabitha Jane Spruce, whom he married in 1971.

After graduation, he worked in an industrial laundry until 1971, when he became an English instructor at a preparatory school in Hampden, Maine. He wrote at night in the trailer he shared with his wife and two children. In the early 1970's, he sold stories to men's magazines. Then, in 1974, he published *Carrie*, which was followed by several best sellers and sales of motion-picture rights.

King settled in Maine with his wife Tabitha King, a novelist and the writer of *Small World* (1981), *Caretakers* (1983), and others. They had three children, Naomi, Joe, and Owen. In addition to writing daily (except Christmas and his birthday), King became active in opposing censorship, composing essays and lecturing on the topic and supporting controversial publications. He also indulged his love of rock and roll, having purchased a local radio station (renamed WZON) and occasionally performing, with writers Dave Barry, Amy Tan, and others, in a group named the Rock-Bottom Remainders.

In 1999, King was struck by an automobile while walking along a road near his home. His injuries were quite severe, yet the famous author remained upbeat and philosophical during his lengthy recovery. He incorporated this painful accident into much of his subsequent long fiction, including *Song of Susanna*, the *Dark Tower* series, *Lisey's Story*, and *Duma Key*.

ANALYSIS

Stephen King may be known as a horror writer, but he calls himself a "brand name," describing his style as "the literary equivalent of a Big Mac and a large fries from McDonald's." His fast-food version of the "plain style" may smell of commercialism, but that may make him the contemporary American storyteller without peer. From the beginning, his dark parables spoke to the anxieties of the late twentieth century. As a surrogate author in *The Mist* explains King's mission, "When the technologies fail, when . . . religious systems fail, people have got to have something. Even a zombie lurching through the night" is a "cheerful" thought in the context of a "dissolving ozone layer."

King's fictions begin with premises accepted by middle Americans of the television generation, opening in suburban or small-town America—Derry, Maine, or Libertyville, Pennsylvania—and have the familiarity of the house next door and the 7-Eleven store. The characters have the trusted two-dimensional reality of kitsch: They originate in clichés such as the high school "nerd" or the wise child. From such premises, they move cinematically through an atmosphere resonant with a popular mythology. King applies naturalistic methods to an environment created by popular culture. This reality, already mediated, is translated easily into preternatural terms, taking on a nightmarish quality.

King's imagination is above all archetypal: His "pop" familiarity and his campy humor draw on the collective unconscious. In *Danse Macabre*, King's study of the contemporary horror genre that emphasizes the cross-pollination of fiction and film, he divides his subject according to four "monster archetypes": the ghost, the "thing" (or human-made monster), the vampire, and the werewolf. As with his fiction, his sources are the classic horror films of the 1930's, inherited by the 1950's pulp and film industries. He hints at their derivations from the gothic novel, classical myth, Brothers Grimm folktales, and the oral tradition in general. In an anxious era both skeptical of and hungry for myth, horror is fundamentally reassuring and cathartic; the tale-teller combines the roles of physician and priest into the witch doctor as "sin eater," who assumes the guilt and fear of the culture. In the neoprimitivism of the late twentieth century, this ancient role and the old monsters took on a new mystique. In *The Uses of Enchantment: The Meaning and Importance of Fairy Tales* (1976), psychologist Bruno Bettelheim argues that the magic and terrors of fairy tales present existential problems in forms children can understand. King's paranormal horrors have similar cathartic and educative functions for adults; they externalize the traumas of life, especially those of adolescence.

Carrie

Stephen King's first published novel, *Carrie*, is a parable of adolescence. Sixteen-year-old Carrie White is a lonely ugly duckling, an outcast at home and at school. Her mother, a religious fanatic, associates Carrie with her own "sin"; Carrie's peers hate her in a mindless way and make her the butt of every joke. *Carrie* concerns the horrors of high school, a place of "bottomless conservatism and bigotry," as King explains, where students "are no more allowed to rise 'above their station' than a Hindu" above caste. The novel is also about the terrors of passage to womanhood. In the opening scene, in the school shower room, Carrie experiences her first menstrual period; her peers react with abhorrence and ridicule, "stoning" her with sanitary napkins, shouting, "Plug it up!" Carrie becomes the scapegoat for a fear of female sexuality as epitomized in the smell and sight of blood. (The blood bath and symbolism of sacrifice will recur at the climax of the novel.) As atonement for her participation in Carrie's persecution in the shower, Susan Snell persuades her popular boyfriend, Tommy Ross, to invite Carrie to the Spring Ball. Carrie's conflict with her mother, who regards her emerging womanhood with loathing, is paralleled by a new plot by the girls against Carrie, led by the rich and spoiled Chris Hargenson. They arrange to have Tommy and Carrie voted King and Queen of the Ball, only to crown them with a bucket of pig's blood. Carrie avenges her mock baptism telekinetically, destroying the school and the town, leaving Susan Snell as the only survivor.

As in most folk cultures, initiation is signified by the acquisition of special wisdom or powers. King equates Carrie's sexual flowering with the maturing of her telekinetic ability. Both cursed and empowered with righteous fury, she becomes at once victim and monster, witch and White Angel of Destruction. As King has explained, Carrie is "Woman, feeling her powers for the first time and, like Samson, pulling down the temple on everyone in sight at the end of the book."

Carrie catapulted King into the mass market; in 1976, the novel was adapted into a critically acclaimed film directed by Brian De Palma. The novel touched the right nerves, including feminism. William Blatty's *The Exorcist* (1971), which was adapted into a powerful and controversial film, had touched on similar social fears in the 1960's and 1970's with its subtext of the "generation gap" and the "death of God." Although Carrie's destructive power, like that of Regan in *The Exorcist*, is linked with monstrous adolescent sexuality, the similarity between the two novels ends there. Carrie's "possession" is the complex effect of her mother's fanaticism, her peers' bigotry, and her newly realized, unchecked female power. Like Anne Sexton's *Transformations* (1971), a collection of fractured fairy tales in sardonic verse, King's novel explores the social and cultural roots of its evil.

King's *Carrie* is a dark modernization of "Cinderella," with a bad mother, cruel siblings (peers), a prince (Tommy Ross), a godmother (Sue Snell), and a ball. King's reversal of the happy ending is actually in keeping with the Brothers Grimm; it recalls the tale's folk originals, which enact revenge in bloody images: The stepsisters' heels, hands, and noses are sliced off, and a white dove pecks out their eyes. As King knows, blood flows freely in the oral tradition. King represents that oral tradition in a pseudodocumentary form that depicts the points of view of various witnesses and commentaries: newspaper accounts, case studies, court reports, and journals. Pretending to textual authenticity, he alludes to the gothic classics, especially Bram Stoker's *Dracula* (1897). *'Salem's Lot*, King's next novel, is a bloody fairy tale in which Dracula comes to Our Town.

'SALEM'S LOT

By the agnostic and sexually liberated 1970's, the vampire had been demythologized into what King called a "comic book menace." In a significant departure from tradition, he diminished the sexual aspects of the vampire. He reinvested the archetype with meaning by basing its attraction on the human desire to surrender identity in the mass. King's major innovation, however, was envisioning the mythic small town in American gothic terms and then making it the monster; the vampire's traditional victim, the populace, becomes the menace as mindless mass, plague, or primal horde. Drawing on Richard Matheson's grimly naturalistic novel *I Am Legend* (1954) and Jack Finney's novel *The Body Snatchers* (1955), King focused on the issue of fragmentation, reinvesting the vampire with contemporary meaning.

The sociopolitical subtext of *'Salem's Lot* is the ubiquitous disillusionment of the Watergate era, King has explained. Like rumor and disease, vampirism spreads secretly at night, from neighbor to neighbor, infecting men and women, the mad and the senile, the responsible citizen and the infant alike, absorbing into its zombielike horde the human population. King is especially skillful at suggesting how small-town conservatism can become inverted on itself, the harbored suspicions and open secrets gradually dividing and isolating. This picture is reinforced by the town's name, 'Salem's Lot, a degenerated form of Jerusalem's Lot, which suggests the city of the chosen reverted to a culture of dark rites in images of spreading menace.

King's other innovation was, paradoxically, a reiteration. He made his "king vampire," Barlow, an obvious reincarnation of Stoker's Dracula that functions somewhere between cliché and archetype. King uses the mythology of vampires to ask how civilization is to exist without faith in traditional authority symbols. His answer is pessimistic, turning on the abdication of Father Callahan, whose strength is undermined by secret alcoholism and a superficial adherence to form. The two survivors, Ben Mears and Mark Petrie, must partly seek, partly create their talismans and rituals, drawing on the compendium of vampire lore—the alternative, in a culturewide crisis of faith, to conventional systems. (At one point, Mears holds off a vampire with a crucifix made with two tongue depressors.) The paraphernalia, they find, will work only if the handler has faith.

It is significant that the two survivors are, respectively, a "wise child" (Mark Petrie) and a novelist (Ben Mears); only they have the necessary resources. Even Susan Norton, Mears's lover and the gothic heroine, succumbs. As in *The Shining*, *The Dead Zone*, and *Firestarter*, the child (or childlike adult) has powers that may be used for good or for evil. Mears is the imaginative, nostalgic adult, haunted by the past. The child and the man share a naïveté, a gothic iconography, and a belief in evil. Twelve-year-old Mark worships at a shrinelike tableau of Aurora monsters that glow "green in the dark, just like the plastic Jesus" he was given in Sunday school for learning Psalm 119. Mears has returned to the town of his childhood to revive an image of the Marsten House lurking in his mythical mind's eye. Spiritual father and son, they create a community of two out of the "pop" remnants of American culture.

As in fairy tales and Dickens's novels, King's protagonists are orphans searching for their true parents, for community. His fiction may reenact his search for the father who disappeared and left behind a box of *Weird Tales*. The yearned-for bond of parent and child, a relationship signifying a unity of being, appears throughout King's fiction. The weakness or treachery of a trusted parent is correspondingly the ultimate fear. Hence, the vampire Barlow is the devouring father who consumes an entire town.

THE SHINING

In *The Shining*, King domesticated his approach to the theme of parent-child relationships, focusing on the threat to the family that comes from a trusted figure within it. Jack Torrance, a writer, arranges to oversee a mountain resort during the winter months, when it is closed because of heavy snows. He moves his family with him to the Overlook Hotel, where he expects to break a streak of bad luck and personal problems (he is an alcoholic) by writing a play. He is also an abused child who, assuming his father's aggression, in turn becomes the abusing father. The much-beloved "bad" father is the novel's monster: The environment of the Overlook Hotel traps him, as he in turn calls its power forth. As Jack metamorphoses from abusive father and husband into violent monster, King brilliantly expands the haunted-house archetype into a symbol of the accumulated sin of all fathers.

CHRISTINE

In *Christine*, the setting is Libertyville, Pennsylvania, in the late 1970's. The monster is the American Dream as embodied in the automobile. King gives *Christine* all the attributes of a fairy tale for "postliterate" adolescents. *Christine* is another fractured Cinderella story, *Carrie* for boys. Arnie Cunningham, a nearsighted, acne-scarred loser, falls "in love with" a car, a passionate (red and white) Christine, "one of the long ones with the big fins." An automotive godmother, she brings Arnie, in fairy-tale succession, freedom, success, power, and love: a home away from overprotective parents, a cure for acne, hit-and-run revenge on bullies, and a beautiful girl, Leigh Cabot. Soon, however, the familiar triangle emerges, of boy, girl, and car, and Christine is revealed as a femme fatale—driven by the spirit of her former owner, a malcontent named Roland LeBay. Christine is the medium for his death wish on the world, for his all-devouring, "everlasting Fury." LeBay's aggression possesses Arnie, who reverts into an older, tougher self, then into the "mythic teenaged hood" that King has called the prototype of 1950's werewolf films, and finally into "some ancient carrion eater," or primal self.

As automotive monster Christine comes from a variety of sources, including the folk tradition of the "death car" and a venerable technohorror premise, as seen in King's "Trucks" and *Maximum Overdrive*. King's main focus, however, is the mobile youth culture that has come down from the 1950's by way of advertising, popular songs, film, and national pastimes. Christine is the car as a projection of the cultural self, anima for the modern American Adam. To Arnie's late 1970's-style imagination, the Plymouth Fury, in 1958 a midpriced family car, is an American Dream. Her sweeping, befinned chassis and engine re-create a fantasy of the golden age of the automobile: the horizonless future imagined as an expanding network of superhighways and unlimited fuel. Christine recovers for Arnie a prelapsarian vitality and manifest destiny.

Christine's odometer runs backward, and she regenerates parts. The immortality she offers, however—and by implication, the American Dream—is really arrested development in the form of a *Happy Days* rerun and by way of her radio, which sticks on the "golden oldies" station. Indeed, *Christine* is a recapitulatory rock musical framed fatalistically in sections titled "Teenage Car-Songs," "Teenage Love-Songs," and "Teenage Death-Songs." Fragments of rock-and-roll songs introduce each chapter. Christine's burden, an undead 1950's youth culture, means that most of Arnie's travels are in and out of time, a deadly nostalgia trip. As Douglas Winter explains, *Christine* reenacts "the death," in the 1970's, "of the American romance with the automobile."

The epilogue from four years later presents the fairy-tale consolation in a burned-out monotone. Arnie and his parents are buried, Christine is scrap metal, and the true Americans, Leigh and Dennis, are survivors, but Dennis, the "knight of Darnell's Garage," does not woo "the lady fair"; he is a limping, lackluster junior high teacher, and they have drifted apart, grown old in their prime. Dennis narrates the story in order to file it away, all the while perceiving himself and his peers in terms of icons from the late 1950's. In his nightmares, Christine appears wearing a black vanity plate inscribed with a skull and the words "ROCK AND ROLL WILL NEVER DIE." From Dennis's haunted perspective, *Christine* simultaneously examines and is a symptom of a cultural phenomenon: a new American gothic species of anachronism or déjà vu, which continued after *Christine*'s publication in films such as *Back to the Future* (1985), *Peggy Sue Got Married* (1986), and *Blue Velvet* (1986). The 1980's and the 1950's blur into a seamless illusion, the nightmare side of which is the prospect of living an infinite replay.

The subtext of King's adolescent fairy tale is another coming-of-age, from the opposite end and the broader perspective of American culture. Written by King as he approached his forties, *Christine* diagnoses a cultural midlife crisis and marks a turning point in King's career, a critical examination of mass culture. The dual time frame reflects his awareness of a dual audience, of writing for adolescents who look back to a mythical 1950's and also for his own generation as it relives its undead youth culture in its children. The baby boomers, King explains, "were obsessive" about childhood. "We went on playing for a long time, almost feverishly. I write for that buried child in us, but I'm writing for the grown-up too. I want grown-ups to look at the child long enough to be able to give him up. The child should be buried."

PET SEMATARY

In *Pet Sematary*, King unearthed the buried child, which is the novel's monster. *Pet Sematary* is about the "*real* cemetery," he told Winter. The focus is on the "one great fear" all fears "add up to," "the body under the sheet. It's our body." The fairy-tale subtext is the magic kingdom of our protracted American childhood, the Disney empire as mass culture—and, by implication, the comparable multimedia phenomenon represented by King himself. The grimmer, truer text-within-the-text is Mary Wollstonecraft Shelley's *Frankenstein* (1818).

The novel, which King once considered "too horrible to be published," is also his own dark night of the soul. Louis Creed, a university doctor, moves with his wife, Rachel, and their two children (five-year-old Ellie and two-year-old Gage) to Maine to work at King's alma mater; a neighbor takes the family on an outing to a pet cemetery created by the neighborhood children, their confrontation with mortality. Additionally the "sematary," whose "Druidic" rings allude to Stonehenge, is the outer circle of a Native American burial ground that sends back the dead in a state of soulless half life. Louis succumbs to temptation when the family cat Church is killed on the highway; he buries him on the sacred old Native American burial grounds. "Frankencat" comes back with his "purr-box broken." A succession of accidents, heart attacks, strokes, and deaths—of neighbor Norma Crandall, Creed's son Gage, Norma's husband Jud, and Creed's wife Rachel—and resurrections follows.

The turning point is the death of Gage, which Creed cannot accept and which leads to the novel's analysis of modern medical miracles performed in the name of human decency and love. Louis is the father as baby boomer who cannot relinquish his childhood. The larger philosophical issue is Louis's rational, bioethical *creed*; he believes in saving the only life he knows, the material. Transferred into an immoderate love for his son, it is exposed as the narcissistic embodiment of a patriarchal lust for immortality through descendants, expressed first in an agony of sorrow and rage, then ghoulishly, as he disinters his son's corpse and makes the estranging discovery that it is like "looking at a badly made doll." Later, reanimated, Gage appears to have been "terribly hurt and then put back together again by crude, uncaring hands." Performing his task, Louis feels dehumanized, like "a subhuman character in some cheap comic-book."

The failure of Louis's creed is shown in his habit, when under stress, of taking mental trips to Orlando, Florida, where he, Church, and Gage drive a white van as Disney World's "resurrection crew." In these waking dreams, which echo the male bond of "wise child" and haunted father from as far back as *'Salem's Lot*, Louis's real creed is revealed: Its focus is on Oz the Gweat and Tewwible (a personification of death to Rachel) and Walt Disney, that "gentle faker from Nebraska"—like Louis, two wizards of science fantasy. Louis's wizardry is reflected in the narrative perspective and structure, which flashes back in part 2 from the funeral to Louis's fantasy of a heroically "long, flying tackle" that snatches Gage from death's wheels.

In this modernization of *Frankenstein*, King demythologizes death and attacks the aspirations toward immortality that typify the 1980's. King's soulless Lazaruses are graphic projections of anxieties about life-support systems, artificial hearts, organ transplants—what King has called "mechanistic miracles" that can postpone the physical signs of life almost indefinitely. The novel also indicts the "wasteland" of mass culture, alluding in the same trope to George Romero's "stupid, lurching movie-zombies," T. S. Eliot's poem about the hollow men, and *The Wizard of Oz*: "headpiece full of straw." Louis worries that Ellie knows more about Ronald McDonald and "the Burger King" than the "*spiritus mundi*." If the novel suggests one source of community and culture, it is the form and ritual of the children's pet "sematary." Its concentric circles form a pattern from their "own collective unconsciousness," one that mimes "the most ancient religious symbol of all," the spiral.

IT

In *It*, a group of children create a community and a mythology as a way of confronting their fears, as represented in It, the monster as a serial-murdering, shape-shifting boogey that haunts the sewers of Derry, Maine. In 1958, the seven protagonists, a cross-section of losers, experience the monster differently, for as in George Orwell's *Nineteen Eighty-Four* (1949), It derives its power through its victims' isolation and guilt and thus assumes the shape of the each individual victim's worst fear. (To Beverly Rogan It appears, in a sequence reminiscent of "Little Red Riding Hood," as her abusive father in the guise of the child-eating witch from "Hansel and Gretel.")

In a scary passage in *Pet Sematary*, Louis dreams of Walt Disney World, where "by the 1890's train station, Mickey Mouse was shaking hands with the children clustered around him, his big white cartoon gloves swallowing their small, trusting hands." To all of the protagonists in *It*, the monster appears in a similar archetypal or communal form, one that suggests a composite of devouring parent and mass-culture demigod, of television commercial and fairy tale, of 1958 and 1985: as Pennywise, the Clown, a cross between Bozo and Ronald McDonald. As in *Christine*, *Pet Sematary*, and *Thinner*, the monster is mass culture itself, the collective devouring parent nurturing its children on "imitations of immortality." Like Christine, or Louis's patched-up son, Pennywise is the dead past feeding on the future.

Twenty-seven years after its original reign of terror, It resumes its siege, whereupon the protagonists, now professionally successful and, significantly, childless yuppies, must return to Derry to confront as adults their childhood fears. Led by horror writer Bill Denborough (partly based on King's friend and collaborator Peter Straub), they defeat It once more, individually as a sort of allegory of psychoanalysis and collectively as a rite of passage into adulthood and community.

It was attacked in reviews as pop psychology and by King himself as a "badly constructed novel," but the puerility was partly intended. The book summarizes King's previous themes and characters, who themselves look backward and inward, regress and take stock. The last chapter begins with an epigraph from Dickens's *David Copperfield* (1849-1850, serial; 1850, book) and ends with an allusion to William Wordsworth's "Ode: Intimations of Immortality" (1807), from which King takes his primary theme and narrative device, the look back that enables one to go forward. In the 1970's, King's fiction was devoted to building a mythos out of shabby celluloid monsters to fill a cultural void; in the postmodern awareness of the late 1980's, he began a demystification process. *It* is a calling forth and ritual unmasking of motley Reagan-era monsters, the exorcism of a generation and a culture.

OTHER 1980'S NOVELS

As for King the writer, *It* was one important rite in what would be a lengthy passage. After *It*'s extensive exploration of childhood, however, he took up conspicuously more mature characters, themes, and roles. In *The Eyes of the Dragon* (written for his daughter), he returned to the springs of his fantasy, the fairy tale. He told much the same story as before but assumed the mantle of adulthood. This "pellucid" and "elegant" fairy tale, according to Barbara Tritel in *The New York Times Book Review* (February 22, 1987), has the "intimate goofiness of an extemporaneous story" narrated by "a parent to a child." In *The Tommyknockers*, King again seemed to leave familiar territory for science fiction, but the novel more accurately applies technohorror themes to the 1980's infatuation with technology and televangelism. In the *Dark Tower* cycle, he combined the gothic with the Western genre and apocalyptic fiction in a manner reminiscent of *The Stand*. Then, with much fanfare, in 1990 King returned to that novel to update and enlarge it by some 350 pages.

King and Bachman

The process of recapitulation and summing up was complicated by the disclosure, in 1984, of Richard Bachman, the pseudonym under whose cover King had published five novels over a period of eight years. Invented for business reasons, Bachman soon grew into an identity complete with a biography and photographs (he was a chicken farmer with a cancer-ravaged face), dedications, a narrative voice (of unrelenting pessimism), and, if not a genre, a naturalistic mode in which sociopolitical speculation combined or alternated with psychological suspense. In 1985, when the Bachman novels (with one exception) were collected in a single volume attributed to King *as* Bachman, the mortified alter ego seemed buried. Actually Bachman's publicized demise only raised a haunting question of what "Stephen King" really was.

Misery

Misery, which was conceived as Bachman's book, was King's first novel to explore the subject of fiction's dangerous powers. After crashing his car on an isolated road in Colorado, romance writer Paul Sheldon is "rescued," drugged, and held prisoner by a psychotic nurse named Annie Wilkes, who is also the "Number One Fan" of Sheldon's heroine Misery Chastain (of whom he has tired and killed off). This "Constant Reader" becomes Sheldon's terrible "Muse," forcing him to write (in an edition especially for her) Misery's return to life. Sheldon is the popular writer imprisoned by genre and cut to fit fan expectations (signified by Annie's amputations of his foot and thumb). Like Scheherazade, the reader is reminded, Sheldon must publish or literally perish. Annie's obsession merges with the expectations of the page-turning real reader, who demands and devours each chapter, and as Sheldon struggles (against pain, painkillers, and a manual typewriter that throws keys) for his life, page by page.

Billed ironically on the dust jacket as a love letter to his fans, the novel is a witty satire on what King has called America's "cannibalistic cult of celebrity": "You set the guy up, and then you eat him." The monstrous Reader, however, is also the writer's muse, creation, and alter ego, as Sheldon discovers when he concludes that *Misery Returns*—not his "serious" novel *Fast Cars*—was his masterpiece. Just as ironically, *Misery* was King's first novel to please most of the critics.

The Dark Half

It was not a complete surprise, then, when in 1989 King examined the issue from the other side, in *The Dark Half*, an allegory of the writer's relation to his genius. The young writer-protagonist Thaddeus Beaumont has a series of headaches and seizures, and a surgeon removes from his eleven-year-old brain the incompletely absorbed fragments of a twin—including an eye, two teeth, and some fingernails. Nearly thirty years later, Beaumont is a creative-writing professor and moderately successful literary novelist devoted to his family. For twelve years, however, he has been living a secret life through George Stark, the pseudonym under which he emerged from writer's block as the author of best-selling crime novels. Stark's purely instinctual genius finds its most vital expression in his protagonist, the ruthless killer Alexis Machine. Like King, Beaumont is forced to disclose and destroy his now self-destructive pseudonym, complete with graveside service and papier-mâché headstone. A series of murders (narrated in Stark's graphic prose style) soon follows. The pseudonym has materialized, risen from its fictional grave literally to take Thad's wife and children (twins, of course) hostage. What Stark wants is to live in writing, outside of which writers do not exist. The writer is also a demon, vampire, and killer in this dark allegory, possessing and devouring the man, his family, friends, community.

Drawing on the motif of the double and the form of the detective story—on Robert Louis Stevenson's *The Strange Case of Dr. Jekyll and Mr. Hyde* (1886) and Sophocles' *Oedipus Rex* (c. 429 B.C.E.), as well as *Misery* and *Pet Sematary*—King gluts the first half of the book with Stark/Machine's gruesome rampages. The last half is psychological suspense and metafiction in biological metaphor: the struggle of the decently introspective Beaumont against the rawly instinctual Stark for control of both word and flesh, with the novel taking shape on the page as the true author reclaims the "third eye," King's term for both child's and artist's inward vision. Once again, the man buries the terrible child in order to possess himself and his art. The book ends in a "scene from some malign fairy tale" as that child and alter ego is borne away by flocks of sparrows to make a last appearance as a black hole in the fabric of the sky.

In dramatizing the tyrannies, perils, powers, and pleasures of reading and writing, *Misery* and *The Dark Half* might have been written by metafictionists John Fowles (to whose work King is fond of alluding) or John Barth (on whom he draws directly in *It* and *Misery*). Anything but abstract, however, *The Dark Half* is successful both as the thriller that King's fans desire and as an allegory of the writer's situation. Critic George Stade, in his review of the novel for *The New York Times Book Review* (October 29, 1989), praised King for his tact "in teasing out the implications of his parable." *The Dark Half* contains epigraphs instead to the novels of George Stark, Thad Beaumont, and "the late Richard

Bachman," without whom "this novel could not have been written." Thus reworking the gothic cliché of the double, King allows the mythology of his own life story to speak wittily for itself, lending a subtle level of self-parody to this roman à clef. In this instance, his blunt literalness ("word become flesh, so to speak," as George Stark puts it) gives vitality to what in other hands might have been a sterile exercise.

GERALD'S GAME *and* DOLORES CLAIBORNE

Some have criticized King's negative depictions of women, which King himself admitted in 1983 was a weakness. A decade later, King would address, and redress, this weakness in his paired novels *Gerald's Game* and *Dolores Claiborne*. Both present strong but besieged female protagonists, and both feature the total solar eclipse seen in Maine in 1963, during which a moment of telepathy, the books' only supernaturalism, links the two women.

Gerald's Game is the story of Jessie Burlingame, a young wife who submits to her husband's desire for sexual bondage play in a deserted cabin, only to have him die when she unexpectedly struggles. Alone and helpless, Jessie confronts memories (including the secret reason she struck out at Gerald), her own fears and limitations, and a ghastly visitor to the cabin who may or may not be real. In a bloody scene—even by King's standards—Jessie frees herself and escapes, a victory psychological as well as physical. The aptly named Dolores Claiborne is trapped more metaphorically, by poverty and an abusive husband, and her victory too is both violent and a sign of her developing independence and strength.

Initial reaction from critics was sometimes skeptical, especially given the prurient aspect of Jessie's plight and the trendy theme of incestuous abuse in both novels. King, however, had examined family dysfunction in works from *Carrie* and *The Shining* to *It*, and he continued his commitment to women's issues and realistic strong females in *Insomnia*, *Rose Madder*, and other novels. Archetypal themes also strengthen the two books: Female power must overcome male dominance, as the moon eclipses the sun; and each woman must find her own identity and strength out of travail, as the darkness gives way to light again. (King uses mythology and gender issues more explicitly in *Rose Madder*, which evenly incorporates mimetic and supernatural scenes.)

The books are daring departures for King in other ways. In contrast to the sprawling *It* or the encyclopedic *The Stand*, these books, like *Misery*, tightly focus on one setting, a shorter period of time, and a small cast—here *Misery*'s duet is replaced by intense monologues. In fact, all of *Dolores Claiborne* is her first-person narrative, without even chapter breaks, a tour de force few would attempt. Moreover, King challenges our ideas of the genre horror novel, since there is little violence, none of it supernatural and all expected, so that suspense is a function of character, not plot (done previously by King only in short fiction such as the novella *The Body* and the story "The Last Rung of the Ladder").

Character and voice, however, have always been essential to King's books, as Debbie

Notkin, Harlan Ellison, and others have pointed out. Dolores Claiborne is especially successful, her speech authentic Mainer and her character realistic both as the old woman telling her story and as the desperate yet indomitable wife, the past self whose story she tells. In these novels, King reaches beyond childhood and adolescence as themes; child abuse is examined, but only from an adult point of view. Dolores and Jessie—and the elderly protagonists of *Insomnia*—reveal King, perhaps having reconciled to his own history, exploring new social and psychological areas.

BAG OF BONES

Bag of Bones, which King calls a "haunted love story," opens with narrator Mike Noonan recounting the death of his wife, Jo, who collapses outside the Rite Aid pharmacy of a brain aneurysm. Both are relatively young, and Jo, Mike learns, was pregnant. Because Mike is unable to father children, he begins to question whether Jo was having an affair. As Mike slowly adjusts to life without Jo, he is forced to make another adjustment. Formerly a successful writer of gothic romance fiction, he now finds that he is unable to write even a simple sentence. In an attempt to regain his muse and put Jo's death behind him, Mike returns to Sarah Laughs (also referred to as "TR-90" or the "TR"), the vacation cabin he and Jo purchased soon after he became successful. As Mike quickly learns, Sarah Laughs is haunted by ghosts, among them the ghost of blues singer Sarah Tidwell.

While at Sarah Laughs, Mike meets Mattie Devore, her daughter Kyra, and Mattie's father-in-law, Max Devore, a withered old man of incalculable wealth who is accustomed to getting anything he wants. Having rescued Kyra from walking down the middle of Route 68, Mike quickly becomes friends with both Kyra and Mattie. Mattie is the widow of Lance Devore, Max's stuttering son. Lance had nothing to do with his father after learning that his father had tried to bribe Mattie into not marrying him. After Lance's death from a freak accident, Max returned to Mattie's life in an attempt to get acquainted with his granddaughter, Kyra. The truth is, however, that Max wants to gain custody of Kyra and take her away to California; he will do whatever it takes to accomplish that.

To help Mattie fight off Max's army of high-priced lawyers, Mike uses his own considerable resources to retain a lawyer for Mattie named John Storrow, a young New Yorker unafraid to take on someone of Max Devore's social stature. As Mike is drawn into Mattie's custody battle, he is also exposed to the ghosts that haunt the community. As Mike sleeps at night, he comes to realize that there are at least three separate spirits haunting his cabin. One, he is sure, is Jo, and one, he determines, is Sarah Tidwell. The third manifests itself only as a crying child, and Mike cannot tell whether it is Kyra or some other child. Mike and Kyra share a special psychic connection that allows them to share dreams and even to have the same ghosts haunting their homes—ghosts who communicate by rearranging magnetic letters on each of their refrigerator doors.

As Mike becomes further embroiled in the custody battle with Max Devore, his search to determine the truth about Jo's affair finally leads him to a set of journals Jo was keeping, notes from a research project that was her real reason for sneaking away to Sarah Laughs. Jo's notes explain how everyone related to the people who murdered Sarah Tidwell and her son have paid for this sin by losing a child of their own. Sarah Tidwell's ghost is exacting her revenge by murdering the children of those who murdered her own child. Mike, related to one of the people who murdered Sarah's child, has been drawn into this circle of retribution from the beginning, and the death of his unborn daughter, Kia, was not the accident it seemed to be. Mike also realizes that Kyra, the last descendant of this tragedy, is to be the final sacrifice used to put Sarah Tidwell to rest. Mike's return to the ironically named Sarah Laughs, it seems, has been a carefully orchestrated tragedy. Everything is tied to the ghost Sarah Tidwell's purposes, even Mike's writer's block. Mike's writing abilities return while he is at Sarah Laughs, but by the end of the novel he realizes this was simply to lead him to the information he needed to put Sarah's spirit to rest. Sarah's ghost may have destroyed his wife and child, but Jo's ghost gives him the means to save Kyra.

The usual King trademarks that fans have come to expect are present in *Bag of Bones*. The novel, moreover, shares much with the southern novel and its themes. Guilt is a predominant theme of many southern works, especially those of William Faulkner and Tennessee Williams. Racism, not a theme usually associated with northern writers, has been successfully transplanted by King via the traveling Sarah Tidwell. By the end of the novel, the evils of the community have become so entrenched in the soil (another similarity to Faulkner's fiction) that they begin to affect Mike himself, and he has to fight the urge to kill Kyra. Only by reburying the past—in this case, by literally reburying Sarah Tidwell's body—can matters finally be put to rest. Mike dissolves Sarah's body with lye, and her spirit finally leaves Sarah Laughs. Jo's spirit also leaves, and all is quiet once more at the cabin.

By the 1980's, King had become a mass-media guru who could open a television commercial for American Express with the rhetorical question "Do you know me?" At first prompted to examine the "wide perceptions which light [children's] interior lives" (*Four Past Midnight*) and then the cultural roots of the empire he had created, he proceeded to explore the phenomenon of fiction, the situations of reader and writer. In the 1990's, King continued to develop as a writer of both supernatural horror and mimetic character-based fiction. His novels after *Dolores Claiborne*—from *Insomnia* through *The Girl Who Loved Tom Gordon*—all provide supernatural chills while experimenting with character, mythology, and metafiction.

Financially invulnerable, King became almost playful with publishing gambits: *The Green Mile* was published as a serial in six slim paperbacks, in emulation of Charles Dickens and as a self-set challenge; Richard Bachman was revived when *The Regulators* was published in 1996. While he is still thought of as having no style, King actually maintained his compelling storyteller's voice (and ability to manipulate readers emotionally) while maturing in the depth and range of his themes and characters.

King, perhaps more than any other author since William Faulkner and his fictional

Yoknapatawpha County, also creates a sense of literary history within his later novels that ties them all together. In *Bag of Bones*, King references several of his other novels, most notably *The Dark Half*, *Needful Things*, and *Insomnia*. For longtime fans, this serves both to update King's readers concerning their favorite characters and to unify King's body of work. King's ironic sense of humor is also evident. When Mike's literary agent tells him of all the other best-selling novelists who have novels coming out in the fall of 1998, the most notable name missing from the list is that of Stephen King himself.

CELL

After *Bag of Bones*, much of King's work consisted of teleplays. However, in 2006, King produced *Cell*, a grim but subtly gleeful exercise in social criticism and homage to classic works of horror and science fiction. Upon its publication, King spoke openly about his having produced a work that would give his fans his spin on the American zombie film as initiated by director George A. Romero in *Night of the Living Dead* (1968) and its sequels. The plot of *Cell* neatly parallels the story lines of Romero's zombie movies and their numerous imitations: The earth is suddenly stricken by a mysterious plague that turns most of its inhabitants into mindless predatory monsters who prey on the few hapless humans who remain unaffected.

Just as Romero used the original *Night of the Living Dead* to examine Americans' fears in the 1960's during the Cold War and the Vietnam War and *Dawn of the Dead* (1978) to decry the rampant consumerism of the 1970's, so King develops *Cell* as a wry critique of early twenty-first century technomania and self-absorption. A glitch in the nation's mobile-phone system (perhaps a terrorist plot) short-circuits the brains of everyone talking on cell phones at the time. Labeled "the Pulse," this glitch removes people's individuality, higher levels of intelligence, and impulse control, triggering wave after wave of mindless violence. Those unaffected by the Pulse try to reach distant rural areas where cell phones would have been scarce. This is the essential social comment that runs throughout *Cell*: Cell-phone addicts are barbarians who are literal threats to society and a menace to those who do not share their obsession with constant phone chat.

To underscore this satiric element, King has his hero, Clay, minutes before the Pulse occurs, strolling down the streets of Boston reflecting to himself that he is witnessing people with cell phones performing inconsiderate, ungracious acts that would have been unimaginable only a few years earlier. Thus, even before disaster strikes, King depicts modern Americans as divided into "phone-crazies" and others; the Pulse only intensifies and highlights this division. In another allusion, this one to classic science fiction, King has the Pulse occur on October 1, thereby referencing English scientist Fred Hoyle's much-admired science-fiction novel *October the First Is Too Late* (1966), in which an anomaly in the space-time continuum separates humankind into opposing groups living in disparate eras of time and levels of civilization.

THE DARK TOWER

King's major accomplishment of the early twenty-first century was the completion of his novel cycle *The Dark Tower.* Inspired by Robert Browning's long poem "Childe Roland to the Dark Tower Came" (1855) and envisioned as an epic intermingling of the Western genre and fantasy, this septet began with *The Gunslinger* in 1982, with a new volume following approximately every five years until 2003, when King focused on the series' completion, revising *Gunslinger* that year and publishing the fifth installment. The final two volumes appeared the following year.

As with many such expansive series, there is much that is good in the *Dark Tower* cycle, but it is nevertheless a flawed work. Recounting the long journey of gunslinger/knight-errant Roland Deschain toward the Dark Tower, a pivot where thousands of parallel universes meet, the series draws on manifold sources: Western films, science fiction, classic fairy tales, L. Frank Baum, Greek mythology, Celtic and Eastern mysticism, Jungian psychology, Arthurian romance, and King's own hefty canon. When these strands mesh, the effect is dazzling, most especially in the fifth volume, *Wolves of the Calla*, a revisioning of the classic Japanese film *The Seven Samurai* (1954) and its American Western remake, *The Magnificent Seven* (1960). The plot is tight and engaging, taking as its motivation a primary theme of King's fiction: the vulnerability of children in a predatory cosmos. Furthermore, in "the Calla"—farmlands of a parallel United States—King engages in first-rate world making on the order of J. R. R. Tolkien and Frank Herbert, as he portrays in detail the dialects, religions, and folkways of the Calla's residents.

In the sixth and seventh novels, however, the series' central conceit—that our Earth is one of thousands of parallel worlds—begins to overwhelm even careful readers, as Roland and his companions pop in and out of numerous Earths so rapidly and frequently that narrative coherence is compromised. Furthermore, in these two novels, King's increasing references to his own canon begin to cloy when he interjects himself into the text, literally saving the day at one point through a deus ex machina—and cheekily using that term in addressing one of his protagonists. Many fans as well as critics also found King's long-awaited conclusion to Roland's quest unsatisfying. In truth, the implication at the end of *The Dark Tower* that Roland's quest has happened before and will happen again is in keeping with much of the Jungian and mystic underpinnings of the septet, implying as it does that archetypes such as the hero and the quest are eternal and recurrent.

A far more serious flaw in the ending of the series is not the fate of Roland but that of Susannah, the only other surviving member of his "ka-tet," or band of fellow fighters. As they near the Dark Tower, Roland and Susannah stumble upon and rescue a child artist who has the ability to make real whatever he draws. He sketches a portal to another world for Susannah to slip through to a parallel New York City, in which she is united with analogues of her slain friends. The suddenness of this magic boy's appearance and of Susannah's subsequent exit seems jarring and false: Why should she abandon Roland just as they approach the Dark Tower? Does King really think that her joining a posse of parallel-world clones of her dead comrades constitutes a "happy ending," as King's disclaimer in the text at this point indicates?

King clearly learned from whatever mistakes he made in the long narration of Roland's journey, as his subsequent work of horror/fantasy fiction, *Lisey's Story*, a masterwork that drew raves from reviewers, deals with the same themes—the binding power of love and the damage wrought by child abuse—employing the same tropes: the quest motif, the concept of parallel realities, and metafictional conceits. *Lisey's Story*, however, although a long work, addresses King's recurring themes within the framework of a taut plot and with always believable character motivation.

Linda C. Badley; Bernadette Lynn Bosky
Updated by Thomas Du Bose

OTHER MAJOR WORKS

SHORT FICTION: *Night Shift*, 1978; *Different Seasons*, 1982; *Skeleton Crew*, 1985; *Dark Visions*, 1988 (with Dan Simmons and George R. R. Martin); *Four Past Midnight*, 1990; *Nightmares and Dreamscapes*, 1993; *Hearts in Atlantis*, 1999; *Everything's Eventual: Fourteen Dark Tales*, 2002.

SCREENPLAYS: *Creepshow*, 1982 (adaptation of his book; with George Romero); *Cat's Eye*, 1984; *Silver Bullet*, 1985 (adaptation of *Cycle of the Werewolf*); *Maximum Overdrive*, 1986 (adaptation of his short story "Trucks"); *Pet Sematary*, 1989; *Sleep Walkers*, 1992.

TELEPLAYS: *The Stand*, 1994 (based on his novel); *Storm of the Century*, 1999; *Rose Red*, 2002.

NONFICTION: *Danse Macabre*, 1981; *Black Magic and Music: A Novelist's Perspective on Bangor*, 1983; *Bare Bones: Conversations on Terror with Stephen King*, 1988 (Tim Underwood and Chuck Miller, editors); *On Writing: A Memoir of the Craft*, 2000; *Faithful: Two Diehard Red Sox Fans Chronicle the 2004 Season*, 2004 (with Stewart O'Nan).

CHILDREN'S LITERATURE: *The Girl Who Loved Tom Gordon: A Pop-up Book*, 2004 (text adaptation by Peter Abrahams, illustrated by Alan Dingman).

EDITED TEXT: *The Best American Short Stories 2007*, 2007.

MISCELLANEOUS: *Nightmares in the Sky*, 1988.

BIBLIOGRAPHY

Bloom, Harold, ed. *Stephen King: Modern Critical Views*. Philadelphia: Chelsea House, 1998. One of the best single collections of essays about King's fiction, many reprinted from other sources. Offers high-quality critical examination of King's works through *Needful Things*, covering a range of topics and themes. Supplemented with chronology, bibliography, and index.

Collings, Michael R. *Scaring Us to Death: The Impact of Stephen King on Popular Culture*. 2d rev. ed. San Bernardino, Calif.: Borgo Press, 1997. Examines King's influence on the rise of horror fiction in the United States and the effects of such fiction on society. Includes bibliography and index.

_______. *The Work of Stephen King: An Annotated Bibliography and Guide*. San Bernardino, Calif.: Borgo Press, 1996. Provides both a good chronology and useful descriptions of some of King's hard-to-find works as well as a copious annotated list of secondary sources.

Hohne, Karen A. "The Power of the Spoken Word in the Works of Stephen King." *Journal of Popular Culture* 28 (Fall, 1994): 93-103. Discusses the tension in King's work between slang speech, which codifies a knowledge rejected by those in power, and monologic orality, which embodies that power. Argues that King's fiction illustrates the tension between official and unofficial languages and ideologies that exists not only in literature but also throughout society.

Magistrale, Tony. *Stephen King: The Second Decade, "Danse Macabre" to "The Dark Half."* New York: Twayne, 1992. Discusses King's work in the 1980's, including his nonfictional analysis of the horror genre in *Danse Macabre*, his Richard Bachman books, *Misery*, and the novellas of the Dark Tower saga. Features a 1989 interview in which King discusses fairy-tale references in his work as well as his treatment of sexuality, masculinity, and race.

_______, ed. *The Dark Descent: Essays Defining Stephen King's Horrorscape*. Westport, Conn.: Greenwood Press, 1992. Collection of scholarly interpretive essays covers subjects such as homophobia, treatment of female characters, and dialogic narratives in King's novels and short fiction. Includes bibliography and index.

Reino, Joseph. *Stephen King: The First Decade*. Boston: Twayne, 1988. Book-by-book analysis, from *Carrie* to *Pet Sematary*, attempts to show King's literary merits, stressing subtle characterization and nuances of symbolism and allusion. Supplemented by chronology and primary and secondary bibliographies.

Russell, Sharon A. *Revisiting Stephen King: A Critical Companion*. Westport, Conn.: Greenwood Press, 2002. Provides biographical information and a discussion of the horror genre before analyzing King's novels from 1996 through 2001. Includes bibliography and index.

Spignesi, Stephen J. *The Essential Stephen King: A Ranking of the Greatest Novels, Short Stories, Movies, and Other Creations of the World's Most Popular Writer*. Franklin Lakes, N.J.: New Page Books, 2001. Detailed volume by a King enthusiast combines serious critical examination of the author's works with the readable commentary of an unabashed fan. Includes discussion of many of King's novels.

Wiater, Stanley, Christopher Golden, and Hank Wagner. *The Complete Stephen King Universe: A Guide to the Worlds of Stephen King*. Rev. ed. New York: St. Martin's Press, 2006. Comprehensive reference volume explores every aspect of King's work, including the common themes, places, and characters that run through his fiction. Features biographical chronology, bibliography, informative appendixes, and index.

Winter, Douglas E. *The Art of Darkness: The Life and Fiction of the Master of the Macabre, Stephen King*. Rev. ed. New York: New American Library, 1989. Provides a perceptive critical overview of King's work, with long articles on each novel up to *The Talisman*. Includes a short biography of King and extensive bibliographies of King's work and of books and articles written about him.

C. S. LEWIS

Born: Belfast, Ireland (now in Northern Ireland); November 29, 1898
Died: Oxford, England; November 22, 1963
Also known as: Clive Staples Lewis; N. W. Clerk; Clive Hamilton; Jack Lewis

PRINCIPAL LONG FICTION

Out of the Silent Planet, 1938 (with *Perelandra* and *That Hideous Strength*, known as the Space Trilogy)
The Screwtape Letters, 1942
Perelandra, 1943
That Hideous Strength: A Modern Fairy Tale for Grownups, 1945
The Lion, the Witch, and the Wardrobe, 1950
Prince Caspian, 1951
The Voyage of the Dawn Treader, 1952
The Silver Chair, 1953
The Horse and His Boy, 1954
The Magician's Nephew, 1955
The Last Battle, 1956
The Chronicles of Narnia, 1950-1956 (collective title for previous 7 novels)
Till We Have Faces: A Myth Retold, 1956

OTHER LITERARY FORMS

Although his novels for adults and children continue to be widely read and admired, C. S. Lewis is also well known as a religious essayist and literary scholar-critic. His religious writings of three decades include autobiography (*The Pilgrim's Regress*, 1933; *Surprised by Joy: The Shape of My Early Life*, 1955; *A Grief Observed*, 1961) and essays in varying lengths and forms. Some of his essays include *The Personal Heresy* (1939; with E. M. W. Tillyard), *Rehabilitations* (1939), *The Problem of Pain* (1940), *The Abolition of Man* (1943), *Miracles: A Preliminary Study* (1947), *Mere Christianity* (1952), *Reflections on the Psalms* (1958), and *The Four Loves* (1960). His works of a religious nature that were published after Lewis's death include *Letters to Malcolm: Chiefly on Prayer* (1964), *Letters to an American Lady* (1967), *God in the Dock* (1970), and *The Joyful Christian: 127 Readings from C. S. Lewis* (1977).

Lewis's criticism, focused primarily on medieval and Renaissance studies, includes *The Allegory of Love* (1936), *A Preface to "Paradise Lost"* (1942), *English Literature in the Sixteenth Century, Excluding Drama* (1954), *Studies in Words* (1960), *An Experiment in Criticism* (1961), and *The Discarded Image* (1964). Several volumes of criticism appeared posthumously, including *Spenser's Images of Life* (1967), *Selected Literary Essays* (1969), and *Present Concerns* (1986).

Less widely known are Lewis's early volumes of poetry, *Spirits in Bondage* (1919), a collection of lyrics; and *Dymer* (1926), a narrative. The posthumous *The Dark Tower, and Other Stories* (1977) includes an unpublished fragment of a novel. This collection and one other, *Of Other Worlds: Essays and Stories* (1966), contain the only extant fictional pieces not printed during Lewis's lifetime. The Wade Collection at Wheaton College (Illinois) and the Bodleian Library, Oxford, hold many volumes of Lewis papers, including eleven volumes of Lewis family letters written from 1850 to 1930.

ACHIEVEMENTS

C. S. Lewis's achievements as a novelist are hard to separate from his role as a Christian apologist and from his impeccable literary scholarship. Many of Lewis's readers believe that his greatness lies in the unusually wide scope of his work: He wrote so much so well in so many forms. His *Mere Christianity*, for example, is a superb primer on Christian ideas, and *The Four Loves* and *A Grief Observed* are powerful explorations of the endurance of love despite doubt and deep pain. *The Screwtape Letters*, Lewis's most popular book in the United States, continues to enthrall new readers with its witty yet serious study of the war between good and evil in the modern world. Among his critical writings, *The Allegory of Love* remains a classic study of medieval literature and society, while *The Discarded Image* is one of the very best discussions of the contrast between the medieval worldview and the modern mind.

The popularity of Lewis's novels for adults (*Out of the Silent Planet, Perelandra*, and *That Hideous Strength*—known as the Space Trilogy—and *Till We Have Faces*) owes more perhaps to their treatment of themes also developed in his nonfiction than to their literary excellence, although the Space Trilogy is widely read among devotees of fantasy and science fiction who have little acquaintance with Lewis's other works. The extraordinary appeal of Lewis's fiction for children, the Narnia books, is undisputed. Each year, these seven novels gain thousands of new readers of all ages and are, for many, the introduction to Lewis that inspires them to delve into his other works. Indeed, had Lewis never published another word, the Narnia books would have ensured his reputation with both critics and the public.

BIOGRAPHY

Born in Belfast in 1898, the son of Albert Lewis, a successful lawyer, and Flora Hamilton Lewis, a writer and mathematician, Clive Staples Lewis spent his early childhood in an atmosphere of learning and imagination. His mother tutored him in French and Latin before he was seven; his nurse, Lizzie Endicott, taught him the folktales of Ireland. Clive and his brother, Warren, devoted long, often rainy afternoons to exploring the book-lined corridors of Little Lea, their home. As small children, the brothers invented their own country, Boxen, for which they wrote a four-hundred-year chronicle and which they peopled with animal characters who became subjects of individual stories. These early-childhood adventures were of incalculable influence on Lewis's long fiction, written almost half a century later.

With his mother's death from cancer in 1908, Lewis's life changed drastically and irrevocably. A disconsolate, bewildered Albert Lewis sent his sons to boarding school in England, the first of several cruel experiences before age sixteen that nurtured in Lewis a hatred for public school education. At last persuading his father to place him with the demanding but kind tutor W. T. Kirkpatrick in 1914, Lewis developed his great scholarly talents and won a scholarship to University College, Oxford, two years later. Before taking his entrance exams, however, Lewis was recruited into the army and served as a second lieutenant on the front lines in France during World War I.

Surviving a wound and the mental shocks of war, Lewis happily entered Oxford life in 1919, his education financed by his father—whose support in other ways would always be lacking. Perhaps to compensate for this lack of parental affection, Lewis developed a steadfast friendship with a Mrs. Moore, the mother of a friend who had died fighting in France. With Mrs. Moore and her young daughter, Maureen, Lewis set up housekeeping, this arrangement continuing thirty years, until Mrs. Moore's death in 1951. Lewis's tenure at Oxford, as student, tutor, and fellow of Magdalen College, lasted even longer, ending in 1954 with his acceptance of the chair of Medieval and Renaissance Literature at Magdalene College, Cambridge. During the Oxford years, he wrote and published most of his fifty-eight books of adult and children's fiction, literary criticism, essays, Christian apologetics, and poetry. It was there also that Lewis, influenced by such close friends as J. R. R. Tolkien, underwent his conversion to Christianity.

Lewis's Christian fervor led to widely read publications and to a long series of radio talks before and during World War II. His faith also inspired fictional works, including his Space Trilogy, written during the war, and his Narnia books for children. Many of his Oxford colleagues, however, were offended by his overt religiousness—and his popularity. Through these years, they thus denied Lewis the Magdalen professorship that his eminence as a literary scholar warranted.

With his rise to a more esteemed position in the more congenial atmosphere of Cambridge, Lewis completed, among other projects, the books of Narnia, the first of which had been published in 1950, and wrote perhaps his finest novel, *Till We Have Faces*. This last work of fiction was dedicated to Joy Davidman Gresham, an American admirer with whom he had corresponded for several years and who came to England to join him in 1955. They were married in 1956, and, according to Lewis, "feasted on love" for the four years they shared before Joy's death from bone cancer in 1960. Despite his own worsening health, Lewis continued to produce autobiographical and critical works until suffering a heart attack in 1963. He died on November 22, the date of President John F. Kennedy's assassination and of the death of writer Aldous Huxley.

ANALYSIS

The happy fact of C. S. Lewis's creation of long fictional works is that the more of them he wrote, the better he became as a novelist. This is not to say that with each book from *Out of the Silent Planet* to *Till We Have Faces* he measurably improved, but from the early Space Trilogy (1938-1945) through the Narnia tales (1950-1956) to his last novel, there is a clear change in Lewis's conception of fiction. In the early books, characters exemplify definite sides in an ethical debate, and plot is the working out of victory for Lewis's side. In the later books, however, character becomes the battleground of ambiguous values, and plot takes place more and more within the minds of the characters.

THE SPACE TRILOGY

The hero of the Space Trilogy, Cambridge don Elwin Ransom, is often less the protagonist of novels than an embodiment of the Christian and intellectual virtues that Lewis recommended in his essays. Throughout the trilogy, Ransom represents Lewis's ideal of the relentless intellectual, his learning solidly founded on respect for great ideas from earlier ages, who valiantly maintains his integrity despite the powerful temptations posed by modern materialism. In both *Out of the Silent Planet* and *Perelandra*—Ransom's journeys to Mars (Malacandra) and Venus (Perelandra), respectively—Ransom's adversary is as clearly villainous as Ransom himself is heroic. The antagonist is Edward Weston, a brilliant physicist, who represents for Lewis that most insidious modern outgrowth of Renaissance humanism: the belief that the highest goal of humankind is to establish dominance over all forms of life in as many worlds as humans can conquer. This view, which Lewis saw as the root of the boundless ambition of political leaders Adolf Hitler, Joseph Stalin, and Benito Mussolini, is exemplified in Weston's misuse of technology to build a spacecraft that enables him to reach other planets so that he might make them colonies of Earth.

By moving the scene of this attempt away from Earth, Lewis can manipulate material reality so that the limitations of Weston's philosophy become obvious and his actions ludicrous. Assuming the innate superiority of man over all other forms, and thus a perpetual state of war between man and nature, Weston fails to see the simplest, most significant facts of the new worlds he intends to conquer. As Ransom, the Christian student of myths and languages, easily perceives, the forces that rule Mars and Venus are both fully hospitable to humankind and infinitely more powerful. Thus, Weston shoots gentle creatures because they appear strange and, in a parody of the European explorers, tries to bribe with shiny trinkets the Oyarsa of Malacandra, who, as Ransom learns, is second only in power and wisdom to Maleldil, ruler of the universe. In contrast to Weston, Ransom—a far truer scientist than his opponent—befriends and learns the language of these extraterrestrials; hence, mysteries are opened to him. In *Out of the Silent Planet*, he learns that only Earth (Thulcandra), long under the dominance of the "bent eldil," is deprived of clear knowledge of the Oyarsa and Maleldil; Thulcandrans believe themselves enlightened above all others, when in reality they are the most benighted. He learns also that the universe is in a state of becoming: that the creatures of old worlds, such as Malacandra, can no longer be endangered by such forces as those that guide Weston, but that newer worlds, such as Thulcandra, are still theaters of contending principles, while the youngest worlds, such as Perelandra, have yet to achieve spiritual identity.

This is vital knowledge for Ransom, who realizes, in the second book, that he has been given wisdom because he has also been given the responsibility of helping to bring about Maleldil's reign on Perelandra, which places him in open confrontation with Weston, now clearly the mere instrument of the bent eldil. In a probing recapitulation of the temptation of Eve, Lewis has Ransom and Weston contend, somewhat in the mode of the medieval *psychomachia*, for the mind of Tinidril, the first woman of Perelandra. As the confoundingly subtle arguments of the Unman (the spirit that controls Weston) begin to conquer Tinidril, Ransom at last understands that he must physically fight, to the death, his adversary. Despite his slim chance of survival, Ransom attacks the Unman; he ultimately defeats him, though suffering wounds, incredible fatigue, and near despair. It is an epic battle, reminiscent of the Pearl-Poet's fourteenth century manuscript *Sir Gawain and the Green Knight* and Edmund Spenser's *The Faerie Queene* (1590, 1596); Ransom's faith and courage in the fight prepare the reader for his apotheosis in the final chapters, wherein Lewis's paradisiacally lush description of Perelandra takes on an almost beatific vividness and illumination.

In novelistic terms, *Perelandra* surpasses *Out of the Silent Planet* in its attention to the development of Ransom's awareness of his role and his struggle to maintain his integrity in the face of fears and misleading appearances. Nevertheless, its extraterrestrial setting and its clearly demarcated hero and villain make *Perelandra* more an epic romance than a novel. This is not to prefer one book to the other, but it is to distinguish them both from the third part of the trilogy, *That Hideous Strength*, which may be Lewis's most interesting fiction, although not his most consistent. *That Hideous Strength* tries to harmonize heterogeneous elements of romance, epic, and novel. Following the novelist's impulse, Lewis brings his setting back to Earth and localizes it in the sort of place he knew best, a venerable English college town, which he calls Edgestow. He also centers the reader's interest on two authentic protagonists, Jane and Mark Studdock, whose story is their painful, humiliating, sometimes dangerous progress toward faith and self-awareness. They act bravely in the ultimate crisis, both risking torture and death, but they engage in nothing like the epic struggle of Ransom and the Unman.

Still, the events in which they engage are of epic magnitude, and in this thrust of the book Lewis returns to familiar fictional territory. The plot concerns a powerful conspiracy to turn Britain into a totalitarian state. This conspiracy is opposed most strenuously by a small underground directed by Elwin Ransom, now a heroic, almost godlike leader, whose powers are spiritual rather than physical. His main adversaries are men who, like Weston, call themselves scientists, but whose distinguishing traits are lust for power, deviousness, and cruelty. Having established a research institute called the National Institute of Co-ordinated Experiments (N.I.C.E.), these men use the press, political infiltrators, and their own "police" to avoid, placate, or squash opposition to their Nazi-like program of "social planning." Mark Studdock is one of the bright but indecisive minds easily co-opted by the N.I.C.E. Lewis shows convincingly how the leaders play on his ego and his fears of rejection in order to exploit his talent as a journalist. Conversely, Jane Studdock falls in with the resistance group; she weighs its values against those of her husband and gradually comes to see that whichever road she chooses will mean great danger for both of them. She chooses the resistance.

Had Lewis limited the book to the clash between political philosophies and its impact on two ordinary people, he would have had a conventional novel, but he wanted to portray this clash as occurring on a cosmic level, as a war between pure good and pure evil. Since the combatants in this novel are the human representatives of these supernatural forces, the reader necessarily finds himself once more in the realm of romance. Aware of his mixing of genres in *That Hideous Strength*, Lewis called the amalgam a fairy tale, arguing that his work fell into that long tradition in which supernatural events subsume the ordinary activities of realistic characters. What fairy tale means here is that when the N.I.C.E. performs such blatant works as the turning of rivers from their courses, the trapping of huge numbers of animals for vivisection, and the deforestation of ancient preserves, they call down on themselves the wrath of nature, personified in a resurrected Merlin, who pledges allegiance to Ransom as the spiritual successor of Arthur. His obedience allows Ransom to reinvest him with eldilic power, which enables him single-handedly to destroy the N.I.C.E. Add to the appearance of Merlin such important romantic elements as Jane Studdock's clairvoyance and the veneration of a talking head by the N.I.C.E., and *That Hideous Strength* seems almost more romance than novel.

The book should be judged as a fairy tale. Lewis warns the reader in his preface not to be deceived by the "hum-drum scenes and persons" into thinking this a realistic fiction. He merely intends the familiar names and places to heighten the reader's appreciation of the importance of the spiritual battles occurring around and within each individual. Indeed, one explicit purpose of the book is to warn England—here Lewis was prophetic—that radical social evil would not be eradicated with Hitler's defeat. The formal problem, however, is that a bit of realism begets the expectation of total realism, and so readers accustomed to novels will naturally look askance at Merlin's return and the survival of the severed head, while they will accept the generic consistency of the floating islands in *Perelandra*. Even if Lewis had deleted these effects from the third book, however, he would have had to substitute other supernatural manifestations in order to be consistent not only with the pattern of the first two books but also, and more important, with his religious conviction of the immanence of the supernatural in everyday life. Viewing the book as a fairy tale, Lewis felt, would allow the reader sufficient suspension of disbelief to become involved with the characters. Nevertheless, the reader would still face, as in all of

Lewis's other works, the challenge of accepting or rejecting Lewis's position on God, nature, and humanity.

THE CHRONICLES OF NARNIA

Lewis actually began the first book of the Narnia series, *The Lion, the Witch, and the Wardrobe*, in 1939, when four children, inspiration for the Pevensie children in the stories, were evacuated to his home at the start of the war. Returning ten years and many books later to the idea of writing for children, Lewis found the fictional form perhaps best suited to his genius. These tales of ordinary boys and girls transported to another world allowed Lewis to relive in some sense the childhood idyll at Little Lea that had been cut short by his mother's death; moreover, they let him put directly into prose the fantastic images—fauns, castles, golden lions—that came to him, without his having to adapt them, as he had in the Space Trilogy, to the narrower tastes of adult readers. The fairy-tale form restricted him to simpler vocabulary and syntax, as well as to a more exclusively narrative and descriptive mode, but these restrictions freed him to do what he did best in fiction: dialogue, action narrative, and vivid description of select detail. More than anything else, however, the form let him depict given characters as essentially good or evil, though careful readers will observe that these qualities are consistently dramatized in action, not merely posited by authorial fiat. One of the many virtues of these stories is that appearance never defines character; the reader likes or dislikes persons or animals in these books only when he has come to know them.

The seven books traverse some sixty years of English time, roughly between 1895 and 1955, and more than one thousand years of time in Narnia, a land that is the home of Aslan, the Golden Lion, as well as talking animals, dwarves, fauns, satyrs, witches, men and women, boys and girls. The chronicle begins with *The Magician's Nephew* (the sequence of publication differs from the internal chronology of the series), in which young Digory Kirke and Polly Plummer magically enter Narnia at the time of its creation by Aslan. Unfortunately, the curious Digory inadvertently breaks the spell that has bound Jadis, the White Witch, who becomes the main enemy of the Narnians.

In *The Lion, the Witch, and the Wardrobe*, almost fifty English years have passed, but an untold number in Narnia. The visitors are now the four Pevensie children, who enter Narnia through a magical wardrobe in the spacious country home of an old friend of their parents—Professor Digory Kirke. They find a cold world in terror of the Witch. The children eventually join those who are still rebelling against her, and their faith is rewarded when Aslan returns. His conquest is not complete, however, until he has been ritually murdered by the Witch, only to be reborn in far greater splendor. The four children are crowned kings and queens of Narnia.

The Horse and His Boy occurs during the reign of Peter Pevensie as High King of Narnia. It concerns Shasta, a boy of neighboring Calormen, who through various adventures is revealed to be the true prince of Archenland, another Narnian neighbor. The fourth part of the chronicle, *Prince Caspian*, takes place a thousand years forward in Narnian time, but only two or three years after the adventure through the wardrobe. The four children are transported to Narnia from a railway bench, only to find all record of their reign obliterated by time and by the purposeful lies told by invaders. The children's arrival, however, coincides with another coming of Aslan, who, aided by an alliance of all the creatures of Narnia, restores to the throne the true heir, Caspian. He is still king of Narnia when the fifth adventure, *The Voyage of the Dawn Treader*, occurs. This time, the two younger Pevensies, Edmund and Lucy, accompanied by a recalcitrant friend, Eustace Scrubb, reenter Narnia to help Caspian sail the farthest seas to find seven Narnian lords banished by the invaders. On their voyage, they discover lands beyond imagining, including Aslan's country itself. The sixth chronicle, *The Silver Chair*, is another story of a search, this time by Eustace and a friend, Jill Pole, who are called to Narnia to find the dying Caspian's long-lost son, Rilian. Despite many deceptions and dangers, the children eventually discover the prince, by then the rightful king of Narnia.

The chronicles end with *The Last Battle*, the apocalypse of Narnia. King Tirian, Rilian's descendant, is joined by Eustace and Jill in a final battle to save Narnia from invading hordes of hostile neighbors. As they go to certain death, they are suddenly greeted by Aslan, who ushers them into the real Narnia, of which the mere parody is now disappearing as quickly as it had been born centuries before. There they are joined by all the friends of Narnia, including three of the four Pevensies, who, with their parents, have come to the real Narnia thanks to a railway accident in "their" world. Aslan tells them that this Narnia is forever, and that they need never leave: "The term is over; the holidays have begun. The dream is ended; this is the morning."

TILL WE HAVE FACES

Almost nothing of the style of the Space Trilogy is recognizable in *Till We Have Faces*, Lewis's first novel for adults after 1945, and the last of his career. Though Lewis here was reworking an ancient myth, that of Cupid and Psyche, this book can be unambiguously called a novel, in the full modern sense of that word. It begins and ends in the spiritual turmoil of the mind of the narrator, Orual, Queen of Glome, a tiny state somewhere north of Greece, sometime in the centuries just preceding the birth of Christ. The novel is the story of her life, told in two parts. The first, much the longer, is Orual's complaint against the gods for their hatred of humankind, hatred shown most obviously in their failure ever to make themselves clearly known. The second part, a few brief chapters hastily penned by the dying queen and ended in midsentence by her death, repents for the slanders of part 1 and tells of a few pivotal encounters and an extraordinary dream that have resolved her anger.

Part 1 recalls a lifelong source of her rage, her ugliness, which has made Orual hated by her father, the king, and shunned by most others. A far greater injury, however, is the sacrifice of her wonderfully beautiful sister, Psyche, whom the head priest of Glome offers to the god of the Grey Mountain in the hope of ending a drought. Orual cannot forgive the gods for taking the only joy of her life. What irritates her most, however, is her discovery that Psyche has not been devoured by the god of the mountain, as most people believe, but that he has wedded her. Moreover, Psyche is happy. Convincing herself that her sister's happiness can only be a fatal delusion, Orual persuades Psyche, with a threat of suicide, to disobey her lord's one command: that she never look at him. The result is that Psyche is banished and forced to undergo ordeals. Orual is also punished: The god tells her, cryptically, "You also will be Psyche." Never fully comprehending this sentence, and enraged by the ambiguity of the portent, Orual passes the years, eventually succeeding her father and distracting her thoughts by careful attention to government of her people. Orual becomes a wise and masterful ruler, but her mind remains troubled. When, by chance, she discovers that the story of Psyche has given rise to a cult of worshipers, she decides finally to spill her anger and doubt onto paper. The story the sect tells is false, she feels: In it, Psyche's sister is accused of deliberately plotting her fall. She feels that she must write to clear the record, to exonerate herself.

In part 2, she repents. She admits that the very writing of part 1 has brought back disquieting memories: Perhaps she had been jealous of Psyche. Her self-awareness grows when two meetings with longtime observers of her life convince her that her perspective on people and events has always been narrow and selfish. Finally, two terrible dreams—visions, she realizes—bring her crime before her eyes; she understands the sentence of the god. She has indeed been Psyche, in that while her sister has performed the ordeals assigned her, Orual, in her years of suffering, has borne all the anguish of them. Thus, she has both committed the crime and expiated the guilt. Her confession in part 2 gives way to thanksgiving, as she discovers that, washed clear of her guilt, she is as beautiful as the sister whom she is at last free to love.

Critics have likened the richness of Orual's character to the increasing depth of compassion in Lewis's essays of these later years. The striking resonance of these works has been attributed, at least in part, to the influence on Lewis's life at this time of Joy Davidman, to whom he dedicated *Till We Have Faces*. That Lewis's renunciation of bachelorhood late in his life signaled an opening of himself, and his prose, to emotions and ways of seeing that he had not before allowed himself seems plausible; nevertheless, the simple design and straightforward nature of this last novel can as easily be explained as further developments of Lewis's style in the direction taken by the Narnia books. Perhaps the exploration of his own childhood necessitated by writing these books taught him lessons about his writing as profound as those Orual learned in trying to recapture her past. Perhaps he learned that he was truly happy as a writer when he could explore the curious corridors of his personality, just as he had loved to explore the rooms and passages of his boyhood home. It is surely no coincidence that the first part of his autobiography, *Surprised by Joy*, was published in 1955, while he was at work not only on *Till We Have Faces* but also on *The Last Battle*. All three books reveal an exquisite sensitivity that can be attributed to Lewis's deep introspection at this time. This sensitivity, this honesty, makes these books far more memorable in themselves than his more clever experiments in less traditional forms.

Christopher J. Thaiss

OTHER MAJOR WORKS

SHORT FICTION: *The Dark Tower, and Other Stories*, 1977.

POETRY: *Spirits in Bondage*, 1919; *Dymer*, 1926; *Poems*, 1964; *Narrative Poems*, 1969.

NONFICTION: *The Pilgrim's Regress*, 1933; *The Allegory of Love*, 1936; *The Personal Heresy*, 1939 (with E. M. W. Tillyard); *Rehabilitations*, 1939; *The Problem of Pain*, 1940; *Broadcast Talks*, 1942; *Hamlet: The Prince or the Poem*, 1942; *A Preface to "Paradise Lost,"* 1942; *The Abolition of Man*, 1943; *Christian Behaviour*, 1943; *Beyond Personality*, 1944; *The Great Divorce*, 1945; *Miracles: A Preliminary Study*, 1947; *Arthurian Torso*, 1948; *The Weight of Glory, and Other Addresses*, 1949; *Mere Christianity*, 1952; *English Literature in the Sixteenth Century, Excluding Drama*, 1954; *Surprised by Joy: The Shape of My Early Life*, 1955; *Reflections on the Psalms*, 1958; *The Four Loves*, 1960; *Studies in Words*, 1960; *The World's Last Night, and Other Essays*, 1960; *An Experiment in Criticism*, 1961; *A Grief Observed*, 1961; *The Discarded Image*, 1964; *Letters to Malcolm: Chiefly on Prayer*, 1964; *Letters of C. S. Lewis*, 1966; *Studies in Medieval and Renaissance Literature*, 1966; *Christian Reflections*, 1967; *Letters to an American Lady*, 1967; *Spenser's Images of Life*, 1967; *Selected Literary Essays*, 1969; *God in the Dock*, 1970; *The Joyful Christian: 127 Readings from C. S. Lewis*, 1977; *They Stand Together: The Letters of C. S. Lewis to Arthur Greeves, 1914-1963*, 1979; *On Stories, and Other Essays on Literature*, 1982; *C. S. Lewis: Letters to Children*, 1985; *Present Concerns*, 1986; *Letters: C. S. Lewis and Don Giovanni Calabria, a Study in Friendship*, 1988; *Collected Letters*, 2000-2006; *From Narnia to a Space Odyssey: The War of Ideas Between Arthur C. Clarke and C. S. Lewis*, 2003 (Ryder W. Miller, editor).

MISCELLANEOUS: *Of Other Worlds: Essays and Stories*, 1966; *The Business of Heaven*, 1984; *Boxen: The Imaginary World of the Young C. S. Lewis*, 1985; *A Year with C. S. Lewis: Daily Readings from His Classic Works*, 2003.

BIBLIOGRAPHY

Carpenter, Humphrey. *The Inklings: C. S. Lewis, J. R. R. Tolkien, Charles Williams, and Their Friends*. Boston: Houghton Mifflin, 1979. Major study of the lives and works of the Inklings, a name first applied by Lewis, perhaps as early as 1933, to a group of literary friends who met regularly together at Oxford University.

Downing, David C. *Planets in Peril: A Critical Study of C. S. Lewis's Ransom Trilogy*. Amherst: University of Massachusetts Press, 1992. Begins with an introduction that provides a concise, insightful view of Lewis's varied career as literary critic, novelist, philosopher, and theologian. The first chapter shows how his early life influenced the writing of his trilogy, and subsequent chapters explore his Christian vision, his use of classicism and medievalism, his portraits of evil, his treatment of the spiritual pilgrimage, and the overall achievement of the trilogy.

Edwards, Bruce L. *C. S. Lewis: Life, Works, and Legacy.* 4 vols. Westport, Conn.: Praeger, 2007. Comprehensive study aims to provide a more wide-ranging view of Lewis's life and work than had previously been available. Essays in volume 1 focus on Lewis's life, and volumes 2 through 4 discuss Lewis as a "fantasist, mythmaker, and poet," "apologist, philosopher, and theologian," and "scholar, teacher, and public intellectual."

Hooper, Walter. *C. S. Lewis: Companion and Guide.* New York: HarperCollins, 1996. Extremely useful volume contains a biography, a chronology of Lewis's life, summaries of his major works, samples of reviews of his works, explanations of key ideas, and an exhaustive bibliography of Lewis's works.

Lindskoog, Kathryn. *C. S. Lewis: Mere Christian.* 4th ed. Chicago: Cornerstone Press Chicago, 1997. Excellent single-volume work on the life and career of Lewis offers a broad overview as well as provocative evaluation of each of the author's works.

Manlove, C. N. *C. S. Lewis: His Literary Achievement.* New York: St. Martin's Press, 1987. Examination of Lewis's major works of fiction is easily accessible in its consideration of narrative, structure, and themes. Includes an analysis of each of the Narnia books,

Myers, Doris T. *C. S. Lewis in Context.* Kent, Ohio: Kent State University Press, 1994. Readable study views Lewis less as an isolated figure and more as a writer who was reflective of his times. Includes a useful bibliography.

Smith, Robert Houston. *Patches of Godlight: The Pattern of Thought of C. S. Lewis.* Athens: University of Georgia Press, 1981. Offers scholarly but accessible analysis of Lewis's philosophy of religion. Links what is dubbed Lewis's Christian "Objectivism" to the profound influence of Platonism on his views of the nature of humanity and of God. Sympathetic treatment nevertheless finds Lewis to have been flawed as a philosopher, a rational mystic torn between a romantic vision of the absolute and the boundaries of a reasoned faith.

Ward, Michael. *Planet Narnia: The Seven Heavens in the Imagination of C. S. Lewis.* New York: Oxford University Press, 2008. New interpretation of the Narnia novels describes how medieval cosmology offers a key to the seven books, with each book expressing characteristics of the seven medieval planets.

Wilson, A. N. *C. S. Lewis: A Biography.* 1989. Reprint. New York: W. W. Norton, 2002. Iconoclastic biography presents an important interpretation of Lewis and his work from a Freudian perspective. Paints Lewis as neither a saint nor a full-time Christian apologist but as a man of real passions and a contradictory nature unbefitting the cult following that developed after his death. Traces many of Lewis's adult preoccupations to the sometimes traumatic experiences of his early childhood and comes to some controversial conclusions regarding several of Lewis's relationships.

HARUKI MURAKAMI

Born: Kyoto, Japan; January 12, 1949

PRINCIPAL LONG FICTION

Kaze no uta o kike, 1979 (*Hear the Wind Sing*, 1987)
1973: Nen no pinboru, 1980 (*Pinball, 1973*, 1985)
Hitsuji o meguru boken, 1982 (*A Wild Sheep Chase*, 1989)
Sekai no owari to hadoboirudo wandarando, 1985 (*Hard-Boiled Wonderland and the End of the World*, 1991)
Noruwei no mori, 1987 (*Norwegian Wood*, 2000)
Dansu dansu dansu, 1988 (*Dance, Dance, Dance*, 1993)
Kokkyo no minami, taiyo no nishi, 1992 (*South of the Border, West of the Sun*, 1999)
Nejimaki-dori kuronikuru, 1994-1995 (3 volumes; *The Wind-Up Bird Chronicle*, 1997)
Suputoniku no koibito, 1999 (*Sputnik Sweetheart*, 2001)
Umibe no Kafuka, 2002 (*Kafka on the Shore*, 2005)
Afutadaku, 2004 (*After Dark*, 2007)

OTHER LITERARY FORMS

Haruki Murakami (myur-ah-kah-mee) is also an accomplished writer of short fiction, and English translations of his many stories are collected in *The Elephant Vanishes* (1993), *Kami no kodomotachi wa mina odoru* (2000; *After the Quake: Stories*, 2002), and *Blind Willow, Sleeping Woman* (2006). Murakami is also a translator of international reputation, translating the works of American writers such as Raymond Carver, F. Scott Fitzgerald, Truman Capote, Raymond Chandler, Tim O'Brien, and Paul Theroux into Japanese. Finally, Murakami's significant contributions as a journalist should not be overlooked, particularly *Andaguraundo* (1997; *Underground: The Tokyo Gas Attack and the Japanese Psyche*, 2000), his moving account of the 1995 sarin gas attack in a Tokyo subway by members of the religious group Aum Shinrikyo. Considered to be journalistic literature, *Underground* includes a series of interviews with victims and perpetrators of the attacks.

ACHIEVEMENTS

In 1994, for his three-volume novel *The Wind-Up Bird Chronicle*, Haruki Murakami won the Gunzo Literature Prize; he also won the Noma Literary Prize for New Writers for his first novel, *Hear the Wind Sing*, and the Yomiuri Prize for Literature—a prestigious Japanese literary award whose previous recipients included Yukio Mishima and Kobo Abe. The Yomiuri Prize was awarded to him by Nobel Prize winner Kenzaburo Oe, who had long been critical of Murakami. Murakami also received the Tanizaki Prize in 1985 for *Hard-Boiled Wonderland and the End of the World*, and he was a teaching fellow at Princeton University and Tufts University in the United States.

Murakami was awarded the Franz Kafka Prize from the Czech Republic in 2006 for *Kafka on the Shore*, the Frank O'Connor International Short Story Award from Ireland in 2006, the Asahi Prize from Japan in 2006, and honorary doctorates from the University of Liège in 2007 and Princeton in 2008. In 2007, Murakami won the Kiriyama Prize—a literary award given annually to books that encourage greater understanding of and among the peoples and nations of the Pacific Rim and South Asia—for his collection of short stories *Blind Willow, Sleeping Woman*; he declined the award "for reasons of personal principle." Murakami's works have been translated into more than forty languages, including Arabic, Estonian, Icelandic, Russian, Thai, and Vietnamese.

BIOGRAPHY

Born in Kyoto in 1949, Haruki Murakami spent most of his youth in Kobe. Both his father and mother taught Japanese literature, igniting a passion for literature early on in their son. Murakami's father was also a Buddhist priest (meditations on religion and spirituality are key themes in Murakami's work), and his mother was the daughter of a merchant. Murakami showed an affinity for Western culture from an early age, particularly Western literature and music. His favorite writers were Kurt Vonnegut and Richard Brautigan, and his favorite musicians were the Beatles, Bob Dylan, Radiohead, Charlie Parker, and countless jazz and classical musicians, particularly Ludwig van Beethoven. Murakami graduated from Waseda University in Tokyo in 1973, where he studied theater arts, and his first job was at a record store. Just before graduating, Murakami opened a coffeehouse (which served as a jazz bar in the evenings) called Peter Cat in Okobunji, Tokyo, with his wife, Yoko. He is a collector of vinyl records, a full-marathon runner and triathlete, and obsessed with cats (all interests that weigh heavily on his fiction).

Murakami did not start writing until he was twenty-nine years old. Legend has it that he was attending a baseball game in Tokyo when he had a revelation regarding writing. Murakami suddenly realized that he was capable of writing a book after seeing American ballplayer Dave Hilton (playing for the Hiroshima Carps) hit a double. Murakami started working on a novel immediately following the game. After several months he had finished *Hear the Wind Sing*, a short, fragmented book (modeled on Brautigan and written in fits and starts) that introduced many elements that would come to dominate Murakami's style: an embrace of Western influences (especially writers Brautigan and Vonnegut, and Western music), dark humor, anonymity, relationships, loss, and alienation. His success—he won the Gunzo Literature Prize for the novel—encouraged him to keep at it. He next published *Pinball, 1973* and then *A Wild Sheep Chase*, the last two works of what came to be known as the trilogy of the rat.

Hard-Boiled Wonderland and the End of the World marked the beginning of Murakami's career as a writer of international reputation, but it was *Norwegian Wood* that made him a star of the literary world. Initially published in two installments, *Norwegian Wood* sold millions of copies among the youth of Japan, catapulting Murakami to superstar status. Murakami initially was not pleased with the sort of fame he had attained, and he left Japan to travel through Europe, before settling in the United States. He became a writing fellow at Princeton and Tufts, where he worked on and completed *South of the Border, West of the Sun* and *The Wind-Up Bird Chronicle*.

Murakami returned to Japan after the Hanshin earthquake and the poison gas attack in the Tokyo subway in 1995. He worked on two nonfiction books about the gas attack, which were combined to form the English edition of *Underground*. *Sputnik Sweetheart*, *Kafka on the Shore*, and *After Dark* cemented Murakami's reputation as one of the world's most popular and critically successful novelists. Several of his stories and novels have been adapted into films, and *Hashiru koto ni tsuite kataru toki ni boku no kataru koto* (2007; *What I Talk About When I Talk About Running: A Memoir*, 2008), Murakami's memoir about his life as a marathon runner and triathlete, was a highly anticipated step in a new direction for the successful novelist.

Analysis

If it is true that writers and artists should spend their entire lives and careers investigating, examining, and trying to understand the same themes, then Haruki Murakami is a prime example of how to do this successfully. Like a jazz musician building on the same note, Murakami has—from the start—been obsessed with issues of sexual identity and love, loss and detachment, history and war, and nostalgia and fate. He has been deeply influenced by Western culture, and his themes, in some ways, are distilled from his favorite writers and musicians. Murakami changed the face of Japanese fiction. He was the first to incorporate Western influences in such an immediate way and he introduced a broad, spare, and raw style that Japanese readers had never before seen. His flirtation with Magical Realism, surrealism, and the fantastic is evidence of his fearlessness as a writer. Never one to be pigeonholed, Murakami is that rarest of literary figures, a writer who revels in telling a good and exciting story without sacrificing his severe vision of what literature is and should be.

Notably, Murakami's novels often have musical themes and often speak of the power and beauty of music. More than that, his titles are often taken directly from songs. The three volumes comprising *The Wind-Up Bird Chronicle* refer to works by Gioachino Antonio Rossini, Robert Schumann, and Wolfgang Amadeus Mozart. *Norwegian Wood*, possibly Murakami's most famous work, is named after a song by the Beatles, and *Dance Dance Dance*, a sort of sequel to *A Wild Sheep Chase*, is named after a song by the Beach Boys.

Murakami's work is the highwater mark at the intersection of popular culture and serious literature. As a writer who has filtered such a variety of influences into his work, he is a complete original. He is also a writer who has sought to understand Japanese history (especially Japan's role in World War II), but he has done so without attempting to make political statements. He examines, explores, and dissects history, war, love, and identity with the same complex (and sometimes confusing) gracefulness. Murakami, like Georges Simenon and Charles Bukowski, has become his own brand name. Though his work has been described in many different ways—as Magical Realism, surrealism, hard-boiled mystery, love story, cyberpunk—it is almost entirely impossible to identify one of his books as anything other than a "Murakami."

Murakami goes where a novel takes him, where history takes him. He goes to the place where love and memory and fear take him. As an independent artist with a singular vision, he is unrivaled in this generation of world writers.

HARD-BOILED WONDERLAND AND THE END OF THE WORLD

A complex and playful novel, *Hard-Boiled Wonderland and the End of the World* features two separate narratives. The odd-numbered chapters are set in the Hard-Boiled Wonderland and feature a narrator who is a Calcutec, a human data-processing system. The even-numbered chapters take place in a strange, walled-off village called The End of the World, removed from the rest of civilization. The narrator of this story becomes the village's dream reader. Eventually, the two stories merge, and the deep influences here—American hard-boiled detective fiction, cyberpunk, Franz Kafka—come together to make this one of the most complex and yet accessible examples of Magical Realism in world literature.

NORWEGIAN WOOD

Norwegian Wood, the book that made Murakami into a superstar, is a nostalgic story of love and loss. It is also Murakami's most straightforward work. Told from the perspective of Toru Watanabe, who looks back on his days as a college freshman, the novel details Toru's relationships with two beautiful, electric, and unusual women, Naoko and Midori. The title of the book is taken from a 1965 song by the Beatles—"Norwegian Wood (This Bird Has Flown)," which appears several times in the novel's narrative (alongside other allusions to Western music and literature). Set in Tokyo in the late 1960's, the novel also portrays a changing Japan, as students protest against the establishment. While Murakami identifies the student movement as naïve and phony, the setting is just the backdrop for a real and complex love story that—while not supernatural or fantastic like much of Murakami's other work—nonetheless reveals a unique vision of how to live and survive in the world.

SOUTH OF THE BORDER, WEST OF THE SUN

South of the Border, West of the Sun also takes part of its title from a song, this time from one sung by Nat King Cole, "South of the Border." The title comes to mean something wholly mystical and mysterious to the novel's two main characters, Hajime and Shimamoto. The second part of the title is a psychological condition known as "*hysteria siberiana*," which is, as Shimamoto explains to Hajime, something that happens to Siberian farmers when they lose their minds and walk west toward the setting sun until they fall down and die. A melancholic novel rooted in the same sense of nostalgia as *Norwegian Wood*, *South of the Border, West of the Sun* is a meditation on love, choices, and mystery.

THE WIND-UP BIRD CHRONICLE

Widely considered to be Murakami's finest achievement, *The Wind-Up Bird Chronicle* tells the story of Toru Okada, an unemployed man whose cat disappears. Toru is married to Kumiko, who has a successful career in the publishing business. A bizarre chain of events leads him to strange encounters with May Kasahara, a young girl who is obsessed with death and deterioration, and Nutmeg Akasaka, a writer who shares a few strange coincidences with Toru. The novel explores typical Murakami themes, and it is also a story of war and history. Particularly relevant to the story are the Manchukuo war crimes before and during World War II and their deep significance in Japanese history. As always, Murakami revels in mystery—both the mystical and hard-boiled varieties—and his crisp, sharp, and accessible style is at its peak here.

KAFKA ON THE SHORE

Kafka on the Shore is another epic Murakami novel with two different narratives—told in alternating chapters—that eventually come together. The odd-numbered chapters tell the story of Kafka, a fifteen-year-old runaway bent on escaping an Oedipal curse, who takes shelter in a library until police arrest him in connection with an unsolved murder. The even-numbered chapters tell the story of Nakata, a mystical cat finder. Nakata and Kafka move toward each other until their stories combine in a thunderclap.

Murakami examines many of the prominent themes readers have come to expect from him—love, loss, spirituality, dreams, the power of music, redemption, and sexual identity—but he also further investigates Japan's World War II heritage, the notion of reality, and the authority of prophecy, fate, and nature.

William Boyle

OTHER MAJOR WORKS

SHORT FICTION: *The Elephant Vanishes*, 1993; *Kami no kodomotachi wa mina odoru*, 2000 (*After the Quake: Stories*, 2002); *Blind Willow, Sleeping Woman*, 2006.

NONFICTION: *Andaguraundo*, 1997 (*Underground: The Tokyo Gas Attack and the Japanese Psyche*, 2000); *Hashiru koto ni tsuite kataru toki ni boku no kataru koto*, 2007 (*What I Talk About When I Talk About Running: A Memoir*, 2008).

BIBLIOGRAPHY

Amitrano, Giorgio. *The New Japanese Novel: Popular Culture and Literary Tradition in the Work of Murakami Haruki and Yoshimoto Banana*. Boston: Cheng and Tsui, 1996. An accessible introduction to the work of Japan's most famous contemporary novelists, Murakami and Yoshimoto Banana.

Japan Foundation. *A Wild Haruki Chase: Reading Murakami Around the World*. Berkeley, Calif.: Stone Bridge Press, 2008. A collection of essays exploring the "Murakami phenomenon," namely, how Murakami is read and translated throughout the world.

Napier, Susan J. *The Fantastic in Modern Japanese Literature: The Subversion of Modernity*. Florence, Ky.: Routledge, 1996. An examination of the fantastic in contemporary Japanese fiction, film, and comics and how it relates to the nation's anxieties and fears. Part of the Nissan Institute/Routledge Japanese Studies series.

Rubin, Jay. *Haruki Murakami and the Music of Words*. New York: Random House, 2001. Rubin, a professor of Japanese literature at Harvard and one of Murakami's translators, takes an exhaustive look at Murakami's life and works. A concise and complete critical introduction to Murakami's books.

Seats, Michael. *Murakami Haruki: The Simulacrum in Contemporary Japanese Culture*. Lanham, Md.: Lexington Books, 2006. Seats discusses the relationship between contemporary Japanese culture and Murakami's fiction, concluding that there are glaring comparisons to be made between Murakami's works and Japanese modernity and technology.

Strecher, Matthew. *Dances with Sheep: The Quest for Identity in the Fiction of Murakami Haruki*. Flint: University of Michigan, Center for Japanese Studies, 2002. Strecher's critical study argues for Murakami's relevance (rejecting the notion of Murakami as a pop author). Relying heavily on theory, Strecher aims to begin a serious critical discussion of Murakami's work.

_______. *Haruki Murakami's "The Wind-Up Bird Chronicle": A Reader's Guide*. New York: Continuum International, 2002. An accessible and informative guide and companion to Murakami's best-received novel.

Suter, Rebecca. *The Japanization of Modernity: Murakami Haruki Between Japan and the United States*. Cambridge, Mass.: Harvard University, Asia Center, 2008. Discusses Murakami's role as a kind of "mediator" between Japanese and American literature.

JUAN CARLOS ONETTI

Born: Montevideo, Uruguay; July 1, 1909
Died: Madrid, Spain; May 30, 1994

PRINCIPAL LONG FICTION

El pozo, 1939, 1965 (*The Pit*, 1991)
Tierra de nadie, 1941 (*No Man's Land*, 1994; also known as *Tonight*, 1991)
Para esta noche, 1943 (*Tonight*, 1991)
La vida breve, 1950 (*A Brief Life*, 1976)
Los adioses, 1954 (novella; *Goodbyes*, 1990)
Una tumba sin nombre, 1959 (novella; better known as *Para una tumba sin nombre*; *A Grave With No Name*, 1992)
La cara de la desgracia, 1960 (novella; *The Image of Misfortune*, 1990)
El astillero, 1961 (*The Shipyard*, 1968)
Tan triste como ella, 1963 (novella)
Juntacadáveres, 1964 (*Body Snatcher*, 1991)
La muerte y la niña, 1973
Dejemos hablar al viento, 1979 (*Let the Wind Speak*, 1997)
Cuando ya no importe, 1993 (*Past Caring?*, 1995)

OTHER LITERARY FORMS

"Los niños en el bosque," one of Juan Carlos Onetti's unpublished novels, dates from 1936. "Tiempo de abrazar," a novel written in 1933 and circulated in manuscript form among Onetti's friends, was not published, despite the praise it received from respected writers such as Roberto Arlt. The manuscript was entered in the contest for the Rinehart and Farrar Prize in 1941. After coming in second, it disappeared, except for a number of fragments, which were published in various journals over the years. In 1974, the Uruguayan critic Jorge Ruffinelli gathered these fragments, a good portion of the original, along with "Los niños en el bosque" and Onetti's uncollected short stories dating from 1933 to 1950, into one volume titled *Tiempo de abrazar, y los cuentos de 1933 a 1950*. There are to date at least eleven short-story collections, with overlapping items. The most complete of these is *Cuentos completos* (1967; revised 1974), edited by Ruffinelli.

Onetti's *Obras completas* (1970) is far from complete, the title notwithstanding. Still uncollected are the many literary essays written by Onetti for Montevideo's weekly *Marcha*, where the author served as editor for two years (1939-1941). Under a variety of exotic pseudonyms and humorous epithets, Onetti wrote not only essays and criticism but also short pieces of fiction as "fillers" for that weekly, all of which remain uncollected. During his first stint in Buenos Aires, from 1930 to 1934, Onetti wrote a number of film reviews for the periodical *Crítica*, and they also remain uncollected. While he may have attempted genres other than prose, only two poems exist in print: "Y el pan nuestro," in *Cuadernos hispanoamericanos* (1974), and "Balada del ausente," in *Casa de las Américas* (1976).

ACHIEVEMENTS

Until the mid-1960's, when Latin American fiction moved into the international limelight and its younger practitioners acknowledged Juan Carlos Onetti as one of their forerunners, Onetti's popularity was limited to a devoted few. His first published novel, *The Pit*, did not go into a second printing for twenty-six years after its initial edition of five hundred copies. The pivotal work of his career, *A Brief Life*, was not reissued until fifteen years after its publication. Onetti is now internationally acclaimed, with his works translated into many languages and constantly being reissued in Spanish editions.

In the mid-1930's, Onetti was becoming increasingly well known in his native Montevideo. His stint as literary editor of *Marcha* from 1939 to 1941 furnished him with a forum for his literary ideas during what was a very productive period for his own writing. His intellectual activities did not abate when he moved to Buenos Aires for the second time, in 1941—where he would remain for a decade and a half—but the move did sever prematurely his growing influence in his own country.

In 1951, Onetti's countrymen gave their first public recognition of his achievements when the important Montevideo review *Número* dedicated a special issue to his work. Ten years later, *The Shipyard* was selected by a jury in a literary contest sponsored by Compañía General Fabril Editora, which published that novel. In 1962, Onetti was awarded Uruguay's national literary prize, and in 1963, *The Shipyard* received the William Faulkner Foundation Certificate of Merit. Italy awarded the same novel its prize for the best foreign work translated into Italian for the year 1975. In June of 1980, a group of distinguished writers and critics from all over the world gathered at the Universidad Veracruzana de Méjico to pay homage to Onetti and his career on the occasion of his seventieth birthday. Today, Onetti's significance in Latin American letters is established beyond any doubt.

BIOGRAPHY

Juan Carlos Onetti was born in Montevideo, Uruguay, on July 1, 1909. His father, Carlos Onetti, whom Onetti characterized as a "gentleman," was a functionary of Montevideo's customs office. On more than one occasion, Onetti noted that the family name was O'Netty before being corrupted to its present form, a suggestion that would point to early Irish ancestry. Onetti was always cryptic about his ancestors, however, intimating only that his great-grandfather was the personal secretary of General Fructuoso Rivera, who fought in the nineteenth century against Juan Manuel de Rosas and the Argentine dictator's territorial pretensions in Uruguay. His mother, Honoria Borges, was of Brazilian stock, and Onetti says only that she was a "slaveholding lady from the south of Brazil."

Onetti was the second of three children; he had an older brother, Raul, and a younger sister, Raquel. He remembered his childhood as a happy one, during which the family moved often, at least four times in his early school days. Onetti was a high school dropout—in part, he said, because he could not receive a passing grade in drawing. As an adolescent, he worked at a number of odd jobs—doorman, automobile-tire salesman, waiter, ticket taker at a stadium, and watchman at a grain elevator.

At the age of fourteen, Onetti discovered the works of Knut Hamsun, which he read avidly and tried, with adolescent fervor, to emulate. Onetti's first known venture into literature and publishing came in 1928. He was nineteen then and living in Villa Colón, not far from Montevideo. With two friends, Juan Andrés Carril and Luis Antonio Urta, he founded a journal, *La tijera de Colón*. Seven issues of the journal were published between March, 1928, and February, 1929, including Onetti's first five short stories. In 1929, Onetti tried, unsuccessfully, to travel to the Soviet Union "to witness a Socialist system in the making." A year later, he was married for the first time, to a cousin, María Amalia, and moved with her to Buenos Aires. He remained there for four years, during which he worked for a while as an adding-machine salesman—he did not sell a single machine. His son, Jorge, who also became a novelist, was born in 1931.

Onetti wrote the first version of *The Pit* in 1932, a version that was lost. The following year, he published what was once believed to have been his first short story, "Avenida de Mayo—Diagonal—Avenida de Mayo" in the Buenos Aires daily *La prensa*. In 1934, Onetti returned to Montevideo and was married for the second time, to another cousin, María Julia. On October 6, 1935, his short story "El obstáculo" appeared in the Argentine daily *La nación*, whose literary supplement was edited at the time by the distinguished novelist Eduardo Mallea. A year later, with the outbreak of the Spanish Civil War, Onetti attempted, again without success, to travel to Europe to enlist as a volunteer in the international brigades fighting in Spain.

With the founding of the weekly *Marcha* on June 23, 1939, Onetti was given the opportunity to work at the center of one of the most important intellectual enterprises of Uruguay. As literary editor, he made his mark on Montevideo's cultural life. In December of that same year, a reconstituted version of *The Pit* was published in a limited edition. Two years later, Onetti left *Marcha* to work as editor for Reuter's news agency and, in that capacity, was transferred to Buenos Aires. Shortly thereafter, he abandoned Reuter's, though he remained in the Argentine capital from 1941 to 1955. After leaving Reuter's, Onetti worked as an editor for various Argentine magazines, including *Vea y lea* and *Ímpetu*. During this decade and a half, he published some of his most important work.

In 1944, Onetti interviewed the populist strongman of Argentina, Juan Perón, a figure Onetti found fascinating; he indicated on more than one occasion his desire to write a novel about him and his legendary wife, Eva Perón. In this period, Onetti also undertook a number of translations of American works, the first being Phoebe Atwood Taylor's *The Cape Cod Mystery* (1931), which he translated with Elizabeth María Pikelharing, his third wife, whom he married in 1945. Only her name appears on the translation, which was published a year later. Onetti also translated Erskine Caldwell's *This Very Earth* (1948) in 1954, Paul I. Wellman's *The Comancheros* (1952) in 1956, and Henry Burgess Drake's *Children of the Wind* (1954) in 1957. Actually, Onetti's interest in translation dates from 1940, when his Spanish version of William Faulkner's "All the Dead Pilots" appeared in *Marcha*, unsigned.

In 1955, back in Montevideo, Onetti worked for an advertising agency and, subsequently, as editor for the publication *Acción*, in which he had an anonymous literary column. In the same year, he was married for the fourth time, to Dorotea (Dolly) Muhr. Onetti was named director of municipal libraries of Montevideo in 1957, a position he held until his arrest in 1974 and subsequent exile in 1975. In 1962, he was the recipient of Uruguay's Premio Nacional de Literatura, the country's literary prize. With this award and the publication of his two major novels *The Shipyard* and *Body Snatcher*, Onetti began to receive international acclaim. Peruvian novelist Mario Vargas Llosa, after receiving the Romulo Gallegos Novel Prize, declared in his acceptance speech that the prize rightfully belonged to Onetti. Such declarations became common. In 1970, the Mexican publishing firm Editorial Aguilar issued Onetti's *Obras completas*, an incomplete collection but an indication of his growing reputation.

Because of one of those tragic but common political debacles that have become a specialty of Latin America, Onetti was first imprisoned for a short period in 1974 and forced into exile in 1975. Thereafter, he lived in Madrid, Spain. Onetti's crime was to have served on a jury for a literary contest sponsored by *Marcha*, which awarded the prize (against Onetti's own vote) to a story deemed inappropriate by the military dictatorship. While Onetti evinced a great sense of loss in having to live in exile, his work continued. In 1979, his novel *Let the Wind Speak* was published, and *Past Caring?* was published in 1993.

ANALYSIS

"He has the power to say a word, to put in an adjective, to change a destiny . . . until he discovers his power, and then he uses it to enter himself into his imaginary world." This is how Juan Carlos Onetti characterizes one of his heroes and the activity of writing. The depiction is apt for Onetti himself. Beginning with *The Pit*—and even before, with his first published stories—Onetti's career consisted in exploring the enabling possibilities of the "power" he describes here. In the process, he himself has become a body of literature, a world of imagination capable of engendering itself in its imaginary world.

If one can glean a constant from Onetti's long and distinguished career, it has to be the persevering exploration and charting of powers of the imagination. Like their author, all of Onetti's characters inevitably strive for a salvation that can be found only in imagination's potency. The guises, the masks, the shapes that this potency takes in Onetti's fictions are many—fantasy, escapism, imaginary biography, delusion, pathetic and courageous Bovarism. The projects engendered by the energies of this power are also varied—a mythical topography, the perfect whorehouse, a dignified death. Onetti calls this itinerary the "adventure of man," and he says, "I only wish to express the adventure of man."

The "destiny" to be altered by imaginative potency in Onetti's fictional cosmos is "real life," which inevitably emerges in his works as overbearing, vulgar, susceptible to corruption by time and experience. This vision of reality is determined in large measure by the social and historical realities of the 1930's and 1940's, Onetti's formative years as a novelist. The setting of Onetti's works, primarily urban, may also have influenced his somber vision of human circumstances. As in the fiction of the Argentine novelist Roberto Arlt, whose influence helped shape Onetti's work, the metropolitan centers of Buenos Aires and Montevideo assume metaphorical significance in Onetti's vision. Onetti eventually conflated these two urban centers to create the imaginary geography of Santa María, the mythical setting of *A Brief Life* and of all of his subsequent novels.

Buenos Aires and Montevideo, of all the Latin American capitals, have always looked toward Europe, with their backs turned, so to speak, to the vast American continent beyond them. Historical events that befall distant metropolitan centers at the other shores of the Atlantic, then, have always had an immediate effect in these twin Río de la Plata cities: World War I, the economic collapse of the 1930's, Francisco Franco's victory in Spain, the rise of fascism beyond Spain in Europe. The fate of European intellectuals has exerted an equally strong influence: Franco's silencing of José Ortega y Gasset, the murder of Federico García Lorca, the deaths of Miguel de Unamuno y Jugo and Antonio Machado in Spain, Adolf Hitler's march into Paris in 1940, the imprisonment or exile of writers such as Jean-Paul Sartre and André Gide. These and other European calamities confirmed the worst suspicions born of the disillusioned intellectuals of Onetti's generation; Onetti and his contemporaries saw that those suspicions found their concrete objective correlatives in what they thought to be the most urbane centers of civilization.

The urban individual with a conscience finds himself in what one of Onetti's titles from 1941 so succinctly expresses—a *tierra de nadie*, a no-man's-land. Onetti, then, is very much a part of that "lost generation," and his novels inevitably reflect the environment in which they have been created. Onetti, with imaginative potency, seeks and finds an inventive, mythopoeic plane where his characters can confront worldly reality and transform the "given" into redemptive adventure, whether as Bovaristic illusion or as creative, poetic figuration. That mythical, poetic geography is the world of Santa María, invented by one of Onetti's protagonists in *A Brief Life*—a world of the imagination that carries within it the "givens" of historical reality, much like Faulkner's Yoknapatawpha County, and into which Onetti himself enters to chart its annals. Onetti's novels become the record of that itinerary.

THE PIT

Published in December of 1939, Onetti's first novel, *The Pit*, is a reconstituted version of the misplaced and lost original from 1932. As a first novel, it is paradigmatic of the author's oeuvre. *The Pit* dramatizes the trial and error of an attempt at self-mastery. In this sense, it is revealing not only of the hero's circumstances (a protagonist who feels compelled to write his autobiography now that he has reached the age of forty) but also of Onetti's conception of his task as a writer. The protagonist's self-characterizations, his halting and reticent attempts at self-writing, his disengagement from the world of reality and human relationships around him, even as he is obsessed with these things, reflect the circumstances of his author and of other, subsequent protagonists in Onetti's fictional cosmos.

The novel's hero, Eladio Linacero, is obsessed with an autobiography and its self-conscious impossibility. In his reticence and self-deprecation, he confesses to his shortcomings as a writer as well as to the necessarily fictional nature of the details of his life that have become committed to his writing. He thus opts for recording not factual detail, which offers a mere pretense of re-creating reality, but the fantasies that have no such claims and that may well be more "true" as a result. He not only spurns historical particulars but also rejects, with a Sartrean "nausea," the concrete, "objective" details that surround him, including his own bodily existence and his neglected apartment, with its dusty furniture and faded newspapers.

The novel's narrative, then, becomes the record of a juxtaposition between the concrete (whether in historical remembrance or in immediate objectivity) and the imaginary, fantasy world of his daydreams. By the end of the novel and of the night (the span of narrative time is one night), Eladio Linacero admits to the impossibility of autobiography, of self-mastery in writing. What he has produced becomes the record of that impossibility, a record that extends the self in the act of recording what writing attempts to contain. Implacably, time vitiates the attempt to freeze oneself in time: "I would have liked to pin the night on paper, like a nocturnal butterfly. But, in turn, it was the night that carried me off amid its waters, like the livid body of a dead man." The problematics of Linacero's attempt and its vicissitudes attained full significance in later works, such as *A Brief Life* and the subsequent novels from the saga of Santa María.

NO MAN'S LAND

A collective social portrait of a historical period, *No Man's Land* is Onetti's most explicit work. Written in the late 1930's, when the lost generation came of age, Onetti's second novel captures, in the manner of cinematic montage, the ambience of the epoch. Despite the value of the novel as a social document, its technical achievement may be even more significant. If *The Pit* showed Onetti as a master of first-person narration, of a stream of consciousness restricted to a single voice, *No Man's Land* displays his mastery of simultaneity, in the manner of John Dos Passos in *Manhattan Transfer* (1925).

No Man's Land is a congeries of parallel paths, multiple destinies, refracted perspectives, desultory points of view that crowd the world of the novel, that occasionally converge but rarely result in any meaningful human communion. As the title suggests, the urban setting is an anonymous no-man's-land, and its sundry inhabitants are alienated individuals whose relationship to a collective community is all but obliterated by indifference, ennui, and individual fantasies. On occasion, those fantasies converge, even if tangentially, and therein lies the seed for an imaginary world, which becomes a communal fantasy in Onetti's later novels. For the first time, too, certain characters who will emerge as protagonists in works from the saga of Santa María, such as Junta Larsen, hero of *The Shipyard* and of *Body Snatcher*, make a fleeting appearance. *No Man's Land* was hailed at the time of its publication as a genuine Río de la Plata novel, an indication that Buenos Aires and Montevideo had finally produced a novel equal to their teeming life.

Tonight

While *No Man's Land* has been hailed as a social novel, *Tonight*, Onetti's third novel, has often been read as an expression of political solidarity. In the late 1930's, when Onetti was affiliated with *Marcha* and later with Reuter's, he frequented the Café Metro in Montevideo. There, Onetti would meet with other intellectuals and there, too, he encountered a number of exiles from the Spanish Civil War and its infamous aftermath.

Onetti said that his conversations with those exiles found their fictionalized echo in *Tonight*, a novel of political terror and oppression. Onetti had made an attempt in 1936 to go to Spain to fight in the civil war. Perhaps this novel is a form of compensation for his failure in that attempt as well as for his comfortable distance from yet another tragic war that was then under way. Ironically, the state of siege, the military terror, the political machinations and victimization of ideals, and the fugitive haunts of idealistic and ambiguous characters depicted in the novel were all too prophetic of what was to befall Argentina two years after the novel's publication. That state of affairs changed little, with Onetti's Uruguay falling victim to the same fate. Even more ironic is that some thirty years later, Onetti himself became the victim of this scourge and, reversing the pattern, went to Spain as an exile.

Technically, Onetti's third novel is not the most accomplished of his works. It suffers from the rhetorically melodramatic, unambiguous dichotomies of good and evil, the idealistic and the corrupt, the victim and the villain. Nevertheless, the perspectivist juxtaposition of narrative points of view and the intensity of terror that builds with the manhunt and concludes with the hero's death make the novel interesting.

A Brief Life

Onetti's fourth novel, *A Brief Life*, opened a new epoch in his novelistic cycle. Santa María, the mythical realm of this and subsequent works, while adumbrated in earlier pieces, has its genesis in *A Brief Life*. As the title suggests, the narrative consists of a series of brief lives, "real" or fantasized, harking back to the multiple, imaginary lives of Eladio Linacero in Onetti's first novel. In contrast to the predicament of Linacero, however, the hero of *A Brief Life*, Juan María Brausen, succeeds in finding a way out of the worldly "here and now" of space and temporality.

Like Linacero, Brausen is a brooder; unlike Onetti's first hero, however, he is also a man of action. His acts of evasion are not merely fantasized mental states. Brausen breaks out of his humdrum existence by physically breaking into the ambit and life of the prostitute who lives next door. Thus, Juan María Brausen becomes Juan María Arce upon "penetrating" the wall to another life, a life that proves as desolate as the respectable normalcy he has left behind. In oscillating between these two lives, the protagonist discovers the impossibility of evasion and the now compounded nature of his entrapment. Real transcendence from the strictures of the existential trap, Brausen discovers, is to be found only in imaginative potency, in the creative powers of the imagination. As a scriptwriter with a commission for a particular film script, Brausen invents the world of Santa María, an imaginary world into which he flees, a fugitive from the authorities following the murder of the prostitute. Not only does he interpolate himself into his invented world, crossing from a fiction of reality to a reality of fiction, but his created world becomes, thereafter, the novelistic cosmos of his creator, Onetti. In this sense, *A Brief Life* may well be Onetti's most significant novel, the gateway to all of his subsequent works.

THE SHIPYARD *and* BODY SNATCHER

There is common agreement among critics that *The Shipyard*, Onetti's fifth major novel, is his best-formed work; it may well be the masterpiece of his career. *The Shipyard* is the first full-blown treatment of the saga of Santa María; in the internal chronology of the saga, it follows the events related in *Body Snatcher*. Onetti said that when he was halfway through the writing of this latter work in 1957, he was assailed by the vision of the hero's death. He then abandoned *Body Snatcher* and wrote *The Shipyard*.

The novel recounts the story of Junta Larsen and his return to Santa María. He was expelled from there five years earlier by the town fathers because of his less-than-respectable activities in running a brothel. *The Shipyard*, then, is a redemptive work, a seeking after salvation in the ashes of a failed dream. The redemption sought by the hero is not a phoenixlike rebirth but a pursuit of some admissible meaning in failure. Junta Larsen emerges as an ennobled hero, a tragic figure who has already endured the blows of the implacable fates. His deep pessimism is not cynical but philosophical. He accepts fate, not with bitter resignation, but with knowing perspicacity. There is an allegorical parallel to Junta Larsen's search for self-salvation in self-surrender to the inevitable: his engagement in salvaging the hopelessly defunct shipyard of Petrus.

The shipyard is beyond salvation. Its owner and management play out the farce of running a going concern even while they surreptitiously junk useless pieces from the carcass of the shipyard to survive. Junta Larsen shuttles between Santa María and the docks, between his own disintegrated past and the concretely visible disintegration of the shipyard. His attempts to marry Petrus's daughter prove futile; she is dim-witted or downright mad. He settles for a sordid relationship with the maid in the servants' quarters. In the face of an impossible future, the most meaningful acts are recollections of the past. In his lucid flashbacks, in his silent monologue, Junta Larsen emerges as a savior, hopeful but hopelessly fated, and knowingly so, a Christ figure in the house of Petrus: The biblical allusion to Saint Peter and the church built upon a rock is transparent. Petrus's rock, however, has become a heap of sand, and Larsen, the savior, can find only a quietus, a final reckoning, rather than a resurrection.

Although published three years later than *The Shipyard*, the episodes narrated in *Body Snatcher* antedate the events of the earlier novel. Onetti's sixth major novel evinces, at least in the first half, the vigor and dynamism of a pursuit: Junta Larsen's dream to found and operate the perfect whorehouse. The language of the novel is wry, at times satirically imbued with irony and frequent humor. The hero is in his prime, his energies at their apex. The novel begins with Junta Larsen's arrival in Santa María with his female cargo—three or four women in varying degrees of decrepitude. The town dubs the hero with the nickname that gives the work its original title, Juntacadáveres, the Corpse-Gatherer (or body snatcher). The town's reaction to Junta's enterprise ensues, with the final expulsion of the hero and his charges from Santa María and the crumbling of Junta's dream in a bathetic denouement.

Interwoven into the rise and fall of Larsen's enterprise is the story of Jorge Malabia, a young man who was the protagonist of an earlier Onetti novella, *A Grave with No Name*. This novella has often been considered a blueprint for Onetti's fiction: It embraces all of his recurring preoccupations, particularly his obsession with the relativity of truth. In *Body Snatcher*, Jorge Malabia is engaged in a guilt-ridden relationship with the widowed wife of his brother. His attempts to patronize Junta Larsen's establishment and his eventual participation in the downfall of that "institution" also form part of the novel's plot. Thus, *Body Snatcher* is an intricately woven novel that gathers various threads from the annals of Santa María. Uruguayan critic Emir Rodríguez Monegal notes that to appreciate the chronological order of events, one must first read *Body Snatcher*, then *A Grave with No Name*, and then *The Shipyard*. Monegal also noted that the second part of *Body Snatcher* is more somber, its language more weighty, its humor darker; the change is attributed to the fact that this second part was written after Onetti had interrupted the novel's composition to write *The Shipyard*.

La muerte y la niña

If the sequence of publication violates the internal chronology of the saga of Santa María, *La muerte y la niña*, Onetti's seventh novel, violates all logical order with impunity. The result is a hermetic involution, a scrambled code that can have intelligibility only for those already initiated in Onetti's fictional system. *La muerte y la niña* is yet another farce played out with the knowledge of its futility in the face of implacable time, guilt, relative truth, and irrevocable fate. The episodes of the plot (the attempts of Augusto Goerdel to exonerate himself and assuage his guilt for the death of his wife, Helga Hauser, by returning to Santa María with suspect documents aimed to prove that he is not the father of the girl whose birth proved fatal to her mother) are less significant than the "resuscitation" of ghosts from earlier novels in the saga. Onetti deliberately violates objective temporality by having characters whose death was narrated in earlier works and episodes reappear, "posthumously," to reflect on the fate of Santa María.

While not Onetti's best work, *La muerte y la niña* is a significant novel insofar as it divulges the author's deliberate destruction of objective reality even in the world of fiction, to point to yet another level, one more demonstration that literature *is* literature, with no obligations to any order outside itself. Accordingly, the language of the novel is deliberately artificial, studied, and rhetorical.

LET THE WIND SPEAK

Let the Wind Speak takes its title and epigraph from the last fragment of *The Cantos* (1972) of Ezra Pound, who wrote

> I have tried to write Paradise
> Do not move
> Let the wind speak
> that is paradise.
> Let the Gods forgive what I
> have made.
> Let those I love try to forgive
> what I have made.

From the outset, then, there is a sense of an ending, a morbid finality, an intimation of doom in this apocalyptic work. The cycle of Santa María, deliberately scrambled in the previous work, now closes in on itself. Characters return—some from death—to haunt the novel, and whole passages are repeated from earlier volumes in the saga.

In some cases, this recursiveness extends even to works that predated the genesis of Santa María. The protagonist of *Let the Wind Speak*, Medina, who appeared in previous works as a police official, returns from Santa María to Lavanda (a homonymic suggestion of La Banda, Uruguay, which is commonly known as La Banda Oriental). His return, reminiscent of Junta Larsen's return in *The Shipyard*, erases all boundaries between the real world and the world of Onetti's fiction, Santa María. There is a peculiar conflation of worlds when, for example, Medina narrates, word for word, whole passages from Onetti's first novel, *The Pit*, and one recognizes scenes and dialogues from the narrative context of Santa María now outside that phantasmagoric geography. The textual boundaries collapse, the dead and the living intermingle, past and present fuse. The cycle has run its course and begins to overtake its own tracks.

Symbolically, the novel is the apocalypse of a literary career, of its enchanted geography (Santa María is consumed by fire in this novel). All that remains is the specter of language. In the end, if this is indeed the end, Onetti reaffirms once again the creative potency of the imagination (the power to create and to destroy its own invention) and the enabling potency of the author to enter and fade into the world of his imaginary creation.

Djelal Kadir

OTHER MAJOR WORKS

SHORT FICTION: *Un sueño realizado, y otros cuentos*, 1951; *El infierno tan temido*, 1962; *Jacob y el otro: Un sueño realizado, y otros cuentos*, 1965; *Cuentos completos*, 1967 (revised 1974; Jorge Ruffinelli, editor); *La novia robada, y otros cuentos*, 1968; *Cuentos*, 1971; *Tiempo de abrazar, y los cuentos de 1933 a 1950*, 1974 (short stories and fragments of unpublished novels; Ruffinelli, editor); *Tan triste como ella, y otros cuentos*, 1976; *Goodbyes, and Other Stories*, 1990.

NONFICTION: *Réquiem por Faulkner, y otros artículos*, 1975; *Confesiones de un lector*, 1995.

MISCELLANEOUS: *Obras completas*, 1970; *Onetti*, 1974 (articles, interview).

BIBLIOGRAPHY

Adams, M. Ian. *Three Authors of Alienation: Bombal, Onetti, Carpentier.* Austin: University of Texas Press, 1975. This study of the three writers includes an extended discussion of Onetti's novel *The Pit*, showing how Onetti's artistic manipulation of schizophrenia creates the sensation of participating in an alienated world.

Craig, Linda. *Juan Carlos Onetti, Manuel Puig, and Luisa Valenzuela: Marginality and Gender.* Woodbridge, England: Tamesis, 2005. Craig's book analyzes the works of Onetti and two other Latin American writers, describing how they share a sense of "postcolonial emptiness" and constantly question realism.

Harss, Luis, and Barbara Dohmann. "Juan Carlos Onetti or the Shadows on the Wall." In *Into the Mainstream: Conversations with Latin-American Writers*. New York: Harper & Row, 1967. Claims that in Onetti's middle-age protagonists there is a yearning for vanished youth and innocence. Discusses Onetti's pessimism and his Faulknerian style in his novella *Goodbyes*.

Maloof, Judy. *Over Her Dead Body: The Construction of Male Subjectivity in Onetti.* New York: Peter Lang, 1995. A feminist reading of Onetti's novels, in which Maloff explores Onetti's representation of gender, particularly his creation of male protagonists. She discusses these male characters' crises, placing them within the context of social and historical events in Uruguay from the 1930's through the 1960's.

Millington, Mark. "No Woman's Land: The Representation of Woman in Onetti." *MLN* 102 (March, 1987): 358-377. Millington discusses the function of the wife, prostitute, girl, and mad woman in Onetti's fiction, arguing that the subjection of women is one of the major impasses of Onetti's thinking.

_______. *Reading Onetti: Language, Narrative and the Subject*. Liverpool, England: Francis Cairns, 1985. Millington discusses the development of Onetti's work under the "hegemony of international modernism." He focuses on the status of Onetti's fiction as narrative discourse and discusses how *Goodbyes* problematizes the act of reading.

Murray, Jack. *The Landscapes of Alienation: Ideological Subversion in Kafka, Céline, and Onetti*. Stanford, Calif.: Stanford University Press, 1991. In his discussion of alienation in the work of Onetti and two other writers, Murray provides some background about the effect of Uruguay on Onetti's ideological unconscious.

San Román, Gustavo, ed. *Onetti and Others: Comparative Essays on a Major Figure in Latin American Literature*. Albany: State University of New York Press, 1999. A collection of twelve essays written from a variety of perspectives. Several focus on gender relationships in Onetti's work; comparative studies relating Onetti to other Latin American writers also are prominent.

Williams, Raymond L. "The Novels of Leopoldo Marechal and Juan Carlos Onetti." In *The Modern Latin American Novel*. New York: Twayne, 1998. This analysis of Onetti's novels is included in a historical overview of the Latin American novel from the modernist fiction of the mid-1940's through the postmodern novels published in the region since 1968. Includes notes, a bibliography, and an index.

J. K. ROWLING

Born: Chipping Sodbury, Gloucestershire, England; July 31, 1965
Also known as: Joanne Kathleen Rowling; Kennilworthy Whisp; Newt Scamander

PRINCIPAL LONG FICTION

Harry Potter and the Philosopher's Stone, 1997 (also known as *Harry Potter and the Sorcerer's Stone*, 1998)
Harry Potter and the Chamber of Secrets, 1998
Harry Potter and the Prisoner of Azkaban, 1999
Harry Potter and the Goblet of Fire, 2000
Harry Potter and the Order of the Phoenix, 2003
Harry Potter and the Half-Blood Prince, 2005
Harry Potter and the Deathly Hallows, 2007

OTHER LITERARY FORMS

In addition to her series of novels about the boy wizard Harry Potter, J. K. Rowling (ROHL-ihng) has composed the volumes *Fantastic Beasts and Where to Find Them* (2001) and *Quidditch Through the Ages* (2001); she has contributed all proceeds from sales of these works, more than fifty million dollars, to charity. Pretending to be volumes from the library at Rowling's fictional Hogwarts School of Witchcraft and Wizardry, these two works are brief, comic parodies of the kinds of informative books often written for children. For The Children's Voice, a charity that she cofounded, Rowling handwrote and auctioned a book of fairy stories titled *The Tales of Beedle the Bard*, which sold for £1.95 million. One of the stories ("The Tale of the Three Brothers") appears in *Harry Potter and the Deathly Hallows*.

ACHIEVEMENTS

J. K. Rowling has received numerous awards for her writing. *Harry Potter and the Philosopher's Stone* won the Nestlé Smarties Book Prize as well as the British Book Award for Children's Book of the Year and the Children's Book Award. Other prizes for volumes in the Harry Potter series followed, including the Hugo Award and the Whitbread Children's Book of the Year Award, but all of these pale before Rowling's unprecedented achievement that, despite writing in a genre (children's literature) that was not expected to sell well, her Harry Potter series, particularly the last four volumes, so significantly broken sales records as to have changed the publishing industry and probably contributed to a renewed interest in reading for countless children. As millions of large books were put in print at once and delivered throughout the world for the parties that greeted their release, each new Harry Potter volume became a major news event and placed a strain on the avenues of parcel delivery, particularly because of the massive attempt to keep the details of the books secret until they were released. One reason for the popularity of the Harry Potter series is that through these works Rowling has subtly changed the nature of long fiction by showing how it can depict psychological development playfully yet insightfully, in great detail and with myriad interconnections.

Biography

The daughter of Peter James Rowling and Anne Rowling (who met at King's Cross railway station—a major location in the Potter series), Joanne Kathleen Rowling grew up in various Gloucester villages in England. Her best friend, Sean Harris, later served as one model for her character Ron Weasley. She studied classics at the University of Exeter and later became a researcher for Amnesty International, which pressures governments around the world to abandon the use of torture and other brutality.

In 1990, much of the characterization and plot of the Harry Potter series occurred to Rowling as she was traveling by train. After the death of her mother that year, she deepened her sense of Harry's sorrow at his parents' demise. In 1992 in Portugal, where she was teaching, she married a television journalist. The marriage ended in divorce but left her with a baby daughter. She was living in poverty when she finished the first volume of her series, *Harry Potter and the Philosopher's Stone*, in 1995. Rowling has stated that this was a period when she suffered from depression and even thought of suicide. Eventually, however, she found an agent and then a publisher for the book.

As late as 1997, Rowling was able to spend her time writing only because she had received a monetary grant from the Scottish Arts Council. The next year, the American publisher Scholastic bid $105,000 for the right to publish the American edition of the first Harry Potter book—this was the first financial record for children's books that Rowling set. After that time, Rowling focused on completing the series, serving as an adviser on the very large-budgeted film adaptations that were made from the books, engaging in legal suits connected to the series, and raising funds for many charities.

Analysis

In various interviews, J. K. Rowling has discussed her intention to furnish her child characters with increasingly complex abilities and mature emotions with each successive volume. Although various authors—for example, James Joyce in *A Portrait of the Artist as a Young Man* (1916)—have experimented with changing style to depict a protagonist's maturing consciousness, the Harry Potter series does so at extraordinary length and with considerable subtlety while alternating between comedy and adventure in a manner that prevents the author's psychological explorations and moralizing from being intrusive.

Harry Potter and the Philosopher's Stone

Harry Potter and the Philosopher's Stone begins with its title character extremely isolated. He has no friends or sympathy from his foster parents, the Dursleys. He lives in a closet under the stairs, and the closest he comes to social life is playing with hand-me-down toys from his bullying cousin Dudley. Despite the fact that Harry is eleven, his psychological situation is typical of someone much younger, who has not yet fully bonded with parents and has not yet begun to have real companions. For Harry, growing up happens suddenly, as he is on the way to Hogwarts School of Witchcraft and Wizardry. He acquires the first of a number of benign parental figures in the person of the giant Hagrid as well as acquaintance with the two children who are to become his closest friends, Ron Weasley and Hermione Granger. For the first time, he is in the care of adults worthy of trust, but also of some (notably the potions professor, Snape) who arouse suspicion, so that Harry and friends fall into another of the normal activities of childhood, learning to break suspect rules. He meets his chief obstacle in Rowling's favorite chapter, "The Mirror of Erised," in which he resists the temptation to withdraw from his friends and regress to being alone with his daydreams. His victory at the end of the book depends on aid he receives from the school's headmaster, Dumbledore, as well as from Ron and Hermione.

Harry Potter and the Chamber of Secrets

Whereas the first book in the series demonstrates the importance of finding one's group, the next three—each in a darker and more alarming way—show Harry the fallibility of groups despite the need for them. In *Harry Potter and the Chamber of Secrets*, betrayed by his best friend's sister, Ginny Weasley, he also finds less direct aid from Ron, Hermione, and Dumbledore than in the previous ending (although they contribute to the victory). At the climax, Harry fights as a sword-wielding hero against a dragonlike basilisk to save an imprisoned maiden. This is, of course, the realization of a typical adolescent fantasy, which teaches courage and self-reliance.

Harry Potter and the Prisoner of Azkaban

In *Harry Potter and the Prisoner of Azkaban*, these virtues (even when augmented with teamwork) turn out to be insufficient for total victory in a society where legal processes have become somewhat confused and corrupt. Near the opening, Harry is a fleeing criminal, expecting to be occupying a cell in the wizard's prison Azkaban for fighting back illegally against a viciously harassing aunt. His godfather, Sirius Black, despite being innocent of the mass murder for which he was convicted, has spent years in that prison, escaped, and now might lose his soul if caught.

In *Harry Potter and the Prisoner of Azkaban*, Rowling offers a special lesson in dealing with fears so intense that they lead toward depression, personified as Dementors. As one remedy for such fears, Professor Lupin (who has struggled with the terror that the beast within him will overpower him) teaches children to reimagine whatever they fear most into a ridiculous form. To counter Harry's vulnerability to despair, Lupin trains him to employ the even more powerful spell of the "Patronus" (a word derived from the Latin word *pater*, which means father). It requires Harry to remember an intense joy, in his case connected to his parents. It takes the form of the animal into which his father used to transform. Since the book is about overcoming depression by reconnecting with the past, its plot hinges on the manipulation of time itself via Hermione's magic amulet.

HARRY POTTER AND THE GOBLET OF FIRE

In the next volume, *Harry Potter and the Goblet of Fire*, the children are no longer as sheltered as they once were from the intricacies and machinations of the commercial world around them. The book starts with the massively merchandised sporting event the World Quidditch Cup. Although still at school, Fred and George, Ron's older brothers, keep attempting to collect a large wager on the tournament so that they can finance a business. Competition among three schools, conducted with repeated reference to prize money and betting, also involves publicity and a spying reporter, Rita Skeeter, who lies and twists facts to help her newspaper sell copies. This systematic distortion is worse than the occasional injustices exposed by the previous book.

The first books in the Harry Potter series thus present typical stages of human development that most modern people undergo: in the first book, the rise from isolation to companionship; in the second, the transition from dependence to independence; in the third, movement from defiance of law to learning how to deal with its inequities while preserving one's integrity; and in the fourth, the transition from innocence to understanding of the machinations of the modern, commercial world. The remaining books present still more complex visions of human development.

HARRY POTTER AND THE ORDER OF THE PHOENIX

In *Harry Potter and the Order of the Phoenix*, Harry, terrorized by nightmares that merge with the external world, must comprehend the intricate interrelationship of subjective and objective. He has reached an advanced developmental stage, recognizing that each person views the world through a unique subjective perspective, so people are not all experiencing precisely the same world but rather subtly different ones, shaped and colored by their viewpoints. Appropriate to this insight is appreciation of diversity. The Order of the Phoenix has a broad membership: a thief and members of the magical police, a magicless "squib" and professors of magic, a bureaucrat and a werewolf. This volume shows that cooperation among the members of this diverse group is essential if they are to avoid domination by the reactionary "purebloods"—the enemies of diversity. Both the sorting hat and Hermione preach this moral. The brightest of the group, she had already some signs of this stage in the previous volume, but now she campaigns for an alliance of all the school's houses, and her crusade for oppressed house elves intensifies. Agreeing with her, Dumbledore condemns the arrogance that results in the tyranny of one magical race over the others. Although not every character achieves this tolerant perspective, the last two books present even less common understandings.

Harry Potter and the Half-Blood Prince

At the core of *Harry Potter and the Half-Blood Prince* is what Hermione calls Golpalott's Third Law: To counteract a mixture of poisons, an antidote must be more than a sum of antidotes to each poison; the cure must have something to catalyze the individual ingredients into a whole. This lesson in systems dynamics belongs to advanced studies that most of the students do not grasp at first—Harry among them—but it is the metaphor running throughout much of the book. As in the battle at the climax of *Harry Potter and the Order of the Phoenix*, members of that Order have been in individual duels with Voldemort's supporters—that is, have been separate antidotes. To counteract the figurative mixture of poisons with which Voldemort has been corrupting society, something more than such an accumulation is needed. Dumbledore's death becomes a catalyst, transforming the situation and (in the next book) inspiring his followers to equal self-sacrifice.

Harry Potter and the Deathly Hallows

The last book, *Harry Potter and the Deathly Hallows*, is the application of the complex teachings of the preceding book, as a way to make the wizarding community hale and whole again. To achieve this unification, each of the main characters must undergo some deathlike loss of self, so that all can better meld with the community. Snape, Lupin, Dobby, and Fred Weasley are among those giving their lives. Hermione hides her parents and disappears from their memory, thus eradicating one foundation for her identity. In a baptism-like plunge, Ron, in dark, cold waters, purges his previous selfishness, a transformation completed only when he overcomes all the nagging fears of being second best that have limited him. Harry has a near-death experience in which he talks to Dumbledore (or imagines himself doing so) at King's Cross. He comes back from this with the authority and charisma of a self-sacrificing leader (group catalyst), ready to grant magnanimous forgiveness to any repentant enemy and thus to end the divisions of the society.

This final volume is an inconclusive conclusion built around the idea of the Elder Wand (which, at one point, Rowling considered mentioning in the book's title). Dumbledore admits to having wasted much of his life in dreams about possessing it, and Harry must also resist that temptation. It guarantees its rightful master victory in any duel, but this does not keep its possessors from losing—a fact that Voldemort ignores arrogantly, imagining himself somehow pure, immortal, and all-powerful: a personification of stasis. Rowling uses her paradox of the vulnerability of the seemingly unconquerable to show that no power, however magical, can control life, which is fluid, unpredictable, and constantly changing. This is a feature not only of this book's plot but also of the series—a vast river of words, flowing from one surprise to another and interconnected to a sea of publicity.

As she was writing the series, Rowling engaged with her readers through the Internet, giving clues to each future volume; fans of the books tried to guess what would happen next or wrote their own additional sections of the story. Thereby, they participated in

Harry's education. The fans' interest intensified near the time of the publication of *Harry Potter and the Deathly Hallows*, and it did not stop after the book appeared. In interviews, Rowling continued to add to that book's epilogue, providing the further fates of characters as well as additional background information—for example, she revealed Dumbledore's homosexuality. Rowling thus significantly modified the closure that had long been assumed to be a characteristic of the novel genre.

James Whitlark

OTHER MAJOR WORKS

CHILDREN'S LITERATURE: *Fantastic Beasts and Where to Find Them*, 2001 (as Newt Scamander); *Quidditch Through the Ages*, 2001 (as Kennilworthy Whisp); *The Tales of Beedle the Bard*, 2008.

BIBLIOGRAPHY

Colbert, David. *The Magical Worlds of Harry Potter.* New York: Berkley Books, 2008. Provides explanations of the allusions to historical events and myths that Rowling employs throughout the Harry Potter series.

Granger, John. *Unlocking Harry Potter: Five Keys for the Serious Reader.* Allentown, Pa.: Zosima, 2007. Presents analysis of the themes found in the Harry Potter series, particularly that of alchemy.

Heilman, Elizabeth E., ed. *Critical Perspectives on Harry Potter.* New York: Routledge, 2008. Collection of essays addresses the Harry Potter books from the perspectives of various academic disciplines, including popular culture and anthropology.

Killinger, John. *God, the Devil, and Harry Potter: A Christian Minister's Defense of the Beloved Novels.* New York: St. Martin's Griffin, 2004. Offers thoughtful arguments defending the books against charges that they are un-Christian.

Nexon, Daniel H., and Iver B. Neumann, eds. *Harry Potter and International Relations.* Lanham, Md.: Rowman & Littlefield, 2006. Collection of essays by scholars in the field of international relations focuses on the connections made among various nations through the international success of the Harry Potter series.

Sexton, Colleen. *J. K. Rowling.* Minneapolis: Twenty-First Century Books, 2008. Brief, illustrated volume offers biographical information on Rowling.

Thomas, Scott. *The Making of the Potterverse: A Month-by-Month Look at Harry's First Ten Years.* Toronto, Ont.: ECW Press, 2007. Presents a history of the media coverage surrounding the Harry Potter series, with particular focus on the film adaptations. Includes interviews.

Trevarthen, Geo. *The Seeker's Guide to Harry Potter.* Ropley, England: O Books, 2008. Provides information on the various symbols that appear in the book series, particularly Celtic ones.

JOSÉ SARAMAGO

Born: Azinhaga, Ribatejo, Portugal; November 16, 1922
Also known as: José de Sousa Saramago

PRINCIPAL LONG FICTION

Terra do pecado, 1947
Manual de pintura e caligrafia, 1976 (*Manual of Painting and Calligraphy*, 1994)
Levantado do chão, 1980
Memorial do convento, 1982 (*Baltasar and Blimunda*, 1987)
O ano da morte de Ricardo Reis, 1984 (*The Year of the Death of Ricardo Reis*, 1991)
A jangada de pedra, 1986 (*The Stone Raft*, 1994)
História do cerco de Lisboa, 1989 (*The History of the Siege of Lisbon*, 1996)
O Evangelho segundo Jesus Cristo, 1991 (*The Gospel According to Jesus Christ*, 1993)
Ensaio sobre a cegueira, 1995 (*Blindness*, 1997)
Conto da ilha desconhecida, 1997 (*The Tale of the Unknown Island*, 1999)
Todos os nomes: Romance, 1997 (*All the Names*, 1999)
A caverna, 2000 (*The Cave*, 2002)
O homem duplicado, 2002 (*The Double*, 2004)
Ensaio sobre a lucidez, 2004 (*Seeing*, 2006)

OTHER LITERARY FORMS

In addition to his novels, José Saramago (sah-rah-MAH-goh) has written various other literary works, including several collections of poetry, short stories, plays, and an extensive personal diary. He has translated many European authors' works, including those of Colette, Georg Wilhelm Friedrich Hegel, Leo Tolstoy, Charles Baudelaire, Nicos Poulantzas, Guy de Maupassant, Étienne Balibar, Jean Cassou, Henri Focillon, Jacques Roumain, André Bonnard, and Raymond Bayer. Saramago has also worked as an editor for the newspaper *Diário de Noticias* and later published several newspaper articles.

ACHIEVEMENTS

José Saramago received the Prémio Cidade de Lisboa in 1980, an award that is critical to achieving recognition in Portugal. International acclaim came to Saramago with the publication of *Baltasar and Blimunda* in 1982. For this novel, he received Portugal's most prestigious literary honor, the PEN Club Award (1983 and 1984). This award was followed by the Prémio da Crítica da Associação Portuguesa 1986, an important journalism prize. *The Gospel According to Jesus Christ* was nominated for the European Literary Prize (1992), awarded by the European Writers' Congress, but Saramago's name was removed from the list of nominees by the Portuguese government. Later, he earned the Prémio Vida Literária (1993) and the Prémio Camões (1995). Most significant, his novel *The Stone Raft* received the 1998 Nobel Prize in Literature. Saramago is the only native writer in Portuguese to have received this highly coveted award, which includes one million U.S. dollars. *The Stone Raft* and his earlier novels were soon translated into many languages.

BIOGRAPHY

José Saramago was born into a poor family in the village of Azinhaga, Portugal, about sixty miles outside Lisbon on November 16, 1922. His name would actually have been a traditional Portuguese last name (de Sousa), but he accidentally received his father's nickname Saramago (Portuguese for "wild radish"). In 1924, the family moved to Lisbon.

Saramago has said that he was a good student. His family could not afford to provide him with a general education that emphasized grammar and writing. At the age of twelve, he was forced to enter a technical school, where he studied for five years to become a mechanic. Nonetheless, he was able to take courses in French. During this period, he borrowed money to buy Portuguese grammar books. After completion of his training, he became a mechanic for two years. At night, he would frequent the public library, where his interest and skill in reading poetry and prose literature inspired him to advance his writing skills without being mentored.

In 1944, Saramago married Lida Reis; in 1947, Violante, their only child, was born. It was also in 1947 that Saramago published his first novel, *Terra do Pecado*, and his only published work for the next twenty years. Saramago himself said that he did not publish during this period because he had nothing worthwhile to say. In 1951, he started work at a publishing firm (Estúdios Cor), where he would meet Portuguese authors. He then began working as a translator of literary works. From 1955 until 1981, these translations provided him a stable income so that he could also begin to seriously write poetry. In 1966, he published his first collection of poetry, *Possible Poems*. Later, he became a journalist for *Diário de Notiças*. In the late 1970's and early 1980's, he published essays that focused on Portuguese politics.

Saramago had joined the Communist Party in 1969 (an affiliation he has maintained), and he also became an atheist, which was directly counter to the traditionally conservative government of Portugal and the tenets of the Catholic Church. In 1991, Saramago left Portugal to live on the Spanish island of Lanzarote in the Islas Canarias (Canary Islands), off the western coast of North Africa. His self-exile came after the Portuguese government removed his name from a list of nominees for the European Literary Prize. The government believed that his nominated work *The Gospel According to Jesus Christ* was divisive and was offensive to the majority of Portuguese citizens.

Undeterred by the opposition and criticism, Saramago continued to publicly express his views. In 2002, in response to what he believed were immoral Israeli actions in Palestine and Lebanon, he wrote in *El País* (a Spanish newspaper) that the radical Judaism of Israel created an attitude that allowed the brutal suppression of the Palestinians. In addition, during the 2006 Lebanon War, he signed a statement declaring the actions of Israel to be a war of genocide against the Palestinian Nation. In response, the Anti-Defamation League, a Jewish civil-rights group based in the United States, said his remarks were anti-Semitic.

Saramago's play *In Nomine Dei* was published at the beginning of 1993, and in the same year, he started writing a series of diaries. Five volumes have been published as *Cadernos de Lanzarote: Diário* (1994-1998).

Analysis

José Saramago's works are often fantastic and surreal. His readers, and his characters, are forced to confront the basis for the existence of humanity; that is, what it is to be human in ever-changing modern civilizations. His characters struggle to find meaning at precisely the moment of greatest change in their respective social settings. His protagonists must not only justify their interpersonal relationships but also renew and redevelop their individuality, often outside previously understood religious, economic, and political structures. Saramago's use of fantasy settings and situations form, many have argued, a new style of writing that combines the regional Magical Realism (the use of fantastic deeds and settings as commonplace) of Latin America with the global outlook of Europe.

Saramago's style, especially in the novels published after 1986, forms a uniquely individual experiment in writing. His novels often display lengthy sentences—lengthy even for Hispanic literature, which is known for its verbosity. His baroque descriptions of the most minor settings and events often continue for pages and pages. He does not use colons, semicolons, hyphens, or quotation marks in his writing, a style that can confuse the reader as he or she attempts to determine who is speaking (including the narrator). Quotations are difficult to distinguish from the narrative; in marking a quotation, Saramago uses a limited number of commas and capitalizes the first word of a new speaker. Although this style can be frustrating, it forces the reader to pay close attention to who is speaking at any given moment. Oftentimes, Saramago eliminates the use of proper nouns and instead refers to characters with vague descriptive terms, such as "the doctor's wife." This inexactness of terminology reflects one of the author's major themes: the recurring mystery of human impermanence.

The Stone Raft

The Stone Raft addresses Portugal's national identity and its political, cultural, and social destiny. In an almost magical turn of events, a postcolonial Iberian society must confront its open-ended future. *The Stone Raft* is an ethnographic tale that explores modern strategies for survival within a previously isolated population. It is not by coincidence that the work was published the same year that Portugal joined the European Union. Portugal had been Europe's last surviving colonial empire, a nation that had only recently begun its voyage of self-acceptance as one of Europe's most enterprising and progressive member-nations.

Like all of Saramago's fictional works, the novel evolves like a present-day fable. The story begins with an event that marks the end of a fundamental concept of accepted reality. In this case, the entire Iberian Peninsula breaks from the European continent and starts drifting in the Atlantic, first toward the Azores and then toward some unknown destination (and destiny) between Europe and the United States. The story follows five characters who represent the entire population of the strange "stone raft."

Unlike many of his later works, Saramago chooses to use specific names for his characters in *The Stone Raft*. Perhaps representative of the evolution of the populace, one of the characters, a dog, has a name that changes throughout the Atlantic adventure. The dog starts as Pilot, later becomes Faithful, and ultimately is named Constant. The newly formed group of pilgrims, united by their search for answers, roam seemingly without purpose from Lisbon to Galicia. As with other Saramago novels, the focus of *The Stone Raft* is on how humans survive in unknown circumstances.

The pilgrims are ordinary people in extraordinary circumstances. Saramago does not conduct a useless search for cause and blame; instead, he focuses on what occurs with human renewal and adaptation: love and companionship, the ability to find love in the strangest of times, and the timeless determination of humans in situations that seem impossible. Saramago shows his readers that everyone must eventually learn to start anew. This collective renewal is symbolized in the novel by the pregnancies of almost all of the women on the floating landmass.

Drifting west at eighteen kilometers per day, the populace slowly begins to accept that the impossible has occurred and that they must prepare for a future that none could have imagined. The society abruptly faces new geopolitical realities, as it soon becomes obvious that the floating landmass will probably hit the Azores. The populations of Lisbon, Coimbra, Oporto, and other coastal cities are abandoned for inland areas. The collision with the Azores is avoided, however, and the floating landmass, the entire Iberian Peninsula, comes to rest somewhere in the South Atlantic between the United States and South America. Furthermore, it soon becomes clear that the United States and Canada are more interested in the economic and political effects of the newly located Iberian Peninsula than in what the consequences will be for the new nation and its people.

Saramago's approach to narration in this work is somewhat complicated, but effective. The reader is presented with single speaking characters *and* with dual narrators. One narrator speaks in an omnipresent voice, as if to explain the meanderings of the protagonists and the drifting landmass. Another, perhaps the writer himself, speaks directly to the reader, as if to justify the style of the work itself. The characters question themselves and the strange series of events, while the narrators question the values of the changes and of the work itself. In spite of the doubt, the "semimagical" tale proceeds forward into an unknown future. As the end of the work states, the journey continues.

THE GOSPEL ACCORDING TO JESUS CHRIST

In this controversial novel, Saramago brings the reader into a time and space that is located within the Christian world, but not a part of a commonly recognized Christianity. The novel explores themes found in the New Testament, such as pain, suffering, guilt, and the struggle for justice and forgiveness, but does so in a manner that goes far beyond the dogma associated with the Gospels of Jesus Christ. The tone of the work is light, even humorous at times. As with other Saramago novels, Magical Realism is employed throughout the work. The sparse descriptions of the events and characters from the Bible are replaced with detailed and fantastical portrayals. For example, in place of the standard concept of an angel as an enlightened and magical entity, the reader finds humanlike figures acting out the miraculous deeds assigned to them. Mary, the mother of Jesus, is informed of her pregnancy in a magical manner, but the angel appears in the form of a common beggar.

The novel describes the life of Jesus, Mary, and Joseph. In an interesting reinterpretation of biblical accounts, Saramago describes a relationship between Joseph and Jesus that is much closer than that between Mary and Joseph. After the birth of his son, Joseph finds out about the plan by King Herod to kill every child over the age of two years in Bethlehem. Joseph hides his son Jesus in a remote part of a cave, thereby preventing his death. However, Joseph later repents, and his life is filled with guilt. Eventually, in an effort to justify his guilt, Joseph gives his own life to save another. His son Jesus would later meet the same fate. Before his death, however, Jesus confronts his other father, God, and engages in a heated debate about the right of God to demand so much of humanity to gain recognition. He decides to rebel against God's plan for him, but in the end, he is deceived and is crucified.

Several predominant themes, or fundamental doubts and questions, arise from the text. The first is the presence of guilt in Joseph's life. Why did he not warn the other families of the impending slaughter of the young children in Bethlehem? Joseph's inaction displays the theme of limited skepticism, and the consequence of his inaction is used to raise questions about the very nature of a god that justifies his cruelty, hunger for power, and anger to get his way. Other controversial themes in the novel include the mutually beneficial relationship between God and the devil, and the plan by God to use humans as slaves to achieve his goal of a single global religion.

BLINDNESS

The setting for the novel *Blindness* is an unnamed city, where people suddenly start to go blind. The illness is contagious, and as it advances, the city's social fabric degenerates and unravels rapidly. Initially, the blind are rounded up, put in a sanatorium, and left to exist there by whatever means possible. The government then attempts to control the sanatorium and its population by using increasingly repressive and unsuccessful measures. Gangs form within the sanatorium and, eventually, all order collapses. At this time, a doctor and his wife start a group that slowly entices the population to construct a new society, with a new form of existence. Once human-centered harmony is restored, people regain their eyesight.

Saramago's long sentences and limited separation of quotes is present in this work as well. Indeed, here it is most effective, as it requires the reader to navigate speech without the usual visual cues. Paragraphs are extensive and punctuation is sparse. Names are not given. Irony is employed throughout the work. For example, the sanatorium doctor is an eye doctor. The doctor's wife is the only one who can see, but she must hide this fact in order to be persuasive to the others.

The theme of blindness in this novel is used as a means to explore the fragility of human societies. Blindness here mimics how one limited problem in a civilization can lead to a complete breakdown of social systems. The reader becomes a spectator to the negative consequences of "blind" ambitions for power. In the end, however, one of Saramago's literary traits comes into play: The new situation brings about a search for new ways of implementing the dignity of the human race. When forced to rely only upon each other, humans can and do reach out.

Paul Siegrist

OTHER MAJOR WORKS

SHORT FICTION: *Objecto quase*, 1977.

PLAYS: *A noite*, pb. 1979; *Que farei com este livro?*, pb. 1980; *A segunda vida de Francisco de Assis*, pb. 1987; *In nomine Dei*, pb. 1993.

POETRY: *Os poemas possíveis*, 1966; *Provàvelmente alegria*, 1970; *O ano de 1993*, 1975.

NONFICTION: *Deste mundo e do outro*, 1971; *A bagagem do viajante*, 1973; *As opiniões que o DL teve*, 1974; *Os apontamentos*, 1976; *Viagem a Portugal*, 1981 (*Journey to Portugal*, 2000); *Cadernos de Lanzarote: Diário*, 1994-1998 (diaries; 5 volumes); *Discursos de Estocolmo*, 1999; *Folhas politicas, 1976-1998*, 1999; *Candida Höfer: In Portugal*, 2007 (art exhibition catalog; with Shelley Rice).

BIBLIOGRAPHY

Askin, Denise Theresa, and Teresa Méndez-Faith, eds. *On the Eve of a New Millennium: Belief and Unbelief as Expressed in Literature, Philosophy, Theology, and the Visual Arts*. Manchester, N.H.: Saint Anselm College Press, 1999. Selected papers of a regional meeting of the Conference on Christianity and Literature. An interesting viewpoint that incorporates ideas about Saramago's controversial view of God and religion. Includes a short, but well-written chapter on *The Gospel According to Jesus Christ*. Also includes a bibliography.

Bloom, Harold. *José Saramago*. Philadelphia: Chelsea House, 2005. An extensive critical work on Saramago. Bloom finds Saramago to be one of the best living authors. Well written and informative. Includes a bibliography.

Frier, David Gibson. *The Novels of José Saramago: Echoes from the Past, Pathways into the Future.* Cardiff: University of Wales Press, 2007. Good critical analysis of Saramago's novels. Uses a European-based perspective of place and time. Includes a bibliography.

Hart, Stephen M., and Wen-chin Ouyang, eds. *A Companion to Magical Realism.* Rochester, N.Y.: Tamesis, 2005. A good source for an international perspective on Magical Realism, with a chapter devoted to the unique style employed by Saramago. Includes an extensive bibliography.

RAMÓN JOSÉ SENDER

Born: Chalamera de Cinca, Spain; February 3, 1901
Died: San Diego, California; January 15, 1982
Also known as: Ramón José Sender Garcés; Ramon Sender

PRINCIPAL LONG FICTION

Imán, 1930 (*Earmarked for Hell*, 1934; better known as *Pro Patria*, 1935)
Siete domingos rojos, 1932, 1973 (*Seven Red Sundays*, 1936)
La noche de las cien cabezas, 1934
Mr. Witt en el cantón, 1936 (*Mr. Witt Among the Rebels*, 1937)
El lugar del hombre, 1939 (*A Man's Place*, 1940)
O. P.: Orden público, 1941
Epitalamio del prieto Trinidad, 1942 (*Dark Wedding*, 1943)
Crónica del alba, 1942-1966 (3 volumes, 9 parts; volume 1 translated as *Before Noon: A Novel in Three Parts*, 1957; includes *Crónica del alba*, 1942 [*Chronicle of Dawn*, 1944]; *Hipogrifo violenta*, 1954 [*Violent Griffin*, 1957]; *La quinta Julieta* [*The Villa Julieta*])
La esfera, 1947, 1969 (originally as *Proverbio de la muerte*, 1939; *The Sphere*, 1949)
El rey y la reina, 1949 (*The King and the Queen*, 1948)
El verdugo afable, 1952 (*The Affable Hangman*, 1954)
Mosén Millán, 1953 (also known as *Requiem por un campesino español*, 1960; *Requiem for a Spanish Peasant*, 1960)
Los cinco libros de Ariadna, 1957, 1977
Emen hetan, 1958
Los laureles de Anselmo, 1958
El mancebo y los heroes, 1960
En la vida de Ignacio Morel, 1969

OTHER LITERARY FORMS

By the end of 1981, first editions of Ramón José Sender's books, exclusive of an anthology of selections from his works, numbered ninety-six. At the time of his death early in 1982, Destino, the Barcelona publishing house, had scheduled for publication two new novels by Sender; an additional manuscript of a novel, appropriately titled "Toque de Queda" ("Taps"), was found among his papers, ready for publication.

Depending on one's criteria for the determination of literary genre (in Sender's case, a task made all but impossible by the author's disdain for such classifications and his deliberate attempts, at times, to blur traditional genre distinctions), Sender's total production of ninety-nine books (including the three unpublished novels) could be described as including sixty-four novels or novellas, seven collections of short stories, five works of drama, two volumes of poetry, and twenty-one books of essays, personal narratives, and journalistic articles. Almost all of this last category consists of material published earlier in newspaper articles or in Sender's literary column, "Los libros y los días" (books and days), which was syndicated in Spanish-language newspapers throughout Latin America from early in the 1950's until the author's death. More than eight hundred articles appeared in "Los libros y los días."

Achievements

Ramón José Sender surely ranks as one of the greatest Spanish novelists of the twentieth century. Marcelino Peñuelas, the Spanish critic, places him "at the head of the Spanish novelists of our time" and adds, in case there is any doubt, that he means by this to exalt Sender above Pío Baroja, generally held to be the preeminent Spanish novelist of the twentieth century. Few, if any, Spanish writers of all history, except for Miguel de Cervantes and Benito Pérez Galdós, have had their novels so widely translated as has Sender.

Sender's first novel, *Pro Patria*, was translated into ten major languages; by 1970, his novels had appeared in more than eighty foreign translations, according to Peñuelas. Thirteen of his novels have appeared in English, all in both British and American editions. In January, 1936, his first historical novel, *Mr. Witt Among the Rebels*, was awarded the National Prize for Literature, at that time regarded as Spain's highest literary award. In 1966, the first three-volume edition of his monumental autobiographical novel, *Crónica del alba* (chronicle of dawn), received the City of Barcelona Prize. In 1969, Sender won the lucrative Planeta Prize from the Planeta publishing house for his rather mediocre novel *En la vida de Ignacio Morel* (in the life of Ignacio Morel).

Biography

Ramón José Sender, whose full name is Ramón José Sender Garcés, was born in the village of Chalamera de Cinca, in the Aragonese province of Huesca, on February 3, 1901. His father was town clerk of both Chalamera and the nearby town of Alcolea de Cinca. Both his parents' families had long-standing roots in Alcolea, and the Sender family returned there in 1903, moving next to Tauste (Aragon) in 1908 or 1909. A composite of both Alcolea and Tauste can be recognized as the scene of three of the author's finest novels, *A Man's Place*, *Crónica del alba*, and *Requiem for a Spanish Peasant*. His deep attachment to his native region and pride in his Aragonese heritage never left him.

From his earliest years, Sender rebelled against the authoritarian attitude of his father, a strict Catholic whose efforts to force his views upon the future novelist seem to have been decisive in determining Sender's lifelong rebellion against the existing order of things, including his rejection of the Roman Catholic Church. Sender's attitude of rebellion and protest is evident in all of his writings, both journalistic and literary. His protests against the dictatorship of Primo de Rivera in 1927 led to his imprisonment for three months in Madrid, an experience that he novelized in *O. P.*

Difficulties with his father apparently led to Sender's being sent to a Catholic boarding school in Reus (Catalonia) for the academic year 1913-1914, a year that forms the basis for his novel *Violent Griffin*, which later became the second of the three parts of the first volume of his monumental three-volume autobiographical novel *Crónica del alba*. Only volume 1 of the series has appeared in English translation (as *Before Noon: A Novel in Three Parts*, 1957), and its first part initially appeared separately under the same title as the series—*Chronicle of Dawn*.

From 1914 to 1917, Sender attended the Institute of Zaragoza. During the next school year, he worked as a pharmacy clerk in Alcañiz while meeting, through special arrangements with the Institute of Teruel (in Teruel), the remaining requirements for his high school diploma. During the next three years, from 1918 to 1921, he worked on the editorial staff of *La tierra*, a small newspaper in Huesca published by the Association of Farmers and Ranchers of Upper Aragon.

Upon his return in 1924 from fourteen months of service in the Spanish army in the ill-fated Moroccan War, Sender joined the editorial staff of the prestigious liberal newspaper *El sol* in Madrid. Following the success of his first novel, *Pro Patria*, Sender left *El sol* to devote himself full-time to freelance journalistic writing and to writing novels. During the next six years, he published six novels in addition to nearly two hundred articles in the newspaper *La libertad* and numerous articles in *Solidaridad obrera*, the organ of the Confederación Nacional de Trabajo (National Labor Federation) in Barcelona.

During the Spanish Civil War, Sender served in the republican army, rising to the rank of *comandante* (major). His wife was executed by Nationalist forces in Zamora on October 10, 1936. Late in 1938, Sender, seeing that the republican cause was hopeless, fled to France and from there to Mexico City in March of 1939. From Mexico, he entered the United States on a Guggenheim Fellowship in 1942, becoming a naturalized U.S. citizen in 1946 and remaining in the United States until his death in 1982.

From 1947 until 1963, Sender was a professor of Spanish at the University of New Mexico in Albuquerque; from 1965 until 1971, he was a visiting professor of Spanish literature at the University of Southern California. Upon retirement in 1971, he moved to San Diego, California, where he lived until his death.

Sender remained an outspoken enemy of the Nationalist regime in Spain, and it was not until June of 1974 that he returned to his native land, his first visit since his self-imposed exile in 1938. During this three-week stay, he was warmly received and highly praised by the Spanish literary community.

Analysis

Though marked by great diversity, Ramón José Sender's vast novelistic production over five decades reveals a remarkable unity of vision. In substance, one finds that there are continuing, basic Senderian concepts and themes, found in large measure in his first novel, *Pro Patria*, as well as in his posthumously published works. In them all, one finds the author's deep concern with social justice, with the struggle of the individual for self-realization, for love, and for an ideal that gives transcendent value to life. Sender's writings serve as a vehicle for ceaselessly probing certain immutable problems of existence: the question of death or human mortality; the enigma of evil in the individual and in the world at large; the possibility of an ultimate basis for moral judgments; and the function of the mysterious and the nonrational in life. Ordinary realism is in a Senderian novel only the starting point or the springboard for reaching out for transcendent meaning, for discovery of the marvelous and the mysterious, for brief flights of poetic fantasy, and for a constant metaphysical-religious-lyric questioning of the ultimate nature of reality. Sender's novels usually move on three distinct levels: the realistic, the poetic, and the philosophical-religious.

Though neither an orthodox believer in God nor an atheist, Sender reveals in his novels a deep faith in and reverence toward humanity; in *The Sphere*, he elaborates his belief that the essential part of humanity is imperishable, believing (along with Benedict de Spinoza) that "man is an integral part of the infinite intellect of God." An offense to humanity thus becomes an offense to God. Humanity, both its individual persons and in the abstract, is squarely in the center of Sender's novelistic universe. Though his short stories, theatrical pieces, essays, and poetry have received very little critical attention, they all exhibit the same basic view of humans and explore the same fundamental questions to be found in his novels.

Sender's style is that of the author speaking directly and personally to the reader in simple, clear, unaffected language, even when passages of the harshest realism are interrupted with flights of lyric fantasy or dialectical probing of philosophical-religious problems (from which inconclusive and eclectic syntheses are derived; Sender is never dogmatic except to reiterate the impossibility of humanity arriving at absolute truth—at least in this life). In a taped interview at the University of Southern California on June 7, 1966, Sender named four Spanish authors as having greatly influenced him: Fernando de Rojas, Francisco de Quevedo y Villegas, Ramón María del Valle-Inclán, and Baroja. Sender, like Baroja, is a writer of substance, always with something worthwhile to say, and openly disdainful of mere style; he also is preoccupied with social, moral, and metaphysical problems.

The influence of Valle-Inclán can be seen in Sender's occasional juxtaposition of the grotesque and the lyrically innocent and in the use of tragicomedy. His bitter social satire, his tendency to caricature and his austere humor (never far removed from sadness) may owe something to Quevedo, the seventeenth century writer of *Los sueños* (1627; *The Visions*, 1640) and the celebrated picaresque novel, *Historia de la vida del buscón* (1626; *The Life and Adventures of Buscon*, 1657). Sender's peculiar fusion of realistic and nonrealistic elements (fantasy, dreams, hallucinations, the mysterious, the marvelous, the magical, and so on) recalls not only the two levels of realism and fantasy in *La Celestina*

(1499; *The Rogue*, 1634) of Rojas but also those in the greatest Spanish novel of all, Miguel de Cervantes' *Don Quixote de la Mancha* (1605, 1615).

Francisco Carrasquer calls Sender's first novel, *Pro Patria*, a "provisional anticipatory synthesis of all of Sender's work" and adds that it is such a great novel "that one cannot understand how a first work like it did not definitely consecrate its author." Peñuelas also calls it a "great novel," and he told Sender, "You have a few novels the equal of *Imán* [*Pro Patria*], but none better." Until recently, critics have tended to regard the work as simply a realistic account of the Moroccan War much in the style of Erich Maria Remarque's *Im Westen nichts Neues* (1929, 1968; *All Quiet on the Western Front*, 1929, 1969), published one year earlier in Germany. *Pro Patria*'s fantastic, poetic, philosophical, and symbolic dimensions were long overlooked, but masterful studies of the work by both Carrasquer and Peñuelas have helped to correct this misapprehension.

Pro Patria

Pro Patria tells the story of the Spanish military campaign to suppress the rebellion of the Moorish leader Abd-el-Krim in 1921 in Spanish Morocco. The story is told from the perspective of Viance, a Spanish private who attracts misfortune (hence the book's Spanish title, *Imán*, meaning "magnet"), alternating with that of a Spanish journalist, Antonio, and that of an omniscient narrator.

Harsh realism is especially evident in the first of the book's three major divisions, "The Camp—The Relief." In the tone and atmosphere set here for the rest of the narrative, there is an implied denunciation of the utter stupidity and uselessness of war, perhaps not only of the specific Spanish campaign but also of war in general—whether the novel is a pacifist work is subject to debate.

In the second division, "Annual—The Catastrophe," the suffering of Viance from hunger, thirst, and exhaustion reaches the limits of human endurance while the Spanish forces are routed. Through it all, however, Viance, though a common soldier (and symbolic of the Spanish masses), engages in some metaphysical-lyric probing of the meaning of his experience and of human life. Lying in the stinking belly of a horse, hiding from the Moors, he senses "that his own matter is alike to that which encircles him, that there is only one kind of matter, and that all of it is animated by the same blind impulses, obedient to the same law." One dark night inclines Viance "to believe in some kind of justice . . . [in] A kind of bright and translucent justice implicit in all things."

In the third and last division, "Escape—War—Discharge—The Peace of the Dead," Viance escapes from his Moorish captors and returns to the Spanish forces, only to receive inhuman treatment from them and finally to be discharged, a bitter, disillusioned man contemplating suicide. The book's social protest arises from the action itself; Viance's officers treat him as the upper classes have for centuries in Spain treated the lower classes. Because Sender's military service in Morocco occurred two years or more after the crushing defeat of the Spaniards at Annual, the events recorded are not autobiographical but are rather a composite of what the young author heard from others combined with his own vivid imagination.

Mr. Witt Among the Rebels

The first of several historical novels published by Sender over four decades, *Mr. Witt Among the Rebels* portrays an insurrection against the First Spanish Republic in the province of Cartagena in 1873; the action occurs in Murcia and, strangely enough, it seems to foreshadow the Civil War, which was to erupt July 18, 1936, almost immediately after the appearance of the novel. Fused with the outer events of the revolution is the private, inner story of Mr. Witt, a balding English engineer of fifty-three, stationed in Cartagena and married to Milagritos, a charming and vivacious Spaniard eighteen years younger than he; the two contrast sharply in temperament and character. Events from the outside world invade the calm and quiet of their domestic life; Milagritos, passionate and nonreflective, wholeheartedly abandons herself to the uprising, while Mr. Witt, logical, reflective, and timid, retreats further into his private world: His "world" and that of the revolution are the two main poles between which the novel is built.

The characterizations of both Mr. Witt and Milagritos are superb, an admirable study in contrasting human psychology. In the end, the uprising is utterly crushed; though Milagritos knows that during the insurrection her husband acted perfidiously, she suspects that his actions were motivated by jealousy, a jealousy that confirms his love for her. Accordingly, she pardons him, and the two resume normal relations. The objective and the subjective, the outer and the inner, are found here in delicate and subtle balance; a serene work, *Mr. Witt Among the Rebels* is probably Sender's best historical novel and surely one of his finest works.

Crónica del alba

The monumental *Crónica del alba* narrates the author's life from the age of ten to his mid-thirties, the time of the Spanish Civil War. The first part, bearing the title of the novel as a whole—*Chronicle of Dawn*—appeared in 1942 and was well received; it and the second part, *Violent Griffin*, are regarded by Peñuelas as superior to the remaining parts.

The novel is essentially a study in idealism, a returning to one's origins to discover the sources of the idealism that led republican officers such as the protagonist José Garcés (obviously the author's alter ego) to risk their lives in defense of the Second Spanish Republic. José, nicknamed Pepe (Sender himself was called Pepe by members of his family), discovers love in the form of his sweetheart, Valentina, an embodiment of his idealistic values. Though Pepe's grandiose dreams as a ten-year-old boy in the "dawn" of life contrast sharply with the cruel realities of defeat that José the mature man suffers at the end of the series (the "noon" of life), his devotion to Valentina remains firm. Lying ill in a concentration camp in Algiers as the Civil War ends, José writes his autobiography in a desperate attempt to remain a man "of substance." "In a man," he explains, "substance is faith." Purportedly, he gives the three notebooks in which he has written his autobiography to Sender the author, then dies.

Following a chronological order, the series follows José's life from childhood through adolescence, young manhood, and into maturity; through it all, he seeks to live up to the grandiose ideals he had conceived as a child, especially as Valentina's sweetheart. An ancient document found in a castle by the young José declared that the men most needed to ensure the greatness of Spain were saints, poets, and heroes, though "there can be no true saint without a touch of the poet, nor, finally, any of the three without some of the virtues of the others."

In the last volume, Valentina assumes in memory the force of a pure ideal, no longer an entity of flesh and blood but a mysterious influence, a dream, a secret nostalgia for some "lost paradise." It is a longing made all the more poignant by the harsh realities of civil war.

THE SPHERE

A revision and considerable augmentation of an earlier novel, *Proverbio de la muerte*, *The Sphere* could properly be called a new novel; its first Spanish edition appeared in 1947; its definitive edition, slightly augmented and retouched from the first edition, was published in 1969. Sender regarded it as his most serious work; in it, he presents his lifelong belief in the spheroidal nature of all reality. The title of the novel is itself a metaphor of the author's monistic conception of total reality.

While crossing the Atlantic on the way to the Western Hemisphere after having escaped from Spain at the end of the Civil War, Saila, Sender's alter ego, observes that nature is composed of an infinite number of spheres or spheroids. This is true in the infinitely small (atoms), and in the infinitely large (planets, suns, the entire universe). By analogy with observable physical phenomena, Saila imagines that moral life is likewise "spherical," unified but showing two sides or two faces. As day is the other side of night and sound the other side of silence, so hate is the other side of the hate-love sphere, good the other side of evil; even death is only the complementary side of life. Thus, Saila reasons, death does not exist, and this idea becomes the fundamental thesis of the book.

To support his thesis of the nonexistence of death, Sender elaborated in *The Sphere*—and in other works as early as *La noche de las cien cabezas* (the night of one hundred heads), for example—his theory of *hombría* and the "persona." The "persona" is the human mask, the individualization of one's personality, which begins at birth, or soon thereafter, and grows throughout life—human self-consciousness. It is temporal and fears death. On the other hand, *hombría*, or "man-ness," is a mystical essence that endows humans with eternal worth; it is a person's essential self and lives in the unconscious. Upon the death of the individual, it joyfully returns to its source, the Great All or the Great Nothing.

Overladen with metaphysical musings and poetic and symbolic meaning, *The Sphere* loses the reader in a labyrinth of levels, dimensions, and meanings to the detriment of narrative force and direction. As a novel, it fails if a novel is to be judged by traditional criteria—narrative interest, character creation, sense of place, and so on. Perhaps such criteria should not be applied; nevertheless, *The Sphere* is notable for its originality and density of ideas, and it is a key work in understanding Sender's self-made philosophy or what, in all seriousness, amounted to his private religion.

Requiem for a Spanish Peasant

Requiem for a Spanish Peasant (originally titled *Mosén Millán*) is perhaps the most widely read of Sender's novels, at least in the Spanish-speaking world, where it has undergone numerous reprintings in Mexico, Argentina, and Spain; an English-Spanish bilingual edition was issued by Las Americas in New York in 1960. A short novel, it is probably Sender's most perfectly constructed work.

In an unnamed Aragonese village, Mosén Millán, a priest, waits in the sacristy to perform a requiem Mass for Paco, a peasant unjustly executed one year earlier by Nationalist forces in the early days of the Spanish Civil War. This period of waiting while the church bell tolls, calling the villagers to the Mass, lasts about twenty minutes and constitutes the novel's primary plane of action. On this plane, nothing happens except for the arrival of the three men most responsible for Paco's execution, the coming and going of the acolyte (who occasionally recites fragments of a ballad recounting Paco's life and death), the discovery of Paco's colt in the sanctuary and its subsequent ejection, and in the end the priest's moving to the chancel and beginning the Mass—with no one except the acolyte and the dead man's chief enemies (all wealthy) present, while the villagers absent themselves in mute protest against the priest's role, ambiguous and unintentional as it may have been, in the events that led to Paco's execution.

While waiting in vain for people to come to the Mass, the priest in a series of flashbacks reconstructs the story of Paco—the second plane of action—his baptism, childhood, adolescence, marriage, protest against an unjust feudal landholding system, capture, and execution. Past and present are thus skillfully woven together while the ballad recited by the acolyte and interspersed throughout the narrative comes to create what Peñuelas calls a third plane, a legendary one beyond the confines of time.

The structure of *Requiem for a Spanish Peasant*, with the priest and his memories as the focal point, provides it with remarkable unity and compactness; past and present are tightly but unobtrusively interwoven; the classical unities of time, place, and action are almost totally observed; social protest is implicit in the events themselves, related in a sober and objective tone, making such protest all the more effective. Here the author's realism is at its best, and Paco emerges as both an individual and a symbol of the Spanish masses; what happened to him in essence happened throughout Spain during the Civil War. At the same time, Mosén Millán, for whom the events of the narrative constitute a deep personal tragedy, likewise comes to embody the inertia of the Spanish Church and its tragically misguided intervention in secular affairs and lack of social conscience. The ballad, composed anonymously by the villagers, is a projection of the author's idealistic faith in the cause of a just social order. Noble also is the book's vivid and memorable portrayal of the life and customs in a Spanish village early in the twentieth century, its humor—the rough humor of country folk—and its psychological realism in the characterization of Mosén Millán.

Sender was a highly individualistic author who never adhered to any literary movement (nor to any political movement or party, despite some flirtation with the communists in the early 1930's) but who did not hesitate to take whatever seemed useful to him from any and all literary and philosophical movements (existentialism, for example), absorbing and adapting them to his own peculiar mode of expression. The voluminous totality of his production surprises and impresses not only by its great diversity but also by its amazing consistency and unity in outlook and vision as well as its unmistakable style and manner. In a sense to be taken with adequate caution, Sender, like other great writers, wrote only one novel, though he wrote it in more than sixty versions, each revealing a different angle or perspective on that reality called life, the enigma of human existence.

Charles L. King

OTHER MAJOR WORKS

SHORT FICTION: *Novelas ejemplares de Cíbola*, 1961 (*Tales of Cibola*, 1964); *Cabrerizas Altas*, 1965; *Las gallinas de Cervantes, y otras narraciones parabólicas*, 1967.

POETRY: *Las imagenes migratorias*, 1960; *Libro armilar de poesía y memorias bisiestas*, 1974.

NONFICTION: *Viaje a la aldea del crimen*, 1934; *Counter-attack in Spain*, 1937; *Hernán Cortés*, 1940; *Mexicayotl*, 1940; *Examen de ingenios: Los noventayochos*, 1961; *Valle-Inclán y la dificultad de la tragedia*, 1965; *Ensayos sobre el infringimiento cristiano*, 1967; *Tres ejemplos de amor y una teoria*, 1969; *Ensayos del otro mundo*, 1970; *El futuro comenzó ayer*, 1975.

BIBLIOGRAPHY

Devlin, John. *Spanish Anticlericalism: A Study in Modern Alienation*. New York: Las Americas, 1966. Sender is included in this study of anticlerical Spanish literature from the nineteenth and twentieth centuries. Includes a bibliography.

Eoff, Sherman Hinkle. "Ramón J. Sender: *The Sphere* (1949) and *El lugar del hombre* (1939)." In *The Modern Spanish Novel: Comparative Essays Examining the Philosophical Impact of Science on Fiction*. New York: New York University Press, 1961. An analysis of two of Sender's novels, *The Sphere* and *A Man's Place*, is included in this study of Spanish literature.

Hart, Stephen M. *Sender: "Réquiem por un campesino español."* Reprint. 1990. London: Grant & Cutler, 1996. A brief guide to *Requiem for a Spanish Peasant* designed to introduce the novel to graduate and undergraduate students. Includes a revised bibliography.

King, Charles L. *Ramón J. Sender.* New York: Twayne, 1974. An introductory overview to Sender's life, with analysis of his writings. One of the volumes in the Twayne World Authors series. Includes a bibliography.

Lough, Francis. *Politics and Philosophy in the Early Novels of Ramón J. Sender, 1930-1936: The Impossible Revolution.* Lewiston, N.Y.: Edwin Mellen Press, 1996. An analysis of novels published in the early to mid-1930's, in which Sender expressed his concern with the historical background of Spain's social and political problems and with the morality of the anarchists, communists, and other revolutionaries.

Perriam, Chris, et al., eds. *A New History of Spanish Writing, 1939 to the 1990's.* New York: Oxford University Press, 2000. This history of almost sixty years of Spanish writing includes a chapter, "Representing Ordinary Histories: Ramón José Sender and Ignacio Aldecoa," in which Sender's work is discussed.

Trippett, Anthony M. *Adjusting to Reality: Philosophical and Psychological Ideas in the Post-Civil War Novels of Ramon J. Sender.* London: Tamesis Books, 1986. Trippett's analysis of Sender's work focuses on three novels: *The Affable Hangman*, *Emen hetan*, and *Crónica del alba.* Includes a bibliography.

ANDREI SINYAVSKY

Born: Moscow, Russia, Soviet Union (now in Russia); October 8, 1925
Died: Fontenay-aux-Roses, France; February 25, 1997
Also known as: Andrei Donatovich Sinyavsky; Abram Tertz

PRINCIPAL LONG FICTION

Sad idzie, 1959 (in Polish; in Russian as *Sud idyot*, 1960; as Abram Tertz; *The Trial Begins*, 1960)
Lyubimov, 1963 (in Polish; Russian translation, 1964; as Tertz; *The Makepeace Experiment*, 1965)
Kroshka Tsores, 1980 (novella; *Little Jinx*, 1992)
Spokoynoy nochi, 1984 (*Goodnight!*, 1989)

OTHER LITERARY FORMS

Andrei Sinyavsky (sihn-YAHV-skee) is the author of an important book-length essay, *Chto takoe sotsialisticheskii realizm* (1959; *On Socialist Realism*, 1960), published under the pseudonym Abram Tertz, in which he maintains with some humor that realism is not the proper medium for the mythmaking inherent in a communist society. Because he believed that the grandiose neoclassicism inherited from eighteenth century Russian literature had also become inadequate, Sinyavsky proposed that the more appropriate genre would be fantasy, and he himself became a writer of fantasy. His collection *Fantasticheskie povesti* (1961; *Fantastic Stories*, 1963; also known as *The Icicle, and Other Stories*, 1963), including a novella and several short stories, is surrealistic, an excursion into the literature of the absurd. *Mysli vrasplokh* (1966; as Tertz; *Unguarded Thoughts*, 1972), a collection of aphorisms, came as a revelation to Sinyavsky's Western readers, disclosing for the first time his profound faith as a Russian Orthodox believer.

In addition to these works, all of which were signed with the pen name Abram Tertz and published abroad before his arrest, Sinyavsky has published a number of important critical studies, including an introductory essay to Boris Pasternak's *Stikhotvoreniya i poemy* (1965, 1976; verses and poems); an analysis of the nineteenth century writer Nikolai Gogol, *V teni Gogolya* (1975; in the shadow of Gogol); and a book on the poet Alexander Pushkin, *Progulki s Pushkinym* (1975; walks with Pushkin). Sinyavsky's *Golos iz khora* (1973; *A Voice from the Chorus*, 1976), largely composed of letters that he wrote to his wife during his six years in a labor camp, is in the tradition initiated by Fyodor Dostoevski and continued by such twentieth century writers as Aleksandr Solzhenitsyn. The essay "Literaturnii protess v Rossii" (literary process in Russia), published in the dissident journal *Kontinent* in 1976, is both a savage analysis of the Soviet mind and an extraordinary literary manifesto that transcends its occasion. Finally, Sinyavsky's *Little Jinx*, with the Yiddish word *tsores* in the original title, serves as a reminder that he identifies with Jews as alienated people outside the normal parameters of Soviet existence.

ACHIEVEMENTS

The true identity of the elusive writer Abram Tertz (a pen name taken from the hero of an underworld ballad) became known to readers in the Soviet Union and the West only after his arrest in 1965 and subsequent imprisonment. Tertz turned out to be the gifted and sophisticated critic Andrei Sinyavsky. Prior to this catastrophe, Sinyavsky had mastered the extremely difficult task of keeping his two voices, that of the writer Tertz and the critic Sinyavsky, separate. Writing as Tertz, Sinyavsky produced fantastic stories and short novels, as well as the famous essay *On Socialist Realism*, a devastating critique of officially tolerated literary practice.

So accomplished a writer was Sinyavsky that his achievements were considered far superior to those of his contemporaries, and it was even thought for a time that Tertz might be the brilliant prose writer Yury Olesha, from the 1920's. Writing during a period when Russian prose had only just begun to emerge from the stultifying limitations of Socialist Realism, Sinyavsky managed to continue the earlier ornamentalist prose tradition of Andrey Bely, Alexey Remizov, and, ultimately, Gogol.

The sophistication of Sinyavsky's worldview is equal to that of his style, for he presents society with all of its inherent contradictions, limitations, and absurdities, a far cry from the narrow vision peculiar to Socialist Realism and official Soviet ideology. With his stylistic brilliance and metaphysical depth, Sinyavsky has rightly come to be considered one of the finest Russian authors of the post-Stalin period.

BIOGRAPHY

Andrei Donatovich Sinyavsky was born in Moscow in 1925 and grew up there. He served in the Russian army during World War II. After the war, he was a student at the philological faculty of Moscow State University, one of the nation's most prestigious institutions of higher learning. He eventually became a candidate of philological sciences, a degree equivalent to a doctorate in the United States, and he obtained a position as a senior staff member with the Gorky Institute of World Literature in Moscow. Sinyavsky immediately came to be regarded as a gifted critic; his book on postrevolutionary Russian poetry, *Poeziya pervykh let revolyutsii, 1917-1920* (1964), coauthored with A. Menshutin, was considered one of the best studies of its time. His interests extended beyond literature to the plastic arts, and he collaborated with I. N. Golomshtok on a work about Pablo Picasso, *Pikasso* (1960).

Simultaneously with his activities as a critic, Sinyavsky pursued a secret career as a fantasy writer, using the name Abram Tertz; it was the revelations of de-Stalinization in 1956 that converted him from establishment critic to dissident author. Madame Hélène Peltier-Zamoyska, daughter of the French naval attaché in Moscow, had become close friends with Sinyavsky when they were students together at Moscow State University, and it was she who arranged for the publication of the works of "Tertz" in the West. In spite of Sinyavsky's discretion, he was unmasked in 1965. He was tried in February, 1966, with fellow dissident writer Yuli Daniel, who had achieved fame in the West and notoriety in the Soviet Union as Nikolay Arzhak. Sinyavsky was sentenced to six years in prison, spending the time in a labor camp in Mordovia. He left the Soviet Union for France in 1973, thereafter teaching at the Sorbonne. The fine works that he has published since his departure attest Sinyavsky's continued development as a writer.

ANALYSIS

Any attempt to analyze Andrei Sinyavsky's fiction must take the essay *On Socialist Realism* into account, for the ideas developed in that essay provide the basis for his fictional works. Socialist Realism has been defined in the Soviet Union as a depiction of "reality in its revolutionary development," the favored official medium being an anemic descendant of the so-called critical realism of the nineteenth century. This realism, Sinyavsky believes, is inadequate for expressing the heroic purpose, a purpose essential to the ideology forming the basis for the Soviet state. The neoclassicism of the eighteenth century, normally the ideal vehicle for the purpose of the autocratic state, could not be used for contemporary Soviet literature; the debunking of the Stalinist myth and absence of a figure of similar stature robbed the Russians of anyone or anything to glorify. The only remaining method possible is one based on hypothesis instead of purpose, and that method has to be fantasy. It is with this premise in mind that Sinyavsky has approached the novel.

THE TRIAL BEGINS

Sinyavsky's first novel, *The Trial Begins*, is set in Moscow during the last days of Joseph Stalin. It is ostensibly a realistic novel dealing with such well-known phenomena of the time as the "doctors' plot," which resulted in the stepped-up persecution of the Jews, the terrifying inner workings of the secret police, and the mass panic immediately following the death of Stalin. Sinyavsky's principal characters include the public prosecutor Vladimir Petrovich Globov, his idealistic son, Seryozha, and Seryozha's friend, Katya. Globov's second wife, Marina, and Yuri Karlinsky, a defending attorney, eventually manage to become lovers behind Globov's back. Globov's former mother-in-law, Yekaterina Petrovna, is an old Bolshevik idealist.

Globov is scheduled to prosecute the gynecologist S. Y. Rabinovich, who performed an illegal abortion, but the woman in question is Globov's beautiful and sexy but soulless wife, Marina. Rabinovich is Jewish, and his predicament is a transparent reference to Stalin's anti-Semitic campaign in the 1950's. Globov's life is complicated further by the fact that his adolescent son, Seryozha, has written a notebook calling for a new Communist society that will be free of the corruption that has stained the old one, a society in which those in the highest offices would earn the lowest wages, money would be abolished, and everyone would receive "according to his needs." Seryozha shares his ideas with Katya and gives her the notebook. She takes it to Karlinsky for advice, protesting against Seryozha's orthodoxy that a noble end should be served by noble means; Karlinsky counters that power corrupts, with the noble means soon forgotten. After she leaves, he gives vent to his jealous rage against Marina's husband, deciding to strike at him by blowing the whistle on his son, Seryozha. Seryozha is eventually tried and sent to a labor camp, where he is joined by Rabinovich. Finally given the opportunity to consummate his affair with Marina, Karlinsky proves to be impotent. Katya is trampled to death in the mass stampede following Stalin's funeral.

At first glance, *The Trial Begins* appears to be a realistic work that reveals corruption and evil in the Soviet Union, a critique of the system in the tradition of Vladimir Dudintsev's *Ne khlebom yedinym* (1956; *Not by Bread Alone*, 1957) or Ilya Ehrenburg's *Ottepel* (1954; *The Thaw*, 1955). Appearances, however, are deceiving, and *The Trial Begins* stands apart from its fellows by virtue of Sinyavsky's use of fantasy.

The Trial Begins is introduced by a narrator, one of a series of Sinyavsky's quirky, neurotic narrators. He bears a close resemblance to Yury Olesha's hero Kavalerov in the novel *Zavist* (1927; *Envy*, 1936), and it is easy to see why a number of Western critics initially assumed that the novelist and critic known as Tertz was actually Olesha. Tertz's narrator, similar to but not identical with Tertz himself, is the author of the manuscript that constitutes the major portion of the novel. He is a writer, the generic, nonconformist Soviet writer.

The narrator is victimized in the middle of the night by two secret police agents, Vitya and Tolya, who work as a team and bear a strong resemblance to Thompson and Thomson from Hergé's series of children's books on the young French reporter Tintin. Vitya and Tolya, like Thompson and Thomson, are the enemies of freedom and originality, and their purpose is to destroy art. One of them scoops all the letters and punctuation marks off the page and crushes one caught trying to escape. The manuscript they have confiscated is *The Trial Begins*, but the characters and events in the work come to life as if they had been written by an omniscient, not a first-person, narrator. The narrator himself disappears from the story, not to surface again until the end, when he is shown in prison camp with his invented characters Rabinovich and Seryozha. Thus, the body of the novel is sandwiched between the reader's introduction to the narrator at the beginning and the reader's final, sad view of him at the end.

The most fantastic element of the frame technique used by Sinyavsky is that two characters who are part of the body of the novel—that is, part of the manuscript written by the convict author—actually appear with him in prison at the conclusion of the story. The reader is then left with the uneasy sensation that the manuscript has taken over and somehow become actuality, that the omniscient and first-person narrators might possibly be the same individual. The implications of this confusing situation are enormous.

Beneath the surface of an apparent protest novel, a novel peppered with such peculiar events as the appearance of the hand of God to the narrator at the beginning or Marina's gift of liqueur-filled chocolates to Seryozha at the end, other factors are at work. Sinyavsky's novel is only superficially about political events and the illicit love affair between Karlinsky and Marina. It is actually about art, specifically about literature and the intricacies involved in the writing of fiction. As such, it follows in the tradition of Russian works that are consciously but obliquely about literature or art, works such as Olesha's *Envy*—a tradition that ultimately extends back to the subtle plays and short stories of Pushkin.

Sinyavsky is, of course, concerned with political abuses and is clearly against the overwhelming domination of all aspects of Soviet life by Stalin's dictatorship, but he is primarily preoccupied with artistic freedom. The arrest, to which any citizen was subject at any time, without warning, was a commonplace of Soviet life during the Terror of the 1930's and then again after World War II. Sinyavsky's account of the narrator's arrest uncannily anticipates his own later arrest and imprisonment; it is the fictional arrest that sets in motion the events of the novel, for only through the narrator's arrest do the police (and the readers) learn of the existence of the formerly secret manuscript. The apparent fragility of the narrator's creation is touchingly depicted in the opening scene, when an escaping letter is destroyed like a bug. The author of the manuscript is himself fragile, easily trapped by the state and sent to prison.

This leads to the realization that there is yet another layer of fantasy operative here, for the entire novel—including both the frame story and the manuscript—actually resurfaces and is subsequently published; the manuscript of the story is only a larger portion of the real manuscript that exists in the form of Sinyavsky's novel. The captured letters have escaped after all, coming to new life in print. The captured narrator, an unfortunate prisoner who is the product of Sinyavsky's imagination, achieves new life within his larger, real novel. If straightforward art cannot appear, Sinyavsky suggests, then the writer must resort to the art of circumlocution. If a literary work is helpless in a police state, then an entire manuscript can be incorporated into another work, and that novel can somehow escape the predatory actions of official limitation. It is through the cunning of fantasy that art survives at all. This is fitting, because fantasy itself is the product of the artistic imagination, an answer to the superficial strictures enforced by politics. The survival of art is the answer to the state, because the actual reality envisioned by art is of a different order from that of the apparent reality of a political system; the boundary between the visible and the hidden is nowhere better demonstrated than in the encounter between the awesome hand of God and the tiny fist of Stalin in Sinyavsky's initial frame segment. The relative disparity between them is but a symbol of the enormous gulf separating apparent and absolute values, be they religious or aesthetic.

The Makepeace Experiment

Fantastic elements are more easily discernible in *The Makepeace Experiment* than in *The Trial Begins*. The Russian title of Sinyavsky's second novel is *Lyubimov*, the name of the town that provides the setting for the incredible events of the novel. *The Makepeace Experiment* was published three years after *The Trial Begins*, and Sinyavsky's greater expertise as a novelist is reflected in the more intricate characterization, fantastic plot, and convoluted narration.

Like his nineteenth century predecessors, Sinyavsky abandons the setting of Moscow in favor of the small, remote town of Lyubimov. It has the flavor of the innumerable squalid hamlets peppering Gogol's prose masterpieces, but it is especially reminiscent of the town in Mikhail Saltykov's novel *Istoriya odnogo goroda* (1869-1870; *The History of a Town*, 1981). *The Makepeace Experiment*, however, is only ostensibly a story of rural life. As circumstances of the plot make amply clear, the events taking place there are actually a microcosm of the larger politico-historical world. Lyonya Tikhomirov's dictatorship (his name means "peaceful world"), the fruitful result of his ability to apply mass hypnosis to the populace of an entire town, bears a certain resemblance to the larger one bedeviling Russians in hundreds of small towns all across the Soviet Union. Lyonya, however, has heeded the idealism of Seryozha in *The Trial Begins*, for this dictatorship is devoid of corruption, greed, and coercion. Through the magic wand of Lyonya's hypnotic powers, the locals believe that toothpaste has changed into fish paste, the local river runs with champagne for thirty minutes, and ordinary bottled water, the sort normally avoided by most of the residents, seems to have turned into grain alcohol and in fact causes the death of one drinker.

Lyonya's aristocratic ancestor, Samson Samsonovich Proferantsov, owned a leather-bound book from India titled *The Magnet of the Soul*. Having accidentally acquired the book, Lyonya masters the contents and sets out to acquire the two things he desires: mind control over the citizens of Lyubimov and the love of the previously indifferent beauty Serafima Petrovna Kozlova. He celebrates his wedding to Serafima simultaneously with his formal installment as official leader of the town of Lyubimov; for a while, events run smoothly, and Serafima is his willing slave. Lyonya has audiences directly with his citizens, attempting to please all of those under his jurisdiction, and they turn Stakhanovite for the dubious reward of ersatz luxuries. He has an elaborate alarm system installed to foil incursions from the outside, using his magnetic powers to baffle would-be enemies, but he becomes increasingly bored with the obedient Serafima and is exhausted by the heavy demands of his office.

Unwilling to be left out of the action, the original owner of the book asserts himself. He scrambles Lyonya's magnetic powers, and our hero's every thought turns into a command subconsciously transmitted to the residents of Lyubimov. A young man silently commanded to "drop dead" collapses and dies of a heart attack; an old woman rides her broom, having become a witch in accordance with Lyonya's desires. The entire utopian society falls apart, and Lyonya escapes in the end, enabling his town to return to normal.

It is in *The Makepeace Experiment* that Sinyavsky introduces a Jewish character for the first time—Serafima Petrovna. The narrator gossips to Lyonya about her ethnic origins and, in the end, the reader learns that she really is part Jewish and that Kozlov was only the name of her first husband. She had kept the existence of her husband and small daughter secret from Lyonya, and there is a hint that these scandalous facts are all related to her Jewishness. Having warned Lyonya that his intended is not really "Russian," the narrator allows himself a digression about Jews. He admires them; they are survivors. They are scattered in society like indissoluble specks, like "raisins" or "black pepper" but never salt. They have Jewish eyes, sad eyes with *tsores* (trouble); Proferantsov calls them "desert eyes."

Sinyavsky's intense interest in Jews extends even to his selection of a Jewish pseudonym, Abram Tertz, a choice that must be regarded as highly unusual for a Russian writer. There are various reasons for his singular interest. In the first place, Sinyavsky resembles Olesha in regarding the writer as a foreign element in society, particularly Soviet society. The writer is like the Jew in his cosmopolitanism, his resultant separation from the mainstream, and his awareness of "trouble." Sinyavsky even flavors his writing with a Jewish accent when describing the Jewish woman who had once been part of his life, a stylistic touch that does not come across in the English translation.

Sinyavsky, however, has yet another complex reason for his apparent obsession: his sense of history. The Jews encountered in Russian society are a reminder that "history did not begin today and it is still not known how it will end." Those desert eyes are sad because of "historical memories." The Jews—and, by extension, the writer—are somehow outside the deterministic orthodoxy that history has evolved along certain lines from the beginning of time. Official Soviet history centers on the concept that the October Revolution was the great break from the capitalism dominating nineteenth century Europe, an economic and political structure giving way to the socialism and eventual communism that will someday grace the Soviet Union. Sinyavsky counters this supposition through his narrator Proferantsov, stating that no one knows how history will end. This incredible statement flies in the face of Marxist orthodoxy, for the presumed final result is the withering away of the state with the triumph of communism. Reality, says Sinyavsky, is unpredictable and cannot be controlled, and he underlines this firmly by his use of fantasy and multiple narrators.

The seeming ordinariness of life gives way at the conclusion of the novel to the ramblings of the narrator Proferantsov, for *The Makepeace Experiment* is a frame story introduced and ended by a chatty writer, in a genre ultimately going back to Pushkin's stories. The narrative here is complicated by the presence of a second narrator, Samson Samsonovich Proferantsov himself, who intrudes into Proferantsov's story in the form of corrective footnotes; it is an irritating practice that does not endear him to his descendant.

By such devices, Sinyavsky makes it impossible for his readers to maintain that "willing suspension of disbelief" so crucial to the flow of most fictional works. He constantly reminds us that we are reading a work of fiction and have entered an artificial world. He underscores this unreality with his pterodactyl, a creature rumored by Dr. Linde, one of the novel's several eccentrics, to inhabit the swampy woods outside town. The pterodactyl indeed exists; it appears to Colonel Almazov, commander of the forces sent to storm the town, during his final drugged moments and seems to speak perfect French. What better witness to this impossible horror than the supporter of state power, a man who would never allow for the oddities of events outside the orthodox conception of reality. The scene between the two is the high point of the novel, the sort of confrontation for which Sinyavsky himself pushed in creating a fantastic world as rival to the rigidity of the real one.

Sinyavsky's fiction provides an excellent illustration of the sort of fantasy he advocated in his theoretical writing. Serving as an antidote to the rigidity of Socialist Realism, it is a reminder that Russian literature still has room for the incredible and unorthodox. Fantasy for Sinyavsky is a vehicle for addressing crucial questions, for it is by circumventing the real world that he is able to deal with such issues as the role and methods of the writer, the meaning of history, and the problems and inequities of the dictatorship that provided the setting for his works. As both artist and thinker, he must be accounted one of the most interesting and significant of contemporary Russian authors.

Janet G. Tucker

OTHER MAJOR WORKS

SHORT FICTION: *Fantasticheskie povesti*, 1961 (*Fantastic Stories*, 1963; also known as *The Icicle, and Other Stories*, 1963).

NONFICTION: *Istoriya russkoy sovetsky literatury*, 1958, 1961; *Chto takoe sotsialisticheskii realizm*, 1959 (as Abram Tertz; *On Socialist Realism*, 1960); *Pikasso*, 1960 (with I. N. Golomshtok); *Poeziya pervykh let revolyutsii, 1917-1920*, 1964 (with A. Menshutin); *Mysli vrasplokh*, 1966 (as Tertz; *Unguarded Thoughts*, 1972); *For Freedom of Imagination*, 1971 (essays); *Golos iz khora*, 1973 (*A Voice from the Chorus*, 1976); *Progulki s Pushkinym*, 1975 (*Strolls with Pushkin*, 1993); *V teni Gogolya*, 1975; *"Opavshie list'ya" V. V. Rozanova*, 1982; *Soviet Civilization: A Cultural History*, 1990; *Ivan-durak: Ocherk russkoi narodnoi very*, 1991 (*Ivan the Fool: Russian Folk Belief—A Cultural History*, 2007); *The Russian Intelligensia*, 1997.

BIBLIOGRAPHY

Fenander, Sara. "Author and Autocrat: Tertz's Stalin and the Ruse of Charisma." *Russian Review* 58 (April, 1999): 286-297. Examines Sinyavsky in his role as both cultural critic and the provocateur Abram Tertz; claims that by turning the discredited Joseph Stalin into a double for himself, Sinyavsky/Tertz reveals both the artistry of Stalinism and the mythical privileged place of the writer in Russian culture.

Frank, Joseph. "The Triumph of Abram Tertz." *The New York Review of Books*, June 27, 1991. A brief biographical and critical discussion of the events of Sinyavsky's life and the nature of his fiction. Notes the importance of his trial for having his works published outside the Soviet Union.

Genis, Alexander. "Archaic Postmodernism: The Aesthetics of Andrei Sinyavsky" and "Postmodernism and Sots-Realism: From Andrei Sinyavsky to Vladimir Sorokin." In *Russian Postmodernism: New Perspectives on Post-Soviet Culture*, by Mikhail Epstein, Alexander Genis, and Slobodanka Vladiv-Glover. Translated and edited by Vladiv-Glover. New York: Berghahn Books, 1999. These two essays about Sinyavsky's postmodernist writings are included in this examination of Russian fiction, poetry, art, and spirituality after the demise of the Soviet Union.

Grayson, Jane. "Back to the Future: Andrei Siniavskii and Kapitanskaia Dochka." In *Reconstructing the Canon: Russian Writing in the 1980's*, edited by Arnold B. McMillin. Amsterdam: Harwood Academic, 2000. This discussion of Sinyavsky's work is included in a collection of essays examining Soviet writers whose work appeared during the 1980's, a decade in which artists were allowed greater freedom of expression.

_______. "Picture Windows: The Art of Andrei Siniavskii." In *Russian Literature, Modernism, and the Visual Arts*, edited by Catriona Kelly and Stephen Lovell. New York: Cambridge University Press, 2000. Grayson's examination of Sinyavsky's work is included in a collection of essays about the influence of the visual arts on Russian modernist literature, focusing on collaborations between writers and artists, designers, and theater and film directors.

Kolonosky, Walter F. *Literary Insinuations: Sorting Out Sinyavsky's Irreverence*. Lanham, Md.: Lexington Books, 2003. Kolonosky's examination of Sinyavsky's writing focuses on the satire in his work, exploring how the writer uses allegory, parody, and irony to criticize abuses and foolishness.

Lourie, Richard. *Letters to the Future: An Approach to Sinyavsky-Tertz*. Ithaca, N.Y.: Cornell University Press, 1975. Lourie analyzes Sinyavsky's novels, short stories, and other work, placing them within the context of Soviet history and Slavic literature. Compares Sinyavsky's "philosophical satire" to the work of Nikolai Gogol. Includes notes, a bibliography, and an index.

Mathewson, Rufus W., Jr. *The Positive Hero in Russian Literature*. 1975. Reprint. Evanston, Ill.: Northwestern University Press, 1999. Mathewson includes an analysis of Sinyavsky's writing in this examination of the "positive hero," a character who sets an example for readers' behavior. Describes how this model character was a longstanding source of controversy in Russian literature.

Sandler, Stephanie. "Ending/Beginning with Andrei Sinyavsky/Abram Tertz." In *Commemorating Pushkin: Russia's Myth of a National Poet*. Stanford, Calif.: Stanford University Press, 2004. Sandler analyzes Russia's complex relationship with Alexander Pushkin, describing how his work has influenced Sinyavsky and other Russian writers and how his legacy is reflected in museums and other Russian cultural institutions.

Theimer Nepomnyashchy, Catherine. "Sinyavsky/Tertz: The Evolution of the Writer in Exile." *Humanities in Society* 7, no. 314 (1984): 123-142. After providing a brief overview of Sinyavsky's career during his first decade in the West, the author goes on to detail Sinyavsky's concerns with the role of the writer in relationship to reality and society at large. Concludes with a discussion of *Little Jinx*.

JUN'ICHIRO TANIZAKI

Born: Tokyo, Japan; July 24, 1886
Died: Yugawara, Japan; July 30, 1965

PRINCIPAL LONG FICTION

Itansha no Kanashimi, 1917
Chijin no ai, 1924-1925 (serial), 1925 (book; *Naomi*, 1985)
Kojin, 1926
Tade kuu mushi, 1928-1929 (serial), 1936 (book; *Some Prefer Nettles*, 1955)
Manji, 1928-1930
Yoshinokuzu, 1931 (*Arrowroot*, 1982)
Bushoko hiwa, 1931-1932 (serial), 1935 (book; *The Secret History of the Lord of Musashi*, 1982)
Sasameyuki, 1943-1948 (serial), 1949 (book; *The Makioka Sisters*, 1957)
Shosho Shigemoto no haha, 1950 (*The Mother of Captain Shigemoto*, 1956)
Kagi, 1956 (*The Key*, 1960)
Futen rojin nikki, 1961-1962 (serial), 1962 (book; *Diary of a Mad Old Man*, 1965)

OTHER LITERARY FORMS

The history of the novel in Japan is quite different from its history in the West, and the distinctions normally observed between the short story and the novel do not apply there. If, arbitrarily, one refers to Japanese works of fewer than one hundred pages of prose fiction as "short stories," Jun'ichiro Tanizaki (tah-nee-zahk-ee) is as famous for his short stories as for his longer works. Typical of his early period, "Shisei" (1910; "The Tattooer," 1963) indicates his early interest in sexual symbolism. "Akuma" (1912; Satan) deals with male masochism, and "Otsuya goroshi" (1913; a springtime case) deals with murder and amorality in Tokyo. Later, Tanizaki wrote such remarkable stories as "Ashikari" (1932; English translation, 1936), "Shunkinsho" (1933; "A Portrait of Shunkin," 1936), "Momoku monogatari" (1931; "A Blind Man's Tale," 1963), and the exquisite "Yume no ukihashi" (1959; "The Bridge of Dreams," 1963).

Tanizaki also wrote a number of plays, including *Aisureba koso* (pb. 1921; all because of love), *Okumi to Gohei* (pb. 1922), and *Shirogitsune no yu* (pb. 1923; *The White Fox*, 1930). In 1932, he began translating Murasaki Shikibu's *Genji monogatari* (c. 1004; *The Tale of Genji*, 1936-1941, 1951-1954) into modern Japanese; over the years, he produced several revisions of it. *Bunsho tokuhon* (1934; a manual of style), in which he outlined his craftsmanlike attitude toward composing fiction, is often called a minor masterpiece of criticism. Although he published several highly accomplished reviews and essays, he seldom was persuaded to undertake them, believing that he ought to concentrate on his fiction.

ACHIEVEMENTS

Jun'ichiro Tanizaki was recognized as a remarkable talent even in his twenties and continued to be so recognized throughout a long and prolific career, which outlasted several publications of his complete works. At first, he was considered shockingly Western by his contemporaries; during the 1920's, however, he gradually began to incorporate more conservative Japanese literary elements, implicitly warning his readers of the dangers of being overly Westernized. Late in his career, his characters are not endangered by Western culture, enjoying, for example, Western clothes and houses as everyday realities in modern Japan.

Tanizaki's mastery of a carefully composed style and his insight into the psychology of his characters place him among the great writers of twentieth century world literature. A slow, careful writer, Tanizaki argued that one of the most important elements of Japanese is its "vagueness" in comparison to other languages, a vagueness that allows the Japanese author to suggest motives, feelings, and details in delicate strokes rather than in precise exposition. Considering the imagination crucial, Tanizaki often dealt with sensational material and abnormal states of mind; by controlling his style, he did not allow his intensity to become hysterical. Despite their bizarre aberrations, his characters rarely become unbelievable as human beings, because of the objective manner in which he treats them. Like many great writers, Tanizaki was also able to assimilate opposing elements such as tradition and innovation, imagination and realism, and the influences of West and East.

BIOGRAPHY

Jun'ichiro Tanizaki was born in the heart of downtown Tokyo. For generations, his ancestors had lived there as members of the merchant class engaged in rice-brokering and printing and had little of the traditional samurai-class interest in affairs of state. Despite the traditional male-dominated culture of Japan, Tanizaki's grandfather and father were considered feminists, his father nearly worshiping Tanizaki's mother. The boy, as a result, was drawn to his mother very strongly, thus establishing the reverential attitude toward women seen in so many of his works. Tanizaki was also a handsome boy, but not a strong one, and, consequently, was often bullied by older classmates, perhaps encouraging a masochistic streak.

During Tanizaki's primary education, a young teacher noticed the boy's talents and gave him special instruction in Japanese and Chinese classics. It is often reported that Tanizaki became known as the brightest student ever to graduate from the First Municipal Secondary School of Tokyo. He entered Tokyo Imperial University in 1908, where he studied Japanese classical literature. He helped found the literary magazine of the university, *Shinshicho*, in which he published several short stories that received praise from older writers such as Mori Ogai and Nagai Kafu. After only a year, however, because he did not pay his fees, he left the university without finishing his degree.

Tanizaki's unfinished education did not hinder him unduly, because he was becoming known as a writer. A notorious frequenter of the "Bluff," or foreign sections of Yokohama, he wore checked suits and gaudy ties and was strongly under the influence of Decadent Western writers such as Edgar Allan Poe, Charles Baudelaire, and Oscar Wilde; Tanizaki translated Wilde's *Lady Windermere's Fan* (1892) in 1919. This lifestyle changed when he moved to Okamoto in 1923 after the Great Earthquake. In the Hakone mountains south of Yokohama, during the disaster, he first was delighted that all he despised of the old Japan had been destroyed. He predicted a new, modern Tokyo with wide boulevards, film theaters, and citizens wearing comfortable Western clothing. Yet, as time passed, he began to seek the traditional roots of Japanese literature and went, as is often asserted, from being merely a good author to being a great one.

By 1930, Tanizaki was so famous that his complete works were published. His personal life was almost as sensational as his fiction. After encouraging his wife, Chiyoko, to have an affair with his friend, Sato Haruo, they were divorced in 1930 after fifteen years of marriage. In 1931, he married Furukawa Tomiko, a literary student whom he divorced in 1934. In 1935, he married his last wife, Morita Matzuko, formerly married to an Osaka millionaire and patron of several artists and writers, including Tanizaki.

With the rise of militarism in Japan, Tanizaki's work—with its interest in aestheticism and sexuality—was considered improper, and he was forced to suppress the amorous passages of his translation of *The Tale of Genji*, which he had begun in 1935. His longest novel, *The Makioka Sisters*, was not published during the war because of the amorous content, but when it was finally released, it—along with his earlier works—established Tanizaki as possibly the most significant twentieth century Japanese author. In 1949, he received Japan's Imperial Prize for Literature.

During the 1950's and 1960's, Tanizaki returned to some of the themes of his earlier career. The publication of the first episode of *The Key* in the magazine *Chuo koron* in 1956 created a sensation in Japan as customers snatched up copies, partly because of its sexual content. It also became well known in the United States, as did "The Bridge of Dreams" and *Diary of a Mad Old Man*, as a result of a new Western interest in Japanese films (such as Akira Kurosawa's 1951 film of Ryunosuke Akutagawa's "Rashomon") and literature (notably the works of Yasunari Kawabata and Yukio Mishima). In 1960, a film version of *The Key* was released in the United States as *Odd Obsession*. In 1964, Tanizaki was elected honorary member of the American Academy of Arts and Letters and the National Institute of Arts and Letters. He spent his last few years struggling with various illnesses and living in a Western-style house on the Izu Coast. At the time of his death, Tanizaki was one of the leading candidates for a Nobel Prize.

ANALYSIS

Jun'ichiro Tanizaki's early literary career was characterized by a deep interest in Western literature. Although as a student he studied Japanese literature and had a nostalgia for classical Japanese works, he once commented that about 1918, "I had come to detest Japan, even though I was obviously a Japanese." Assiduously reading Baudelaire, Wilde, and especially Poe, he asserted the supremacy of the imagination in literature, as opposed to the naturalism of many of his contemporaries, arguing that even Gustave Flaubert and Émile Zola could not have produced their naturalistic works without being highly imaginative.

Once using Wilde's aphorism "Nature imitates art" as an epigraph to a story, Tanizaki believed that the representation of reality was not the primary function of literature; it was rather the presentation of truth. "The artist," he wrote, "justifies his existence only when he can transform his imagination into truth." This truth, in Tanizaki's view, was primarily psychological. Imagination allowed the author to see the subconscious depths of humanity. The writer perceived what people were, not what they could be. There was no need for a writer to justify his (or her) works for social or moral reasons, and Tanizaki was seen as an exponent of aestheticism.

As might be expected, the early influence of the Decadent authors led to intense, macabre works. They are, by turn, gothic, grotesque, hedonistic, diabolic, and erotic. Tanizaki's first important work, "The Tattooer," is typical. Seikichi is a master tattooer who has become so great he only tattoos according to his vision of his client's character. Further, he delights in the suffering his needles cause his clients. His obsession becomes the creation of a masterwork on the skin of a woman who meets his requirements of character as well as beauty. After four years, he sees the foot of a woman disappear into a palanquin, knows instantly that she is the one he has been searching for, but loses the palanquin in the crowd. The next spring, she appears at his house, and after he reveals her true, vampirish nature, he creates an exquisite tattoo of a black widow spider on her back and finds himself the slave of his own creation.

There are several elements characteristic of Tanizaki's work in this story. In most of his works, a man delights in his utter servitude to the woman he adores. Seikichi goes from sadist to masochist as the result of finding his perfect woman, and although Tanizaki devotes this work to the psychological and artistic obsessions of the tattooer, he was generally more interested in his women characters, because they expressed an ideal before which his men groveled. This subservient role has been frequently associated with Tanizaki's attitude toward his mother, who died in 1917. One will also note the foot fetishism implicit in Seikichi's first noticing the young girl. Throughout Tanizaki's career, women's feet play a large role in the sexual relationships between his characters. This is obvious in such works as "Fumiko no ashi" in which an old man is infatuated with the feet of his mistress and dies in ecstasy as Fumiko presses his forehead under her foot, but it reveals itself in other ways as well: Frequently, Tanizaki devotes more detail to his description of a woman's feet than he does to his description of her face.

Despite Tanizaki's interest in Western writers, many elements of his early work were derived from traditional Japanese literature. Throughout his career, he felt no hesitation in setting his stories in the Japanese past. "The Tattooer," for example, occurs in the

Tokugawa period of the seventeenth century. In 1919, in the middle of his Decadent interests, the same year as "Fumiko no ashi" and his translation of *Lady Windermere's Fan*, he published a volume of erotic stories in the style of the Japanese 1830's and two novellas in the Chinese style. As they are depicted in works by Tanizaki, women are often portrayed as treacherous, cruel creatures in classical Japanese literature. The seventeenth century novelist Ihara Saikaku wrote many risqué stories, in some of which the heroine's insatiable sexual appetite exhausts the hero. Finally, grotesque and diabolic motifs are very common in classical Japanese literature, and it is perhaps too easy to overemphasize the influence of Poe's and Wilde's content on Tanizaki, when he was more interested in adapting their conception of art in his reaction against naturalism.

There is no doubt, however, that Tanizaki's work changed at the beginning of the 1920's, particularly after he moved from Tokyo to the more conservative Kansai (Kyoto, Osaka, and Kobe) region after the Great Earthquake. Although in his later work he retained his masochistic heroes, characters for whom there are few precedents in traditional Japanese literature, he began to acknowledge more strongly the values and practices of his culture.

NAOMI

Naomi marks the division between Tanizaki's Westernized period and his more tradition-oriented works from the 1920's through the 1940's. Although, like so many of his works, *Naomi* tells of a man's quest for the ideal woman, there is much implied criticism of Japanese worship of the West, despite the fact that the novel seems to have been based on W. Somerset Maugham's *Of Human Bondage* (1915).

Joji, the narrator in *Naomi*, is attracted to a European-looking waitress named Naomi. Her features make him think of Mary Pickford, and he asks her if she would like to go to a film. Instead of the usual polite evasions, she says (like Mildred in *Of Human Bondage*), "I don't mind if I do." Eventually, he takes her home with the intention of remaking her into his ideal of beauty—a woman he will not be ashamed of in front of blond foreigners—and marrying her within a few years. Naomi is given Western clothes, practices playing the piano, speaking English, and dancing. All of this merely encourages her decadent tendencies. He learns she has been unfaithful and attempts to leave her. He discovers he cannot, however, and gives in completely to her. She can do as she wishes, have whatever lover she wishes, as long as she remains his wife.

Joji is a fool as much in his obsessive love of Western things as in his love of the girl. He is ashamed of his racial identity. His shortness, his protruding teeth, his dark complexion, and other typically Japanese features embarrass him, but he is proud of his European-style Yokohama house. He is degraded by his sense of both cultural and sexual inferiority. Often offended by Naomi's crudity, he excuses it because of his fascination with her; to be humiliated by her is an honor. Even when she dresses and behaves like a prostitute, he is filled with masochistic pride that she is his.

Some Prefer Nettles

Tanizaki's next major novel, *Some Prefer Nettles*, deals with similar themes. This work tells of a character, Kaname, whose superficial Western tastes are gradually replaced by an appreciation of traditional Japanese culture. Kaname is unhappily married to Misako. He has lost sexual interest in her but is tormented by uncertainty over what to do about it. He encourages her to have an affair while he finds sexual satisfaction with a Eurasian prostitute. There is a superficial resemblance between this plot and certain events in Tanizaki's own life. Bored with his first wife, Chiyoko, one night at dinner he calmly asked Sato Haruo, poet and friend, if he would like to marry her. In 1930, after encouraging the affair, Tanizaki divorced Chiyoko, and she married Sato. Obviously, this arrangement was on his mind during the writing of *Some Prefer Nettles*, and his ambivalence is perhaps reflected by the book itself.

Far more important, however, in assessing the book, is the struggle in Kaname between his appreciation of Western culture and his appreciation of the merchants' culture of old Japan surviving in Osaka, particularly represented in this novel by the Bunraku, or puppet theater. At the end of the novel, Kaname confuses a puppet with the Osaka beauty O-hisa, showing perhaps that the old way of life is a fantasy that cannot be recaptured. Edward G. Seidensticker, who translated the novel, argues that Kaname (and Tanizaki) is attempting to return to the peace of childhood, although the adult knows the new world is here to stay. In his essay "In'ei raisan" (1934; *In Praise of Shadows*, 1955), Tanizaki wrote "I know as well as anyone that I am dreaming, and that, having come this far, we cannot turn back."

It should also be noted that whatever ambivalence or vagueness readers might find in *Some Prefer Nettles* and other Tanizaki novels is as much a reflection of his aesthetic as of any personal feelings. He always insisted on exploiting the vagueness of Japanese and objected to writers who were too clear. One cannot, for example, know exactly what will happen to Kaname the day after the novel closes. Primary among Tanizaki's goals in writing was to achieve poetic suggestiveness, which the last scene certainly does.

The Makioka Sisters

During the late 1930's, Tanizaki continued his rediscovery of traditional Japanese culture by beginning his translation of *The Tale of Genji*, a work that, in many ways, influenced the composition of *The Makioka Sisters*, his longest and, many argue, his greatest novel. Although Tanizaki was always a slow, very careful writer, wartime circumstances forced him to work even more slowly than usual. He spent many years on *The Makioka Sisters*, and censorship prevented complete publication of the work until 1948.

Before Tanizaki began writing the novel, he delineated a precise plan and followed it nearly to the conclusion. Despite this detailed planning, *The Makioka Sisters*—unlike his usual lean, straightforward novels—is a sprawling, indirect novel in the episodic form often favored by Japanese authors. Complex characterization and diverse social forces create many layers of action and emotion to give the book a texture quite different from that of Tanizaki's typical works, which focus on a single character.

In the novel, the four Makioka sisters represent various aspects of Japanese culture during the 1930's. Once a rich Osaka merchant family, the Makiokas have declined. Tsuruko, the eldest, is the most conservative, trying to hang on to a way of life they have outlived. Taeko, the youngest, seems the brightest, the most talented, and the most corrupted by the Tokyo-style intelligentsia with its Western fads. Sachiko, with her husband, Teinosuke, holds the family together by mediating between the impulses that tear at it. Yukiko, despite her traditional beauty, is too shy to deal effectively with her sisters or the world about her.

Most of the novel concerns the attempt to find the aging Yukiko a husband; the Japanese title *Sasameyuki* (thin snow) refers to the number of *miai* (marriage arrangements) that fail. Tsuruko generally insists on going through the slow traditional investigation of potential husbands, while Sachiko recognizes the diminishing value of Yukiko as a bride and tries to carry the arrangements out in a reasonable, though not hurried, time. Taeko, who intends to marry a Westernized playboy, must wait for her elder sister's marriage before marrying on her own. Yukiko is so introverted that she often seems indifferent to the whole struggle, except when she rejects another candidate.

This plot, however, is not Tanizaki's main concern. Using details from his wife Tomiko's family history, he re-creates Osaka as it was before the war, revealing foreign influences that would inevitably destroy that way of life—the clothing, the foreign films, the German neighbors, the visit to the White Russians, Taeko's desire to go to Paris to learn dressmaking—and the traditional Japanese customs as they were then practiced. Attention is devoted to the cherry blossom festival, Taeko's dollmaking, Kabuki, Japanese dance, and the old house of the Makiokas. The elegant Osaka dialect is spoken by the main characters and the Tokyo dialect is portrayed as being corrupted. Despite these contrasts, *The Makioka Sisters* is not a didactic work that preaches the superiority of the old ways over the new. It captures a particular way of life at a certain period in a certain place. Free of the grotesqueness that characterizes his early works and of the obsessive characters that populate most of his works, *The Makioka Sisters* is a panoramic view of diverse characters with complex motivations, a work unusual in Tanizaki's oeuvre but indisputably a masterpiece.

Unlike many writers, who, once they have achieved an integrated work such as *The Makioka Sisters*, run out of things to say, Tanizaki remained as creative in the final decades of his life as he had earlier. Entering the third phase of his career, he returned to many of the themes that had occupied him in his youth; with a more detached and sometimes ironic point of view, he dealt with the obsessions of sex in old age. Composed of the parallel diaries of a fifty-six-year-old professor and his forty-five-year-old wife, *The Key* progresses through the former's attempt to expand the sexual abilities of the latter, a woman whom he loves madly but who no longer satisfies him. Once again, one might note the autobiographical resonance of the professor's gradually directing his wife into the young Kimura's arms. One might also note the return of the devouring woman as the wife encourages the eating of beef and incites his jealousy, in spite of her knowledge of her husband's rising blood pressure, which eventually kills him.

The Key

The Key created a sensation on its publication, no doubt largely because of its frank treatment of sex; like other works of literature—Gustave Flaubert's *Madame Bovary* (1857) and D. H. Lawrence's *Lady Chatterley's Lover* (1928)—which achieved notoriety before their literary merits were admitted, *The Key*'s craftsmanship can now be assessed more objectively. Presenting one diary in the *katakana* script and the other in the *hiragana* script, Tanizaki exploits the differences between the two characters' perceptions of the situation. Further, he complicates the ostensibly sincere presentations of the diaries by having each character aware that the other may be reading what is written. This complex treatment of point of view turns an apparently simple, short work into a multilayered psychological study.

Diary of a Mad Old Man

Tanizaki's last novel, *Diary of a Mad Old Man*, also consists mainly of a diary, but by a man even older than the protagonist of *The Key*. Also suffering from high blood pressure, he is sexually impotent as well. Nevertheless, he is attracted to his daughter-in-law, Satsuko, estranged from her husband and having an affair with another man. As in many of Tanizaki's works, the narrator devotes much attention to Satsuko's feet as sexual objects, and he thinks often of his mother. He compares Satsuko's feet many times with those of his mother, and he delights in kissing Satsuko's feet and biting her toes when she comes from the shower. Her feet also become associated with the Buddhist goddess of mercy, and the old man plans for his daughter-in-law's footprints to be carved on his tombstone.

Objectively treated, *Diary of a Mad Old Man* is a great deal less sensational than it would appear from a plot summary. The artistic coolness that Tanizaki worked so hard to achieve saves the work from any pornographic content. Further, the novel is comic in its attitude toward the main character, satirizing the high intensity of Tanizaki's early works. Several of his works have comic elements—he was fond of cats and often wrote of them in a lighthearted vein—and Tanizaki seems to have ended his career looking back on his extraordinary achievements with a whimsical detachment.

J. Madison Davis

Other major works

SHORT FICTION: "Kirin," 1910; "Shonen," 1910; "Shisei," 1910 ("The Tattooer," 1963); "Hokan," 1911; "Akuma," 1912; "Kyofu," 1913 ("Terror," 1963); "Otsuya goroshi," 1913; "Haha o kouruki," 1919 ("Longing for Mother," 1980); "Watakushi," 1921

("The Thief," 1963); "Aoi Hano," 1922 ("Aguri," 1963); "Momoku monogatari," 1931 ("A Blind Man's Tale," 1963); "Ashikari," 1932 (English translation, 1936); "Shunkinsho," 1933 ("A Portrait of Shunkin," 1936); *Hyofu*, 1950; "Yume no ukihashi," 1959 ("The Bridge of Dreams," 1963); *Yume no ukihashi*, 1960 (collection); *Kokumin no bungaku*, 1964; *Tanizaki Jun'ichiro shu*, 1970; *Seven Japanese Tales*, 1981; *The Gourmet Club: A Sextet*, 2001 (Anthony H. Chambers and Paul McCarthy, translators).

PLAYS: *Aisureba koso*, pb. 1921; *Okumi to Gohei*, pb. 1922; *Shirogitsune no yu*, pb. 1923 (*The White Fox*, 1930); *Mumyo to Aizen*, pb. 1924; *Shinzei*, pb. 1949.

NONFICTION: *Bunsho tokuhon*, 1934; "In'ei raisan," 1934 ("In Praise of Shadows," 1955); *Kyo no yume, Osaka no yume*, 1950; *Yosho-jidai*, 1957 (*Childhood Years: A Memoir*, 1988).

TRANSLATION: *Genji monogatari*, 1936-1941, 1951-1954 (of Murasaki Shikibu's medieval novel).

MISCELLANEOUS: *Tanizaki Jun'ichiro zenshu*, 1930 (12 volumes); *Tanizaki Jun'ichiro zenshu*, 1966-1970 (28 volumes).

BIBLIOGRAPHY

Chambers, Anthony Hood. *The Secret Window: Ideal Worlds in Tanizaki's Fiction*. Cambridge, Mass.: Harvard University Press, 1994. Chambers analyzes seven of Tanizaki's novels and novellas, focusing on the characters' attempts to create "ideal worlds" and the elements of fantasy in these works. Includes notes and a bibliography.

Gessel, Van C. *Three Modern Novelists: Soseki, Tanizaki, Kawabata*. New York: Kodansha International, 1993. The sixty-five-page chapter on Tanizaki concentrates on his approach to modernism. Includes detailed notes but no bibliography.

Golley, Gregory L. "Tanizaki Junichiro: The Art of Subversion and the Subversion of Art." *Journal of Japanese Studies* 21 (Summer, 1995): 365-404. Examines the "return to Japan" inaugurated by Tanizaki's *Some Prefer Nettles*. Discusses themes and images in the work and suggests that Tanizaki's traditionalist fiction both championed and undermined the idea of an essential Japanese traditional culture.

Ito, Ken K. *Visions of Desire: Tanizaki's Fictional Worlds*. Stanford, Calif.: Stanford University Press, 1991. A critical biography, with chapters arranged in chronological order of Tanizaki's life and work. Ito primarily focuses his analysis on Tanizaki's best-known works that have been translated into English, and pays special attention to Tanizaki's language, narrative style, and his male characters' projection of their desires upon women. Includes notes, a bibliography, and a section on names and sources.

Keene, Donald. *Dawn to the West: Japanese Literature of the Modern Era—Fiction*. New York: Holt, Rinehart and Winston, 1984. A massive study of the fiction produced since the Japanese enlightenment of the nineteenth century. Chapter 20 is devoted exclusively to Tanizaki, and he is discussed in the introduction and in several other chapters in association with other writers and literary movements.

_______. *Five Modern Japanese Novelists*. New York: Columbia University Press, 2003. Keene devotes a chapter to Tanizaki in his tribute to five twentieth century Japanese novelists. Includes his personal recollections of Tanizaki, with whom he was acquainted, and discusses the writer's works.

_______. *Japanese Literature: An Introduction for Western Readers*. New York: Grove Press, 1955. Unlike the comprehensive treatment in *Dawn to the West*, this is a brief introduction to Japanese literature. Tanizaki is briefly mentioned in the introduction and chapter 4, "The Japanese Novel," but is discussed throughout chapter 5, "Japanese Literature Under Western Influence."

Lippit, Noriko Miuta. *Reality and Fiction in Modern Japanese Literature*. White Plains, N.Y.: M. E. Sharpe, 1980. Lippit considers the struggle of several Japanese writers to define the function of art and literature, both socially and personally. The sections on Tanizaki deal with his aesthetic preference for fantasy and complex structure, with a comparison to Edgar Allan Poe. Includes notes.

Suzuki, Tomi. *Narrating the Self: Fictions of Japanese Modernity*. Stanford, Calif.: Stanford University Press, 1996. Two of the chapters are devoted to Tanizaki: "Allegories of Modernity in Tanizaki Jun'ichiro's *Fool's Love*" (also known as *Naomi*) and the epilogue, "Tanizaki's Speaking Subject and the Creation of Tradition." Includes notes and a bibliography.

Ueda, Makoto. "Tanizaki Jun'ichiro." In *Modern Japanese Writers and the Nature of Literature*. Stanford, Calif.: Stanford University Press, 1976. Discusses Tanizaki as one of the eight major writers who make up the majority of modern Japanese fiction familiar to Western readers. Provides an introduction to major literary theories underlying Japanese novels and stories. Supplemented by source notes, a bibliography, and an index.

Yamanouchi, Hisaaki. *The Search for Authenticity in Modern Japanese Literature*. New York: Cambridge University Press, 1978. Discusses twelve modern Japanese writers, analyzing the ways each dealt with difficult personal, social, and intellectual questions in art. The sections on Tanizaki focus on the concept of eternal womanhood in his works. Includes notes, a bibliography, and an index.

J. R. R. TOLKIEN

Born: Bloemfontein, South Africa; January 3, 1892
Died: Bournemouth, England; September 2, 1973
Also known as: John Ronald Reuel Tolkien

PRINCIPAL LONG FICTION

The Hobbit: Or, There and Back Again, 1937
The Fellowship of the Ring, 1954
The Two Towers, 1954
The Return of the King, 1955
The Lord of the Rings, 1955 (collective title of previous 3 novels)
The Silmarillion, 1977
The Children of Húrin, 2007

OTHER LITERARY FORMS

The novels that J. R. R. Tolkien (TAHL-keen) produced represent only a small part of the complicated matrix from which they evolved. During Tolkien's lifetime, he published three volumes of novellas and short stories, *Farmer Giles of Ham* (1949), *Tree and Leaf* (1964), and *Smith of Wootton Major* (1967). Some of these tales had originally been bedtime stories for his own children, such as those in the posthumously published *The Father Christmas Letters* (1976) and *Roverandom* (1998). *The Silmarillion* and *Unfinished Tales of Numenor and Middle-Earth* (1980) both contain stories Tolkien composed early in his life, material that sets the stage for the events in his novels. His poetry collections, *Songs for the Philologists* (1936), *The Adventures of Tom Bombadil* (1962), and *The Road Goes Ever On: A Song Cycle* (1967), link Tolkien's poetic formulations of Middle-earth's themes with the historical and linguistic themes of which both his professional work and much of his dreams were made, "the nameless North of Sigurd of the Völsungs, and the prince of all dragons." Tolkien's academic publications dealt with the history of the English language and Middle English literature: *A Middle English Vocabulary* (1922) and editions of *Sir Gawain and the Green Knight* (1925; with E. V. Gordon) and the *Ancrene Wisse* (1962). His seminal essay "Beowulf: The Monsters and the Critics" (1936) and his only play, *The Homecoming of Beorhtnoth Beorhthelm's Son* (pb. 1953), offer fresh interpretations of ancient English epic poems.

Tolkien's novels have been adapted for cinema and television, and many, though not all, of his fragmentary stories, articles, and letters have been published since his death. His histories of Middle-earth, a remarkable invented mythology comprising chronicles, tales, maps, and poems, were edited as a series by his son, Christopher Tolkien. Volumes include *The Book of Lost Tales*, *The Lays of Beleriand*, *The Shaping of Middle-Earth*, and *The Lost Road, and Other Writings*.

ACHIEVEMENTS

J. R. R. Tolkien's fiction dismayed most of his fellow scholars at the University of Oxford as much as it delighted most of his general readers. Such reactions sprang from their recognition of his vast linguistic talent, which underlay both his professional achievements and his mythical universe. Tolkien led two lives at once, quietly working as an Oxford tutor, examiner, editor, and lecturer while concurrently Middle-earth and its mythology were taking shape within his imagination.

For twenty years after he took first-class honors in English language and literature at Oxford, Tolkien's teaching and linguistic studies buttressed his scholarly reputation. Editing the fourteenth century text of *Sir Gawain and the Green Knight* with E. V. Gordon helped bring Tolkien the Rawlinson and Bosworth Professorship of Anglo-Saxon at Oxford in 1925. His lecture "Beowulf: The Monsters and the Critics" approached the Anglo-Saxon epic poem from an entirely new perspective and is considered a landmark in criticism of Western Germanic literature. As he was shaping his linguistic career, however, Tolkien was also formulating an imaginary language that, as early as 1917, had led him to explore its antecedents, its mythology, and its history, all of which he molded into the tales of *The Silmarillion*. Over the years, he shared these stories with friends, but he never finished putting them into a unified structure.

His preoccupation with Middle-earth and the practical demands of his teaching distracted Tolkien from scholarship, and between his celebrated essay *On Fairy Stories* in 1939 and his edition of the Middle English *Ancrene Wisse* in 1962, Tolkien published only fiction, a circumstance acknowledged with polite forbearance by most of Oxford's scholarly community, although his novels eventually met with astonishing popular success. *The Hobbit*, originally a children's story, was published in 1937 after a six-year gestation, and by 1949, *The Lord of the Rings* was complete. Its sales, though steadily increasing after its publication in 1954-1955, did not soar until 1965, when an unauthorized American printing proved a disguised blessing, resulting in a campus cult responsible for the sale of three million copies by 1968.

Most critics of *The Lord of the Rings* have not achieved moderation. As W. H. Auden observed, "People find it a masterpiece of its genre, or they cannot abide it." Auden himself and C. S. Lewis, Tolkien's Oxford friend, headed the "masterpiece" faction, while Edwin Muir in England and Edmund Wilson in the United States deplored Tolkien's style and aims.

Honorary fellowships, an honorary doctorate of letters from Oxford, and the honor of being made a Commander of the Order of the British Empire by Queen Elizabeth II all descended on Tolkien with the unexpected wealth of his last years, which were nevertheless darkened by his reluctance to complete *The Silmarillion*. His reputation rests not on his academic talent or his scholarly production, or even on his brilliant linguistically oriented "mythology for England," but on the novels that began as tales for his children and blossomed into a splendid imaginative tree of fiction whose roots feed on the archetypes of northern European civilization and whose leaves shelter its finest aspirations.

BIOGRAPHY

John Ronald Reuel Tolkien was born in Bloemfontein, South Africa, on January 3, 1892. The piano-manufacturing firm of his father's family, originally descended from German aristocracy, had gone bankrupt, and the elder Tolkien had taken a South African bank position in the hope of improving his shaky finances. Tolkien's mother, Mabel Suffield, joined her husband at Bloemfontein, but when the climate strained Ronald's health, she took their two sons home to England in 1895. Less than a year later, Arthur Tolkien died in South Africa, leaving his widow and children nearly penniless.

In the summer of 1896, Mabel Tolkien rented a rural cottage at Sarehole Mill, close to Birmingham, and for the next four years she taught her boys French, Latin, drawing, and botany, to save school expenses. Much later, Tolkien called these "the longest-seeming and most formative part" of his life. Mabel Tolkien's attraction to Roman Catholicism led to her conversion in 1900, and she moved to a Birmingham suburb from which Ronald attended one of England's then leading grammar schools, King Edward's, on a scholarship. Already, he was demonstrating the fascination with ancient languages that was to determine his career. He was involved in learning such northern European languages as Norse, Gothic, Finnish, and Welsh, as well as the Old and Middle English in which he achieved his academic reputation. He later claimed this philological bent dated from the time he was five or six years old.

In 1904, his mother died at the age of thirty-four, leaving her children in the care of Father Francis Morgan, her friend and pastor. Tolkien's devotion to his mother was inextricably intertwined with his own Catholic faith, and both played vital roles in the development of his fiction. Thus at sixteen, Ronald Tolkien looked back on a series of grievous losses: his father, whom he considered as "belonging to an almost legendary past"; the Sarehole countryside he loved; his mother, whom he considered a martyr to her faith. Not surprisingly for a lonely boy, Tolkien fell in love early when he met Edith Bratt, another orphan, in his Birmingham boardinghouse. She was three years older than he, and she had just enough inheritance to support herself modestly while she dreamed of becoming a musician. Recognizing the boy's scholarly talent and fearing for his future, Father Morgan finally stopped all communication between Ronald and Edith until Ronald was twenty-one. Tolkien himself commented thirty years later, "Probably nothing else would have hardened the will enough to give such an affair (however genuine a case of true love) permanence." When he and Edith were reunited in 1913, they seemed to have little in common, but on the eve of his military departure to France in 1916, they were married.

By this time Tolkien had won a scholarship to Oxford University and had graduated with first-class honors in 1913. He enlisted in the Lancashire Fusiliers in 1915, embarking for France in 1916. He survived the Battle of the Somme but was invalided back to England suffering from trench fever. While in a military hospital in 1917, Tolkien began *The Book of Lost Tales*, the genesis of *The Silmarillion*, although he dated the original ideas for the complete oeuvre from as early as 1910 and the original story of Beren and Tinuviel back to 1913. By 1918 he had read a version of "The Fall of Gondolin" to a college group.

After demobilization, Tolkien gained employment working on the new *Oxford English Dictionary*, until in 1921 he was appointed to the University of Leeds in Yorkshire to lecture in Old English. While there he began to establish his academic reputation with *A Middle English Vocabulary* and an edition of *Sir Gawain and the Green Knight* done with Professor E. V. Gordon. On the strength of these and his connections back at Oxford, he was appointed the Rawlinson and Bosworth Professor of Anglo-Saxon Studies at Oxford in 1925, a post he held until 1945, when he was appointed Merton Professor of English Language and Literature at the same university. He held this post until his belated retirement in 1959. Various honorary degrees were bestowed on him, and in 1938 he was Andrew Lang Lecturer at the University of St. Andrews, where he gave his famous lectures on fairy stories.

The central part of Tolkien's life, however, lay in his secret creation of the mythology of Middle-earth. It was initially the demands of his growing family (three sons and a daughter) that brought any of this to light, particularly in *The Hobbit*, which was first drafted, according to his close friend and science-fiction novelist C. S. Lewis, by the beginning of 1930. Then it was through the influence of the Inklings, a group of like-minded university friends that included Lewis and Tolkien, that *The Hobbit* was reformulated and sent for eventual publication in 1937. The importance of the Inklings cannot be stressed enough, especially the friendship of Lewis, who encouraged Tolkien's work on *The Lord of the Rings* during World War II and immediately after, and who reviewed it in glowing terms. In a sense, Lewis was repaying the enormous debt he owed Tolkien for his conversion to Christianity. The Inklings continued until Lewis's death in 1963, though the two men had drifted apart somewhat by then.

Even so, the vast bulk of Middle-earth mythology lay in a constant state of revision, expansion, and rearrangement, and despite the best efforts of friends and publishers, it was unpublished at his death. In fact, after the publication of *The Lord of the Rings* in 1956, he concentrated again on his academic work, and only after retirement did he make any serious inroads again into the mythology. In the end, it was left to his third son, Christopher, also an academic, to order the material and have it published, as he did with a number of incomplete academic studies. Tolkien's death in 1973 had been preceded by his wife's in 1971. They were both buried outside Oxford, their graves suitably inscribed with the names Beren and Lúthien. The year before his death he had been made a Commander of the Order of the British Empire by Queen Elizabeth II.

Analysis

Looking back on his Middle-earth around 1951, J. R. R. Tolkien commented, "I do not remember a time when I was not building it . . . always I had the sense of recording what was already 'there,' somewhere: not of inventing." He conceived of fantasy as a profound and powerful form of literature with intense philosophical and spiritual meaning, serious purposes, and eternal appeal. He believed the imagination, the mental power of making images, could be linked by art to "subcreation," the successful result of image making, and so he regarded the genuine artist as partaking in the Creator's divine nature.

Three major factors of Tolkien's personality and environment combined to shape the theory of fantasy underlying his novels, as first enunciated in the essay "On Fairy-Stories" (1938). His love of language for its singular rewards, his delight in the English countryside, and his shattering experience of trench warfare during World War I all provided the seeds for his three longest pieces of fiction. They also contributed to the points of view, astonishingly nonhuman and yet startlingly convincing, of *The Silmarillion*, *The Hobbit*, and *The Lord of the Rings*, where Elves and Hobbits illuminate the world of Men.

Even as a boy, Tolkien had been enchanted by Welsh names on railway coal cars, a sign of his unusual linguistic sensitivity, and as a mature scholar, he devoted himself to the mystery of the word in its northern manifestations. In "On Fairy-Stories," he wrote that "*spell* means both a story told, and a formula of power over living men." Tolkien cast his spells in the building blocks of words drawn from the imaginary languages he had been constructing as long as he could remember. The two languages he formulated for his Elves, the Elder Race, both derived from a common linguistic ancestor as human languages do, and this "nexus of languages" supplied the proper names for his fiction, so that despite their considerable length and complication they possess "cohesion, consistency of linguistic style, and the illusion of historicity." The last was possibly the greatest achievement of Tolkien's mastery of language in his novels, fostering vital credence in his imaginary world. He felt that the finest fairy stories "open a door on Other Time, and if we pass through . . . we stand outside our own time, outside Time itself, maybe." In his own childhood, a "troublous" one Tolkien said, he had "had no special 'wish to believe'"; he instead "wanted to know," as, perhaps, do his readers, aided by the resonance of his masterful use of words.

The memory of his years at Sarehole, the happiest of his boyhood, gave Tolkien an abiding love of nature, "above all trees," which formed the basis for one of his principal concepts, "the inter-relations between the 'noble' and the 'simple.'" He found "specially moving" the "ennoblement of the ignoble," a theme that recurs throughout his fiction. Tolkien's Elves practice love and respect toward nature, as do his Hobbits, "small people" connected closely to "the soil and other living things" who display both human pettiness and unexpected heroism "in a pinch." The Elves, Hobbits, and good Men are countered in Tolkien's Middle-earth by the threat of the machine, by which he meant "all use of external plans or devices," as opposed to "the development of inner powers or talents." The evil of the machine in Tolkien's eyes (he did not own a car after World War II) derived from the misguided human desire for power, itself a rebellion against the Creator's laws, a Fall from Paradise, another recurring theme in his fiction.

The horrors of World War I must have struck Tolkien as evil incarnate, with new military technology that devastated the countryside, struck down the innocent, and left no place for chivalry, heroism, or even common decency. Unlike Andrew Lang, an early Scottish collector of fairy tales, who felt children most often ask, "Is it true?," Tolkien declared that children far more often asked him of a character, "Was he good? Was he wicked?" Tolkien shared G. K. Chesterton's conviction that children "are innocent and love justice; while most of us are wicked and naturally prefer mercy." The child's stern perception of right and wrong, as opposed to the "mercy untempered by justice" that leads to "falsification of values," confirmed Tolkien's long-held inclination toward the steely world of the northern sagas, where human heroism faces inevitable defeat by the forces of evil, and the hero, according to Edith Hamilton, "can prove what he is only by dying." From his basic distrust of the machine and his firsthand memories of the Somme, Tolkien drew one of the major lessons of his fiction: "that on callow, lumpish and selfish youth peril, sorrow, and the shadow of death can bestow dignity, and even sometimes wisdom."

Reconciling this harsh northern *Weltbild* with his Roman Catholic faith did not seem to be difficult for Tolkien. An indispensable element of his theory of fantasy is the "sudden joyous 'turn'" of a "eucatastrophic" story, a moment in fiction accompanied by "a catch of the breath, a beat and lifting of the heart, near to (or indeed accompanied by) tears." By inserting the "turn" convincingly into his tale, the subcreator "denies universal final defeat" and gives "a fleeting glimpse of Joy, Joy beyond the walls of the world, poignant as grief." Hence, Tolkien believed that such a joy was the "mark of the true fairy story," the revelation of truth in the fictional world the subcreator built. It might even be greater, "a far-off gleam or echo of *evangelium* in the real world." Tolkien was able to see the Christian Gospels as "the greatest and most complete conceivable eucatastrophe," believing that in fantasy the human subcreator might "actually assist in the effoliation and multiple enrichment of creation."

Tolkien's *The Silmarillion*, *The Hobbit*, and *The Lord of the Rings* form, as he always hoped, one coherent and archetypal whole. His "creative fantasy" effectively shows the three dissimilar faces his theory demanded: "the Mystical towards the Supernatural; the Magical towards Nature; and the Mirror of scorn and pity toward Man." Humanity's "oldest and deepest desire," the "Great Escape" from death, is satisfied in Tolkien's major fiction, not by denying Mortality but by accepting it gracefully as a gift from the Creator, a benefit to humankind that Tolkien's immortal Elves envied. The Elves' own magic is actually art, whose true object is "subcreation" under God, not domination of lesser beings whose world they respectfully share. Scorn for fallen people (and fallen Elves and Hobbits as well) abounds in Middle-earth, but pity, too, for guiltless creatures trapped in the most frightful evil Tolkien could envision, evil that he believed arises "from an apparently good root, the desire to benefit the world and others—speedily—and according to the benefactor's own plans." Middle-earth lives forever in Tolkien's novels, and with it an affirmation of what is best, most true, and most beautiful in human nature.

For almost fifty years, mostly in the quiet academic atmosphere of Oxford, Tolkien built his resounding tales of "a body of more or less connected legend, ranging from the large and cosmogonic, to the level of romantic fairy-story." He consciously dedicated the work simply "to England; to my country." The intellectual absorption with language he had always enjoyed gave him the starting place for his mythology, which he implemented in *The Silmarillion*, whose unifying theme is the Fall of Elves and Men. His happiness in the English countryside seems to have provided him the landscape from which *The Hobbit* grew, perhaps his most approachable "fairy-story" for both children and adults, illustrating the happiness to be gained from simplicity and the acceptance of the gift of mortality. The chivalric dreams of noble sacrifice shattered for Tolkien's generation by World War I were redeemed for him by his realization that the humble may effectively struggle against domination by the misguided technological values of modern civilization. The heroic legend of *The Lord of the Rings* best illustrates Tolkien's resolution of the conflict between the northern values he had admired from youth and the Roman Catholic religion of hope and consolation to which he was devoted. Tolkien wanted to illuminate the simplest and the highest values of human existence, found in a human love that accepts and transcends mortality. Tolkien's "mythology for England," a unique gift of literature and language, has earned its immense popular success by appealing to humanity's eternal desire to understand its mortal lot. As Hilda Ellis Davidson commented of the great northern myths, so like Tolkien's own, "In reaching out to explore the distant hills where the gods dwell and the deeps where the monsters are lurking, we are perhaps discovering the way home."

THE SILMARILLION

Both in Tolkien's life and in the chronology of Middle-earth, the tales of *The Silmarillion* came first, but the book was not published until four years after his death. The volume called *The Silmarillion* contains four shorter narratives as well as the "Quenta Silmarillion," arranged as ordered chronicles of the Three Ages of Tolkien's Middle-earth by his son Christopher, following his father's explicit intention.

Tolkien began parts of *The Silmarillion* in 1917 after he had been invalided home from France. The work steadily evolved after more than forty years, and, according to Christopher Tolkien, "incompatibilities of tone" inevitably arose from his father's increasing preoccupation with theology and philosophy over the mythology and poetry he had originally favored. Tolkien himself never abandoned his work on *The Silmarillion*, even though he found himself unable to complete it. As Christopher Wiseman had suggested to Tolkien, "Why these creatures live to you is because you are still creating them," and so Tolkien painstakingly revised, recast, and polished these stories, unwilling to banish their characters from his imagination.

The Silmarillion opens with "Ainulindalë," a cosmogonical myth revealing the creation of Middle-earth by God ("Iluvatar") in the presence of the Valar, whom Tolkien described as angelic powers. He wanted "to provide beings of the same order . . . as the 'gods' of higher mythology" acceptable to "a mind that believes in the Blessed Trinity." The universe to which Middle-earth belonged was set in living motion by music, "beheld as a light in the darkness."

The short "Valaquenta" enumerates the individual Valar, whose personal responsibilities covered all created things of Middle-earth, stopping short of the act of creation itself. One of the Valar, Melkor, rebelled in the First Age; Tolkien believed that "there cannot be any 'story' without a fall." Melkor "began with the desire of Light, but when he could not possess it for himself alone, he descended . . . into a great burning." One of Melkor's servants was Sauron, who later embodied evil in the Third Age of Middle-earth.

The twenty-four chapters of the "Quenta Silmarillion" recount the legendary history of the immortal Elves, the First-Born of Iluvatar, whom Tolkien elsewhere called "rational incarnate creatures of more or less comparable stature with our own." After writing *The Lord of the Rings*, Tolkien clearly indicated that the Elves were "only a representation of an apprehension of a part of human nature" from which art and poetry spring, but, he said, "that is not the legendary mode of talking." The Elves originally share the Paradise of the Valar, Valinor, but the Elves suffer a fall from that grace in the "Quenta Silmarillion," the rebellion and exile to Middle-earth of one of the great families of Elves, led by their chief, the artificer Fëanor, who has captured the primal light of Iluvatar in the three Silmarils. Tolkien described these great jewels as aglow with the "light of art undivorced from reason, that sees things both scientifically (or philosophically) and imaginatively (or subcreatively) and 'says that they are good'—as beautiful." Fëanor's lust to possess the Silmarils for himself leads to their capture by Melkor, and in the struggle to redeem them, splendid deeds are performed by Beren, a Man of Middle-earth beloved of the Elvish princess Lúthien. Tolkien called this "the first example of the motive (to become dominant in Hobbits) that the great policies of world history . . . are often turned . . . by the seemingly unknown and weak." The union of Beren and Lúthien is the first between mortal Man and immortal Elf; they win Paradise together, and eventually Earendil the Elven Mariner closes the "Quenta Silmarillion" by bringing the gem Beren painfully rescued from Melkor to the land of the Valar. His Silmaril was set into the sky as its brightest star, while the others were lost in the depths of the earth and sea, and the First Age of Middle-earth came to its end.

Tolkien saw the Second Age of Middle-earth as dark, and he believed "not very much of its history is (or need be) told." The Valar continued to dwell at Valinor with the faithful Elves, but the exiled Elves with Fëanor were commanded to leave Middle-earth and live in the lonely Isle of Eressëa in the West. Some of them, however, ignored the order and remained in Middle-earth. Those Men of Middle-earth who had aided the Elves to redeem the Silmarils were given the Atlantis-like realm of Númenor as their reward, as well as life spans three times the normal age of Men. Though Melkor was chained, his servant Sauron remained free to roam Middle-earth, and through his evil influence, both Men of Númenor and the Delaying Elves came to grief.

The decay of Númenor is told in the *Akallabeth*, a much briefer illustration of

Tolkien's belief that the inevitable theme of human stories is "a Ban, or Prohibition." The long-lived Númenoreans were prohibited by the Valar from setting foot on "immortal" lands in the West. Their wrongful desire to escape death, their gift from Iluvatar, causes them to rebel and bring about their own watery destruction through the worship of Sauron, Melkor's servant. At the same time, the Elves who delayed in Middle-earth suffered the painful consequences of their flawed choice. Tolkien said they "wanted to have their cake without eating it," enjoying the perfection of the West while remaining on ordinary earth, revered as superior beings by the other, lesser races. Some of them cast their lot with Sauron, who enticed them to create three Rings of Power, in the misguided hope of making Middle-earth another Valinor. Sauron secretly made another ring himself, one with the power to enslave all the others. The ensuing war between Sauron and the Elves devastated Middle-earth, but in the Last Alliance of Elves and Men against Sauron, the One Ring was lost. Tolkien calls this the "catastrophic end, not only of the Second Age, but of the Old World, the primeval age of Legend."

The posthumous collection called *The Silmarillion* ends with Tolkien's résumé "Of the Rings of Power and the Third Age," which introduces the motives, themes, and chief actors in the next inevitable war between Sauron and the Free Peoples of Middle-earth. Although *The Hobbit* and *The Lord of the Rings* have proved vastly more popular, and both can be enjoyed without the complicated and generally loftily pitched history of *The Silmarillion*, its information is essential to a thorough understanding of the forces Tolkien set at work in the later novels. Even more important, *The Silmarillion* was for Tolkien, as his son Christopher has said, "the vehicle and depository of his profoundest reflections," and as such, it holds the bejewelled key to the autobiography Tolkien felt was embedded in his fiction.

The Hobbit

Around 1930, Tolkien jotted a few enigmatic words about "a hobbit" on the back of an examination paper he was grading. "Names always generate a story in my mind," he observed, and eventually he found out "what hobbits were like." The Hobbits, whom he subsequently described as "a branch of the specifically *human* race (not Elves or Dwarves)," became the vital link between Tolkien's mythology as constructed in *The Silmarillion* and the heroic legend that dominates *The Lord of the Rings*. Humphrey Carpenter, Tolkien's official biographer, has written that Bilbo Baggins, hero of *The Hobbit*, "embodied everything he [Tolkien] loved about the West Midlands." Tolkien himself once wrote, "I am in fact a hobbit, in all but size," and beyond personal affinities, he saw the Hobbits as "rustic English people," small in size to reflect "the generally small reach of their imagination—not the small reach of their courage or latent power."

Tolkien's Hobbits appear in the Third Age of Middle-earth, in an ominously quiet lull before a fearful storm. Sauron had been overthrown by the Elflord Gil-galad and the Númenorean King Elendil, but since evil is never completely vanquished, Sauron's creatures lurk in the margins of Middle-earth, in the mountain-enclosed region of Mordor, while a few Elves keep watch on its borders. Descendants of a few Númenoreans were saved from their land's disaster (Atlantean destruction was a recurrent nightmare for both Tolkien and his son Christopher), and they rule in the Kingdoms of Arnor in the North of Middle-earth and Gondor of the South. The former Númenoreans are allies of the Homeric Riders of Rohan, whose human forefathers had remained in Middle-earth when Númenor came to be. The three Elven Rings of Power secretly guard Rivendell and Lothlórien, which Tolkien called "enchanted enclaves of peace where Time seems to stand still and decay is restrained, a semblance of the bliss of the True West."

The Hobbits live in the Shire, in "an ordered, civilised, if simple rural life." One day, the Hobbit Bilbo Baggins receives an odd visitor, Gandalf the Wizard, who sends Bilbo off with traveling dwarves, as a professional burglar, in search of Dragon's Gold, the major theme of the novel. In the process, Tolkien uses the humble Hobbit to illustrate one of his chief preoccupations, the process by which "small imagination" combines with "great courage." As he recalled from his months in the trenches, "I've always been impressed that we are here, surviving, because of the indomitable courage of quite small people against impossible odds."

Starting from the idyllic rural world of the Shire, *The Hobbit*, ostensibly a children's book, traces the typical quest of the northern hero about whom Tolkien himself had loved to read in his youth. Gandalf shares certain characteristics with the Scandinavian god Odin, said to wander among people as an "old man of great height," with a long grey cloak, a white beard, and supernatural powers. Gandalf, like Odin, understands the speech of birds, being especially fond of eagles and ravens, and his strange savage friend Beorn, who rescues the Hobbits at one critical point, recalls the berserkers, bearskin-clad warriors consecrated to Odin who fought with superhuman strength in the intoxication of battle. The Dwarves of Middle-earth distinctly resemble their Old Norse forebears, skilled craftsmen who made treasures for the gods. Smaug the Dragon, eventually slain by the human hero Bard, is surely related to "the prince of all dragons" who had captured Tolkien's boyish imagination and who would reappear in *Farmer Giles of Ham*. The Germanic code of the *comitatus*, the warrior's fidelity unto death, celebrated in the tenth century Anglo-Saxon poem "The Battle of Maldon," inspired Tolkien's only play and applies to *The Hobbit*, too, since Bilbo's outward perils are overshadowed by the worst threat of all to the northern hero, the inward danger of proving a coward.

Bilbo's hard-won self-knowledge allows him to demonstrate the "indomitable courage of small people against great odds" when he saves Dwarves, Men, and Elves from suicidal war against one another, after the Dragon has been slain and its treasure freed. *The Hobbit* far exceeded its beginnings as a bedtime story for Tolkien's small sons, since it is also a fable about the child at the heart of every person, perceiving right and wrong as sternly as did the heroes of the North.

In late 1937, at the suggestion of his British publisher, Stanley Unwin, Tolkien began a sequel to *The Hobbit*. To the East, a malignant force was gathering strength in the Europe that even the mammoth sacrifices of World War I had not redeemed from oppression, and while Tolkien often cautions against interpreting his works allegorically, the apprehensive atmosphere of prewar England must have affected his own peace of mind. He described his intention in *The Lord of the Rings* as "an attempt to . . . wind up all the elements and motives of what has preceded." He wanted "to include the colloquialism and vulgarity of Hobbits, poetry and the highest style of prose." The moral of this novel, not a "trilogy" but, he stressed, "conceived and written as a whole," was "obvious": "that without the high and noble the simple and vulgar is utterly mean; and without the simple and ordinary the noble and heroic is meaningless."

THE LORD OF THE RINGS

The Lord of the Rings is a vast panoramic contest between good and evil played out against the backdrop of Tolkien's mythology as presented in *The Silmarillion*. The One Ring of Sauron, long lost, was found by little Bilbo Baggins, and from him it passed to his kinsman Frodo, who becomes the central figure of the quest-in-reverse: Having found the Ring, the allied Men, Elves, Dwarves, and Hobbits must destroy it where it was forged, so that its power can never again dominate Middle-earth. Another quest takes place simultaneously in the novel, as the mysterious Strider who greets the Hobbits at Bree on the first stage of their perilous journey is gradually revealed as Aragorn, son of Arathorn and heir to Arnor in the North, descendant of Elendil who kept faith with the Valar; he is the human King of Middle-earth who must reclaim his realm. Sauron's minions rise to threaten the Ringbearer and his companions, and, after many adventures, a great hopeless battle is fought before the Gates of Mordor. As Tolkien stated in "Of the Rings of Power and the Third Age," "There at the last they looked upon death and defeat, and all their valour was in vain; for Sauron was too strong." This is the paradoxical defeat-and-victory of the northern hero, whose glory is won in the manner of his death. As a practicing Christian, however, Tolkien had to see hope clearly in the ultimate struggle between right and wrong, "and help came from the hands of the weak when the Wise faltered." Frodo the Hobbit at last manages to carry the Ring to Mount Doom in spite of Sauron, and there it is destroyed, and "a new Spring opened up on Earth." Even then, Frodo's mission is not completed. With his three Hobbit companions, he has to return to the Shire and undo the evil that has corrupted the hearts, minds, and landscape of that quiet region. Only after that may Frodo, with the Elves, depart for the far west.

In retrospect, Tolkien acknowledged that another central issue of *The Lord of the Rings* is "love in different modes," which had been "wholly absent from *The Hobbit*." Tolkien considered the "simple 'rustic' love" between Sam, Frodo's faithful batman, and his Rosie was "*absolutely essential*" both to the study of the main hero of the novel and "to the theme of the relation of ordinary life . . . to quests, to sacrifice, causes, and the 'longing for Elves,' and sheer beauty." The evidence of Tolkien's own life indicates the depth of his ability to love, like Beren, always faithful to his Lúthien. Such love that makes all sacrifice possible forms the indestructible core of *The Lord of the Rings*, which moved C. S. Lewis to speak of "beauties which pierce like swords or burn like cold iron . . . a book that will break your heart."

Love exemplified in two important romances softens the necromancy and the battles of *The Lord of the Rings*: the poignant "mistaken love" of Eowyn for Aragorn, as Tolkien described it, and the novel's "highest love-story," the tale of Aragorn and Arwen, daughter of Elrond, leader of the Elves of Middle-earth. Eowyn is niece to Theoden, King of Rohan, the land of the horsemen that Tolkien patterned on ancient Anglo-Saxon tribes, which he first encountered through William Morris's *The House of the Wolfings* (1888). In Theoden's decline, the shield-maiden Eowyn gives her first love to the royalty-in-exile she senses in Aragorn, and although he in no sense encourages her, Eowyn's tragedy is one only he can heal once he is restored as King. In contrast, Tolkien merely alludes to the love of Aragorn and Arwen in *The Lord of the Rings*, since it seems almost too deep for tears. Arwen must forsake her Elven immortality and join Aragorn in human death, paralleling the earlier story of Beren and Lúthien. Like Tolkien's own love for Edith, Aragorn's for Arwen is temporarily prevented from reaching fruition until he can return to her in full possession of his birthright. The shadow of her possible loss lends stature to the characterization of Aragorn, the hero of *The Lord of the Rings*.

In 1955, Tolkien observed that "certain features . . . and especially certain places" of *The Lord of the Rings* "still move me very powerfully." The passages he cited sum up the major means by which the novel so strongly conveys love, redemption, and heroism achieved in the face of overwhelming odds. "The heart remains in the description of Cerin Amroth," he wrote, the spot where Aragorn and Arwen first pledged their love and where, many years later at the beginning of his fearful quest, "the grim years were removed from the face of Aragorn, and he seemed clothed in white, a young lord tall and fair." Tolkien magnifies this small epiphany of love through the eyes of the Hobbit Frodo. Another key episode, the wretched Gollum's failure to repent because Sam interrupts him, grieved Tolkien deeply, he said, for it resembled "the *real* world in which the instruments of just retribution are seldom themselves just or holy." In his favorite passage, however, Tolkien was "most stirred by the sound of the horns of the Rohirrim at cockcrow," the great "turn" of *The Lord of the Rings*, a flash of salvation in the face of all odds that comes beyond hope, beyond prayer, like a stroke of unexpected bliss from the hand of the Creator.

The "turn" that makes *The Lord of the Rings* a "true fairy-story" in Tolkien's definition links fidelity to a vow, a Germanic value, to the Christian loyalty that animated many of the great Anglo-Saxon works Tolkien had spent his scholarly life studying. By weaving the immensely complex threads of Elves, Hobbits, Men, and Dwarves into his heroic legend of the last great age of Middle-earth, he achieved a valid subcreation, sharing in the nature of what for him was most divine.

THE HISTORY OF MIDDLE-EARTH

Tolkien's son Christopher undertook the massive task of editing and commenting on the many drafts and manuscripts Tolkien left unpublished. These volumes, grouped under the title *The History of Middle-Earth*, became commentary of a painstaking, scholarly kind, such as Tolkien himself would have enjoyed, no doubt, though it leaves the average reader rather befuddled. Each volume reprints, compares, and comments on original draft material in chronological order. One interesting feature is the emergence of the *Annals*, running alongside the stories; another is the evolution of the Elvish languages and etymologies. Tolkien's original attempt to make this a mythology of England through the character of Aelfwine, an Anglo-Saxon who had somehow reached Middle-earth and then translated some of its material into Old English, can also be seen. *The Lost Road* (1937) emerges as a fragment produced as part of an agreement with C. S. Lewis for a science-fiction story on time travel that would complement a story by Lewis on space. The latter produced *Out of the Silent Planet* (1938), but Tolkien gave up on his, though the attempt to connect it to the *Akallabeth* can be seen clearly.

Christopher Tolkien also edited the childhood stories and poetry; others have dealt with Tolkien's drawings, illustrations, and mapmaking predilections. The production of such works is perhaps in some danger of overshadowing the myth that gave them life. Tolkien saw all of his writings as unfinished and imperfect. As C. S. Lewis saw too in his *Chronicles of Narnia* (1950-1956), our myths can only ever be the first page of the Great Myth that goes on forever.

Mitzi M. Brunsdale
Updated by David Barratt

OTHER MAJOR WORKS

SHORT FICTION: *Tree and Leaf*, 1964 (revised 1988); *Unfinished Tales of Numenor and Middle-Earth*, 1980 (Christopher Tolkien, editor).

PLAY: *The Homecoming of Beorhtnoth Beorhthelm's Son*, pb. 1953.

POETRY: *Songs for the Philologists*, 1936 (with E. V. Gordon et al.); *The Adventures of Tom Bombadil*, 1962; *The Road Goes Ever On: A Song Cycle*, 1967 (music by Donald Swann); *Poems and Stories*, 1980.

NONFICTION: *A Middle English Vocabulary*, 1922; *The Letters from J. R. R. Tolkien: Selection*, 1981 (Humphrey Carpenter, editor); *The Monsters and the Critics, and Other Essays*, 1983.

TRANSLATIONS: *"Sir Gawain and the Green Knight," "Pearl," and "Sir Orfeo,"* 1975; *The Old English Exodus*, 1981; *Finn and Hengest: The Fragment and the Episode*, 1982.

CHILDREN'S LITERATURE: *Farmer Giles of Ham*, 1949; *Smith of Wootton Major*, 1967; *The Father Christmas Letters*, 1976; *Roverandom*, 1998.

EDITED TEXTS: *Sir Gawain and the Green Knight*, 1925 (with E. V. Gordon); *Ancrene Wisse: The English Text of the Ancrene Riwle*, 1962.

MISCELLANEOUS: *The Tolkien Reader*, 1966; *The History of Middle-Earth*, 1983-1996 (Christopher Tolkien, editor; includes *The Book of Lost Tales I*, 1983; *The Book of Lost Tales II*, 1984; *The Lays of Beleriand*, 1985; *The Shaping of Middle-Earth*, 1986; *The Lost Road, and Other Writings*, 1987; *The Return of the Shadow: The History of "The Lord of the Rings," Part One*, 1988; *The Treason of Isengard: The History of "The Lord of the Rings," Part Two*, 1989; *The War of the Ring: The History of "The Lord of the Rings," Part Three*, 1990; *Sauron Defeated, the End of the Third Age: The History of "The Lord of the Rings," Part Four*, 1992; *Morgoth's Ring*, 1993; *The War of the Jewels*, 1994; *The Peoples of Middle-Earth*, 1996).

BIBLIOGRAPHY

Carpenter, Humphrey. *Tolkien: A Biography*. Winchester, Mass.: Allen & Unwin, 1977. Standard biography was written with access to Tolkien's unpublished letters and diaries; the mostly chronological narrative traces the development of the world of Middle-earth from Tolkien's philological work. Includes an extensive section of black-and-white photographs, a detailed bibliography, a family genealogy, and an index.

Clark, George, and Daniel Timmons, eds. *J. R. R. Tolkien and His Literary Resonances: Views of Middle-Earth*. Westport, Conn.: Greenwood Press, 2000. Collection of fourteen essays is devoted to Tolkien's Middle-earth works. Includes an examination of Tolkien's images of evil, discussion of his use of medieval allegory, and comparisons of his works to those of John Milton and C. S. Lewis.

Crabbe, Katharyn W. *J. R. R. Tolkien*. Rev. ed. New York: Continuum, 1988. Study of Tolkien's writings is unified by a vision of "the quest." After a brief biographical chapter, Crabbe considers Tolkien's use of languages to delineate character in his major works.

Curry, Patrick. *Defending Middle-Earth: Tolkien, Myth, and Modernity*. New York: HarperCollins, 1997. Examines the relevance of Tolkien's mythological creation, especially in terms of its depiction of the struggle of community, nature, and spirit against state. Includes discussion of politics, ecology, and spirituality in Tolkien's works.

Dickerson, Matthew T., and Jonathan Evans. *Ents, Elves, and Eriador: The Environmental Vision of J. R. R. Tolkien*. Lexington: University Press of Kentucky, 2006. Focuses on Tolkien's view of the natural world and environmental responsibility, arguing that the lifestyles of his fictional creations anticipated many of the tenets of modern environmentalism and agrarianism.

Drout, Michael D. C., ed. *J. R. R. Tolkien Encyclopedia: Scholarship and Critical Assessment*. New York: Routledge, 2007. Comprehensive reference volume contains five hundred entries on a wide range of subjects, including Tolkien's biography, characters, influence, and critical reception. Also addressed are the topics of scholarship about the writer and adaptations of his writings to the screen and other media.

Foster, Robert. *The Complete Guide to Middle-Earth: From "The Hobbit" to "The Silmarillion."* Rev. ed. New York: Ballantine, 1978. Alphabetical annotated compendium includes entries on each of the proper names in Tolkien's major works, including persons, places, and things, with page references to standard editions of the works. This invaluable reference guide, written from a perspective within the world created by Tolkien, also provides translations of Middle-earth tongues, chronologies as appropriate, and masterful summaries of complex events.

Haber, Karen, ed. *Meditations on Middle-Earth.* New York: St. Martin's Press, 2001. Collection of essays by a number of fantasy writers, including Ursula K. Le Guin, provides discussion of Tolkien's influence. Also offers an overview of the novelist's work by Tolkien scholar Douglas Anderson.

Johnson, Judith A. *J. R. R. Tolkien. Six Decades of Criticism.* Westport, Conn.: Greenwood Press, 1986. Thorough and well-annotated bibliography of Tolkien scholarship treats all phases of Tolkien's work. Well-indexed volume is especially informative regarding the more obscure periodicals dealing with Tolkien's work.

Lobdell, Jared. *The Rise of Tolkienian Fantasy.* Chicago: Open Court, 2005. Examines Tolkien's fantasy fiction, discussing the writers who influenced him, the elements of his fantasy literature, and his literary heirs, including writers Ursula K. Le Guin, Stephen King, and J. K. Rowling.

Rosebury, Brian. *Tolkien: A Cultural Phenomenon.* 2d ed. New York: Palgrave Macmillan, 2003. Traces the development of Tolkien's writing over several decades, devoting a lengthy analysis to *The Lord of the Rings.* Also addresses Tolkien scholarship in general and discusses director Peter Jackson's film adaptation of *The Lord of the Rings.*

Shippey, T. A. *J. R. R. Tolkien: Author of the Century.* Boston: Houghton Mifflin, 2001. Critical review of Tolkien's work argues that the writer is deserving of both popular and critical acclaim. Demonstrates how, although Tolkien produced fantasy fiction, he addressed real twentieth century issues in his works.

AMOS TUTUOLA

Born: Abeokuta, Nigeria; June 20, 1920
Died: Ibadan, Nigeria; June 8, 1997

PRINCIPAL LONG FICTION

The Palm-Wine Drinkard, 1952
My Life in the Bush of Ghosts, 1954
Simbi and the Satyr of the Dark Jungle, 1955
The Brave African Huntress, 1958
Feather Woman of the Jungle, 1962
Ajaiyi and His Inherited Poverty, 1967
The Witch-Herbalist of the Remote Town, 1981
The Wild Hunter in the Bush of Ghosts, 1983 (wr. c. 1948)
Pauper, Brawler, and Slanderer, 1987

OTHER LITERARY FORMS

Excerpts from the novels of Amos Tutuola (tew-tew-OH-lah) have appeared in numerous anthologies of African literature, but only a handful of short stories have been published. Most of these stories were, until the 1980's, either earlier or later versions of tales included in the novels. These stories include "The Elephant Woman" (in *The Chicago Review*, 1956), "Ajaiyi and the Witchdoctor" (*The Atlantic Monthly*, 1959), "The Duckling Brothers and Their Disobedient Sister" (*Présence africaine*, 1961), "Akanke and the Jealous Pawnbroker" (*Afriscope*, 1974), and "The Pupils of the Eyes" (*Confrontation: A Journal of Third World Literature*, 1974). In 1984, two new stories about a character called Tort, the Shell Man, were published in a popular fantasy anthology in the United States, indicating the possibility of an entirely new audience in the 1980's. Those stories, "The Strange Fellows Palm-Wine Tapster" and "Tort and the Dancing Market Woman," published in *Elsewhere* in 1984, reprise themes found in Tutuola's earliest writings.

ACHIEVEMENTS

Amos Tutuola, who was unknown to both African and Western readers at the time of the publication of *The Palm-Wine Drinkard*, occupies a unique place in the literary world. While his novels have been praised by serious writers and literary critics, he is, quite literally, one of a kind. Despite a limited command of Standard English (which, coupled with his depictions of a "backward" and "superstitious" Africa, has drawn the wrath of many educated Africans), he produced a body of work that stands at the very beginning of the increasingly impressive body of anglophone African literature. Combining the rich folkloric traditions of his Yoruba people with a powerful imagination, his stories supply the Nigerian Bushman with heroes and heroines who face television-handed ghosts, half-bodied babies, bloodthirsty satyrs, and witch-mothers.

Few writers have achieved such serious attention while remaining as unsophisticated in their literary style as did Tutuola. There is no question that Tutuola is, in the truest sense of the word, a "natural," yet he is more than a literary curiosity. In a number of ways, he is a crossroads figure. He succeeded as a writer not by imitating the West but by depending on local sources (mixed with a number of influences from the West but never overwhelmed by them). This helped create a climate in which other Africans could write about the African experience and be accepted both in their own nations and abroad. His dependence on Yoruba folk stories, and such Yoruba-language writers as Chief Daniel O. Fagunwa, continues to draw attention to the richness and variety of African folk traditions.

The depth of Tutuola's debt to those folk stories and the writings of Fagunwa has yet to be fully explored. Extensive passages in several of Tutuola's books appear to be in large part translated or paraphrased from Fagunwa's *The Forest of a Thousand Daemons: A Hunter's Saga* (1950), a title that in itself suggests both Tutuola's second published novel, *My Life in the Bush of Ghosts*, and his first-written novel, *The Wild Hunter in the Bush of Ghosts*. It cannot be said, however, that Tutuola was merely plagiarizing. In a sense, he continued—on paper—the time-honored storytellers' practice of drawing on existing and remembered material to make the old tales new again. Moreover, Tutuola's stories are possessed of a human warmth that makes them more than simply entertaining embellishments of the folk heritage. Despite hardships—which sometimes make the sufferings of Job appear insignificant—his men and women persevere and eventually triumph against all odds. Like all great cultural heroes, they stand up to a potentially destructive universe and struggle to preserve themselves and their people. Their mythic successes are rather like Tutuola's own achievement—wildly unexpected and strangely gratifying.

Biography

There was little in Amos Tutuola's early life to indicate that he would be a world-famous author. Born in 1920, in Abeokuta, Nigeria, in the township of Iporo-Ake, he eagerly listened to the folktales told to him in the evenings by his mother and his aunt. At the age of ten, he was enrolled in the nearby Salvation Army school, where he first began to study English. English is the official language of Nigeria (whose people speak many different African languages), but Tutuola's first language was Yoruba. Furthermore, the everyday English spoken by uneducated Nigerians is either pidgin or affected by West African idiom. Like many other Nigerians, Tutuola combined the deep grammar of his native language with English surface grammar. "I had no other work more than to drink," for example, the statement made by the Palm-Wine Drinkard at the start of his story, is typical Yoruba syntax.

When his family could no longer afford to send him to school, Tutuola began to work as a houseboy for a government clerk. In return for his services, the clerk enrolled Tutuola in Ake Central School and, later, in Lagos High School. There, Tutuola became familiar with the Yoruba writings of Fagunwa and simplified versions of such classics as John Bunyan's *The Pilgrim's Progress* (1678, 1684). Apparently he was not an outstanding student, for he decided to leave school and learn the trade of blacksmith, finding a job as a metalworker for the Royal Air Force at Oshodi. When this job ended, the only work Tutuola could find was as a junior messenger for the labor department in Lagos in 1946. Much of his time was spent sitting in the offices, waiting for messages to carry. To combat his boredom, he began scribbling down stories on scraps of paper. Around 1948, he sent his first completed manuscript, *The Wild Hunter in the Bush of Ghosts*, to a photography publisher in London, the Focal Press. The book, he explained to them in a letter, was written to accompany a collection of photographs of ghosts. Those photographs, he said, would follow shortly. The photographs turned out to be of drawings of ghosts, and Focal Press dumped both text and "ghost photos" into their files. There they remained for more than thirty years.

Although Tutuola may have been discouraged by that early failure (which he did not mention to anyone for decades), he continued to write. Upon seeing an advertisement for books from the United Society for Christian Literature in a newspaper, he decided to send to that organization a manuscript, the first draft of which had been written in lead pencil over the course of several days. After three months of enlarging the story, he made a copy of it in ink and sent it off. The society did not publish books but, making one of those small decisions that have unexpectedly large effects, it sent the manuscript to the publishing house Faber and Faber. Slightly more than one year later, in 1952, it was published as *The Palm-Wine Drinkard*. Three months after its publication, Faber and Faber received a second Tutuola manuscript. After a small amount of editing by Geoffrey Parrinder, it was published as *My Life in the Bush of Ghosts*. It is clear now that it drew freely on Tutuola's memories of his first, "lost" manuscript.

Enchanted by his fresh West African idiom, critics praised the book and went so far as to urge other African writers to follow Tutuola's example—a difficult task; indeed, Tutuola himself found it hard to do. He continued for a time to work as a messenger (who was visited now and then by distinguished white scholars, to the disapproving surprise of his employers) but was now concerned about his own shortcomings. He acknowledged that his English was imperfect, so he attended night school to improve it. His renown brought him a great deal of attention, but he remained a shy, retiring person. A job working as a storekeeper for the Nigerian Broadcasting Corporation was given to him in 1956, and in 1957, he arranged to be transferred to the Ibadan offices of the corporation so that he could work with Professor Collis at the University of Ibadan in producing a play version of *The Palm-Wine Drinkard*. This version was translated into Yoruba and successfully staged throughout West Africa in the early 1960's.

Married in 1947 and the father of several children, Tutuola was never comfortable playing the part of a celebrity. He had little to say to interviewers and did not like to go on lecture tours or even have much to do with other writers (though he was a self-effacing charter member of the Mbari Club, a seminal writers' and publishers' group in Nigeria). A six-month scholarship was offered to him in 1963 by West Germany, but he did not accept it.

By the time Tutuola's third novel was published, there was some improvement in his standard of English, but there also was a growing disenchantment with his work. Africans continued to criticize both his bad habits and his borrowings, and Europeans intimated that his "improvement" had a negative effect on his work, which they also criticized for being repetitive. To some, he was now deliberately childish, whereas before he had been pleasingly childlike.

By the 1970's, however, Tutuola was again receiving praise from both African and European critics, who were beginning to see his writings for what they were: not true novels, but linked stories in the monomythic tradition. Some see him as the equivalent for world literature of the *akpala kpatita* (professional storyteller) of Nigeria. (Jorge Amado, the popular Brazilian writer, shows the influence of Tutuola in his own writing.) This renewed and more balanced attention directed toward Tutuola is surely one of the factors that led to his publishing a book in 1981, the first in more than a decade, and an extended tour of the United States in the 1980's, during which he spoke and took part in symposia. Thanks to some fine scholarly detective work by Bernth Lindfors, the handwritten original manuscript of what was to be Tutuola's first novel, *The Wild Hunter in the Bush of Ghosts*, was found; it was then published in 1983. As a result, both scholars and biographers of the Yoruba writer had to do considerable backtracking. Published by Three Continents Press with a typeset script facing photocopies of the original handwritten pages, it is significant as a minor work at an early stage of Tutuola's development. Furthermore, as Lindfors puts it in his introduction to the book, it is "the first long piece of prose fiction written for publication in English by a Nigerian author."

Analysis

Although it is certainly possible to enjoy Amos Tutuola's novels on their own merits—merits that include economy of language, a strong storytelling voice, a marvelous self-assurance on the part of his narrators (almost always in the first person), fantastic imagination, and virtually nonstop action—it is useful to look at him within the context of Yoruba culture. The Yorubas are a people of western Nigeria who both have embraced Western culture and have remained intensely connected to traditional ways. The Yoruba people make up about 20 percent of the population of Nigeria, Africa's most populous nation and one of its best educated. Although Christianity is the religion of virtually all Yoruba people, there is a deep undercurrent of animism.

As with Tutuola's narrators, contemporary Yoruba people see nothing unusual in a world where churches coexist with magical charms (*juju*) and the deepest and most impassable jungles (the bush) are filled with spirits, both those of the dead and those of nonhuman beings. Yoruba folklore is characterized by a belief in a distant but benevolent supreme deity and the presence on the earth of numerous smaller "gods" and powers, often anthropomorphic. It is still common practice for both adults and children to sit around in the evening and listen to folk stories much like those in Tutuola's books. In some cases, they do so while drinking palm wine, a mildly alcoholic beverage made from the sap of palm trees.

Inexpensive or "free" primary education in British-style schools, often run by churches, was common when Tutuola was a child, and this exposure, from his tenth year until his late teens, provided Tutuola with the necessary tools—literacy and a knowledge of literary forms (from simplified classics in the schools to books published in Yoruba)—to begin his career as a writer. One thing those schools did not give him, however, was the confidence of one who knows a good story and is not afraid to tell it. It was that self-assurance (so clearly echoed in the gentle strength of all of his various protagonists) that led a junior clerk, a man in a lowly position in an extremely class-conscious colonial society, to dare to send his first writings to a publisher.

THE PALM-WINE DRINKARD

The Palm-Wine Drinkard begins with the narrator telling us a bit about himself. "I was a palm-wine drinkard since I was a boy of ten years of age. I had no other work more than to drink palm-wine in my life." These first words hardly prepare readers for the mythic dimensions of the character seen later in the book, but the prodigious amounts of palm wine he consumes (225 kegs every twenty-four hours) give us the hint that he is no ordinary human. When his palm-wine tapster falls from a tree and dies, the Drinkard sees that the only thing he can do is seek out his tapster in the land of the Dead. This sets the mythic tone of the book and all the rest of Tutuola's work. The Drinkard enters the bush, a netherworld inhabited by spirits and strange creatures. His first encounter, with an old man who sets him the Herculean task of capturing Death, reveals to us the Drinkard's superhuman powers. His other name, he tells us, is "Father of gods who could do everything in this world," and his success in capturing Death (who then escapes, which is why "we are hearing his name about in the world") proves that his title is no idle boast. The Drinkard's next exploit is to rescue his wife-to-be from a skull who has borrowed body parts to masquerade as a "Complete Gentleman." Thereafter, he and his wife continue on his quest, but not before she becomes pregnant (in her thumb) and gives birth to a miraculous and dangerous half-bodied child who must be destroyed before they can continue on their way. They do eventually reach the town of the Dead, despite the menace of such beasts as a Spirit of Prey with eyes like searchlights and with the help of the Drinkard's powerful jujus and such beings as the Faithful Mother, whose servants buy the Drinkard's death and rent his fear.

Novelistic plot development in the conventional sense does not exist in this or Tutuola's other romances; the various episodes are almost interchangeable. The Drinkard, however, does learn a lesson at the end of the novel. His tapster has now (like a student in a European school or an apprentice blacksmith) "qualified" as a full dead man. He cannot return to the living. Instead, he gives the Drinkard and his resourceful wife, who has developed into something of a Sibyl, a miraculous egg. The Drinkard and his wife return to the land of the living. There he finds a famine and, sending a sacrifice to Heaven, brings rain to the people—an ending that seems to recapitulate the conclusion of a traditional creation story.

In one of the best analyses of Tutuola's style, Lindfors concludes that his books are not novels at all; instead, they are, in content, structure, and style, concatenated folktales. Both African and English critics have noted the structure of the quest and the rite of passage that also characterize Tutuola's extended narratives. They always begin with the introduction of a main character; the sending out of that character into the world, where many hardships are encountered; the overcoming of all obstacles; and the return of the hero or heroine in triumph. This structure is both that of *The Pilgrim's Progress* and that of the epic stories of Yoruba (and other African) cultural heroes as they overcome death, use their personal magic to change themselves into animals or objects, and travel through a world fully as hostile as real life. To describe either Tutuola's stories or African folklore as escapism, in fact, is quite inaccurate. The worlds of Simbi, of the Brave Huntress, and of the Drinkard are graphically horrifying. They are no more an escape than would be a series of vivid nightmares.

The flavor of the stories is that of the naïve tall tale. Almost anything is possible in such accounts, even turning oneself into a stone and then throwing oneself to escape. The reader (or the listener, for the voice in Tutuola is that of an oral storyteller) is carried along by the headlong rush of events, the total acceptance of this illogical world by the narrators (who always live well within this world, playing and winning by its rules), the humor and humanity that are among the author's greatest virtues. Furthermore—and here both Tutuola's Christian faith (which is very real) and the folktale tradition come into play—these are moral tales. There are always lessons to be learned. No one commits a foolish action without having to pay the consequences. Good is always eventually rewarded; evil is always strong but eventually defeated.

There is a clear structure to each of Tutuola's books, a beginning and an end that are carefully linked. The Drinkard's search for his tapster ends with his finding him and learning a lesson as a result of all of his efforts—a lesson that was unexpected on the protagonist's part but that the reader responds to and understands. *My Life in the Bush of Ghosts* begins with the central character not knowing what "good" or "bad" or hatred is. It ends, after twenty-four years of trials and wandering in the bush, with these words: "This is what hatred did."

A cornucopia of horrifically memorable menaces confronts Tutuola's protagonists in each of the books. Indeed, this may be one of the more serious of Tutuola's failings, the very abundance of monsters and fabulous encounters in each of his stories (although those monsters are invariably memorable and individually characterized with surprising economy). After a certain point, especially when one reads a series of Tutuola's novels in a short space of time, events and characters begin to blur and one feels overwhelmed. It was probably with this overabundance in mind that the dramatic version of *The Palm-Wine Drinkard* was created out of only eight of the twenty episodes found in the book. In his essay "Amos Tutuola: A Nigerian Visionary," Gerald Moore characterizes the first two novels as quest romances and ties them to the monomyth of Joseph Campbell's *The Hero with a Thousand Faces* (1949). Considering that Tutuola's stories follow the pattern of Yoruba storytelling sessions, only a bit more extended, and those stories often relate creation myths, it is not surprising that Moore should find that pattern.

MY LIFE IN THE BUSH OF GHOSTS

It is difficult to use conventional critical apparatus in dealing with Tutuola. It is equally difficult to summarize easily any of his books, for they consist, like his first book, of a loosely organized, helter-skelter collection of fantastic events that have their own logic.

My Life in the Bush of Ghosts presents its readers with another character like the Drinkard, but possessed of less magic. He is, however—like the Drinkard—resourceful, plucky, and often very shrewd. He is not fortunate enough to have a wife like the Drinkard's, but Tutuola makes up for that in the characters of both Simbi and the Brave African Huntress in his later books. They are women of purpose, wonderfully self-reliant, and as capable as his male heroes. Simbi engages in heroic combat with a "Satyr" (Tutuola's names for his mythic creatures are often drawn from Western mythology but have nothing at all to do with the original beings in Western myth) who is ten feet tall, covered with blood and feathers, "an impatient and ill-tempered, impenitent and noxious creature." The Brave African Huntress vows death to all the "pygmies" (small creatures that resemble the various dwarflike forest creatures of African myth rather than human beings) who have either killed or "detained" her four brothers. She proceeds to do so with bloodthirsty efficiency, burning the pygmy town, blowing it up with gunpowder, and then picking off the pygmies one by one with her gun as they run from the ruins. After rescuing her brothers, she proceeds to sell the minerals found in the Jungle of the Pygmies and becomes wealthy.

The world that is inhabited by the characters in all of Tutuola's writing is an interesting one in another way. It contains no Caucasians. Aside from one brief reference to a set of footprints made in the rocks near Ife by "the first white men who had traveled from heaven through that rock to the earth," one finds no Europeans in his books. Instead, the books are set in an African Africa, albeit an Africa affected by Western inventions and institutions such as newspapers, gunpowder, the Methodist Church, and airplanes. Though it may be unintentional, certain sections of Tutuola's novels—such as the description of the Dead Cousin who has become a Methodist bishop in the "10th Town of Ghosts"—seem to be parodies of real events in Nigerian history. More often than not, Western objects appear in Tutuola's similes—as when he compares the sound of the skulls chasing the Drinkard to "a thousand petrol drums pushing along a hard road." His is thus not an ideal Africa, but one rather like the West Africa of the early nineteenth century, when the influence of the slave trade had deepened rivalries between such African states as Oyo and Dahomey and created a climate of continual warfare and uncertainty. In this world, Tutuola's heroes and heroines are much like many Yoruba people of today, men and women who deal with an increasingly complicated world with pragmatism, shrewdness, and even humor.

Joseph Bruchac

OTHER MAJOR WORKS

SHORT FICTION: "The Elephant Woman," 1956; "Ajaiyi and the Witchdoctor," 1959; "The Duckling Brothers and Their Disobedient Sister," 1961; "Akanke and the Jealous Pawnbroker," 1974; "The Pupils of the Eyes," 1974; "The Strange Fellows Palm-Wine Tapster," 1984; "Tort and the Dancing Market Woman," 1984; *Yoruba Folktales*, 1986; *The Witch Doctor, and Other Stories*, 1990.

NONFICTION: *Tutuola at the University: The Italian Voice of a Yoruba Ancestor*, 2001 (lectures; Alessandro Di Maio, editor).

BIBLIOGRAPHY

Achebe, Chinua. "Work and Play in Tutuola's *The Palm-Wine Drinkard*." In *Hopes and Impediments: Selected Essays*. New York: Doubleday, 1989. Novelist Achebe's perceptive article about Tutuola's novel *The Palm-Wine Drinkard* is included in this collection of essays examining art and literature.

Afolayan, A. "Language and Sources of Amos Tutuola." *In Perspectives on African Literature*, edited by Christopher Heywood. New York: African Publishing, 1971. Afolayan's essay assesses Tutuola's contribution to Yoruba literature from a Yoruba perspective.

Ajayi, Jare. *Amos Tutuola: Factotum as a Pioneer*. Ibadan, Nigeria: Creative Books, 2003. Ajayi, a Nigerian journalist, spent sixteen years researching and writing this first English-language biography of Tutuola, which discusses, among other subjects, the novelist's motivations for creative writing and how he was exploited by publishers. Also includes interpretations of Tutuola's work.

George, Olakunle. *Relocating Agency: Modernity and African Letters*. Albany: State University of New York Press, 2003. George examines writings by Tutuola and three other Nigerian writers—Daniel O. Fagunwa, Wole Soyinka, and Chinua Achebe. He uses several modern critical theories, including poststructuralism and postcolonialism, to interpret these writers' works.

Gera, Anjali. *Three Great African Novelists: Chinua Achebe, Wole Soyinka, and Amos Tutuola*. New Delhi, India: Creative Books, 2001. Gera's examination of Tutuola—along with novelists Chinua Achebe and Wole Soyinka—focuses on the use of the Yoruba and Igbo storytelling traditions in his work. Gera describes how Tutuola adapts these traditions to define himself and his society.

Irele, Abiola. "Tradition and the Yoruba Writer: Daniel O. Fagunwa, Amos Tutuola, and Wole Soyinka." In *Perspectives on Wole Soyinka: Freedom and Complexity*, edited by Biodun Jeyifo. Jackson: University Press of Mississippi, 2001. Irele's essay compares Tutuola's work with that of two other Yoruba writers. The essay should be read with Afolayan's essay in *Perspectives on African Literature*.

Lindfors, Bernth, ed. *Critical Perspectives on Amos Tutuola*. Washington, D.C.: Three Continents Press, 1975. This collection of essays, edited by a respected Tutuola scholar, provides critical insight into Tutuola's individual novels. Includes a bibliography.

Onyeberechi, Sydney E. *Critical Essays: Achebe, Baldwin, Cullen, Ngugi, and Tutuola*. Hyattsville, Md.: Rising Star, 1999. Essays on African and African American literature, featuring critical commentary on Tutuola, Chinua Achebe, Ngugi wa Thiong'o, Countee Cullen, and James Baldwin.

_______. "Myth, Magic, and Appetite in Amos Tutuola's *The Palm-Wine Drinkard*." *MAWA Review* 4 (1989): 22-26. Often cited as one of the best studies of Tutuola's masterpiece. A brief but comprehensive study.

Owomoyela, Oyekan. *Amos Tutuola Revisited*. New York: Twayne, 1999. An excellent introduction to Tutuola's life and works, written by a Yoruba writer and scholar. Owomoyela argues that Tutuola symbolizes the African tradition from the time of colonialism to postcolonialism. Includes notes, references, a selected bibliography, and an index.

Quayson, Ato. "Treasures of an Opulent Fancy: Amos Tutuola and the Folktale Narrative." In *Strategic Transformation in Nigerian Writing: Orality and History in the Work of Rev. Samuel Johnson, Amos Tutuola, Wole Soyinka, and Ben Okri*. Bloomington: Indiana University Press, 1997. A sound treatment of the element of orality in fiction by Tutuola and three other Nigerian writers. Quayson focuses on Tutuola's novels *The Palm-Wine Drinkard* and *My Life in the Bush of Ghosts*.

T. H. WHITE

Born: Bombay (now Mumbai), India; May 29, 1906
Died: Piraeus, Greece; January 17, 1964
Also known as: Terence Hanbury White; James Aston

PRINCIPAL LONG FICTION

Darkness at Pemberley, 1932
First Lesson, 1932 (as James Aston)
They Winter Abroad, 1932 (as Aston)
Farewell Victoria, 1933
Earth Stopped: Or, Mr. Marx's Sporting Tour, 1934
Gone to Ground, 1935
The Sword in the Stone, 1938
The Witch in the Wood, 1939
The Ill-Made Knight, 1940
Mistress Masham's Repose, 1946
The Elephant and the Kangaroo, 1947
The Master: An Adventure Story, 1957
The Candle in the Wind, 1958
The Once and Future King, 1958 (includes *The Sword in the Stone*, *The Witch in the Wood*, *The Ill-Made Knight*, and *The Candle in the Wind*)
The Book of Merlyn: The Unpublished Conclusion to "The Once and Future King," 1977

OTHER LITERARY FORMS

T. H. White's first literary productions were two poetry collections. Several short stories enclosed within the satiric frame narrative of *Gone to Ground* were reprinted along with later items in the posthumously issued *The Maharajah, and Other Stories* (1981). The majority of White's nonfiction books celebrate his strong interest in field sports; *The Goshawk* (1951), which describes his experiments in falconry, is the most notable. The title *The Godstone and the Blackymor* (1959) refers to a legendary monument on the island of Inniskea. White also wrote two books on famous scandals, *The Age of Scandal: An Excursion Through a Minor Period* (1950) and *The Scandalmonger* (1952).

ACHIEVEMENTS

T. H. White labored long and hard in relative obscurity before achieving literary success. His most successful work, *The Sword in the Stone*, was considered by many a children's book. White intended from the very beginning, however, that the story should be the introduction to a comprehensive modern rendering of the Arthurian legend. The second and third volumes became increasingly adult in their concerns and much darker in their implications. The fourth part languished unpublished for nearly twenty years, but after it was finally revised to form the conclusion of *The Once and Future King*, the collection was eventually recognized as a masterpiece of modern fantasy. Even that version lacked the original fifth part, however, which remained unpublished for another nineteen years—thirteen years after the author's death. Although the animated film of *The Sword in the Stone* (1963) and the film version of the *Once and Future King*-based stage musical *Camelot* (1967) have reached a far wider audience than the original novels, the Arthurian sequence can now be seen as a work comparable in ambition and quality to the similar endeavors of fantasy novelist J. R. R. Tolkien.

BIOGRAPHY

T. H. White, whose full name was Terence Hanbury White, was born in Bombay, India, the son of a district supervisor of police and the grandson of a judge. He spent his first five years on the Indian subcontinent before moving to England with his mother, Constance. His childhood was difficult because Constance—who eventually obtained a judicial separation from her husband but not the divorce that would have allowed her to marry her live-in lover—was mentally disturbed, and White was frightened of her. Removal to Cheltenham College in 1920 provided no relief; mistreatment from classmates maintained his misery, but he still won admission to Queen's College in Cambridge. He might have been happier there were it not for certain anxieties, in which homosexual feelings and alcoholism were joined by the total loss of his early religious faith and irrepressible sadomasochistic fantasies. Also, he contracted tuberculosis while in his second year at Cambridge, and his teachers had to donate money to send him to Italy to convalesce; it was there that he wrote his first novel.

White returned from Italy in much better condition. His determination to stay fit and healthy cemented his interest in field sports, but his triumph over physical frailty was shadowed by an exaggerated awareness of his mortality, which added furious fuel to all his activities. After obtaining a first-class degree with distinction in 1929, he became a schoolmaster—concluding with a four-year stint at one of England's best public schools, Stowe, in 1932-1936—before the autobiographical potboiler *England Have My Bones* (1936) sold well enough to win him a commission to deliver a book every year to his publisher, Collins. He rented a gamekeeper's cottage on the Stowe estate to pursue his new career.

Fearful of conscription into a war he desperately did not want to be involved in, White moved to Ireland (which remained neutral throughout World War II) in 1939, lodging in Doolistown in county Meath and at Sheskin Lodge in county Mayo. In these two locations, living as an exile, he wrote the fourth and fifth parts of the Arthurian series, but Collins ended the book-per-year arrangement after issuing *The Ill-Made Knight*; the subsequent hiatus in his career lasted until 1946. In that year he relocated to the Channel Islands, living briefly in Jersey before settling in Aldernay in 1947; he died in his cabin, apparently of heart failure, while on a Mediterranean cruise in 1964.

ANALYSIS

T. H. White's first five novels, one of which was written in collaboration with R. McNair Scott and two of which were concealed under the pseudonym James Aston, were all naturalistic. White wrote his first novel—*They Winter Abroad*—under the pseudonym Aston. This work is of some interest for the insight it offers into his youthful state of mind. Also as Aston he published his second novel, *First Lesson*. His first novel as White was *Darkness at Pemberley*. All three novels were published in 1932. The only one of White's novels from this period that is now remembered is his nostalgic panorama of the Victorian era, *Farewell Victoria*; it is also the only one not solidly rooted in his own experiences.

EARTH STOPPED *and* GONE TO GROUND

Earth Stopped is a satiric comedy paying respectful homage to the works of English novelist Robert Smith Surtees, whose addiction to hunting, shooting, and fishing was shared by White. White's similarly addicted friend, Siegfried Sassoon, had introduced him to a reprint of Surtees' 1845 novel *Hillingdon Hall* in 1931. Sassoon's autobiographical novel *Memoirs of a Fox-Hunting Man* (1928) reflects sarcastically on the fact that he had been sent to a sanatorium to save him from a court-martial when he refused to return to the front after being wounded in action in 1917; his influence on White's attitudes was profound.

Earth Stopped introduces the inept revolutionary Mr. Marx into a Surtees-like party gathered for a weekend's sport at an English country house. The party remains blithely good humored until the final chapters, when a world war abruptly precipitated by the forces of communism and fascism breaks out, at which point "the universe split open like a pea-pod, informed by lightning but far transcending thunder."

The story continues in *Gone to Ground*, in which the survivors of the house party swap tall tales while they hide from the catastrophe, taking psychological refuge in fantasy while taking physical refuge underground. Although its prophetic pretensions were supposedly impersonal, this provided an ironic metaphorical account of the subsequent shape of White's life and career. The book ends with the conclusion of the final tale—reprinted in *The Maharajah, and Other Stories* as "The Black Rabbit"—in which Keeper Pan, who was the inventor of panic as well as the god of nature, asserts his ultimate dominion over the objects of human sport.

THE ONCE AND FUTURE KING

Anticipation of a new world war, which many imaginative people expected to put an end to civilization, overwhelmed English fantastic fiction in the late 1930's. Other English writers were writing apocalyptic fantasies far more terrifying than *Earth Stopped*, but

White decided to go in the opposite direction, becoming a connoisseur of playful escapism. The account of the boyhood and education of Arthur set out in *The Sword in the Stone* is as firmly rooted in personal experience as White's earliest novels are, but it is a calculated magical transformation of the oppressions that afflicted the author and his ultimate redemption from them.

The Sword in the Stone begins with an exotic schoolroom syllabus devised for the future Sir Kay by his governess, who cannot punish her noble student but can and does take out her frustrations on his whipping boy, the Wart, who is not recognized as the future embodiment of England and the chivalric ideal until he acquires a far more inspiring tutor in Merlyn. The debt that White owed to his tutor at Cambridge and longtime correspondent L. J. Potts is acknowledged in the fact that Merlyn, whose prophetic gifts result from living his life in reverse, actually served as a Cambridge tutor in the twentieth century, which lay in his distant past.

The account of the childhood of Gareth and his brothers contained in *The Witch in the Wood* is far darker—in spite of comic relief provided by the alcoholic lapsed saint Toirdealbhach and King Pellinore's obsessive pursuit of the Questing Beast—because their lustful, neglectful, and unbalanced mother is a transfiguration of White's own. The characterization of Lancelot in *The Ill-Made Knight* probably owes something to Sassoon as well as to White's perception of himself, and it is significant that the text explicitly compares the greatest of all the Arthurian knights to one of the great sportsmen of the late 1930's, the Australian cricketer Donald Bradman. Lancelot's obsessive anxiety that his forbidden love for Guenevere will sap the strength that makes him England's champion and deny him the chance to find the Holy Grail is a transfiguration of White's anxieties about his homosexuality and terror of military service (both of which were implicated in his decision to live as a recluse as soon as it became economically viable).

Given the deep personal significance of the first three volumes, it is hardly surprising that the dourly harrowing *The Candle in the Wind*, which White wrote in the latter months of 1940, is saturated with his anxiety for the blitzkrieg-devastated England that he had left and the civilization that it represented. He wrote to Potts on December 6, 1940, that he had discovered that "the central theme of the *Morte d'Arthur* is to find an antidote to war." In the fifth volume, Arthur goes underground with his old tutor, and they analyze the dismal failure of the Grail quest and look for a new way forward. While they do so, in *The Book of Merlyn*, they are surrounded by the animals Arthur loved so much as a boy, and Keeper Pan is certainly present in spirit, if not in person. Two key sequences from *The Book of Merlyn* were transposed into the version of *The Sword in the Stone* contained in *The Once and Future King*, and other elements were grafted onto the new version of *The Candle in the Wind* to supply the sense of an ending, but these devices distorted the balance and meaning of the whole, which was not published in its intended form.

J. R. R. Tolkien set out to expand his children's fantasy *The Hobbit: Or, There and Back Again* (1937) into an epic at almost exactly the same time White began to elaborate

The Once and Future King. Tolkien was a Catholic and an Old English scholar who carefully excluded everything that had arrived in Great Britain with the Norman Conquest (1066) from the mythos of his fantastic secondary world, Middle-earth; however, it was precisely that imported tradition of chivalric romance that White chose for the heart of his own exercise. There is, therefore, a curious sense that the two resultant masterpieces of fantasy are as complementary and opposed as the Universities of Oxford, which was Tolkien's home, and Cambridge, White's spiritual home, to which he remained anchored by his correspondence with Potts.

One might also compare and contrast *The Once and Future King* with the fantasies of an older Cambridge man, John Cowper Powys. Powys, also troubled by inescapable sadomasochistic fantasies, eventually followed up the Grail epic *A Glastonbury Romance* (1932) with a more explicit transfiguration of Arthurian myth, *Porius* (1951), which was never issued in its entirety. Powys tackled the problem of designing a mythology for the much-conquered island of Britain by producing his own syncretism of Anglo-Saxon and Anglo-Norman elements with earlier Celtic and Greek myths.

All three of these writers were trying to construct or reconstruct a neomythological epic for an island that had somehow never contrived to produce a real one, which would also embody and allegorize the crisis at which the contemporary British nation had arrived in the pause between World War I and World War II. Of the three, White's is by far the most lighthearted but also—by virtue of its precipitous plunge into tragedy in *The Candle in the Wind*—the most emotional. It is perhaps ironic that Tolkien, who was not nearly as committed to the politics of escapism as White, should have become the parent of a whole genre of escapist fantasy, while White became best known as the inspirer of a Walt Disney film and a musical comedy. Because of the University of Texas edition of *The Book of Merlyn*, however, modern readers and critics can reconstruct White's masterpiece as he intended it to be read, and to judge its true worth as an epic for the isle of Britain.

LATER NOVELS

The three fantasies that White wrote after he recovered from the disappointment of Collins's initial refusal to publish *The Candle in the Wind* are best regarded as footnotes to the main sequence of his novels, displaying a gradual acceptance of the fact that he was seen as a children's writer. *The Elephant and the Kangaroo* is an allegorical comedy in which an English atheist in Ireland witnesses a visitation by the archangel Michael and sets out to build an ark in response to the threat of an impending second deluge. In *Mistress Masham's Repose*, a young girl discovers descendants of the Lilliputians of Jonathan Swift's *Gulliver's Travels* (1726) living on an island and sets out to defend them from commercial exploitation by Hollywood filmmakers. *The Master* is a science-fiction story for children, whose juvenile heroes thwart the eponymous island-based villain's plans for world domination.

Brian Stableford

Other major works

nonfiction: *England Have My Bones*, 1936 (autobiography); *The Age of Scandal: An Excursion Through a Minor Period*, 1950 (anecdotes); *The Goshawk*, 1951; *The Scandalmonger*, 1952 (anecdotes); *The Godstone and the Blackymor*, 1959 (autobiography); *America at Last*, 1965 (autobiography).

translation: *The Book of Beasts*, 1954 (of medieval bestiary).

Bibliography

Brewer, Elisabeth. *T. H. White's "The Once and Future King."* Cambridge, England: D. S. Brewer, 1993. Brewer examines White's tetralogy, with separate chapters on each of the four novels and another on the fifth, unfinished work, *The Book of Merlyn*. She discusses comedy in the tetralogy and places White's work within the context of other Arthurian romances, historical fiction, and fantasy literature. Includes a bibliography and an index.

Crane, John K. *T. H. White*. New York: Twayne, 1974. A competent introductory overview of White, with biographical information, discussion of his works, and a bibliography. Very useful for the beginning student.

Gallix, François. "T. H. White and the Legend of King Arthur: From Animal Fantasy to Political Morality." In *King Arthur: A Casebook*, edited by Edward Donald Kennedy. New York: Garland, 1996. This analysis of *The Once and Future King* is one of sixteen essays that examine how the legend of King Arthur has been recounted in medieval romances, nineteenth century art, and twentieth century literature.

Kellman, Martin. *T. H. White and the Matter of Britain: A Literary Overview*. Lewiston, N.Y.: Edwin Mellen Press, 1988. Kellman discusses all of White's historical fiction, the lesser-known works as well as *The Once and Future King*. Includes a bibliography and an index.

Manlove, C. N. *The Impulse of Fantasy Literature*. Kent, Ohio: Kent State University Press, 1983. Manlove's study of fantasy fiction includes a chapter examining *The Once and Future King*, placing the tetralogy within the context of British fantasy literature.

Matthews, Richard. "Shining Past and Future: The Persistence of Camelot (T. H. White's *The Once and Future King*)." In *Fantasy: The Liberation of Imagination*. New York: Twayne, 1997. A study of fantasy fiction, containing a discussion of the genre's origins and development from antiquity to the present as well as analyses of works by White and other writers. Includes a bibliographic essay, a list of recommended fantasy titles, and an index.

Sprague, Kurth. *T. H. White's Troubled Heart: Women in "The Once and Future King."* Rochester, N.Y.: Boydell & Brewer, 2007. An analysis of the female characters in White's tetralogy. Sprague describes White's misogyny, which was a reaction to his difficult mother, but notes that White also was able to create a charming portrait of Queen Guenevere.

JEANETTE WINTERSON

Born: Manchester, England; August 27, 1959

PRINCIPAL LONG FICTION

Boating for Beginners, 1985
Oranges Are Not the Only Fruit, 1985
The Passion, 1987
Sexing the Cherry, 1989
Written on the Body, 1993
Art and Lies: A Piece for Three Voices and a Bawd, 1994
Gut Symmetries, 1997
The PowerBook, 2000
Lighthousekeeping, 2004
Weight: The Myth of Atlas and Hercules, 2005
The Stone Gods, 2007

OTHER LITERARY FORMS

Jeanette Winterson has dramatized several of her own books, most notably *Oranges Are Not the Only Fruit* (1990) for British television. She has written original radio drama and worked on a documentary, *Great Moments in Aviation* (1994), also for British television. She has written short stories, essays, and columns for *The Guardian* and *The Times*. One of her earlier books was a comic book, and she has published several works of children's fiction, including *The King of Capri* (2003) and *Tanglewreck* (2006).

ACHIEVEMENTS

Jeanette Winterson has been in the public eye from the time her first novel won the Whitbread Prize. She was named by *Granta* magazine one of the twenty best young British writers. Other prizes include the Prix d'Argent at the Cannes Film Festival, the Prix Italia, and the BAFTA Best Drama Award for her television adaptation of *Oranges Are Not the Only Fruit*. She won the John Llewellyn Rhys Memorial Prize for *The Passion* and the E. M. Forster Award from the American Academy of Arts and Letters for *Sexing the Cherry*. In 2006, she was awarded the Order of the British Empire (OBE) for services to literature. Her books have been translated into more than one dozen languages.

BIOGRAPHY

Jeanette Winterson was born in 1959 in Manchester, in the northwest of England, and adopted by a childless Pentecostal couple from Accrington, a mill town just outside Manchester. She was raised under strict religious principles and shaped for a career as a missionary. By the age of eight, she was preaching at evangelist tent meetings held by the family's small chapel, and was making converts. Her reading material at home was limited to the Bible and Sir Thomas Malory's *Le Morte d'Arthur* (1485), a strange combination from which she developed a strong feeling for literary style.

At the age of fifteen, Winterson had a lesbian relationship with one of her converts that was strongly denounced by the church. At the age of sixteen, she decided to leave home and took a number of part-time jobs to pay for the academic high school where she was enrolled. When she was eighteen years old, she enrolled at St. Catherine's College, Oxford University, to major in English. She worked for one year at a mental hospital to pay tuition.

After graduation in 1981, Winterson worked in various theaters and began writing what would become her first novel, *Oranges Are Not the Only Fruit*. She finished the novel at the young age of twenty-three years. After it was published in 1985, she began working as an assistant editor for Pandora Press (her early publisher). She began a romantic relationship with Pat Kavanagh, her literary agent. In 1987, Winterson published her second novel, *The Passion*. Its successful reception by readers and critics inspired her to become a full-time writer. The next year she entered a long-term relationship with Peggy Reynolds, an academic and a radio broadcaster. The following year, Winterson published *Sexing the Cherry*.

In 1990, Winterson adapted *Oranges Are Not the Only Fruit* for television in a highly acclaimed dramatization. Her work was embraced in the American market with *Written on the Body* in 1993, ensuring a worldwide readership. Honors and prizes followed, and she became a regular columnist, essayist, writer of children's fiction, and broadcaster. She also bought a delicatessen in central London and a house in Gloucestershire.

Analysis

Jeanette Winterson's novels are at the cusp of modernism, postmodernism, and Magical Realism. Her sheer verbal skills, so evident in her fiction, led to the novels' initial popularity. The novels also were popular because they filled the desire in the mid-1980's for a new lesbian narrative subgenre. In some ways, Winterson steered the postfeminist novel into uncharted territories, especially in terms of narrative. She made gender, along with plot, history, and even narrator, sources of uncertainty. The one certainty in her novels is the story of the truth of love. Other consistent themes include myth and the fairy tale.

Oranges Are Not the Only Fruit, an immediate popular success, is an autobiographical story of lesbian sexuality. The heroine, simply called Jeanette (and later Jess), relates her experiences with a narrow-minded religious sect. With this novel, Winterson joined a long line of writers who were liberated from narrow religious upbringings. (D. H. Lawrence is perhaps the most obvious and most acknowledged of these writers.)

Winterson inherited far more from her religious upbringing than she rejected. She admitted that her readings as a child, narrow and limited as they were, led to her love of words and her sense of style. She became an evangelist, not for religion but for the books themselves, much like the "religion of literature" that the poet Matthew Arnold sought to construct out of the ruins of his childhood faith. Winterson has said that literature, and specifically postmodernist literature, has to redefine the boundaries of truth in terms of love and do so beyond the norms of common sense. As in Lawrence, that love has to be defined in terms of sexuality and passion.

Winterson's next two novels, *The Passion* and *Sexing the Cherry*, play with history, with *The Passion* set in the Napoleonic era. Her fourth novel, *Written on the Body*, is a more somber exploration of what became her typical plot structure, the love triangle of a married couple and a single woman, usually lesbian. Love is challenged by disease, as the heroine is diagnosed with cancer. Love and disease break down boundaries, demanding new ones be constructed. The novel has no plot line and the narrator is not clearly gendered. *Art and Lies* and *Gut Symmetries* are similarly constructed.

After publishing the novels *The Power Book* and *Lighthousekeeping*, Winterson turned to children's science fiction. By invitation of a small Scottish press, she turned to pure myth in the novel *Weight*, which is a retelling of the story of Atlas and Hercules. A growing concern with ecological issues led to the novel *The Stone Gods*, set partly in space in the science fiction format and partly on Easter Island, which suffered desertification at the hands of humans.

Sexing the Cherry

Sexing the Cherry is an experiment in postmodern fiction, interweaving strands of history, myth, fairy tale, and Magical Realism. The main plot concerns an orphan named Jordan and his adoptive mother, a large Rabelaisian earth-mother type of woman who lives by the river Thames in London. The time is the seventeenth century, and London is in the throes of civil war. Winterson shows herself with this novel to be deeply reactionary in her politics, siding with King Charles against the Puritans. The tale's search, as it develops, is both for new fruit for Jordan and for love and identity, which includes gender identity, for his mother. A banana comes to symbolize the phallus, and Jordan's mother literally bites off a penis as one would bite off part of a banana. The London portrayed is gross, sordid, and decaying, yet the mythic elements, the search for Fortunata the dancer in particular, prioritize the spiritual. The novel is a bold experiment, and it is left to readers to piece together the fragments.

The Power Book

Winterson considers *The Power Book* the last of a seven-novel cycle of long fiction. The work is another conscious effort to rewrite the English novel on postmodern terms, this time using the metaphor of the computer and, as one of its loci, cyberspace. In *The Power Book*, word processors are shown to erase what one has written and rewrite what one has erased. Networks are shown to help one find parallel information to the story one is working on, but the information comes in fragments. Nothing is whole or finished.

This process of writing becomes a metaphor for individual lives. Winterson's life is consciously "queer," a term she prefers to lesbian. Queer suggests strange, not straightforward, and it also suggests the ambiguity of the phallus. The novel's opening motif is the tulip, which is used as a phallus for the female body to become male. The consciousness of the presence or absence of the phallus in terms of connection and identity runs throughout the book. The novel's subtexts include the story of gender change and ambiguity in Virginia Woolf's *Orlando: A Biography* (1928). The story's themes are the lifelong search for the grand passion, whether for love or tulips, and how humans keep reinventing themselves to find that grand passion; in finding it, one finds one's true identity.

The main plot, such as it is, centers on two lesbian lovers (one of them married) as they meet in Paris and then continue to Capri. In the second half of the book, Winterson introduces autobiographical fragments from *Oranges Are Not the Only Fruit.* A mother tells her adopted orphan daughter that treasure exists out there in the world, if only one searches for it and even if one has to begin that search in muck and filth. This determination to find the treasure through layers of time and meaning, symbolized by the Thames and London archaeology (as in *Sexing the Cherry*), leads to the realization that the treasure lies within.

LIGHTHOUSEKEEPING

By Winterson's own admission, *Lighthousekeeping* uses the remnants of her autobiography that are not resolved in *Oranges Are Not the Only Fruit.* Silver, the narrator of *Lighthousekeeping*, is an illegitimate orphan girl who finds a home in the Cape Wrath lighthouse in the far north of Scotland, where several different seas meet, setting up dangerous currents. The lighthouse keeper, the blind man Pew, teaches her to tell stories, and local history is constructed as narrative. The novel interweaves several stories toward a personal resolution for Silver as she seeks her identity.

The main story weaves around Babel Dark, a Victorian clergyman who was a minister in the local village of Salts and who knew Charles Darwin and the writer Robert Louis Stevenson. Dark lives a double life and is portrayed as the inspiration for Stevenson's classic novel *The Strange Case of Dr. Jekyll and Mr. Hyde* (1886), which forms one of the novel's subtexts. Dark's own life reverses the Jekyll and Hyde scenario, in that the respectable minister suppresses the former fashionable son of a Bristol merchant who had a passionate affair with Molly, a shop assistant. Dark has escaped the affair by retreating to the north of Scotland and living almost a dead man's life, suppressing all emotion. However, he kept two diaries, one respectable and the other wild and passionate, revealing his inner turmoil. Molly reappears twice to offer Dark a second chance, but he refuses, compromising by going to live with her in Bristol for two months under the alias Lux (or light). In the end, he commits suicide. One of Pew's ancestors, also a lighthouse keeper, recounts Dark's confession.

Dark represents some of the emotional suppression of Winterson's own upbringing. In the other main story, Silver has to find her own identity, especially when the lighthouse is automated and Pew and she are out of a job. She goes to Bristol to seek out some of Dark's roots, then undergoes a number of encounters, some of which seem quite autobiographical. She takes a trip to Capri, where she steals a parrot because the parrot can say "Silver," representing the one thing that knows her name and, therefore, her. Eventually, she has a lover and then resolves to return to the lighthouse, say farewell, and realize the strength of love and the choice for passion which must be made to continue living.

David Barratt

OTHER MAJOR WORKS

SHORT FICTION: *The World and Other Places*, 1998.

PLAY: *The Power Book*, pr. 2002 (based on her novel).

TELEPLAYS: *Oranges Are Not the Only Fruit*, 1990 (based on her novel); *Great Moments in Aviation* (1994).

RADIO PLAYS: *Static*, 1988; *Text Message*, 2001.

NONFICTION: *Art Objects: Essays on Ecstasy and Effrontery*, 1995.

CHILDREN'S LITERATURE: *The King of Capri*, 2003; *Tanglewreck*, 2006.

EDITED TEXT: *Passion Fruit: Romantic Fiction with a Twist*, 1986.

BIBLIOGRAPHY

Andermahr, Sonya. *Jeanette Winterson*. New York: Palgrave Macmillan, 2008. Late biography of Winterson by a scholar of her work. Places her fiction in historical, critical, and theoretical context and analyzes her experimentation with technique and form.

_______, ed. *Jeanette Winterson: A Contemporary Critical Guide*. Harrisburg, Pa.: Continuum International, 2007. Collection of scholarly essays covering the key themes and styles in Winterson's fiction.

Lopez, Gemma. *Seductions in Narrative: Subjectivity and Desire in the Works of Angela Carter and Jeanette Winterson*. Youngstown, N.Y.: Cambria Press, 2007. Scholarly treatise examining through a poststructuralist lens the themes of desire and self-searching in the novels of Winterson and Angela Carter.

Makinen, Merja. *The Novels of Jeanette Winterson*. New York: Palgrave Macmillan, 2005. Traces the reception to Winterson's novels and places them in the context of modern literary debate. Part of the Readers' Guide to Essential Criticism series.

Onega, Susana. *Jeanette Winterson*. New York: Manchester University Press, 2006. Examines the forms, themes, and ideologies of Winterson's novels within the context of the modern British novel. The first full-length study of Winterson's complete oeuvre.

Reynolds, Margaret, and Jonathan Noakes. *Jeanette Winterson: The Essential Guide*. New York: Vintage Press, 2003. Series of interviews with Winterson in which she discusses four of her most popular novels. Includes a biography, questions for discussion, suggestions for further reading, extracts from reviews, a bibliography, and a glossary of literary terms.

Bibliography

Every effort has been made to include studies published in 2000 and later. Most items in this bibliography contain a listing of secondary sources, making it easier to identify other critical commentary on novelists, movements, and themes.

Theoretical, thematic, and historical studies

Altman, Janet Gurkin. *Epistolarity: Approaches to a Form.* Columbus: Ohio State University Press, 1982. Examines the epistolary novel, explaining how novelists use the letter form to develop characterization, further their plots, and develop meaning.

Beaumont, Matthew, ed. *Adventures in Realism.* Malden, Mass.: Blackwell, 2007. Fifteen essays explore facets of realism, which was critical to the development of the novel. Provides a theoretical framework for understanding how novelists attempt to represent the real and the common in fiction.

Brink, André. *The Novel: Language and Narrative from Cervantes to Calvino.* New York: New York University Press, 1998. Uses contemporary theories of semiotics and narratology to establish a continuum between early novelists and those of the postmodern era in their conscious use of language to achieve certain effects. Ranges across national boundaries to illustrate the theory of the development of the novel since the seventeenth century.

Brownstein, Rachel. *Becoming a Heroine: Reading About Women in Novels.* New York: Viking Press, 1982. Feminist survey of novels from the eighteenth century through the latter half of the twentieth century. Examines how "becoming a heroine" defines for women a sense of value in their lives. Considers novels by both men and women, and discusses the importance of the traditional marriage plot.

Bruzelius, Margaret. *Romancing the Novel: Adventure from Scott to Sebald.* Lewisburg, Pa.: Bucknell University Press, 2007. Examines the development of the adventure novel, linking it with the medieval romance tradition and exploring readers' continuing fascination with the genre.

Cavallaro, Dani. *The Gothic Vision: Three Centuries of Horror, Terror, and Fear.* New York: Continuum, 2005. Study of the gothic novel from its earliest manifestations in the eighteenth century to the early twenty-first century. Through the lenses of contemporary cultural theories, examines readers' fascination with novels that invoke horror, terror, and fright.

Doody, Margaret Anne. *The True Story of the Novel.* New Brunswick, N.J.: Rutgers University Press, 1996. Traces the roots of the novel, traditionally thought to have been developed in the seventeenth century, to classical Greek and Latin texts that exhibit characteristics of modern fiction.

Hale, Dorothy J., ed. *The Novel: An Anthology of Criticism and Theory, 1900-2000.* Malden, Mass.: Blackwell, 2006. Collection of essays by theorists and novelists. Includes commentary on the novel form from the perspective of formalism, structuralism, poststructuralism, Marxism, and reader response theory. Essays also address the novel through the lenses of sociology, gender studies, and feminist theory.

_______. *Social Formalism: The Novel in Theory from Henry James to the Present*. Stanford, Calif.: Stanford University Press, 1998. Emphasizes the novel's special ability to define a social world for readers. Relies heavily on the works of contemporary literary and cultural theorists. Provides a summary of twentieth century efforts to identify a theory of fiction that encompasses novels of many kinds.

Hart, Stephen M., and Wen-chin Ouyang, eds. *A Companion to Magical Realism*. London: Tamesis, 2005. Essays outlining the development of Magical Realism, tracing its roots from Europe through Latin America to other regions of the world. Explores the political dimensions of the genre.

Hoffman, Michael J., and Patrick D. Murphy, eds. *Essentials of the Theory of Fiction*. 2d ed. Durham, N.C.: Duke University Press, 1996. Collection of essays by influential critics from the late nineteenth century through the twentieth century. Focuses on the essential elements of fiction and the novel's relationship to the world it depicts.

Lodge, David. *The Art of Fiction: Illustrated from Classic and Modern Texts*. New York: Viking Press, 1993. Short commentaries on the technical aspects of fiction. Examples from important and minor novelists illustrate literary principles and techniques such as point of view, suspense, character introduction, irony, motivation, and ending.

Lynch, Deirdre, and William B. Walker, eds. *Cultural Institutions of the Novel*. Durham, N.C.: Duke University Press, 1996. Fifteen essays examine aspects of long fiction produced around the world. Encourages a redefinition of the genre and argues for inclusion of texts not historically considered novels.

Moretti, Franco, ed. *The Novel*. 2 vols. Princeton, N.J.: Princeton University Press, 2006. Compendium exploring the novel from multiple perspectives, including as an anthropological, historical, and sociological document; a function of the national tradition from which it emerges; and a work of art subject to examination using various critical approaches.

Priestman, Martin, ed. *The Cambridge Companion to Crime Fiction*. New York: Cambridge University Press, 2003. Essays examine the nature and development of the genre, explore works by writers (including women and ethnic minorities) from several countries, and establish links between crime fiction and other literary genres. Includes a chronology.

Scaggs, John. *Crime Fiction*. New York: Routledge, 2005. Provides a history of crime fiction, explores key subgenres, and identifies recurring themes that suggest the wider social and historical context in which these works are written. Suggests critical approaches that open crime fiction to serious study.

Shiach, Morag, ed. *The Cambridge Companion to the Modernist Novel*. New York: Cambridge University Press, 2007. Essays explaining the concept of modernism and its influence on the novel. Detailed examination of works by writers from various countries, all influenced by the modernist movement. Includes a detailed chronology.

Vice, Sue. *Holocaust Fiction*. New York: Routledge, 2000. Examines controversies generated by novels about the Holocaust. Focuses on eight important works, but also offers observations on the polemics surrounding publication of books on this topic.

Zunshine, Lisa. *Why We Read Fiction: Theory of Mind and the Novel*. Columbus: Ohio State University Press, 2006. Applies theories of cognitive psychology to novel reading, explaining how experience and human nature lead readers to constrain their interpretations of a given text. Provides numerous examples from well-known novels to illustrate how and why readers find pleasure in fiction.

Laurence W. Mazzeno

Glossary of Literary Terms

absurdism: A philosophical attitude, pervading much of modern drama and fiction, that underlines the isolation and alienation that humans experience, having been thrown into what absurdists see as a godless universe devoid of religious, spiritual, or metaphysical meaning. Conspicuous in its lack of logic, consistency, coherence, intelligibility, and realism, the literature of the absurd depicts the anguish, forlornness, and despair inherent in the human condition. Counter to the rationalist assumptions of traditional humanism, absurdism denies the existence of universal truth or value.

allegory: A literary mode in which a second level of meaning, wherein characters, events, and settings represent abstractions, is encoded within the surface narrative. The allegorical mode may dominate an entire work, in which case the encoded message is the work's primary reason for being, or it may be an element in a work otherwise interesting and meaningful for its surface story alone. Elements of allegory may be found in Jonathan Swift's *Gulliver's Travels* (1726) and Thomas Mann's *Der Zauberberg* (1924; *The Magic Mountain*, 1927).

anatomy: Literally the term means the "cutting up" or "dissection" of a subject into its constituent parts for closer examination. Northrop Frye, in his *Anatomy of Criticism* (1957), uses the term to refer to a narrative that deals with mental attitudes rather than people. As opposed to the novel, the anatomy features stylized figures who are mouthpieces for the ideas they represent.

antagonist: The character in fiction who stands as a rival or opponent to the *protagonist*.

antihero: Defined by Seán O'Faoláin as a fictional figure who, deprived of social sanctions and definitions, is always trying to define himself and to establish his own codes. Ahab may be seen as the antihero of Herman Melville's *Moby Dick* (1851).

archetype: The term "archetype" entered literary criticism from the psychology of Carl Jung, who defined archetypes as "primordial images" from the "collective unconscious" of humankind. Jung believed that works of art derive much of their power from the unconscious appeal of these images to ancestral memories. In his extremely influential *Anatomy of Criticism* (1957), Northrop Frye gave another sense of the term wide currency, defining the archetype as "a symbol, usually an image, which recurs often enough in literature to be recognizable as an element of one's literary experience as a whole."

atmosphere: The general mood or tone of a work; atmosphere is often associated with setting but can also be established by action or dialogue. A classic example of atmosphere is the primitive, fatalistic tone created in the opening description of Egdon Heath in Thomas Hardy's *The Return of the Native* (1878).

bildungsroman: Sometimes called the "novel of education," the bildungsroman focuses on the growth of a young *protagonist* who is learning about the world and finding his or her place in life; typical examples are James Joyce's *A Portrait of the Artist as a*

Young Man (1914-1915, serial; 1916, book) and Thomas Wolfe's *Look Homeward, Angel* (1929).

biographical criticism: Criticism that attempts to determine how the events and experiences of an author's life influence his or her work.

bourgeois novel: A novel in which the values, preoccupations, and accoutrements of middle-class or bourgeois life are given particular prominence. The heyday of the bourgeois novel was the nineteenth century, when novelists as varied as Jane Austen, Honoré de Balzac, and Anthony Trollope both criticized and unreflectingly transmitted the assumptions of the rising middle class.

canon: An authorized or accepted list of books. In modern parlance, the literary canon comprehends the privileged texts, classics, or great books that are thought to belong permanently on university reading lists. Recent theory—especially feminist, Marxist, and poststructuralist—critically examines the process of canon formation and questions the hegemony of white male writers. Such theory sees canon formation as the ideological act of a dominant institution and seeks to undermine the notion of canonicity itself, thereby preventing the exclusion of works by women, minorities, and oppressed peoples.

character: Characters in fiction can be presented as if they were real people or as stylized functions of the plot. Usually characters are a combination of both factors.

classicism: A literary stance or value system consciously based on the example of classical Greek and Roman literature. While the term is applied to an enormous diversity of artists in many different periods and in many different national literatures, "classicism" generally denotes a cluster of values including formal discipline, restrained expression, reverence for tradition, and an objective rather than a subjective orientation. As a literary tendency, classicism is often opposed to *Romanticism*, although many writers combine classical and romantic elements.

climax/crisis: The term "climax" refers to the moment of the reader's highest emotional response, whereas "crisis" refers to a structural element of plot, a turning point at which a resolution must take place.

complication: The point in a novel when the *conflict* is developed or when the already existing conflict is further intensified.

conflict: The struggle that develops as a result of the opposition between the *protagonist* and another person, the natural world, society, or some force within the self.

contextualist criticism: A further extension of *formalist criticism*, which assumes that the language of art is constitutive. Rather than referring to preexistent values, the artwork creates values only inchoately realized before. The most important advocates of this position are Eliseo Vivas (*The Artistic Transaction*, 1963) and Murray Krieger (*The Play and Place of Criticism*, 1967).

conventions: All those devices of stylization, compression, and selection that constitute the necessary differences between art and life. According to the Russian Formalists, these conventions constitute the "literariness" of literature and are the only proper concern of the literary critic.

deconstruction: An extremely influential contemporary school of criticism based on the works of the French philosopher Jacques Derrida. Deconstruction treats literary works as unconscious reflections of the reigning myths of Western culture. The primary myth is that there is a meaningful world that language signifies or represents. The deconstructionist critic is most often concerned with showing how a literary text tacitly subverts the very assumptions or myths on which it ostensibly rests.

defamiliarization: Coined by Viktor Shklovsky in 1917, this term denotes a basic principle of Russian Formalism. Poetic language (by which the Formalists meant artful language, in prose as well as in poetry) defamiliarizes or "makes strange" familiar experiences. The technique of art, says Shklovsky, is to "make objects unfamiliar, to make forms difficult, to increase the difficulty and length of perception. . . . Art is a way of experiencing the artfulness of an object; the object is not important."

detective story: The so-called classic detective story (or mystery) is a highly formalized and logically structured mode of fiction in which the focus is on a crime solved by a detective through interpretation of evidence and ratiocination; the most famous detective in this mode is Arthur Conan Doyle's Sherlock Holmes. Many modern practitioners of the genre, however, such as Dashiell Hammett, Raymond Chandler, and Ross Macdonald, have de-emphasized the puzzlelike qualities of the detective story, stressing instead characterization, theme, and other elements of mainstream fiction.

determinism: The belief that an individual's actions are essentially determined by biological and environmental factors, with free will playing a negligible role. (See *naturalism.*)

dialogue: The similitude of conversation in fiction, dialogue serves to characterize, to further the *plot*, to establish *conflict*, and to express thematic ideas.

displacement: Popularized in criticism by Northrop Frye, this term refers to the author's attempt to make his or her story psychologically motivated and realistic, even as the latent structure of the mythical motivation moves relentlessly forward.

dominant: A term coined by Roman Jakobson to refer to that which "rules, determines, and transforms the remaining components in the work of a single artist, in a poetic canon, or in the work of an epoch." The shifting of the dominant in a *genre* accounts for the creation of new generic forms and new poetic epochs. For example, the rise of *realism* in the mid-nineteenth century indicates realistic conventions becoming dominant and *romance* or fantasy conventions becoming secondary.

doppelgänger: A double or counterpart of a person, sometimes endowed with ghostly qualities. A fictional character's doppelgänger often reflects a suppressed side of his or her personality. One of the classic examples of the doppelgänger motif is found in

Fyodor Dostoevski's novella *Dvoynik* (1846; *The Double*, 1917); Isaac Bashevis Singer and Jorge Luis Borges, among others, offer striking modern treatments of the doppelgänger.

epic: Although this term usually refers to a long narrative poem that presents the exploits of a central figure of high position, the term is also used to designate a long novel that has the style or structure usually associated with an epic. In this sense, for example, Herman Melville's *Moby Dick* (1851) and James Joyce's *Ulysses* (1922) may be called epics.

episodic narrative: A work that is held together primarily by a loose connection of self-sufficient episodes. *Picaresque novels* often have episodic structure.

epistolary novel: A novel made up of letters by one or more fictional characters. Samuel Richardson's *Pamela: Or, Virtue Rewarded* (1740-1741) is a well-known eighteenth century example. In the nineteenth century, Bram Stoker's *Dracula* (1897) is largely epistolary. The technique allows for several different points of view to be presented.

euphuism: A style of writing characterized by ornate language that is highly contrived, alliterative, and repetitious. Euphuism was developed by John Lyly in his *Euphues, the Anatomy of Wit* (1578) and was emulated frequently by writers of the Elizabethan Age.

existentialism: A philosophical, religious, and literary term, emerging from World War II, for a group of attitudes surrounding the pivotal notion that existence precedes essence. According to Jean-Paul Sartre, "Man is nothing else but what he makes himself." Forlornness arises from the death of God and the concomitant death of universal values, of any source of ultimate or a priori standards. Despair arises from the fact that an individual can reckon only with what depends on his or her will, and the sphere of that will is severely limited; the number of things on which he or she can have an impact is pathetically small. Existentialist literature is antideterministic in the extreme and rejects the idea that heredity and environment shape and determine human motivation and behavior.

exposition: The part or parts of a fiction that provide necessary background information. Exposition not only provides the time and place of the action but also introduces readers to the fictive world of the story, acquainting them with the ground rules of the work.

fantastic: In his study *The Fantastic* (1970), Tzvetan Todorov defines the fantastic as a *genre* that lies between the "uncanny" and the "marvelous." All three genres embody the familiar world but present an event that cannot be explained by the laws of the familiar world. Todorov says that the fantastic occupies a twilight zone between the uncanny (when the reader knows that the peculiar event is merely the result of an illusion) and the marvelous (when the reader understands that the event is supposed to take place in a realm controlled by laws unknown to humankind). The fantastic is thus essentially unsettling, provocative, even subversive.

feminist criticism: A criticism advocating equal rights for women in political, economic, social, psychological, personal, and aesthetic senses. On the thematic level, the feminist reader should identify with female characters and their concerns. The object is to provide a critique of phallocentric assumptions and an analysis of patriarchal ideologies inscribed in a literature that is male-centered and male-dominated. On the ideological level, feminist critics see gender, as well as the stereotypes that go along with it, as a cultural construct. They strive to define a particularly feminine content and to extend the *canon* so that it might include works by lesbians, feminists, and women writers in general.

flashback: A scene in a fiction that depicts an earlier event; it may be presented as a reminiscence by a character in the story or may simply be inserted into the narrative.

foreshadowing: A device to create suspense or dramatic irony in fiction by indicating through suggestion what will take place in the future.

formalist criticism: Two particularly influential formalist schools of criticism arose in the twentieth century: the Russian Formalists and the American New Critics. The Russian Formalists were concerned with the conventional devices used in literature to defamiliarize that which habit has made familiar. The New Critics believed that literary criticism is a description and evaluation of its object and that the primary concern of the critic is with the work's unity. Both schools of criticism, at their most extreme, treated literary works as artifacts or constructs divorced from their biographical and social contexts.

genre: In its most general sense, this term refers to a group of literary works defined by a common form, style, or purpose. In practice, the term is used in a wide variety of overlapping and, to a degree, contradictory senses. Tragedy and comedy are thus described as distinct genres; the novel (a form that includes both tragic and comic works) is a genre; and various subspecies of the novel, such as the *gothic* and the *picaresque*, are themselves frequently treated as distinct genres. Finally, the term "genre fiction" refers to forms of popular fiction in which the writer is bound by more or less rigid conventions. Indeed, all these diverse usages have in common an emphasis on the manner in which individual literary works are shaped by particular expectations and conventions; this is the subject of genre criticism.

genre fiction: Categories of popular fiction in which the writers are bound by more or less rigid conventions, such as in the *detective story*, the *romance*, and the *Western*. Although the term can be used in a neutral sense, it is often used dismissively.

gothic novel: A form of fiction developed in the eighteenth century that focuses on horror and the supernatural. In his preface to *The Castle of Otranto* (1765), the first gothic novel in English, Horace Walpole claimed that he was trying to combine two kinds of fiction, with events and story typical of the medieval romance and character delineation typical of the realistic novel. Other examples of the form are Matthew Gregory

Lewis's *The Monk: A Romance* (1796; also known as *Ambrosio: Or, The Monk*) and Mary Wollstonecraft Shelley's *Frankenstein: Or, The Modern Prometheus* (1818).

grotesque: According to Wolfgang Kayser (*The Grotesque in Art and Literature*, 1963), the grotesque is an embodiment in literature of the estranged world. Characterized by a breakup of the everyday world by mysterious forces, the form differs from fantasy in that the reader is not sure whether to react with humor or with horror and in that the exaggeration manifested exists in the familiar world rather than in a purely imaginative world.

Hebraic/Homeric styles: Terms coined by Erich Auerbach in *Mimesis: The Representation of Reality in Western Literature* (1953) to designate two basic fictional styles. The Hebraic style focuses only on the decisive points of narrative and leaves all else obscure, mysterious, and "fraught with background"; the Homeric style places the narrative in a definite time and place and externalizes everything in a perpetual foreground.

historical criticism: In contrast to *formalist criticism*, which treats literary works to a great extent as self-contained artifacts, historical criticism emphasizes the historical context of literature; the two approaches, however, need not be mutually exclusive. Ernst Robert Curtius's *European Literature and the Latin Middle Ages* (1940) is a prominent example of historical criticism.

historical novel: A novel that depicts past historical events, usually public in nature, and features real as well as fictional people. Sir Walter Scott's Waverley novels established the basic type, but the relationship between fiction and history in the form varies greatly depending on the practitioner.

implied author: According to Wayne Booth (*The Rhetoric of Fiction*, 1961), the novel often creates a kind of second self who tells the story—a self who is wiser, more sensitive, and more perceptive than any real person could be.

interior monologue: Defined by Édouard Dujardin as the speech of a character designed to introduce the reader directly to the character's internal life, the form differs from other kinds of monologue in that it attempts to reproduce thought before any logical organization is imposed on it. See, for example, Molly Bloom's long interior monologue at the conclusion of James Joyce's *Ulysses* (1922).

irrealism: A term often used to refer to modern or postmodern fiction that is presented self-consciously as a fiction or a fabulation rather than a mimesis of external reality. The best-known practitioners of irrealism are John Barth, Robert Coover, and Donald Barthelme.

local colorists: A loose movement of late nineteenth century American writers whose fiction emphasizes the distinctive folkways, landscapes, and dialects of various regions. Important local colorists include Bret Harte, Mark Twain, George Washington Cable, Kate Chopin, and Sarah Orne Jewett. (See *regional novel*.)

Marxist criticism: Based on the nineteenth century writings of Karl Marx and Friedrich Engels, Marxist criticism views literature as a product of ideological forces determined by the dominant class. However, many Marxists believe that literature operates according to its own autonomous standards of production and reception: It is both a product of ideology and able to determine ideology. As such, literature may overcome the dominant paradigms of its age and play a revolutionary role in society.

metafiction: This term refers to fiction that manifests a reflexive tendency, such as Vladimir Nabokov's *Pale Fire* (1962) and John Fowles's *The French Lieutenant's Woman* (1969). The emphasis is on the loosening of the work's illusion of reality to expose the reality of its illusion. Other terms used to refer to this type of fiction include "irrealism," "postmodernist fiction," "antifiction," and "surfiction."

modernism: An international movement in the arts that began in the early years of the twentieth century. Although the term is used to describe artists of widely varying persuasions, modernism in general was characterized by its international idiom, by its interest in cultures distant in space or time, by its emphasis on formal experimentation, and by its sense of dislocation and radical change.

motif: A conventional incident or situation in a fiction that may serve as the basis for the structure of the narrative itself. The Russian Formalist critic Boris Tomashevsky uses the term to refer to the smallest particle of thematic material in a work.

motivation: Although this term is usually used in reference to the convention of justifying the action of a character from his or her psychological makeup, the Russian Formalists use the term to refer to the network of devices that justify the introduction of individual *motifs* or groups of motifs in a work. For example, "compositional motivation" refers to the principle that every single property in a work contributes to its overall effect; "realistic motivation" refers to the realistic devices used to make a work plausible and lifelike.

multiculturalism: The tendency to recognize the perspectives of those traditionally excluded from the canon of Western art and literature. In order to promote multiculturalism, publishers and educators have revised textbooks and school curricula to incorporate material by and about women, members of minority groups, persons from non-Western cultures, and homosexuals.

myth: Anonymous traditional stories dealing with basic human concepts and antinomies. According to Claude Lévi-Strauss, myth is that part of language where the "formula *tradutore, tradittore* reaches its lowest truth value. . . . Its substance does not lie in its style, its original music, or its syntax, but in the story which it tells."

myth criticism: Northrop Frye says that in myth "we see the structural principles of literature isolated." Myth criticism is concerned with these basic principles of literature; it is not to be confused with mythological criticism, which is primarily concerned with finding mythological parallels in the surface action of the *narrative*.

narrative: Robert Scholes and Robert Kellogg, in *The Nature of Narrative* (1966), say that by "narrative" they mean literary works that include both a story and a storyteller. The term "narrative" usually implies a contrast to "enacted" fiction such as drama.

narratology: The study of the form and functioning of *narratives*; it attempts to examine what all narratives have in common and what makes individual narratives different from one another.

narrator: The *character* who recounts the *narrative*, or story. Wayne Booth describes various dramatized narrators in *The Rhetoric of Fiction* (1961): unacknowledged centers of consciousness, observers, narrator-agents, and self-conscious narrators. Booth suggests that the important elements to consider in narration are the relationships among the narrator, the author, the characters, and the reader.

naturalism: As developed by Émile Zola in the late nineteenth century, naturalism is the application of the principles of scientific *determinism* to fiction. Although it usually refers more to the choice of subject matter than to technical conventions, those conventions associated with the movement center on the author's attempt to be precise and scientifically objective in description and detail, regardless of whether the events described are sordid or shocking.

New Criticism: See *formalist criticism.*

novel: Perhaps the most difficult of all fictional forms to define because of its multiplicity of modes. Edouard, in André Gide's *Les Faux-monnayeurs* (1925; *The Counterfeiters*, 1927), says the novel is the freest and most lawless of all *genres*; he wonders if fear of that liberty is the reason the novel has so timidly clung to reality. Most critics seem to agree that the novel's primary area of concern is the social world. Ian Watt (*The Rise of the Novel*, 2001) says that the novel can be distinguished from other fictional forms by the attention it pays to individual characterization and detailed presentation of the environment. Moreover, says Watt, the novel, more than any other fictional form, is interested in the "development of its characters in the course of time."

novel of manners: The classic examples of this form might be the novels of Jane Austen, wherein the customs and conventions of a social group of a particular time and place are realistically, and often satirically, portrayed.

novella, novelle, nouvelle, novelette, novela: Although these terms often refer to the short European tale, especially the Renaissance form employed by Giovanni Boccaccio, the terms often refer to that form of fiction that is said to be longer than a short story and shorter than a novel. "Novelette" is the term usually preferred by the British, whereas "novella" is the term usually used to refer to American works in this *genre*. Henry James claimed that the main merit of the form is the "effort to do the complicated thing with a strong brevity and lucidity."

phenomenological criticism: Although best known as a European school of criticism practiced by Georges Poulet and others, this so-called criticism of consciousness is also propounded in the United States by such critics as J. Hillis Miller. The focus is less on individual works and *genres* than it is on literature as an act; the work is not seen as an object but rather as part of a strand of latent impulses in the work of a single author or an epoch.

picaresque novel: A form of fiction that centers on a central rogue figure, or picaro, who usually tells his or her own story. The plot structure is normally *episodic*, and the episodes usually focus on how the picaro lives by his or her wits. Classic examples of the mode are Henry Fielding's *The History of Tom Jones, a Foundling* (1749; commonly known as *Tom Jones*) and Mark Twain's *Adventures of Huckleberry Finn* (1884).

plot/story: "Story" refers to the full *narrative* of *character* and action, whereas "plot" generally refers to action with little reference to character. A more precise and helpful distinction is made by the Russian Formalists, who suggest that "plot" refers to the events of a narrative as they have been artfully arranged in the literary work, subject to chronological displacement, ellipses, and other devices, while "story" refers to the sum of the same events arranged in simple, causal-chronological order. Thus story is the raw material for plot. By comparing the two in a given work, the reader is encouraged to see the narrative as an artifact.

point of view: The means by which the story is presented to the reader, or, as Percy Lubbock says in *The Craft of Fiction* (1921), "the relation in which the narrator stands to the story"—a relation that Lubbock claims governs the craft of fiction. Some of the questions the critical reader should ask concerning point of view are the following: Who talks to the reader? From what position does the narrator tell the story? At what distance does he or she place the reader from the story? What kind of person is he or she? How fully is he or she characterized? How reliable is he or she? For further discussion, see Wayne Booth, *The Rhetoric of Fiction* (1961).

postcolonialism: Postcolonial literature emerged in the mid-twentieth century when colonies in Asia, Africa, and the Caribbean began gaining their independence from the European nations that had long controlled them. Postcolonial authors, such as Salman Rushdie and V. S. Naipaul, tend to focus on both the freedom and the conflict inherent in living in a postcolonial state.

postmodernism: A ubiquitous but elusive term in contemporary criticism, "postmodernism" is loosely applied to the various artistic movements that followed the era of so-called high modernism, represented by such giants as James Joyce and Pablo Picasso. In critical discussions of contemporary fiction, the term "postmodernism" is frequently applied to the works of writers such as Thomas Pynchon, John Barth, and Donald Barthelme, who exhibit a self-conscious awareness of their modernist predecessors as well as a reflexive treatment of fictional form.

protagonist: The central *character* in a fiction, the character whose fortunes most concern the reader.

psychological criticism: While much modern literary criticism reflects to some degree the impacts of Sigmund Freud, Carl Jung, Jacques Lacan, and other psychological theorists, the term "psychological criticism" suggests a strong emphasis on a causal relation between the writer's psychological state, variously interpreted, and his or her works. A notable example of psychological criticism is Norman Fruman's *Coleridge, the Damaged Archangel* (1971).

psychological novel: A form of fiction in which *character*, especially the inner lives of characters, is the primary focus. This form, which has been of primary importance at least since Henry James, characterizes much of the work of James Joyce, Virginia Woolf, and William Faulkner. For a detailed discussion, see *The Modern Psychological Novel* (1955) by Leon Edel.

realism: A literary technique in which the primary convention is to render an illusion of fidelity to external reality. Realism is often identified as the primary method of the novel form: It focuses on surface details, maintains a fidelity to the everyday experiences of middle-class society, and strives for a one-to-one relationship between the fiction and the action imitated. The realist movement in the late nineteenth century coincides with the full development of the novel form.

reception aesthetics: The best-known American practitioner of reception aesthetics is Stanley Fish. For the reception critic, meaning is an event or process; rather than being embedded in the work, it is created through particular acts of reading. The best-known European practitioner of this criticism, Wolfgang Iser, argues that indeterminacy is the basic characteristic of literary texts; the reader must "normalize" the text either by projecting his or her standards into it or by revising his or her standards to "fit" the text.

regional novel: Any novel in which the character of a given geographical region plays a decisive role. Although regional differences persist across the United States, a considerable leveling in speech and customs has taken place, so that the sharp regional distinctions evident in nineteenth century American fiction have all but disappeared. Only in the South has a strong regional tradition persisted to the present. (See *local colorists*.)

rhetorical criticism: The rhetorical critic is concerned with the literary work as a means of communicating ideas and the means by which the work affects or controls the reader. Such criticism seems best suited to didactic works such as satire.

roman à clef: A fiction wherein actual people, often celebrities of some sort, are thinly disguised.

romance: The romance usually differs from the novel form in that the focus is on symbolic events and representational characters rather than on "as-if-real" characters and events. Richard Chase says that in the romance, character is depicted as highly stylized, a function of the plot rather than as someone complexly related to society. The romancer is more likely to be concerned with dreamworlds than with the familiar world, believing that reality cannot be grasped by the traditional novel.

Romanticism: A widespread cultural movement in the late eighteenth and early nineteenth centuries, the influence of which is still felt. As a general literary tendency, Romanticism is frequently contrasted with *classicism.* Although many varieties of Romanticism are indigenous to various national literatures, the term generally suggests an assertion of the preeminence of the imagination. Other values associated with various schools of Romanticism include primitivism, an interest in folklore, a reverence for nature, and a fascination with the demoniac and the macabre.

scene: The central element of *narration*; specific actions are narrated or depicted that make the reader feel he or she is participating directly in the action.

science fiction: Fiction in which certain givens (physical laws, psychological principles, social conditions—any one or all of these) form the basis of an imaginative projection into the future or, less commonly, an extrapolation in the present or even into the past.

semiotics: The science of signs and sign systems in communication. According to Roman Jakobson, semiotics deals with the principles that underlie the structure of signs, their use in language of all kinds, and the specific nature of various sign systems.

sentimental novel: A form of fiction popular in the eighteenth century in which emotionalism and optimism are the primary characteristics. The best-known examples are Samuel Richardson's *Pamela: Or, Virtue Rewarded* (1740-1741) and Oliver Goldsmith's *The Vicar of Wakefield* (1766).

setting: The circumstances and environment, both temporal and spatial, of a *narrative.*

spatial form: An author's attempt to make the reader apprehend a work spatially in a moment of time rather than sequentially. To achieve this effect, the author breaks up the *narrative* into interspersed fragments. Beginning with James Joyce, Marcel Proust, and Djuna Barnes, the movement toward spatial form is concomitant with the *modernist* effort to supplant historical time in fiction with mythic time. For the seminal discussion of this technique, see Joseph Frank, *The Widening Gyre* (1963).

stream of consciousness: The depiction of the thought processes of a *character,* insofar as this is possible, without any mediating structures. The metaphor of consciousness as a "stream" suggests a rush of thoughts and images governed by free association rather than by strictly rational development. The term "stream of consciousness" is often used loosely as a synonym for *interior monologue.* The most celebrated example of stream of consciousness in fiction is the monologue of Molly Bloom in James Joyce's *Ulysses* (1922); other notable practitioners of the stream-of-consciousness technique include Dorothy Richardson, Virginia Woolf, and William Faulkner.

structuralism: As a movement of thought, structuralism is based on the idea of intrinsic, self-sufficient structures that do not require reference to external elements. A structure is a system of transformations that involves the interplay of laws inherent in the system itself. The study of language is the primary model for contemporary structuralism. The structuralist literary critic attempts to define structural principles that operate intertextually throughout the whole of literature as well as principles that operate in *genres* and in individual works. One of the most accessible surveys of structuralism and literature available is Jonathan Culler's *Structuralist Poetics* (1975).

summary: Those parts of a fiction that do not need to be detailed. In *Tom Jones* (1749), Henry Fielding says, "If whole years should pass without producing anything worthy of . . . notice . . . we shall hasten on to matters of consequence."

thematics: According to Northrop Frye, when a work of fiction is written or interpreted thematically, it becomes an illustrative fable. Murray Krieger defines thematics as "the study of the experiential tensions which, dramatically entangled in the literary work, become an existential reflection of that work's aesthetic complexity."

tone: The dominant mood of a work of fiction. (See *atmosphere.*)

unreliable narrator: A narrator whose account of the events of the story cannot be trusted, obliging readers to reconstruct—if possible—the true state of affairs themselves. Once an innovative technique, the use of the unreliable narrator has become commonplace among contemporary writers who wish to suggest the impossibility of a truly "reliable" account of any event. Notable examples of the unreliable narrator can be found in Ford Madox Ford's *The Good Soldier* (1915) and Vladimir Nabokov's *Lolita* (1955).

Victorian novel: Although the Victorian period extended from 1837 to 1901, the term "Victorian novel" does not include the later decades of Queen Victoria's reign. The term loosely refers to the sprawling works of novelists such as Charles Dickens and William Makepeace Thackeray—works that frequently appeared first in serial form and are characterized by a broad social canvas.

vraisemblance/verisimilitude: Tzvetan Todorov defines vraisemblance as "the mask which conceals the text's own laws, but which we are supposed to take for a relation to reality." Verisimilitude refers to a work's attempts to make the reader believe that it conforms to reality rather than to its own laws.

Western novel: Like all varieties of *genre fiction*, the Western novel—generally known simply as the Western—is defined by a relatively predictable combination of *conventions*, *motifs*, and recurring themes. These predictable elements, familiar from many Western films and television series, differentiate the Western from *historical novels* and idiosyncratic works such as Thomas Berger's *Little Big Man* (1964) that are also set in the Old West. Conversely, some novels set in the contemporary West are regarded as Westerns because they deal with modern cowboys and with the land itself in the manner characteristic of the *genre.*

Charles E. May

Guide to Online Resources

Web Sites

The following sites were visited by the editors of Salem Press in 2009. Because URLs frequently change, the accuracy of these addresses cannot be guaranteed; however, long-standing sites, such as those of colleges and universities, national organizations, and government agencies, generally maintain links when sites are moved or updated.

American Literature on the Web

http://www.nagasaki-gaigo.ac.jp/ishikawa/amlit

Among this site's features are several pages providing links to Web sites about specific genres and literary movements, southern and southwestern American literature, minority literature, literary theory, and women writers, as well as an extensive index of links to electronic text collections and archives. Users also can access information for five specific time periods: 1620-1820, 1820-1865, 1865-1914, 1914-1945, and since 1945. A range of information is available for each period, including alphabetical lists of authors that link to more specific information about each writer, time lines of historical and literary events, and links to related additional Web sites.

Books and Writers

http://www.kirjasto.sci.fi/indeksi.htm

This broad, comprehensive, and easy-to-use resource provides access to information about hundreds of authors throughout the world, extending from 70 B.C.E to the twenty-first century. Links take users from an alphabetical list of authors to pages featuring biographical material, lists of works, and recommendations for further reading about individual authors; each writer's page also includes links to related pages on the site. Although brief, the biographical essays provide solid overviews of the authors' careers, their contributions to literature, and their literary influences.

The Canadian Literature Archive

http://www.umanitoba.ca/canlit

Created and maintained by the English Department at the University of Manitoba, this site is a comprehensive collection of materials for and about Canadian writers. It includes an alphabetical listing of authors with links to additional Web-based information. Users also can retrieve electronic texts, announcements of literary events, and videocasts of author interviews and readings.

A Celebration of Women Writers
http://digital.library.upenn.edu/women

This site presents an extensive compendium of information about the contributions of women writers throughout history. The "Local Editions by Authors" and "Local Editions by Category" pages include access to electronic texts of the works of numerous writers, including Louisa May Alcott, Djuna Barnes, Grazia Deledda, Edith Wharton, and Virginia Woolf. Users can also access biographical and bibliographical information by browsing lists arranged by writers' names, countries of origin, ethnicities, and the centuries in which they lived.

Contemporary Writers
http://www.contemporarywriters.com/authors

Created by the British Council, this site offers "up-to-date profiles of some of the U.K. and Commonwealth's most important living writers (plus writers from the Republic of Ireland that we've worked with)." The available information includes biographies, bibliographies, critical reviews, news about literary prizes, and photographs. Users can search the site by author, genre, nationality, gender, publisher, book title, date of publication, and prize name and date.

Internet Public Library: Native American Authors
http://www.ipl.org/div/natam

Internet Public Library, a Web-based collection of materials, includes this index to resources about writers of Native American heritage. An alphabetical list of authors enables users to link to biographies, lists of works, electronic texts, tribal Web sites, and other online resources. The majority of the writers covered are contemporary Indian authors, but some historical authors also are featured. Users also can retrieve information by browsing lists of titles and tribes. In addition, the site contains a bibliography of print and online materials about Native American literature.

LiteraryHistory.com
http://www.literaryhistory.com

This site is an excellent source of academic, scholarly, and critical literature about eighteenth, nineteenth, and twentieth century American and English writers. It provides numerous pages about specific eras and genres, including individual pages for eighteenth, nineteenth, and twentieth century literature and for African American and postcolonial literature. These pages contain alphabetical lists of authors that link to articles, reviews, overviews, excerpts of works, teaching guides, podcast interviews, and other materials. The eighteenth century literature page also provides access to information about the eighteenth century novel.

Literary Resources on the Net

http://andromeda.rutgers.edu/~jlynch/Lit

Jack Lynch of Rutgers University maintains this extensive collection of links to Internet sites that are useful to academics, including numerous Web sites about American and English literature. This collection is a good place to begin online research about the novel, as it links to hundreds of other sites with broad ranges of literary topics. The site is organized chronically, with separate pages for information about the Middle Ages, the Renaissance, the eighteenth century, the Romantic and Victorian eras, and twentieth century British and Irish literature. It also has separate pages providing links to Web sites about American literature and to women's literature and feminism.

LitWeb

http://litweb.net

LitWeb provides biographies of more than five hundred world authors throughout history that can be accessed through an alphabetical listing. The pages about each writer contain a list of his or her works, suggestions for further reading, and illustrations. The site also offers information about past and present winners of major literary prizes.

The Modern Word: Authors of the Libyrinth

http://www.themodernword.com/authors.html

The Modern Word site, although somewhat haphazard in its organization, provides a great deal of critical information about writers. The "Authors of the Libyrinth" page is very useful, linking author names to essays about them and other resources. The section of the page headed "The Scriptorium" presents "an index of pages featuring writers who have pushed the edges of their medium, combining literary talent with a sense of experimentation to produce some remarkable works of modern literature." The site also includes sections devoted to Samuel Beckett, Umberto Eco, Gabriel García Márquez, James Joyce, Franz Kafka, and Thomas Pynchon.

Novels

http://www.nvcc.edu/home/ataormina/novels/default.htm

This overview of American and English novels was prepared by Agatha Taormina, a professor at Northern Virginia Community College. It contains three sections: "History" provides a definition of the novel genre, a discussion of its origins in eighteenth century England, and separate pages with information about genres and authors of nineteenth century, twentieth century, and postmodern novels. "Approaches" suggests how to read a novel critically for greater appreciation, and "Resources" provides a list of books about the novel.

Outline of American Literature

http://www.america.gov/publications/books/outline-of-american-literature.html

This page of the America.gov site provides access to an electronic version of the ten-chapter volume *Outline of American Literature*, a historical overview of prose and poetry from colonial times to the present published by the U.S. Department of State. The work's author is Kathryn VanSpanckeren, professor of English at the University of Tampa. The site offers links to abbreviated versions of each chapter as well as access to the entire publication in PDF format.

Voice of the Shuttle

http://vos.ucsb.edu

One of the most complete and authoritative places for online information about literature, Voice of the Shuttle is maintained by professors and students in the English Department at the University of California, Santa Barbara. The site provides thousands of links to electronic books, academic journals, association Web sites, sites created by university professors, and many, many other resources about the humanities. Its "Literature in English" page provides links to separate pages about the literature of the Anglo-Saxon era, the Middle Ages, the Renaissance and seventeenth century, the Restoration and eighteenth century, the Romantic age, the Victorian age, and modern and contemporary periods in Britain and the United States, as well as a page focused on minority literature. Another page on the site, "Literatures Other than English," offers a gateway to information about the literature of numerous countries and world regions.

Electronic Databases

Electronic databases usually do not have their own URLs. Instead, public, college, and university libraries subscribe to these databases, provide links to them on their Web sites, and make them available to library card holders or other specified patrons. Readers can visit library Web sites or ask reference librarians to check on availability.

Canadian Literary Centre

Produced by EBSCO, the Canadian Literary Centre database contains full-text content from ECW Press, a Toronto-based publisher, including the titles in the publisher's Canadian fiction studies, Canadian biography, and Canadian writers and their works series, *ECW's Biographical Guide to Canadian Novelists*, and *George Woodcock's Introduction to Canadian Fiction*. Author biographies, essays and literary criticism, and book reviews are among the database's offerings.

Literary Reference Center

EBSCO's Literary Reference Center (LRC) is a comprehensive full-text database designed primarily to help high school and undergraduate students in English and the humanities with homework and research assignments about literature. The database contains massive amounts of information from reference works, books, literary journals, and other materials, including more than 31,000 plot summaries, synopses, and overviews of literary works; almost 100,000 essays and articles of literary criticism; about 140,000 author biographies; more than 605,000 book reviews; and more than 5,200 author interviews. It also contains the entire contents of Salem Press's MagillOnLiterature Plus. Users can retrieve information by browsing a list of authors' names or titles of literary works; they can also use an advanced search engine to access information by numerous categories, including author name, gender, cultural identity, national identity, and the years in which he or she lived, or by literary title, character, locale, genre, and publication date. The Literary Reference Center also features a literary-historical time line, an encyclopedia of literature, and a glossary of literary terms.

MagillOnLiterature Plus

MagillOnLiterature Plus is a comprehensive, integrated literature database produced by Salem Press and available on the EBSCO*host* platform. The database contains the full text of essays in Salem's many literature-related reference works, including *Masterplots*, *Cyclopedia of World Authors*, *Cyclopedia of Literary Characters*, *Cyclopedia of Literary Places*, *Critical Survey of Long Fiction*, *Critical Survey of Short Fiction*, *World Philosophers and Their Works*, *Magill's Literary Annual*, and *Magill's Book Reviews*. Among its contents are articles on more than 35,000 literary works and more than 8,500 writers, poets, dramatists, essays, and philosophers, more than 1,000 images, and a glossary of more than 1,300 literary terms. The biographical essays include lists of authors' works and secondary bibliographies, and almost four hundred overview essays offer information about literary genres, time periods, and national literatures.

NoveList

NoveList is a readers' advisory service produced by EBSCO. The database provides access to 155,000 titles of both adult and juvenile fiction as well information about literary awards, book discussion guides, feature articles about a range of literary genres, and "recommended reads." Users can search by author name, book title, or series title or can describe the plot to retrieve the name of a book, information about the author, and book reviews; another search engine enables users to find titles similar to books they have enjoyed reading.

Rebecca Kuzins

GEOGRAPHICAL INDEX

CARIBBEAN AND WEST INDIES
Arenas, Reinaldo, 18
CHILE
Donoso, José, 71
CUBA
Arenas, Reinaldo, 18

ENGLAND
Adams, Richard, 11
Carroll, Lewis, 54
Carter, Angela, 62
Hartley, L. P., 108
Lewis, C. S., 160
Rowling, J. K., 189
Tolkien, J. R. R., 232
White, T. H., 256
Winterson, Jeanette, 262

FRANCE
France, Anatole, 85
Green, Julien, 97

GERMANY
Hoffmann, E. T. A., 129

JAPAN
Murakami, Haruki, 171
Tanizaki, Jun'ichiro, 222

NIGERIA
Tutuola, Amos, 247

PORTUGAL
Saramago, José, 195

RUSSIA
Bulgakov, Mikhail, 32
Sinyavsky, Andrei, 212

SPAIN
Sender, Ramón José, 202

UNITED STATES
Bradley, Marion Zimmer, 24
Cabell, James Branch, 42
Green, Julien, 97
Heinlein, Robert A., 116
Hoffman, Alice, 123
King, Stephen, 139
Sender, Ramón José, 202
URUGUAY
Onetti, Juan Carlos, 177

SUBJECT INDEX

Adams, Richard, 11-17
Adventure novels, 11
Aestheticism, 225
Akutagawa, Ryunosuke, 224
Alice's Adventures in Wonderland (Carroll), 57
Allegory
  James Branch Cabell, 49
  José Donoso, 72
  Stephen King, 149
Antagonists, 63
Archetypes, 6
  Stephen King, 144
  J. R. R. Tolkien, 233
Arenas, Reinaldo, 18-23
Asimov, Isaac, 118
Aston, James. *See* White, T. H.
At Risk (Hoffman), 126
Atmosphere
  Mikhail Bulgakov, 33
  Julien Green, 98
  Ramón José Sender, 206
Auden, W. H., 233

Bachman, Richard. *See* King, Stephen
Bag of Bones (King), 153
Balzac, Honoré de, 131
Baroja, Pío, 203, 205
Barth, John, 151
Batista, Fulgencio, 19
Baudelaire, Charles, 131, 224
Bergson, Henri, 74
Bernanos, Georges, 98
Biblical themes, 36, 65, 79, 185, 199
Bildungsromans
  L. P. Hartley, 113
  E. T. A. Hoffmann, 135
  J. K. Rowling, 190
Biography of the Life of Manuel, The (Cabell), 47
Black Snow (Bulgakov), 36
Blindness (Saramago), 199
Boat, The (Hartley), 112
Body Snatcher (Onetti), 184
Book of Merlyn, The (White), 259
Bradley, Marion Zimmer, 24-31
Brief Life, A (Onetti), 183
Brontë, Emily, 126
Brothers Grimm, 143
Bulgakov, Mikhail, 32-41
Bunyan, John, 249

Cabell, James Branch, 42-53
Caldwell, Erskine, 180
Candle in the Wind, The (White), 259
Carrie (King), 143
Carroll, Lewis, 54-61
Carter, Angela, 62-70
Castro, Fidel, 19
Catholic themes
  Julien Green, 105
  E. T. A. Hoffmann, 134
  J. R. R. Tolkien, 238
Cell (King), 155
Censorship, 19
Cervantes, Miguel de, 203, 206
Chesterton, G. K., 237
Christine (King), 146
Chronicles of Narnia, The (Lewis), 166
Clarke, Arthur C., 118
Closed Garden, The (Green), 101
Cocteau, Jean, 102
Cold War, 155
Colum, Padraic, 44
Contemporary History (France), 92

Coronation (Donoso), 74
Crime fiction, 151
Crime of Sylvestre Bonnard, The (France), 89
Crónica del alba (Sender), 207
Cyberpunk fiction
  Haruki Murakami, 174
  Jeannette Winterson, 264

Dark Half, The (King), 151
Dark Journey, The (Green), 102
Dark Tower, The (King), 156
Darkover Landfall (Bradley,), 26
Decadence, 6, 225
De la Mare, Walter, 12
Devil's Elixirs, The (Hoffmann), 134
Diary of a Mad Old Man (Tanizaki), 229
Didactic novels, 252
Dodgson, Charles Lutwidge. *See* Carroll, Lewis
Dolores Claiborne (King), 152
Donoso, José, 71-84
Dostoevski, Fyodor, 131, 212
Double Star (Heinlein), 119

Earth Stopped (White), 258
Elephant and the Kangaroo, The (White), 260
Ellison, Harlan, 153
Eustace and Hilda (Hartley), 112
Eustace and Hilda trilogy (Hartley), 111
Existentialism, 210

Fairy tales, 5
  Angela Carter, 63
  Alice Hoffman, 125
  E. T. A. Hoffmann, 129
  Stephen King, 144
  C. S. Lewis, 165
Fantastic, 1
  Angela Carter, 62
  E. T. A. Hoffmann, 130
  Haruki Murakami, 173
  José Saramago, 197, 199
  Ramón José Sender, 206
  Andrei Sinyavsky, 213
  T. H. White, 258
Fantasy fiction, 1-10
  Richard Adams, 13
  Marion Zimmer Bradley, 26
  Lewis Carroll, 56
  Angela Carter, 66
  Robert A. Heinlein, 118
  E. T. A. Hoffmann, 133
  Stephen King, 156
  C. S. Lewis, 161
  J. K. Rowling, 190
  J. R. R. Tolkien, 235
  T. H. White, 257
Farewell to the Sea (Arenas), 22
Faulkner, William, 180
Feminist fiction, 28
Figures of Earth (Cabell), 48
Firebrand, The (Bradley,), 29
Flashbacks
  Mikhail Bulgakov, 37
  Robert A. Heinlein, 120
  Juan Carlos Onetti, 184
  Ramón José Sender, 209
Forest House, The (Bradley,), 29
Fowles, John, 151
France, Anatole, 85-96
Freud, Sigmund, 129

Galdós, Benito Pérez, 203
Gay and lesbian novels
  Julien Green, 105
  Jeanette Winterson, 263
Gerald's Game (King), 152
Girl in a Swing, The (Adams), 14
Go-Between, The (Hartley), 113
Gods Are Athirst, The (France), 92

Goethe, Johann Wolfgang von, 131
Gogol, Nikolai, 131, 212
Gone to Ground (White), 258
Gospel According to Jesus Christ, The (Saramago), 199
Gothic fantasy, overview, 6
Gothic novel, 1
- Angela Carter, 62
- Julien Green, 98
- L. P. Hartley, 108
- E. T. A. Hoffmann, 133
- Stephen King, 143
- Jun'ichiro Tanizaki, 225

Great Depression, 46
Green, Julien, 97-107
Greene, Graham, 110
Grotesque
- Mikhail Bulgakov, 37
- Angela Carter, 64
- José Donoso, 76
- Julien Green, 103
- Ramón José Sender, 205
- Jun'ichiro Tanizaki, 225

Hamsun, Knut, 37
Hard-Boiled Wonderland and the End of the World (Murakami), 174
Harris, Joel Chandler, 12
Harry Potter and the Chamber of Secrets (Rowling), 191
Harry Potter and the Deathly Hallows (Rowling), 193
Harry Potter and the Goblet of Fire (Rowling), 192
Harry Potter and the Half-Blood Prince (Rowling), 193
Harry Potter and the Order of the Phoenix (Rowling), 192
Harry Potter and the Philosopher's Stone (Rowling), 190
Harry Potter and the Prisoner of Azkaban (Rowling), 191
Harry Potter and the Sorcerer's Stone. See *Harry Potter and Philosopher's Stone*
Hartley, L. P., 108-115
Heart of a Dog, The (Bulgakov), 39
Heinlein, Robert A., 116-122
Hell Has No Limits (Donoso), 79
Here on Earth (Hoffman), 126
Heroes and Villains (Carter), 66
Historical novels, 203
History of Middle-Earth, The (Tolkien), 244
Hobbit, The (Tolkien), 240, 259
Hoffman, Alice, 123-128
Hoffmann, E. T. A., 129-138
Hope, Anthony, 119
Horror fiction
- L. P. Hartley, 108
- E. T. A. Hoffmann, 133
- Stephen King, 142

Horse and His Boy, The (Lewis), 166
House in the Country, A (Donoso), 81

Ill-Made Knight, The (White), 259
Illumination Night (Hoffman), 127
Impressionism, 110
Infernal Desire Machines of Doctor Hoffman (Carter), 66
Interior monologues, 77
It (King), 149

Jurgen (Cabell), 50

Kafka on the Shore (Murakami), 175
Kawabata, Yasunari, 224
Key, The (Tanizaki), 229
King, Stephen, 139-159

Lady of Avalon (Bradley,), 30
Last Battle, The (Lewis), 167

Let the Wind Speak (Onetti), 186
Lewis, C. S., 160-170, 233
Lewis, Matthew Gregory, 134
Life and Opinions of Kater Murr, The (Hoffmann), 135
Lighthousekeeping (Winterson), 265
Lion, the Witch, and the Wardrobe, The (Lewis), 166
Lord of the Rings, The (Tolkien), 242

Magic Toyshop, The (Carter), 64
Magical Realism, 8
  Reinaldo Arenas, 20
  Robert A. Heinlein, 118
  Haruki Murakami, 173
  José Saramago, 197
  Jeannette Winterson, 263
Magician's Nephew, The (Lewis), 166
Maia (Adams), 15
Makepeace Experiment, The (Sinyavsky), 217
Makioka Sisters, The (Tanizaki), 227
Mallea, Eduardo, 179
Mariel Boat Lift, 19
Master and Margarita, The (Bulgakov), 37
Master, The (White), 260
Maugham, W. Somerset, 226
Mauriac, François, 98
Metafiction, 151
Misery (King), 150
Mishima, Yukio, 224
Mistress Masham's Repose (White), 260
Mists of Avalon, The (Bradley,), 28
Modernism, 263
Moira (Green), 105
Motifs
  Lewis Carroll, 58
  Angela Carter, 64
  José Donoso, 75
  L. P. Hartley, 113
  Stephen King, 151
  Jun'ichiro Tanizaki, 226
Mr. Witt Among the Rebels (Sender), 207
Muerte y la niña, La (Onetti), 185
Murakami, Haruki, 171-176
Murasaki Shikibu, 222
My Life in the Bush of Ghosts (Tutuola), 253
Mystery novels, 174
Mysticism, 6

Naomi (Tanizaki), 226
Naturalism
  James Branch Cabell, 46
  Jun'ichiro Tanizaki, 225
Nerval, Gérard de, 131
Nights at the Circus (Carter), 67
No Man's Land (Onetti), 182
Norwegian Wood (Murakami), 174

Obscene Bird of Night, The (Donoso), 80
Oe, Kenzaburo, 171
O'Hara, John, 102
Once and Future King, The (White), 258
Onetti, Juan Carlos, 177-188
Oranges Are Not the Only Fruit (Winterson), 263
Orlando (Woolf, Virginia), 265
Orwell, George, 149
Out of the Silent Planet (Lewis), 163

Palace of the White Skunks, The (Arenas), 21
Palm-Wine Drinkard, The (Tutuola), 251
Passion of New Eve, The (Carter), 66
Passion, The (Winterson), 264
Passos, John Dos, 182
Pasternak, Boris, 212
Pentagonía (Arenas), 20
Perelandra (Lewis), 163
Pet Sematary (King), 147
Philosophical novels, 205

Picaresque novel, 205
Pit, The (Onetti), 181
Plague Dogs, The (Adams), 14
Poe, Edgar Allan, 131, 224
Point of view
  Anatole France, 90
  Stephen King, 153
  Jun'ichiro Tanizaki, 228
Political novels, 21
Postcolonialism, 197
Postmodernism, 263
Pound, Ezra, 186
Powell, Anthony, 110
Power Book, The (Winterson), 264
Priestess of Avalon (Bradley,), 30
Prince Caspian (Lewis), 167
Prisoner of Zenda (Hope, Anthony), 119
Pro Patria (Sender), 206
Pulp fiction, 117
Puppet Masters, The (Heinlein), 119
Pushkin, Alexander, 131, 212

Realism, 1
  James Branch Cabell, 44
  José Donoso, 71
  L. P. Hartley, 110
  C. S. Lewis, 165
  Ramón José Sender, 205
  Andrei Sinyavsky, 212
  Jun'ichiro Tanizaki, 223
Red Lily, The (France), 94
Religious novels, 111
Remarque, Erich Maria, 206
Requiem for a Spanish Peasant (Sender), 209
Roman à clef
  Mikhail Bulgakov, 34
  Stephen King, 152
Romance novels, 4
Rowling, J. K., 189-194

'Salem's Lot (King), 144
Saramago, José, 195-201
Sassoon, Siegfried, 258
Satire
  Richard Adams, 14
  Mikhail Bulgakov, 38
  Angela Carter, 66
  Ramón José Sender, 205
Schiller, Friedrich, 131
Science fiction, 1, 8
  Marion Zimmer Bradley, 26
  Angela Carter, 66
  Robert A. Heinlein, 117
  Stephen King, 150
  C. S. Lewis, 161
  Jeanette Winterson, 264
Scott, Sir Walter, 131
Sender, Ramón José, 202-211
Several Perceptions (Carter), 65
Sexing the Cherry (Winterson), 264
Shardik (Adams), 13
Shattered Chain, The (Bradley,), 27
Shelley, Mary Wollstonecraft, 147
Shining, The (King), 145
Shipyard, The (Onetti), 184
Shrimp and the Anemone, The (Hartley), 111
Silmarillion, The (Tolkien), 238
Silver Chair, The (Lewis), 167
Singing from the Well (Arenas), 19-20
Sinyavsky, Andrei, 212-221
Sixth Heaven, The (Hartley), 111
Solzhenitsyn, Aleksandr, 212
Some Prefer Nettles (Tanizaki), 227
Sophocles, 151
South of the Border, West of the Sun (Murakami), 174
Southern novel, 154
Space Trilogy (Lewis), 163
Speculative fiction, 119
Spenser, Edmund, 164

Sphere, The (Sender), 208
Starship Troopers (Heinlein), 120
Stevenson, Robert Louis, 151
Stone Raft, The (Saramago), 197
Stowe, Harriet Beecher, 12
Strange Case of Dr. Jekyll and Mr. Hyde, The (Stevenson, Robert Louis), 265
Strange River, The (Green), 103
Stranger in a Strange Land (Heinlein), 118, 121
Stream of consciousness, 182
Surrealism, 173
Sword in the Stone, The (White), 259
Sylvie and Bruno (Carroll), 58
Sylvie and Bruno Concluded (Carroll), 58

Tan, Amy, 142
Tanizaki, Jun'ichiro, 222-231
Tertz, Abram. *See* Sinyavsky, Andrei
That Hideous Strength (Lewis), 163
Thaïs (France), 90
This Sunday (Donoso), 77
Through the Looking-Glass and What Alice Found There (Carroll), 58
Till We Have Faces (Lewis), 167
Tolkien, J. R. R., 12, 162, 232-246, 257, 259
Tolstoy, Leo, 131
Tonight (Onetti), 183
Tragicomedy, 205
Traveller (Adams), 15
Trial Begins, The (Sinyavsky), 214
Tutuola, Amos, 247-255

Valle-Inclán, Ramón María del, 205
Verisimilitude, 35
Vigny, Alfred de, 85
Voyage of the Dawn Treader, The (Lewis), 167

Watership Down (Adams), 12
Waugh, Evelyn, 110
Weird Tales (periodical), 5
White Guard, The (Bulgakov), 35
White, T. H., 256-261
Wilde, Oscar, 224
Wind-up Bird Chronicle, The (Murakami), 175
Winterson, Jeanette, 262-266
Wise Children (Carter), 68
Witch in the Wood, The (White), 259
Woolf, Virginia, 265
Wordsworth, William, 149
Written on the Body (Winterson), 264

Yiddish literature, 212
Young adult fiction
  Lewis Carroll, 56
  J. K. Rowling, 190